Writing History

General Editors: Stefan Berger
Heiko Feldner
Kevin Passmore

Also in the *Writing History* series

Published:

Writing History: Theory and Practice
Edited by Stefan Berger, Heiko Feldner and Kevin Passmore

Writing Early Modern History
Garthine Walker

Writing Gender History
Laura Lee Downs

Writing Medieval History
Nancy Partner

Forthcoming:

Writing Postcolonial History
Rochona Majumbar and Dipesh Chakrabarty

Writing Contemporary History

Edited by: Robert **Gildea**
Anne **Simonin**

HODDER
EDUCATION
PART OF HACHETTE LIVRE UK

First published in Great Britain in 2008 by
Hodder Education, part of Hachette Livre UK,
338 Euston Road, London NW1 3BH

www.hoddereducation.com

Hachette Livre UK's policy is to use papers that are natural, renewable and
recyclable products and made from wood grown in sustainable forests.
The logging and manufacturing processes are expected to conform to the
environmental regulations of the country of origin.

The advice and information in this book are believed to be true and
accurate at the date of going to press, but neither the authors nor the publisher
can accept any legal responsibility or liability for any errors or omissions.

British Library Cataloguing in Publication Data
A catalogue record for this book is available from the British Library

Library of Congress Cataloging-in-Publication Data
A catalog record for this book is available from the Library of Congress

ISBN 978 0340 95000 5

1 2 3 4 5 6 7 8 9 10

Cover photo © Jean Ayissi AFP/Getty Images

Typeset in 11/13 Adobe Garamond by Dorchester Typesetting Group Ltd
Printed and bound in Great Britain by CPI Antony Rowe, Chippenham, Wiltshire

What do you think about this book? Or any other Hodder
Education title? Please send your comments to the feedback
section on www.hoddereducation.com

Contents

Acknowledgements

We would like to thank the Maison Française, Oxford, and in particular its director, Alexis Tadié, for hosting the conference in June 2006 that provided the forum and springboard for this volume. Teena Stabler of the Modern European History Research Centre (MEHRC) at Oxford put in a huge amount of work organising the conference. We also wish to thank those who played a leading role in that workshop, namely Christine Bard, Martin Conway, Sudhir Hazareesingh, Colin Jones, Jan Matlock, Marie-Claire Lavabre and Stéphane Van Damme.

Generous grants from the British Academy, the Europaeum, the History Faculty of the University of Oxford and the Maison Française made this international workshop possible. We are greatly indebted to all these institutions.

On the publishing side Stefan Berger, the series editor, took up our idea with enthusiasm and helped to develop the project. For all their help and hard work at Hodder Arnold we are keen to thank Deborah Edwards, Susan Millership, Tamsin Smith and Chrissie Taylor. We are indebted to Lyn Ward for her careful copy-editing. The bibliography was compiled with great speed and skill by Gabi Maas of the Politics and International Relations Department of the University of Oxford.

Notes on contributors

Alya Aglan is Assistant Professor in Modern History at University of Paris X Nanterre. A specialist in the French Resistance, she has published *Mémoires résistantes: histoire du réseau Jade-Fitzroy 1940–1944* (Le Cerf, 1994); *La résistance sacrifiée. Histoire du mouvement Libération-Nord* (Flammarion, 1999); *Jean Cavaillès résistant ou la pensée en actes* with Jean-Pierre Azéma (eds.) (Flammarion, 2002); *Le temps de la résistance* (Actes-Sud, 2008).

David Andress is Reader in Modern European History at the University of Portsmouth. He has published extensively on the problems of violence, popular culture and politics in and around the French Revolution. His books include *Massacre at the Champ de Mars* (Boydell & Brewer, 2000); *The French Revolution and the People* (Hambledon & London, 2004); *The Terror* (Abacus, 2006); and *1789: the threshold of the modern age* (Little, Brown, 2008), which explores transatlantic and global currents at the opening of the revolutionary era.

Raphaëlle Branche is Assistant Professor in Modern History at University of Paris 1 Panthéon-La Sorbonne. She is an authority on French colonialism and the Algerian war, and has published *La torture et l'armée pendant la guerre d'Algérie, 1954–1962* (Gallimard, 2001); *La guerre d'Algérie: une histoire apaisée* (Le Seuil, 2005); and 'The state, historians and memories: the Algerian war in France, 1992–2002', in H. Jones, K. Ostberg and N. Randeraad (eds.), *History on Trial: The Public Use of Contemporary History in Europe since 1989* (Manchester University Press, 2007), pp.159–73.

Patricia Clavin is Tutor and Fellow in History at Jesus College and a Lecturer in the Faculty of History at Oxford University. Her recent publications include 'Transnationalism and the League of Nations: understanding the work of its economic and financial organisation', *Contemporary European History* 14/4 (2005) 465–492; and 'The League of Nations and Europe', in R. Gerwarth (ed.), *Europe, 1914–1945* (Oxford University Press, 2007). In 2008–9 she will be the Thank-Offering to Britain Fellow of the British Academy, completing her book, *Bread and Butter Internationalism and the League of Nations, 1919–1945.*

Laura Lee Downs is Directeur d'études at the École des Hautes Études en Sciences Sociales in Paris. She is the author of *Manufacturing Inequality: Gender Division in the French and British Metalworking Industries, 1914–1939* (Cornell University Press, 1995); *Childhood in the Promised Land: Working-Class Movement and the Colonies de Vacances in France, 1880–1960* (Duke University Press); *Writing Gender History* (London: Hodder Arnold); and, with Stéphane Gerson, *Why France? American Historians of France Reflect on their Enduring Fascination* (Cornell University Press, 2006).

Martin Evans is Professor of Contemporary History at the University of Portsmouth. He is the author of *Memory of Resistance: French Opposition to the Algerian War* (Berg, 1997), which has been translated into French (L'Harmattan, 2008). He is the co-author (with John Phillips) of *Algeria: Anger of the Dispossessed* (Yale University Press, 2007). He is presently writing a history of the Algerian war, to be published by Oxford University Press in 2009.

Robert Gildea is Professor of Modern History at the University of Oxford. He is the author of *The Past in French History* (Yale University Press, 1994); *Marianne in Chains. In Search of the German Occupation, 1940–1944* (Macmillan, 2002); and *Children of the Revolution. The French, 1799–1914* (Allen Lane, 2008). He is currently directing an AHRC- and Leverhulme-funded international research project on militants in Europe in 1965–75, entitled 'Around 1968: Activism, Networks, Trajectories'.

Ruth Harris is Fellow and Tutor of New College, Oxford. She is the author of works on the history of Modern France and ranges in her interests across the fields of gender history, history of religion, and history of medicine and science. She is currently completing a major revisionist study of the Dreyfus Affair, to be published by Allen Lane/Penguin Press next year.

Dominique Kalifa is Professor of Contemporary History at the University of Paris 1 Panthéon-Sorbonne and co-director of the Centre d'Histoire du XIXe siècle (Paris 1–Paris 4). He is the author of *L'encre et le sang: récits de crimes et société à la Belle Epoque* (Fayard, 1995); *Naissance de la police privée: detectives et agences de recherches en France* (Plon, 2000); *La culture de masse en France: 1860–1930* (La Découverte, 2001); *Vidal le tueur de femme: essai de biographie sociale* (with Philippe Artières, Perrin 2001); and *Crime et culture au XIXe siècle* (Perrin). He is also co-editor of several books, including *Les exclus en Europe, 1830–1930* (L'Atelier, 1999); *Imaginaire et sensibilité au XIXe siècle* (Créaphis, 2005); and the recent *L'enquête judiciaire en Europe au XIXe siècle* (Créaphis, 2007). He is currently completing a book on the colonial penitentiary system of the French army.

Michael Kelly is Professor of French and Head of the School of Humanities at the University of Southampton. He is a founder member of the Editorial Board of the journal *French Cultural Studies* and edited *Introduction to French Cultural Studies* (Oxford University Press, 2005) with Jill Forbes. He is author of *The Cultural and Intellectual Rebuilding of France after the Second World War* (Palgrave Macmillan, 2004), and coordinator of CultureFB, a Network on Franco-British cultural relations funded by the Arts and Humanities Research Council (AHRC). He is currently co-investigator in an AHRC-funded project on 'Languages at War', examining the role of languages in conflicts in Western Europe in 1945–47 and in Bosnia in 1995–98. He also plays a prominent role in Europe, particularly in the UK, in developing public policy on languages.

Michel Margairaz is Professor of Contemporary History at the University of Paris 8 Saint-Denis and member of a research unit of the CNRS (IDHE: *Institutions et dynamiques historiques de l'économie*). He is author of *Essai historique sur le capitalisme en France au XXème siècle*, which has been translated into Japanese by Yasuo Gonjo and Isao Hirota as *Nihon Keizaï Hyoron Sha* (Tokyo, 2004). He is co-author with Danielle Tartakowsky of *'L'avenir nous appartient'. Une histoire du Front populaire* (Larousse, 2006); and is co-editor with Alya Aglan and Philippe Verheyde of *1816 ou La genèse de la Foi publique. La fondation de la Caisse des dépôts et consignations* (Librairie Droz, 2006).

Gérard Noiriel is Directeur d'études at the École des Hautes Études en Sciences Sociales in Paris. He has written widely on labour history and immigration. His most recent work includes *Immigration, antisémitisme et racisme en France. Discours publics, humiliations privées* (Fayard, 2007); and he has edited *L'identification. Genèse d'un travail d'Etat* (Belin, 2007).

Jean-Frédéric Schaub is Directeur d'études at the École des Hautes Études en Sciences Sociales in Paris, and Visiting Professor at the Oxford History Faculty, Modern European History Research Centre, in 2006–8. He is author of several books in early modern studies, of which the two latest are *La France espagnole. Les racines hispaniques de l'absolutisme français* (Le Seuil, 2003) and *Oroonoko, prince et esclave. Roman de l'incertitude coloniale* (Le Seuil, 2008).

Anne Simonin is Senior Researcher at the French National Centre for Scientific Research, appointed at the Maison Française d'Oxford for the last three years. Her recent publications include: 'L'écrivain, l'éditeur et les mauvaises moeurs' in Boris Gobille et al. (eds.), *Mai Juin 68* (L'Atelier, 2008), pp.411–27, and 'Le droit au mensonge: comment dire le vrai pendant la guerre d'Algérie', in Luc Boltanski et al. (eds.), *Affaires, scandales et grandes causes. De Socrate à Pinochet*

(Stock, 2007), pp.249–77. Her *L'Honneur dans la République. Une histoire de l'indignité de la Révolution française aux années cinquante* will be published by Grasset in 2008.

Sophie Wahnich is a research professor at Laios-EHESS/CNRS. She is a specialist in the French Revolution and works on the actions, language, emotion, rituals and violence of sovereignty. She has published *L'impossible citoyen: l'étranger dans le discours de la Révolution française* (Albin Michel, 1997); *La liberté ou la mort, essai sur la Terreur et le terrorisme* (La Fabrique Éditions, 2003); and *La longue patience du peuple* (Payot, 2008).

Chris Waters is Professor of History and Chair of the Department of History at Williams College in Massachusetts. He is the co-editor of *Moments of Modernity: Reconstructing Britain, 1945–1964* (Rivers Oram Press, 1999); and author of *British Socialists and the Politics of Popular Culture, 1884–1914* (Stanford University Press, 1990) and numerous articles on various topics in the social and cultural history of modern Britain. He is currently at work on a study of psychiatry, the regulation of sexuality and the shaping of the modern self in twentieth-century Britain.

Introduction

Robert Gildea

In 1974 a group of French historians published a two-volume collection of essays entitled *Faire de l'histoire*. Many of these essays were subsequently translated in a volume called *Constructing the Past*.[1] The team responsible for this collection, thirty-two men and one woman, were linked to the *Annales* school of history which took its name from the journal of that name founded in 1929 by Marc Bloch and Lucien Febvre. From 1947 the school was dominated by Fernand Braudel, head of the sixth section of the École Pratique des Hautes Études in Paris, which became in 1975 the École des Hautes Études en Sciences Sociales (EHESS). After 1968 a new generation of historians emerged, headed by medievalists Georges Duby and Jacques Le Goff, which was keen to define and make its mark upon what it called 'the new history'.[2]

Each generation in a new discipline brings fresh ideas, and in June 2006 a group of 16 historians met at the Maison Française in Oxford to discuss the state of writing contemporary history, by which they understood history from the French Revolution onward, and to explore the possibility of a common 'tool-box' with which to tackle historical questions at the beginning of the twenty-first century. Eight of them were French, eight British or American, and male and female historians were also in equal proportion. Much had happened in the discipline of history in the intervening thirty years – the decline of Marxist history and the *Annales* school, the revival of narrative history, the rise of women's history, gender history, the history of memory and post-colonial history, the 'anthropological turn', 'cultural turn' and 'linguistic turn'. These have all thrown down challenges to historians. Should they jump on bandwagons, rethink their approaches, or simply continue as before? The contributors to this volume belong to a younger generation of historians who have made their mark at the turn of the twentieth and twenty-first centuries. They explore what it means to write contemporary history, in the sense both of writing about the recent past and writing in the new century. Coming with expertise in a wide range of sub-disciplines – social, economic, cultural, gender, political and colonial history –

they offer new insights and explore new directions of research for the benefit of the history student of today.

Annales: from pomp to panic

In 1974 the authority of the *Annales* school was beyond question. It was commonly regarded in the UK and the USA as the powerhouse of the most exciting and innovative work in the discipline. It aspired to write 'total history', a history not only of populations, economies and societies, but of the body, the unconscious, public opinion, art, literature and science, film and festivals, sounds and smells. It was keen to respond to the accusation of 'hard' social sciences such as demography, economics and sociology, that history was 'soft' – that it narrated events rather than analysed problems, and that it had no serious theory or methodology. The theory it therefore developed was that human activity was determined by deep and broad historical 'structures'. These might be the ecological balance between population and resources, the slowly changing climate, or the mindsets or 'mentalities' which shaped the way people thought in previous centuries. The method it preached was quantitative, statistical, with a passion for tracking the economic cycles of good and bad harvests, price fluctuations and the rise and fall of international trade in what became known as 'serial history'. 'Tomorrow's historian', declared Emmanuel Le Roy Ladurie in 1968, 'will have to be able to programme a computer in order to survive'.[3] Political history, the story of kings and queens, battles and peace treaties, was sidelined by the *Annales* school as *l'histoire événémentielle*, the history of events, which could only be narrated, not quantified, and were seen to be merely froth on the slow swell of population movements and climate change.

Twenty years later, however, the 'Annales' school was in a state of panic. 'We are in a time of uncertainty', announced the journal's editorial in 1988.[4] In the first place, the ambition to write 'total history', to embrace every possible topic from climate to cooking, had resulted in the fragmentation or 'crumbling' of the historical discipline, which now lacked a central topic of concern. Second, there was a 'general crisis of the social sciences', a distrust of the view that human activities were determined by material forces and subject to historical laws. With that went a feeling that while quantitative history could answer questions about *how* things happened, it could not answer such questions as *why* people decided to limit the size of their families or change religion or regime. Having announced the triumph of the computer and of 'immobile history' in which only changeless structures counted, Le Roy Ladurie published a best-seller, *Montaillou*, in 1975, a study of Cathar heresy and life in a single Pyrenean village in the thirteenth century, which explored the complex lives, loves and beliefs of a small community of people brought eerily back to life thanks to the records of the Inquisition.[5]

He was not the only member of the *Annales* school to jump ship. For there was, finally, a move back in favour of political history and narrative that were not discarded as meaningless events. In 1973 Georges Duby published *Le Dimanche de Bouvines,* an account of a battle in 1214 that moved beyond the event by setting it in the context of 'the sociology of war at the beginning of the thirteenth century in north-west Europe', and exploring what it meant to violate contemporary taboos by killing on a Sunday.[6] In *Faire de l'histoire* Jacques Julliard argued that political power was a decisive force in society and could be studied quantitatively if need be through public opinion polls and electoral geography, while Pierre Nora announced the 'return of the event', with 'the Six Day war, May 68, the invasion of Prague, the departure and death of General de Gaulle, and the American moon landing'.[7]

Dethroning Marx

The *Annales* school was particularly strong in medieval and early modern history, before the French Revolution and Industrial Revolution, when agrarian society dominated and state power was limited. French historians dealing with later periods were more likely to be Marxist in inspiration, following Ernest Labrousse, who studied the economic trends and crises that led up to the French Revolution, and who dominated the Sorbonne in the immediate post-war period, and then Albert Soboul, a Communist who portrayed the revolutionary sans-culottes as a proto-working class and became Professor of the History of the French Revolution at the Sorbonne in 1968. In the UK, by contrast, the Communist Party Historians' Group, founded in 1946, which broke with Moscow over the invasion of Hungary in 1956, included medievalists such as Rodney Hilton and early modernists such as Christopher Hill, as well as modernists Eric Hobsbawm and E. P. Thompson.

Marxist historians saw people above all as workers, who learned to produce more efficiently by revolutionising the means of production, for example replacing the windmill by the steam mill, but whose fate was determined by whether they owned the means of production – land, capital, tools – and could thus exploit labour, or whether they were that exploited labour. New technologies gave rise to new classes, such as the bourgeoisie, who challenged the feudal landowners for political power in order to drive through their economic and social revolution. The English Civil War in the 1640s was thus a class war for Christopher Hill, a bourgeois revolution against feudalism and absolute government; the French Revolution of 1789 was a bourgeois revolution, helped along by the peasants and sans-culottes, for Albert Soboul, while according to the laws of history, nineteenth-century labour movements were rehearsals for the great proletarian revolution in Russia in 1917. Ideology, the dominant thought forms in any period, was a class consciousness – religion for feudal lords, the rights of man for the middle class, socialism for the working class. The Marxist interpretation of history was highly influential from the 1950s to the 1970s in the Sorbonne, where Labrousse's students included Maurice Agulhon, who defended his thesis in 1969 on the emergence of republicanism before 1851 in the small towns and countryside of Provence, and Michelle Perrot, whose 1968 thesis was on industrial workers' strikes in 1870–1914. In British universities it was the most forceful radical position to challenge the orthodoxy which held that political narrative should be the backbone of all historical writing.

Marxism, like the *Annales* school, suffered from a reaction against the notion that human activity and ideas were determined by material conditions and subject to historical laws of development. Often attacked by non-Marxists, the real problem came when Marxist orthodoxy was challenged from within Marxism itself. In 1963, E. P. Thompson published *The Making of the English Working Class*, in which he set out to show that the class consciousness of the English in the wake of the French Revolution was not an automatic reflection of the creation of an industrial working class, but evolved from their common experience as workers fighting oppression. 'Class consciousness', he wrote, 'is the way in which these experiences are handled in cultural terms: embodied in traditions, value-systems, ideas and institutional forms', and he explored the making of a working-class radical culture between the 1790s and the Chartism of the 1830s.[8] Once a gap had been opened between class formation and consciousness, it could be forced wider. Gareth Stedman Jones, who had written a book on casual labour in London in 1971, but had witnessed British workers vote in droves for Thatcherite conservatism, argued that radical culture could not be understood independently of the language in which it was expressed. Chartism, he suggested, did not arise from workers' struggles against industrialisation but from struggles with the state for wider political representation, and the language used was that of a political radicalism that went back to the English Civil War.[9]

In France, François Furet, who had himself broken with the Communist Party in 1956 and was keen to demonstrate 'the disastrous experiment of twentieth-century communism', attacked the Marxist interpretation of the French Revolution defended by Albert Soboul, first in an article in 1971, then in a polemical book, *Penser la Révolution française* (1978), translated as *Interpreting the French Revolution* in 1981. He argued first that the Revolution was not caused by the material force of class struggle but was a cultural revolution, the shaping and evolution of a language and culture of political democracy. Then, after the acclaim given to Alexander Solzhenitsyn's exposure of the Soviet Gulag system in 1973, Furet argued that the Terror of 1793–94, during which the French revolutionaries had eliminated their enemies, was not a response to the 'circumstances' of war and invasion, as Marxists claimed, but the natural consequence of the revolutionaries' language of paranoia and exclusion, which was faithfully reproduced by the communist totalitarian system.[10] He found allies for his revisionist cause in American and British universities to impose it as the new orthodoxy in time for the bicentenary of the Revolution in 1989.

Discourses and practices

The 1960s and 1970s saw a much wider and sharper engagement with the question of mentalities and ideologies than what was happening within the Marxist and *Annales* schools. This was associated with three powerful French philosophers and sociologists, Michel Foucault, Pierre Bourdieu and Michel de Certeau, whose radical ideas about the nature of discourse and practice in society obliged historians to rethink their own methodology.

In a series of books starting with his *Madness and Civilisation* (1961, translated 1971), Foucault developed the view that individuals were conditioned not by economic and social forces but by ways in which society thought about and described itself, called discourses, and by social practices elaborated to impose them. In medieval times, he said, people thought in terms of correspondences between things, but from the seventeenth century arose a mania for measuring, classifying and ordering. Mad people, who had previously been seen as holy fools and humoured by society, were now seen as the antithesis of rationality and excluded from society in asylums.[11] In his *Discipline and Punish. The Birth of the Prison* (1975, translated 1977), he linked discourse and practice.[12] Knowledge, he famously said, was power, and the Enlightenment, far from enshrining the liberty of the individual, divided the rational from the irrational, the healthy from the sick, the idle from the infirm, the criminal from the law-abiding, the military from the civil, the young from the adult, and the state incarcerated half of humanity in asylums, hospitals, workhouses, prisons, barracks and schools. His work stimulated a wide range of work on criminality, madness and degeneration, such as Michael Ignatieff's *Just Measure of Pain* (1978), Daniel Pick's *Faces of Degeneration* (1989) and Ruth Harris's *Murders and Madness* (1989).[13]

In his *Outline of a Theory of Practice* (translated 1977) and *Logic of Practice* (translated 1990) French sociologist Pierre Bourdieu rethought what external social conditioning might amount to and strengthened the notion of individual and social agency that had been squeezed by Marxist historical materialism. He argued that although individuals and groups were constrained by an internalised 'habitus' or sense of how things were done learned from the group they belonged to, they were nevertheless able to elaborate strategies to obtain their ends. He highlighted the importance of 'cultural capital' alongside economic capital and 'symbolic goods' such as prestige in the negotiation of advantage and domination. His work is much less cited by historians than by sociologists and anthropologists, and yet his understanding of strategies and practices has been disinterred in order to counter the tyranny of 'discourse' that emerged with the linguistic turn.[14]

More popular with historians has been the work of the philosopher Michel de Certeau, who took up ideas from both Foucault and Bourdieu and played with them. His *Practices of Everyday Life* (1980, translated 1984) suggested that the bodies and minds of individuals were not entirely controlled by the agencies of the state, as Foucault argued, since the individual was subversive and creative, and able to counteract the networks of discipline by weaving a 'network of anti-discipline'. Likewise, whereas Bourdieu spoke of strategies, which presupposed a secure base of group practice from which to operate, de Certeau spoke of tactics, which individuals at the margins of society, from a position of weakness, were able to improvise in opportunistic ways, turning the tables on those in power.[15] He stimulated works such as James C. Scott's *Weapons of the Weak. Everyday Forms of Peasant Resistance* (1985), which explored the footdragging, pilfering and sabotage favoured by oppressed peasants in Malaysia to overt revolt.[16]

Anthropological history and the cultural turn

Another development in the 1960s and 1970s, in the UK and the USA perhaps more than in France, was a turning to social and cultural anthropology in order to breathe new life into the study of history. Anthropology allowed historians to place society at the centre of their focus, brushing aside both the traditional orthodoxy that political narrative must hold centre stage, and the Marxist idea that social relations and conflicts were determined by the economic 'substructure'. Rather than a 'top-down' political approach or a 'bottom-up' materialist approach, anthropology proposed an 'inside-out' model, which started with social beliefs and practices and then explored what they might mean for the society. Whereas sociology concentrated on modern industrial societies and dealt in classes, bureaucracies and political parties, anthropology studied 'primitive' societies in which the state was weak and social stratification fluid – models that were more readily transferable to medieval or early modern societies studied by historians.

Not all anthropologists, of course, thought in the same way. Evans-Pritchard belonged to the 'functionalist' school, which held that social beliefs and practices served a function of maintaining social coherence. Thus belief in witchcraft, though it might give rise to witch-hunts, also protected vulnerable people for fear that refusing charity to an old woman would result in an evil spell being cast on the miscreant. His 1961 lecture, 'Anthropology and history', greatly influenced a young researcher at his Oxford college, Keith Thomas, who replied with an article on 'History and anthropology', which he put to good use in his pathbreaking book of 1971, *Religion and the Decline of Magic*.[17] Thomas's next work, *Man and the Natural World*, was much more influenced by Claude Lévi-Strauss, who argued that social beliefs and practices were less *for* something than simply a way of classifying and structuring the world. The totemic system, by which certain individuals or groups were identified with certain animals or plants, was above all a way of representing the world and mapping social organisation onto it. For Thomas, the ordering of the natural world in early modern England was thus a projection of the social structure as it was imagined by contemporaries.[18] Even more persuasive was the work of British anthropologist Victor Turner and American anthropologist Clifford Geertz. These were interested in rituals, myths and practices which made society into a social drama, a theatre which made manifest a society's beliefs and relationships and allowed their meaning to be decoded. In his study of a Balinese cockfight, for example, Geertz used the technique of 'thick description' to demonstrate that the cockfight was a dramatisation of rivalries between social strata and villages, members of which placed bets on the cockerels, and argued that the outcome was a 'status bloodbath' for the players as well as a literal one for the birds.[19] Geertz taught a course on history and anthropology at Princeton University with Robert Darnton, who in 1984 brought out his *Great Cat Massacre*. Using the account of an eighteenth-century Paris artisan about the mock trial and execution by himself and his fellow apprentices of a number of cats who were better cared for in the household by the master's wife than they were, Darnton traced the association of cats with witchcraft and sexuality in the *Ancien Régime* in order to understand the ritual massacre, and linked it as a historian to the worsening conditions suffered by workers with the onset of industrialisation.[20]

The surge of interest in anthropology stimulated a take-off of cultural history. Culture was no longer art, literature and music, but ways in which societies imagined class, regime, nation and gender, ritual and religious practices, stylised revolts such as the carnival or charivari, the production and consumption of popular reading matter, material culture such as clothing and home-building, how societies remembered their past, and what was now called political culture.[21] Geertz argued that culture was 'symbols, rituals, events, historical artefacts, social arrangements and belief systems', 'webs of significance that [man] himself had spun' and whose meaning he must now elicit.[22] William Sewell, who was influenced by Geertz at Princeton, energised studies of the labour movement by studying not only trade unions and strikes, but 'ritual gestures, work practices, methods of struggle, customs and actions that give to the workers' world a comprehensible shape'.[23] In France, although with very little exposure to contemporary anthropology, historians such as Mona Ozouf and Maurice Agulhon stimulated work on the Revolution and Republic through studies of political festivals and the political symbolism of Marianne. In their shadow,

American historian Lynn Hunt moved on from studying political mobilisation in the French Revolution to the Revolution's rhetoric, symbols and imagery.[24] A conference at the University of California, Berkeley, in 1987, sponsored by Lynn Hunt, announced the arrival of the New Cultural History.[25] A series of conferences to mark the bicentenary of the French Revolution in Chicago, Oxford and Paris, organised by François Furet, Mona Ozouf, Keith Baker and Colin Lucas, designed to lay to rest the ghost of Marx, took as their theme political culture, defined as the discourses and practices which defined and legitimated political communities.[26] Finally, after the *Annales* expressed its doubts about the future of history, Roger Chartier replied that salvation lay in a shift 'from the social history of culture to a cultural history of the social'. A history of the book, for example, would start not with the text itself but with the 'interpretative communities' that read and reflected on it.[27]

New voices: gender and race

One of the dominant ideas of conventional history, that it was possible to write a single objective account acceptable to everyone, came under fire in the 1970s as, under the impetus of civil rights and feminist movements, ethnic minorities and women began to criticise the standard view as written by whites, males and westerners, and demanded that other voices be heard. Black and women's studies departments mushroomed in American universities, and black historians took back writing about slavery from the white economic and social historians. From this point, traditional historians began to express concerns about the loss of consensus and objectivity as every group seemed to have its own historians.[28]

'Becoming visible' was the title of one of the early collections which flagged up the history of women as a historical subject. Its intention was 'to restore women to history and to explore the meaning of women's unique historical experience'.[29] Since E. P. Thompson saw the working class as male, the first task was to demonstrate that women had been present as workers in the Industrial Revolution and as revolutionaries, at least in so far as rioting for bread was concerned. To begin with, patriarchy was under attack as the source of all women's ills; then historians of women discovered that social life was gendered into a public sphere, occupied by men, and a private sphere, left to women. Bonnie Smith for France and Catherine Hall and Leonore Davidoff for England demonstrated how the formation of the middle class in England during the nineteenth century removed women from the world of work to install them as domestic goddesses, and in 1989 Leonore Davidoff founded a new journal, *Gender and History*.[30] In France, women's history asserted itself with more difficulty than in Britain and America. At the new university of Vincennes, founded after 1968, Michelle Perrot moved on from labour history to women's history, teaching a course from 1973 on 'Do women have a history?' and breaking the silence of the *Annales* on women's history by co-signing a manifesto that appeared there in 1986 and argued that the study of 'feminine culture' was the way forward.[31] Women's history approached the mainstream in the early 1990s when Michelle Perrot joined forces with *Annales* historian Georges Duby, who approached the subject of women through the study of marriage, the family and inheritance, to edit a five-volume *History of Women in the West*, which was published in both French and English.[32]

In the colonial world, history was written until about 1950 from the point of view of the imperialist and was underpinned by a faith in the West's 'civilising mission'. Christopher Bayly has spoken of a 'redemptive history' that took it as axiomatic that the West redeemed the East and South from backwardness, faction and the wrong faith or no faith at all. After the Second World War a new generation of western historians became interested in social history, breaking down the old interface between coloniser and colonised, and studying peasant communities, notables, and ordinary towns and districts. Through social history, the social organisation and mentalities of indigenous populations were studied, while anthropologists such as Jan Vansina insisted on the need in 'societies without history' to study oral testimonies, which transmitted the oral tradition, alongside the official record. In the 1980s, young historians originating from the Indian subcontinent who worked in the UK, Australia and America, and led by Ranajit Guha, founded the Subaltern Studies project. They criticised the way in which Indian history had been written either by white historians of the Raj or Indian historians of the elite, and told a story of a negotiated transition to independence which did not involve the masses, except to suppress trouble. They set out to rewrite the story of the struggle for independence as a violent struggle in which peasant uprisings, urban revolt and women had played the main part, from the point of view of the masses, and to recover the consciousness of the masses from popular memory as well as the official record.[33] Increasingly, the dominant narrative of the western, white male was under attack.

Sites of memory

One of the veins mined by cultural history as it developed was the way in which societies remembered their pasts. Memory, it was argued, was not simply what came into the mind of an individual, for what was remembered, how it was remembered and for what purpose was determined by society or a smaller social group within it. The French sociologist Maurice Halbwachs, who died in a German concentration camp in 1945, wrote two key texts on 'The social framework of memory' (1925) and *The Collective Memory*, published in 1950. In these he argued that while dreams were individual, memories were selected, ordered and erased by social groups in order to define the group, bind it together and legitimate its claims. These groups might be families, religious groups or classes. At the level of the nation there was history, which was a single objective record, written by historians, and different from the multiple and subjective memories held by social groups. These texts were translated in 1980 and 1992 and became the obligatory reference point for any historian writing on the history of memory.[34]

In France, Pierre Nora masterminded a vast study of the 'sites of memory' which had structured the French Republic and nation, published between 1984 and 1992. He maintained Halbwachs' distinction between history, which was universal and objective, and memories, which were partial and subjective. However, he argued that there was a collective memory at the level of the republic and the nation, embodied in certain canonical texts, buildings, emblems and commemorations which had defined and legitimated them. As history accelerated, he argued, memories dissolved, and so it was up to historians to step in and reconstitute these 'sites of memory' before the republic and nation lost their identity and legitimacy.[35]

In the UK there was also an outpouring of works on collective memory, although historians took a rather different view from that of Nora. They were inspired in part by anthropologists such as Terence Ranger and James Fentress, who explored the myths or 'usable pasts' which societies used in order to define and legitimate themselves. They were often Marxist historians who, since E. P. Thompson, were interested in the way in which working people drew on an imaginary Golden Age in the past in order to think about an imaginary New Jerusalem in the future. They were open to what could be offered by the witness of ordinary people, accessed through oral history, which secured a bridgehead with the formation of the Oral History Society in 1971. The seminal texts, each co-edited by an anthropologist and a historian, were Terence Ranger's and Eric Hobsbawm's *Invention of Tradition* (1983), and *Social Memory* (1992), edited by James Fentress and Chris Wickham.[36] This openness to a more democratic view of how history was constructed, and by whom, was regarded in France as a threat to the position of the professional, 'scientific' historian.

The revival of narrative

The purists of the *Annales* school had tried to eliminate the political event, on the grounds that it was powerless against the deep structures and relentless cycles that conditioned human affairs, and that it privileged a political history that was narrative rather than analytical, and therefore scientific. Even in the early 1970s, as we have seen, there were dissident voices close to the *Annales*, but in the Anglo-Saxon world the stir was caused by Lawrence Stone's 1979 article on 'The revival of narrative'. Here he argued that, perhaps since the recession of 1973, there was 'a widespread disillusionment' with the determinist models of the Marxists, the *Annales* school and the American 'cliometricians' who claimed to quantify how the American economy would have developed in the nineteenth century had there been no railways. Quantification was losing its appeal, because books such as Fogel and Engerman's *Time on the Cross* told a great deal about the material conditions of slavery but nothing about what it felt like to be a slave. With the new cultural history, inspired by anthropology, and micro-studies such as Le Roy Ladurie's *Montaillou* or Carlo Gizburg's *The Cheese and the Worms* (1980), historians were telling new stories, exploring the bottom of society rather than the top, using new sources such as trial records to lay bare what people thought and how they interacted, exploring on a small scale 'the internal workings of a past culture and society'.[37]

Many narrative historians of the old school, who had never departed from political narrative, breathed a sigh of relief. One work which Stone did not cite, however, was Hayden White's *Metahistory. The Historical Imagination in Nineteenth Century Europe.* (1973). White drew on the work of Northrop Frye, whose 1957 *Anatomy of Criticism* proposed that literature was shaped by four generic plots – the comedy, the tragedy, the romance and irony or satire – and argued that far from being 'scientific', historians consciously or unconsciously reproduced the same plot forms. A series of events such as the French Revolution were not intrinsically comic, romantic or tragic, but while Michelet's history, in which the French people struggle for liberation against evil tyranny and redeem themselves, was romance, Tocqueville's story of the French striving for liberty but thwarted by their stronger desire for equality and finding despotism, was tragic.[38] This revelation, that historians used literary tropes in order to shape their narratives, echoed the work of some historians such as Natalie Davis, who scripted *The Return of Martin Guerre*, or Lynn Hunt, who published *The Family Romance of the French Revolution*.[39] It was one thing, however, to explore the style of historical writing, and quite another to suggest that the sources historians were using were also fiction.

The linguistic turn

'Linguistics is a growth industry', declared a contributor to *Faire de l'histoire* in 1974, 'and it has an imperialist attitude'. These lessons had been learned by Lévi-Strauss and Foucault, he said, but historians had yet to awake to what was in store for them.[40] Drawing on the work of Swiss linguist Ferdinand de Saussure, linguistic theory focused on the gap between a word itself and what it signified. There was no logical reason, it claimed, why 'pen' should indicate both a writing tool and a place to keep hens, or that 'pencil' should be another writing tool while 'pennant' should be a flag. Meaning was generated by the internal logic of the language, the way in which it differentiated 'pencil' from 'pennant', and the world could only be grasped through the medium of language. Theorists such as Derrida introduced even more complications: language was slippery and ambiguous, sliding over a meaning that was not made clear, and on a timer, so that the full meaning would not be clear until the sentence or book was over. He only reinforced the idea that the world was constructed by language in his statement that 'il n'y a pas de hors-texte', 'there is nothing outside the text', and 'there has never been anything but writing'.[41]

The impact of this linguistic theory was felt progressively by historians during the 1980s, and by the 1990s many were in a state of alarm. Linguistic theorists, with both literary and historical works in their sights, argued that the texts or sources studied by literary scholars and historians were palimpsests – compilations, borrowings or quotations from other texts.[42] There could be no such thing as the 'original' author, creating a totally new idea or genre, since the author was only rewriting what others had written before. The author, indeed, was now dead.[43] The 'reality' described by a realist novelist such as Balzac or Dickens was simply a 'reality effect', using forms of description to create an illusion of reality. By the same token, the serried ranks of footnotes and quotations used by historians to underpin their argument and to repel those who might question their interpretation, was also a 'reality effect'.[44] The footnotes and quotations sent the reader in search of other sources, but never would there be a point at which 'reality' emerged as a 'fact' to demonstrate the 'truth' of the historian's interpretation. What separated one historian from another, indeed, was not the number of footnotes they wrote, but the apparent originality, persuasiveness, even passion of their writing.[45] There could be no objective or definitive account of history. Everything was relative: each culture had its own story and one story was as valid as another. Indeed, the 'definitive' interpretation laid claim to by established academics could easily be dismissed as imperialist, sexist and bourgeois. It did not give voice to women or black people, to gay people or slaves, and the accounts of these minorities, systematically ignored or censored, must now be privileged.[46]

The linguistic turn had an enormous impact on historical writing, as historians woke up to the hurricane in whose path they stood. In some respects it was revolutionary and liberating, in others distressing and destructive. Sub-disciplines such as economic and social history, which were based on the crunching of facts and figures, were suddenly told that the categories with which they worked, such as the market, social classes, unemployment, even statistics themselves, were only cultural constructs, with no real existence at all. Social historians such as Lawrence Stone protested at the idea that 'there is nothing besides the text … texts thus become a hall of mirrors reflecting nothing but each other and throwing no light on the "truth", which does not exist'.[47] Victoria Bonnell, an expert on the Russian Revolution, and Lynn Hunt organised conferences on the future of history after the linguistic turn in the USA in 1994 and 1996, calling for a 'redefinition or revitalization of the social'.[48] Marxist historians were completely discountenanced. Exploitation and class struggle could not be reduced to the language of politics, said Bryan Palmer, 'language is not life'.[49] Political history fell under the spell of political discourse. The French Revolution, for example, was now caused not by economic crisis or social struggle but by the rhetoric of the sovereignty of the people and the rights of man, which of its own momentum swept away the *Ancien Régime*, while the descent into revolutionary violence was explained not by genuine threats to the Revolution but by 'the cumulative radicalisation of speeches', each orator seeking to be more extreme than the one before.[50] Historians of social groups such as the peasantry took to their tents for at least a decade. Cultural history, on the other hand, now laid claim to the hegemonic role that had belonged to economic and social history when Marxism and the *Annales* had ruled the roost. Every other publication had 'representation', 'construction', 'invention' or 'imagination' in the title. Cultural history was only one star in the firmament of cultural studies departments which proliferated in the universities under the banner of postmodernism, studying not the dead modernist icons of Abstract Impressionism and Le Corbusier, James Joyce and Jean-Luc Godard, but mass culture and mass entertainment, pastiche and parody, rejoicing in the death of the author and the perpetual present of the consumer society.[51]

Women's history, which dealt in the sufferings and struggles of women in the past, was replaced by gender history. This seized on the notion that gender was a cultural construct to argue that all political and religious documents were 'gendered' and could be read as ways of defining women's identity and place in society. Gender now ruled alongside class and ethnicity as the three principal ways in which society was imagined and structured, and all historians, male and female, had to take account of the gender dimension of history on pain of extreme political incorrectness. Colonial history now became post-colonial history, 'deconstructing' the formerly straightforward relationship between colonisers and colonised. Edward Said's *Orientalism* (1978) set out to demonstrate that behind the ideology of Enlightenment and the rights of man, European powers formulated a discourse of 'the Other' which represented non-Europeans as uncivilised and backward, fit only to be dominated and exploited. A later version of post-colonialism explored the interface between colonial and colonised societies which was seen not in terms of the domination of one culture and the oppression or elimination of another, but in terms of borrowings, translations and the emergence of hybrid forms. Moreover, encounters could be studied not only at the periphery, in former colonial territories, but in the heartland, where former colonised populations were now immigrants.[52]

The linguistic turn, which instructed historians that historical writing could not be controlled by reference to historical reality but was 'made up' according to the rules of any narrative, upset many of them. Richard Evans, Professor of Modern History at the University of Cambridge, who had taken on Holocaust denier David Irvine and now feared that a legion of Holocaust deniers would arise, rejected the view that 'there is no reality beyond [texts] except other texts', and that 'in all this theorization, the historical fact more or less disappears from view'. The socio-economic determinism of the Marxists had been replaced by an 'intellectual reductionism' and yet he insisted on 'the past as extra-textual reality'.[53] Even more explicit was the work of Australian historian and journalist Keith Windschuttle, *The Killing of History. How Literary Critics and Social Theorists Are Murdering our Past.*[54] That said, the linguistic turn in fact freed up historians to experiment with narrative technique. If all historical writing obeyed fictional conventions, why not experiment with different fictional forms? If there could be no objective and definitive account of history by the omniscient historian, since every culture had its own history, why not let the spokespeople of those cultures tell their own stories? This, of course, opened the door to the idea that the memory of any community or group, such as Holocaust survivors, or the descendants of slaves, or immigrants from former colonies, or working-class women, was as valid as that of any historian, and probably more valid if the historian were white, Protestant, middle class and sexist. History now became a battlefield not only in which professional historians refuted each other's theories, but in which those whose community had been exploited, persecuted or decimated in the past sought a rewriting of history privileging their memory, leading to a formal apology and compensation from former exploiters, persecutors or decimators, or from states deemed to speak for them. Historians might now be called upon to change roles, no longer to follow the guidance of academic debate as they went about their research, but to bow to the pressure of those in society who demanded justice in the courtroom of history.

The essays in this volume explore ways in which different schools of the discipline of history have reacted to challenges such as the linguistic turn and are reinventing themselves for the twenty-first century. Historians from British, American and French academic backgrounds propose ways in which historians can develop new approaches which take into account new developments while remaining faithful to tried and tested historical methods. In the first chapter Gérard Noiriel and Chris Waters confront the 'crisis' afflicting social history after the linguistic turn claimed that social reality was only a construction of language. Chris Waters shows how social history has been reinvigorated in the UK and the USA by building bridges to cultural history, while still prioritising social relations. Gérard Noiriel proposes a new version of social history, 'socio-history', which is open to culture but regards it as a power relationship alongside other social and power relations that are constructed in society.

In the second chapter, Patricia Clavin and Michel Margairaz explore the way in which economic history became separated from mainstream history as 'cliometrics', the application of complex economic theory to historical problems. Since then, they argue, economic history has moved closer to social and cultural history, studying businesses as well as economies, and consumption rather than production. They point out that economic historians invented approaches now regarded as cutting-edge, such as global and transnational history, and urge social, cultural and political historians to take more account of economic dimensions and of models which recognise the 'interconnectedness of things'.

In Chapter 3, Dominique Kalifa and Michael Kelly examine the growing popularity of cultural history and ask what cultural history is now about. For Michael Kelly it is the study of cultural forms or products such as literature, the press, theatre, music and film in their wider social, religious and political context. He gives the example of the way in which across a range of media a new national identity was created in France after its Liberation in 1944, healing the wounds of war and civil war. For Dominique Kalifa cultural history is 'the social history of representations', that is, ways in which society represents the world to itself. He gives as examples from nineteenth-century France the social construction of crime by police and judges, witnesses and medical experts, the press and even the criminal himself, and the way in which the press not only reported and entertained, but changed the way people saw the world and experienced the passage of time.

Ruth Harris and Laura Lee Downs, in Chapter 4, examine the way in which the linguistic turn was seized upon by historians of women in order to transform the history of women's experiences into gender history and thus to move it from the margins of the discipline to the cutting-edge of historical enquiry. This happened earlier in the USA and the UK than in France, which was long resistant to women's and gender history. Harris and Downs argue, however, that there has been a shift in recent years away from seeing gender entirely as a product of discourse, and that women are now located in a wider context, including the family, labour market, religion and politics, and that they have been restored to their bodies, shaped by biology as much as by culture.

The linguistic turn, calling into question the existence of an extra-textual reality, has moved the spotlight onto historical writing itself. Chapter 5 explores ways in which historical writing has moved beyond the stages of 'critical history', reconstructing facts from objective study of documents, and of 'scientific history', imitating social sciences such as economics and sociology, to become a branch of imaginative literature as it was in the Romantic period of the nineteenth century. Robert Gildea explores how this revival of interest in the narrative has encouraged historians' to experiment with a variety of narrative styles in their own work. Jean-Frédéric Schaub shows how historians are using skills of literary criticism to extract greater historical meaning from works of fiction, a theme returned to by Anne Simonin in the conclusion.

Political history, which was sidelined as 'the history of events' without purchase of the broader trends of history when 'scientific history' was in the ascendancy, has made a return to centre stage through the study of extreme political change, or revolution, and political violence. In Chapter 6, David Andress and Sophie Wahnich take the French Revolution as a case study. Andress shows how political violence was regarded by Marxist historians as the inevitable by-product of revolution, and by right-wing historians as its very essence, and that only recently has it been studied seriously as an integral part of the political process opposing revolution and counter-revolution. Wahnich explores how violence, in the minds of the revolutionaries themselves, was part of the difficult and extended transition from old to new society, suspended between experience and hope, yet also how revolutionary violence was governed by rules, resorted to only when political means had failed.

In Chapter 7, Raphaëlle Branche and Martin Evans show how violence has returned to the centre of colonial history, as post-colonial views have highlighted the brutal and oppressive methods of colonial powers, long masked by the rhetoric of the white man's burden and civilising mission. They show how former colonial powers and former colonised countries have had to come to terms with the painful legacy of decolonisation. They demonstrate also how colonial history has moved from the periphery to the centre of historical studies, as the legacy of colonial occupation and war is manifest in the suburbs of French and British cities, and the colonial past now has to be integrated into any consideration of national identity.

In the final chapter, Alya Aglan and Robert Gildea ask whether the past is no longer dead and buried, to be picked over by professional historians, but will not go away, and indeed is constantly used to fight contemporary battles for legitimacy by groups in today's civil society. Since the linguistic turn it has been argued that the memory or subjective 'take' of these groups on the past is of equal value to that of professional historians, whose objectivity as members of the establishment has been called into question. These memories are often accounts of victimisation in the past, for which compensation and apology is sought in the present. The Jewish memory of the Holocaust and the black memory of slavery have set the standard for the memory of all groups of victims. This chapter explores how the memory of competing groups can be integrated into a coherent narrative which takes account of their suffering, and how the historian can explore the difficult question of how societies confront and work through their past.

Notes

1 Jacques Le Goff and Pierre Nora, eds., *Faire de l'histoire. Nouveaux problèmes. Nouvelles approches. Nouveaux objets* (Paris, Gallimard, 1974). English translation, *Constructing the Past* (Cambridge and Paris, Cambridge University Press and Editions de la Maison des Sciences de l'Homme, 1985).

2 Jacques Le Goff, Roger Chartier and Jacques Revel, eds., *La Nouvelle Histoire* (Paris, CEPL, 1978).

3 Emmanuel Le Roy Ladurie, 'The Historian and the Computer', *Le Nouvel Observateur,* 8 May 1968, in *The Territory of the Historian* (Hassocks, Harvester Press, 1979), 6.

4 'Histoire et sciences sociales: un tournant critique?', *Annales ESC* 43/2 (March–April 1988), 291–3.

5 Emmanuel Le Roy Ladurie, 'History that stands still', inaugural lecture at the Collège de France, 30 Nov. 1973, in *The Mind and Method of the Historian* (Brighton, Harvester Press, 1981), 1–27; *Montaillou, village Occitan de 1294 à 1324* (Paris, Gallimard, 1975), translated as *Montaillou, Cathars and Catholics in a French village* (London, Scolar Press, 1981).

6 Georges Duby, *Le Dimanche de Bouvines* (Paris, Gallimard, 1973), translated as *The Legend of Bouvines. War, Religion and Culture in the Middle Ages* (Cambridge, Polity Press, 1990).

7 Jacques Julliard, 'La politique', in *Faire de l'histoire* I, 210–28, and Pierre Nora, 'Le retour de l'événement', in *Faire de l'histoire* II, 229–50.

8 E. P. Thompson, *The Making of the English Working Class* (London, Penguin, 1968), 10.

9 Gareth Stedman Jones, 'Rethinking Chartism' in *The Languages of Class* (Cambridge University Press, 1983), 95–129 His earlier book was *Outcast London. A Study of the Relationship between Classes in Victorian London* (Oxford, Clarendon Press, 1971).

10 François Furet, 'The revolutionary catechism' (originally published in *Annales* 26/2 (March–April 1971), 255–89 and 'The Revolution is over', in *Interpreting the French Revolution* (Cambridge University Press, 1981), 81–131 and 1–79.

11 Michel Foucault, *Folie et déraison: histoire de la folie à l'âge classique* (Paris, Plon, 1961); *Madness and Civilisation: A History of Insanity in the Age of Reason* (London, Tavistock & New York, Mentor, 1965).

12 Michel Foucault, *Surveiller et punir: naissance de la prison* (Paris, Gallimard, 1975); *Discipline and Punish: The Birth of the Prison* (New York, Pantheon, 1977).

13 Michael Ignatieff, *A Just Measure of Pain: The Penitentiary in the Industrial Revolution, 1750–1850* (London, Macmillan, 1978); Daniel Pick, *Faces of Degeneration: A European Disorder, c.1948–c.1914* (Cambridge University Press, 1989); Ruth Harris, *Murders and Madness: Medicine, Law and Society in the Fin de Siècle* (Oxford, Clarendon Press, 1989).

14 For an anthropological use of Bourdieu, see Deborah Reed-Danahay, *Education and Identity in Rural France. The Politics of Schooling* (Cambridge University Press, 1996). For his recent use by historians see Gabrielle M. Spiegel, *Practising History. New Directions in Historical Writing after the Linguistic Turn* (New York and London, Routledge, 2005) and below, p.111

15 Michel de Certeau, *L'invention du quotidien I. Arts de faire* (Paris, 1980); *The Practice of Everyday Life* (Berkeley and Los Angeles, University of California Press, 1984).

16 James C. Scott, *Weapons of the Weak. Everyday Forms of Peasant Resistance* (New Haven and London, Yale University Press, 1985).

17 E. E. Evans-Pritchard, *Anthropology and History* (Manchester University Press, 1961), reprinted in *Essays in Social Anthropology* (London, Faber and Faber, 1962); Keith Thomas, 'History and anthropology', *Past & Present* 24 (1963), 3–24; Thomas, *Religion and the Decline of Magic. Studies in Popular Belief in Sixteeenth and Seventeeth Century England* (London, Weidenfeld & Nicolson, 1971).

18 Keith Thomas, *Man and the Natural World. Changing Attitudes in England, 1500–1800* (London, Allen Lane, 1983); Peter Burke, *What Is Cultural History?* (Cambridge, Polity Press, 2004), 34–5.

19 Clifford Geertz, 'Deep play: notes on the Balinese cockfight' in his *The Interpretation of Cultures* (New York, Basic Books, 1973), 412–53.

20 Robert Darnton, *The Great Cat Massacre and Other Episodes in French Cultural History* (London, Penguin, 1985), 79–104.

21 Peter Burke, *Varieties of Cultural History* (Cambridge, Polity Press, 1997), 183–212; Burke, *What Is Cultural History?*, 44–104.

22 Geertz, *The Interpretation of Cultures*, 5.

23 William Sewell, *Work and Revolution in France: The Language of Labour from the Old Regime to 1848* (Cambridge University Press, 1980), 12.

24 Mona Ozouf, *La fête révolutionnaire, 1789–1799* (Paris, Gallimard, 1976), translated as *Festivals and the French Revolution* (Cambridge, Mass., Harvard University Press, 1988); Maurice Agulhon, *Marianne au*

combat. L'imagerie et la symbolique républicaines de 1789 à 1848 (Paris, Flammarion, 1979), translated as *Marianne into Battle: Republican Imagery and Symbolism in France, 1789–1880* (Cambridge University Press, 1981); Lynn Hunt, *Politics, Culture and Class in the French Revolution* (Berkeley and London, University of California Press, 1984).

25 Lynn Hunt, ed., *The New Cultural History* (Berkeley, Los Angeles and London, University of California Press, 1989).

26 *The French Revolution and the Creation of Modern Political Culture I. The Political Culture of the Old Regime*, ed. Keith Michael Baker (Oxford, Pergamon, 1987); *II. The Political Culture of the French Revolution,* ed. Colin Lucas (Oxford, Pergamon, 1988); *III. The Tranformation of Political Culture, 1789–1848,* ed. François Furet and Mona Ozouf (Oxford, Pergamon, 1990); *IV. The Terror,* ed. Keith Baker (Oxford, Pergamon, 1994).

27 Roger Chartier, 'Le monde comme représentation', *Annales ESC* 44 (1989), 1511.

28 See for example John Blassingame, *The Slave Community. Plantation Life in the Antebellum South* (New York and Oxford, Oxford University Press, 1972); Peter Novick, *That Noble Dream. The 'Objectivity Question' and the American Historical Profession* (Cambridge University Press, 1988).

29 Renate Bridenthal and Claudia Koonz, *Becoming Visible: Women in European History* (Boston, Houghton Mifflin, 1977), 1.

30 Bonnie G. Smith, *Ladies of the Leisure Class. The Bourgeoises of Northern France in the Nineteenth Century* (Princeton University Press, 1981); Catherine Hall and Leonore Davidoff, *Family Fortunes: Men and Women of the English Middle Class, 1780–1850* (London, Routledge, 1987).

31 Michelle Perrot, *Les femmes ou les silences de l'histoire* (Paris, Flammarion, 1998), ix–xv; Cécile Dauphin et al., 'Culture et pouvoir des femmes: essai d'historiographie', *Annales ESC* 41 (1986), 271–93.

32 Georges Duby and Michelle Perrot, eds., *Une histoire des femmes en occident* (5 vols., Paris, Plon, 1991–92), translated as *A History of Women in the West* (Cambridge Mass. and London, Belknap Press of Harvard University Press, 1992–94).

33 Henk Wesserling, 'Overseas history', in Peter Burke ed., *New Perspectives on Historical Writing* (Cambridge, Polity Press, 1991), 67–92; C. A. Bayly, 'The Orient: British historical writing since 1890', in Peter Burke, ed., *History and Historians in the Twentieth Century* (Oxford University Press, 2002), 88–119; Ranajit Guha and Gayatri Chakravorty Spivak, eds., *Selected Subaltern Studies* (New York and Oxford, Oxford University Press, 1988).

34 Maurice Halbwachs, *Les cadres sociaux de la mémoire* (Paris, Alcan, 1925), translated as *On Collective Memory* (Chicago and London, University of Chicago Press, 1992) and *La mémoire collective* (Paris, PUF, 1950, 2nd edn, 1968), translated as *The Collective Memory* (New York, Harper and Row, 1980).

35 Pierre Nora, *Les lieux de mémoire I. La République; II. La Nation; III. Les France* (Paris, Gallimard, 1984–92), translated as *Realms of Memory: Rethinking the French Past* (New York, Columbia University Press, 1996–98)

36 Eric Hobsbawm and Terence Ranger, eds., *The Invention of Tradition* (Cambridge University Press, 1983); James Fentress and Chris Wickham, eds., *Social Memory* (Oxford, Blackwell, 1992).

37 Lawrence Stone, 'The revival of narrative', *Past & Present* 85 (1979), 3–24.

38 Northrop Frye, *Anatomy of Criticism. Four Essays* (Princeton,1957); Hayden White, *Metahistory. The Historical Imagination in Nineteenth Century Europe* (Baltimore, Johns Hopkins University Press, 1973). See also White, *Tropics of Discourse* (Baltimore, Johns Hopkins University Press, 1978).

39 Natalie Davis, *The Return of Martin Guerre* (Cambridge, Mass. and London, Harvard University Press, 1983); Lynn Hunt, *The Family Romance of the French Revolution* (London, Routledge, 1992).

40 Jean-Claude Chevalier, 'La langue', in *Faire de l'histoire* III, 95–114.

41 Jacques Derrida, *Of Grammatology* (Baltimore, Johns Hopkins University Press, 1997), 158–9. In general see Anne Jefferson and David Robey, *Modern Literary Theory* (second edn., Batsford, 1988); Elizabeth A. Clark, *History, Theory, Text. Historians and the Linguistic turn* (Cambridge, Mass. and London, Harvard University Press, 2004).

42 Gérard Genette, *Palimpsestes. La littérature au second degree* (Paris, Le Seuil, 1962), translated as *Palimpsests. Literature in the Second Degree* (Lincoln, University of Nebraska Press, 1997).

43 Roland Barthes, 'The death of the author' in *Image Music Text* (London, HarperCollins, 1977), 142–8, and in *The Rustle of Language* (Oxford, Blackwell, 1986), 49–55.

44 Barthes, 'Le discours de l'histoire' and 'L'effet du reel' in *Le bruissement de la langue* (Le Seuil, 1984), translated as 'The discourse of history' and 'The reality effect' in *The Rustle of Language*, 127–48.

45 F. R. Ankersmit, *Narrative Logic. A Semiotic Analysis of the Historian's Language* (Groningen, 1981), 252–8.

46 Robert Berkhofer, 'The point of view on viewpoints in historical practice', in Frank Ankersmit, ed., *The*

New Philosophy of History (London, Reaktion Books, 1995), 174–91.

47 Lawrence Stone, 'History and postmodernism', *Past & Present* 131 (1991), 217–18.
48 Victoria Bonnell and Lynn Hunt, *Beyond the Cultural Turn. New Directions in the Study of Society and Culture* (Berkeley and London, 1999), 11.
49 Bryan D. Palmer, *Descent into Discourse. The Reification of Language and the Writing of Social History* (Philadelphia, Temple University Press, 1990), xiv.
50 William H. Sewell, *A Rhetoric of Bourgeois Revolution. The Abbé Sieyes and* What Is the Third Estate? (Durham and London, Duke University Press, 1994); Patrice Gueniffey, *La politique de la Terreur. Essai sur la violence révolutionnaire, 1789–1794* (Paris, Fayard, 2000), 230.
51 Frederic Jameson, *The Cultural Turn. Selected Writings on the Postmodern, 1983–1998* (London and New York, Verso, 1988).
52 Homi K. Bhabha, *The Location of Culture* (London, Routledge, 1994); Gayatri Chakravorty Spivak, *The Post-Colonial Critic. Interviews, Strategies, Dialogues* (New York and London, Routledge, 1990).
53 Richard Evans, *In Defence of History* (London, Granta, 1997), 101, 186.
54 Keith Windschuttle, *The Killing of History. How Literary Critics and Social Theorists Are Murdering our Past* (New York, The Free Press, 1997).

1

Is there still a place for social history?

Chris Waters and Gérard Noiriel

Social history, often predicated on Marxist notions of the primacy of material reality and the economic determinants of social change, had the wind behind its sails between the 1950s and the 1970s. It endured something of a crisis from the 1980s as postmodernists brought to the fore new questions about the constructed nature of social reality, drawing attention to the importance of language and representation. More recently, social history has been reinvigorated, often incorporating the cultural dimension but never losing sight of the importance of social relationships. Chris Waters shows how in Britain and the United States social history has revived by allowing barriers between social and cultural history to become more porous, while from a French perspective, Gérard Noiriel makes the case for a more combative 'socio-history' which, while more sensitive to the cultural, still insists on the importance of power relations and social domination.

Chris Waters

The heyday of social history

In 1970, back in the days when it was a good time to be a social historian – when social history appeared to enjoy a flourishing present and could look forward to a golden future – Eric Hobsbawm, the British Marxist historian, reflected on the rapid, post-war expansion of the field and held out hopes for its continued success. Repudiating the notion that, as G. M. Trevelyan had loosely put it in his *English Social History* in 1942, social history was 'the history of a people with the politics left out', Hobsbawm argued for a history that was nothing less than a comprehensive history of society. While rejecting formal research models derived from the social sciences, Hobsbawm grounded his own notion of what a social historian should be doing in a practice that linked the economic, the social and the political in ways Marx himself would have recognised. Hobsbawm insisted that one 'starts with the material and historical environment', and then studied 'the forces and techniques of production' and 'the structure of the consequent economy'. Then, working 'outwards and upwards from the process of social production', one eventually came to an understanding of broader social structures, and thus to 'the phenomena which are traditionally the subject of interest to the social historians – for example, collective consciousness, social movements and the social dimension of intellectual and cultural change.'[1]

Hobsbawm's expansive definition of his practice attempted both to bring together and move beyond what he saw to be the three overlapping understandings of social history then in circulation: a record of the lives of the poor and of the social movements linked to them; an account of the manners, customs and everyday life of a past society; and an appendage of economic history, a field fully institutionalised in Britain with the establishment of the Economic History Society in 1928. Although Thomas Babington Macaulay had pioneered the 'manners and morals' school of social history in the famous third chapter of his *History of England from the Accession of James II* in the 1840s, and although historians between the wars, from G. D. H. Cole to R. H. Tawney and John and Barbara Hammond, contributed to the study of the poor and various social movements, it was not until the 1950s and after – much later than in France – that social history would emerge as a coherent sub-discipline, complete with its own journals and academic networks. Harold Perkin claims to have been the first lecturer appointed to a post in social history in Britain (at Manchester University) in the early 1950s.[2] Although elsewhere the *International Review of Social History* was founded in 1956 and *Comparative Studies in Society and History* in 1958, it would be another decade before the *Journal of Social History* appeared in the United States (1967), and two decades before Perkin would establish the Social History Society in Britain (1976), the same year that witnessed the publication of the first issue of two journals that more than any others came to shape the field in Britain, *Social History* and *History Workshop Journal*.

Inspired by E. P. Thompson's 1963 classic, *The Making of the English Working Class*, and growing out of the workshops that, since 1967, had reconstructed the lived experiences of workers in Britain, *History Workshop Journal*, claimed its editorial collective, would 'address itself to the fundamental elements of social life – work and material culture, class relations and politics, sex divisions and marriage, family, school and home.' Echoing Hobsbawm in his call for social history as a comprehensive history of society, the collective insisted it would elaborate these themes 'and attempt to coordinate them within an overall view of capitalism as a historical phenomenon, both as a mode of production and as a system of social relations.'[3] Even without the socialist commitment that informed *History Workshop*, many of the new journal's fields of enquiry had already yielded an impressive array of scholarly work by this time, including Brian Harrison's study of the temperance question in the nineteenth century, *Drink and the Victorians* (1971), and the essays in the pioneering collection edited by H. J. Dyos and Michael Wolff, *The Victorian City* (1973). And yet the more such work appeared – and it was now being published with great rapidity in the 1970s – the more it appeared to some that a balkanisation of historical practice was taking place, that social history was turning into a narrow sub-discipline that failed to challenge the hegemonic role of political or economic history, let alone transform those fields. As both Thompson and Keith Thomas saw it, declining to support the initial formation of the Social History Society, social history needed to be promoted less as a branch of history than as a way of doing history.[4]

Whether a way of doing history or a mere branch of history, there can be no disputing the fact that it was a good time to be a social historian in Britain between the mid 1960s and the early 1980s – something that might not be said of subsequent years. The end of the golden age of the expansion of higher education in Britain, the decline of actually existing socialism and the marginalisation of left debate – and, more importantly, the epistemological challenges to many of the very assumptions on which social history rested that emanated from what broadly might be termed postmodern theory – all served to halt the advance of social history that Hobsbawm celebrated at the beginning of the 1970s. It is with these challenges, and the future of social history in the wake of them, that the rest of this essay is concerned.

The challenge of the linguistic turn

Even though in Britain the transatlantic geographer and social theorist, David Harvey, had published his masterful summation (and critique) of the changes taking place in the cultural landscape of modern western societies, *The Condition of Postmodernity*, in 1989, it was in the United States that debates about the impact of postmodern thought on the practice of history were most widespread.[5] The year 1989 marked not only the demise of the Iron Curtain and the actually existing communist regimes of eastern Europe, but also the appearance in the United States of what would soon become a highly influential collection of essays, *The New Cultural History*. As Lynn Hunt wrote in her introduction, influenced much more by current French than by British historiographical practice, the new cultural history promised (or threatened) a move away from the social to a new concern with the constitutive nature of language, a new emphasis on the close reading of the products of culture, broadly defined – all of which, she argued, would help decipher the complexity of meaning in the past without erecting any new master narrative to replace those forms of materialist reductionism that had been central to many works of social history.[6] The sceptics were not convinced, and in the United States, 1989 also saw a number of crucial debates in the academic journals about the impact of the cultural and linguistic turns on the writing of history. In *History and Theory*, the Dutch advocate of postmodern theory, Frank Ankersmit, slogged it out with the more traditional historian of early modern Britain, Perez Zagorin. Each merely asserted and reasserted the importance of their own epistemological assumptions, Zagorin at one point simply noting that his fellow historians and graduate students were not favourably disposed to the new work they encountered.[7] More fruitful, perhaps, was the debate that took place between David Harlan and Joyce Appleby in the *American Historical Review* in the same year, although at the end of her rejoinder to Harlan, Appleby admitted the limits of their exchange: 'No logical argument is presented by Harlan, nor have I offered one for my counter-assertions. I appeal to experience.'[8]

What is remarkable about this debate as it unfolded in the United States in the 1980s – in such a way that few historians could ignore it (even if they might wish it would go away) – is the extent to which so little of it infiltrated mainstream historical circles in Britain. The debates aired in journals such as the *American Historical Review* in 1989 were wholly absent in their British counterparts that year. Neither the *English Historical Review*, nor *Historical Research*, nor the *Historical Journal*, nor *History* paid any attention to those issues being debated in the USA. Still, while *Past & Present* also did not engage in the debates that inflamed American tempers, it did, in that seminal year, carry an article by James Epstein – a portent of things to come – on the symbolic meaning of those caps of liberty displayed by early nineteenth-century radicals in Britain.[9] Epstein was slowly moving away from more orthodox forms of social history, experimenting with the new departures in cultural history that were being showcased in books like Hunt's. Others would soon follow, leading to an increasing rupture between historians of modern Britain based in Britain and those at work in the United States – a rupture that has yet to be studied in much depth, but that can in part be related to the greater influence of postmodern theories in American academic circles than in Britain – something Patrick Joyce has since attributed to the greater 'polyphony of American academic life'.[10] Ironically, in Britain, it was the journal that was the first to celebrate and champion 'history from below' as central to the new practices of social history – *History Workshop Journal* – that was also among the first to engage seriously with the linguistic turn and its impact on the work of practising historians, in 1989 publishing a special feature on 'Language and History'.[11]

If, in her critique of Harlan's enthusiasm for the possibility of a new historical practice made possible by the linguistic turn, Appleby appealed to her own 'experience' as a practising historian, the very category of 'experience' – central to the work of those social historians who devoted their energies to recounting the experience of various subaltern groups – came under increasing attack in the 1990s. As Joan Scott insisted in her seminal critique of an ever-growing number of historical works that documented the experience of social groups in the past, the practitioners of such studies often took as self-evident the identities of those whose experience they documented. Social historians, according to Scott, treated experience in an unproblematic manner – it was what individuals had and what historians often viewed unproblematically as their starting point. Such work, she argued, avoided dealing with more important questions 'about the constructed nature of experience'. At her most polemical, Scott argued that historians now needed 'to attend to the historical processes, that, through discourse, position subjects and produce their experiences. It is not individuals who have experience, but subjects who are constituted through experience. Experience in this definition then becomes not the origin of our explanation …, but rather that which we seek to explain.'[12] Scott's arguments drew a flurry of dismissive responses. More orthodox social historians were especially apt to counter her claims, or at least to reiterate the importance of their own work. In the USA, for example, Gordon Chang attempted to counter what he viewed as the postmodern challenge to the work of social history simply by reiterating his own epistemological assumptions: one of the 'original and still basic purposes of Asian American Studies', he wrote, was 'the effort to reclaim minority voice, to uncover the "buried past," to recover collective, lived experience.'[13]

Despite such reiterations of the traditional goals of social history – the uncovering of the 'buried past', the reclamation of minority voice and the resurrection of collective experience – those goals were rendered problematic by the new theoretical onslaughts, at least for those who cared to take an interest in the debates. To be sure, many social historians who came of age in the 1960s and 1970s continued to practise their craft in the ways they knew best, while many historical journals, notably the *International Review of Social History*, continued on the well-worn path they had long trodden, publishing work that seemed increasingly remote from the debates now taking place. But particularly for many younger historians – and also for those who were becoming uncomfortable with the central methodological practices and operative assumptions on which they had been raised – a number of works that rethought the practice of social history as it had developed in Britain began to acquire an iconic importance. Close to a decade before Joan Scott offered her own critique of the category of 'experience' in the USA, Gareth Stedman Jones had published his seminal article, 'Rethinking Chartism'. The single most important work in marking the 'linguistic turn' in the writing of British social history, it argued, provocatively, that the demands of the Chartists in the 1830s and 1840s must be seen not merely as a response to their personal experience of class and exploitation, but much more broadly in terms of a political language of eighteenth-century radicalism that pre-dated them. In

1986, Carolyn Steedman's path-breaking *Landscape for a Good Woman* also abandoned the terrain of straightforward reconstruction work to offer elaborate musings about how and in what ways individuals come into a sense of self, understand themselves, and negotiate their lives based on that knowledge. By the early 1990s, their work was joined by that of Patrick Joyce, who devoted his energies to repudiating the importance of class as a marker of self-identification in Britain. In so doing, he implicitly – and sometimes not so implicitly – attacked the work of a host of post-Thompsonian social historians for whom the reconstruction of the lived experience of class remained the bedrock of their own intellectual commitments.[14]

Not all social historians in Britain engaged with the work of Stedman Jones, Steedman or Joyce, or with that of those who followed loosely in their footsteps. But certainly, by the 1990s, debates about the future of social history in the wake of the linguistic turn were being aired more frequently in Britain than ever before, especially in the pages of the journal that took the new departures seriously, *Social History*. It was there that the work of Stedman Jones was debated; it was there, too, that Joyce could write not of the 'end of history', as Francis Fukuyama had after the end of the cold war in 1992, but of the end of social history as we had hitherto known it.[15] Obviously, despite Joyce's insistence, it was not (yet) the end of social history as it had been practised in Britain from the 1960s to the early 1980s. Indeed, by the close of the decade those social historians who had been most hostile to the new trends could celebrate what they perceived to be the end of the attacks on social history by the contemporary theorists. Certainly, by the turn of the millennium the debates had died down, prompting Lynn Hunt to co-edit a new collection of essays, *Beyond the Cultural Turn*, and, as president of the American Historical Association, to ponder the question, 'Where have all the theories gone?'[16] But while the debates were less shrill, while the polemics had become muted, and while for many 'the postmodern' increasingly seemed like a mere passing phase we (or some of us) were going through, the victory claimed by the forces of the more traditional practitioners of social history was pyrrhic at best. It was not the case that the more orthodox historians in general and social historians in particular had 'won' the battles of the 1980s and early 1990s. While some remained oblivious to the intellectual debates taking place around them, others were absorbing many of the new ideas. Those most likely to respond enthusiastically to the work of a Carolyn Steedman or a Patrick Joyce were already more than aware of the intellectual transformations taking place in the wake of the cultural turn, and the emergence of radically new work being undertaken in geography, anthropology and feminist theory, and in literary, post-colonial and cultural studies. As Alun Munslow succinctly put it in a debate in 1999 on history and postmodernism, hosted by the Institute of Historical Research in London, 'History is not what it was.'[17]

Rethinking social history

But if history wasn't what it was, what was it now – and how did the future of social history look at the beginning of the new millennium? In the United States, the *Journal of Social History* ran a series of articles on the state of social history in 2003. Marcel van der Linden, of the International Institute of Social History, began his contribution, 'More than thirty years ago, Eric Hobsbawm remarked that it was "a good moment to be a social historian." Few people would say the same now.'[18] Maybe van der Linden was right; maybe by 2003 it was not a good time to be the kind of social historian that flourished in the 1960s and 1970s – even if intellectual outlets for the work undertaken by such historians were still to be found in the *Journal of Social History* and in the journal of van der Linden's own institute, the *International Review of Social History.* Certainly the giddy days of expansion in the higher education sector characteristic of the 1960s were no more, and a whole generational cohort of social historians were gracefully (or not so gracefully) growing older together, their ranks increasingly depleted. Certainly, too, the confidence with which social historians from that moment once strutted their wares had been eroded by the various challenges outlined earlier. Moreover, even the highly specialised centre for the study of social history was fast becoming a relic of another age. While E. P. Thompson was a founder of the Centre for the Study of Social History at the University of Warwick in the mid 1960s, that centre, and others like it – and social history in general in Britain – ceased to enjoy the quasi-independent status it had slowly carved out for itself, reabsorbed into more mainstream departments of history, often for financial reasons, often for pedagogical reasons. Notwithstanding these changes, however – and some-times as a result of them – one could argue that social history was in the midst of a much-needed transformation and revitalisation, even if the new work that was being undertaken increasingly bore little resemblance to the work of the so-called golden age of the 'new' social history.

Many of the changes taking place can be seen unfolding in the pages of the new journal, *Cultural and Social History*, the 'official' organ of the Social History Society in Britain. Though the Society had already been in existence for 28 years before the launch of its journal, and though during that time it had published both a newsletter and a bulletin, the journal marked a new departure – both in scope and scale, and, more importantly, in its broader epistemological assump-tions. As the editorial board wrote in the first issue of *Cultural and Social History*, the new journal was committed to 'furthering the dialogue between social and cultural historians', thereby contributing to the 'reinvigoration of the discipline' in the wake of those 'epistemological challenges' that had confronted the profes-sion. 'We believe', wrote the board members, 'that an appreciation of the con-stellation of cultural forces that confer meaning on the lives of historical actors is necessary if we are to understand more fully the social experience of individuals and groups in the past.'[19] While 'experience' might still be central to the concerns of the Society and its members, the ways in which the category of experience had been rendered problematic was echoed in this editorial statement. On the one hand, this could certainly be seen as a capitulation of social history to the new cultural history that had risen so dramatically since the 1980s. But on the other it simply recognised a reality that was already clearly in evidence when one perused the journals and book catalogues – namely that the best social historical practice was already in the process of taking a 'cultural turn': a sharp turn in some cases, a mild bend in many others. In short, we had all (or at least a good number of us) become cultural historians. Even Asa Briggs, president of the Social History Society, could write, 'many social historians, who were I believe pioneers of social history in Britain, have for many years come to consider themselves principally as cultural historians'.[20]

What does it mean though, to say that social history was taking a cultural turn and that social historians were increasingly coming to view themselves as cultural historians? Perhaps some examples taken from *Cultural and Social History* during the first four years of its existence can be used to illustrate this gradual transition. During this period (2004–8) the journal conveyed an impression of a broader and more eclectic field than had hitherto been the case in the Society's old *Bulletin*; indeed, 'cultural and social history' became an amorphous and expansive rubric, incorporating a number of divergent operative assumptions and historiographical practices that depended for their momentum on the radical transformations in the broader profession during the past twenty years. This can be seen if we turn to several articles in particular and the ways in which they contributed to a rethinking of various sub-fields of social historical practice.

Borrowing from the extensive work that has in the last two decades emerged in the field of collective memory, a field that nicely straddles some of the concerns of social history (using oral history as a means of reconstructing past experience) and cultural history (looking at the ways in which group memories are socially mediated), Penny Summerfield has studied how the investigative subjects of oral history have drawn on public discourses to construct their accounts of the past. More specifically, turning to oral history accounts of experience in Britain during the Second World War, Summerfield examines the relationship between personal narratives and broader cultural silences about gender in society at the time. In so doing, she focuses on those expressive languages of selfhood that were available to women in the past, moving deftly back and forth between personal narratives and the cultural context in which they were composed.[21] Expanding rapidly in the 1960s, oral history became central to the writing of social history in the 1970s. The Oral History Society's journal *Oral History* was established in 1972, listed in terms of British Library cataloguing information as first and foremost concerned with 'social conditions – historical sources', while Paul Thompson's seminal work, *The Voice of the Past* (1978), soon became the cornerstone for work in the field. In part fueled by the History Workshop Movement, numerous local history projects in Britain were established in the 1970s and early 1980s, with the goal of getting 'the people' to remember the past – particularly the working-class past. In recent years it has been the work of scholars interested in the operations of memory, of the ways in which the past has come to be remembered and the narrated forms through which those memories have become more widely available – work along the lines of Summerfield's contribution – that has slowly, but radically, changed the face of the field.[22]

The cultural turn in social history can also be charted in the work of Andrew Davies. In 1992, Davies published his study of leisure in the working-class communities of Manchester and Salford between the wars, a recognisable work of post-Thompsonian social history.[23] Beginning in the later 1970s, the study of popular culture and leisure emerged as a major focus of social historical research in Britain, and in many respects Davies' work fits squarely within the confines of the general paradigm of the earlier work. To be sure, it is on some levels a revisionist text. It suggests, for example, that working-class experiences of leisure were much more diverse than Hobsbawm had previous implied in articles that stressed the importance of a homogeneous class, increasingly enthralled by the products of a new, mass culture.[24] More importantly, it paid much more attention to the gendering of class relationships than hitherto had been the case, focusing on the ways in which the experience of leisure was stratified along lines of gender as well as class. But at the end of the day it remained a methodologically traditional text, committed to the reconstruction of the experience of leisure, primarily via the tools of oral history. Fifteen years later, however, in an article in *Cultural and Social History*, Davies' focus had shifted, away from the reconstruction of everyday life to an examination of a series of linguistic codes through which particular aspects of everyday life were understood and rendered intelligible. To be more precise, Davies charted how various groups in Glasgow understood themselves and the world around them through the sensational media depictions of the gangster in the United States, a series of depictions that they strategically deployed in their own quest for influence, power and self-understanding in the local community.[25]

Davies' newer work is representative of a number of shifts taking place in a field once known as 'social history', shifts unfolding at numerous sites, including in the pages of *Cultural and Social History*. Central to those shifts are a heightened awareness of issues of language and representation; central, too, is a new attention to the political, an awareness that social history is anything but history with the politics left out. That *Cultural and Social History* should itself carry a debate on the ways in which diplomatic history is being transformed by the cultural turn, giving rise to an emphasis on the cultural politics of foreign relations, among other things, is itself testimony to the broader shifts taking place in the discipline of history and to the erosion of the boundaries between various disciplinary sub-fields.[26] Moreover, as those boundaries come to be seen as more porous and artificial, so has an interest in the history of their origins and development grown. That historians should now be calling for a history of 'the social', a history of how the very terrain on which social historians operate has been constituted as a domain of knowledge and a site for the exercise of power, is testimony to the changes taking place.[27]

In the forty years since the institutionalisation of social history in the British academy the field has changed beyond recognition. Nowhere can this be seen more clearly than through a comparison of two books that ostensibly deal with similar topics – hunger, food, diet – written at both ends of this period, *Plenty and Want*, published in 1966 by the late John Burnett, a former chair of the Social History Society, and *Hunger: A Modern History*, published by James Vernon in 2007.[28] The former marked a late-stage intervention into the standard-of-living debate during and in the wake of the Industrial Revolution. In meticulous detail, Burnett charted who ate what, and when, amassing an array of figures with respect to consumption patterns during a century and a half of rapid social change. Reconstructing the diets of different social classes in Britain, Burnett was eager to dispel widely circulated myths about the consumption of food: 'Stripped of its mythology, the story of dietary change in England may be less colourful than we would wish. The facts must speak for themselves. It is important that our social history should not be based on fiction, and that the facts should be put together before they vanish completely.'[29] Vernon, by contrast, sets himself a radically different task, one of tracing the concept of hunger and how it has changed over time, from the early nineteenth century, when it was viewed as either a result of the moral failing of individuals or an unavoidable natural phenomenon, to the later twentieth century – to a period when, in the wake of the intervention of all kinds of 'experts' and political authorities, hunger was viewed as a global social problem requiring state and humanitarian assistance. From a focus on suffragette hunger strikes to the politics of school meals, from famines in Ireland and India to the rise of nutritional science, Vernon casts his net broadly, focusing on two simple questions: 'How has the meaning of hunger changed over time, and what were the causes and consequences of those changes?'[30]

Vernon's work cannot be viewed as 'social history', at least not in the way Burnett saw it. Indeed, his work makes a mockery of sub-disciplinary boundaries, and in many respects aspires to the kind of 'total' history Hobsbawm called for in the essay with which this chapter opened (albeit without the same degree of commitment to those forms of economic determinism that framed Hobsbawm's work). As Vernon describes his own practice, 'I have combined social, cultural, political, and imperial history with histories of science, technology, and other material forms, without ever trying to reconcile them in any grand framing statement.' It is a book, he insists, written after both the cultural and imperial turns in the writing of British history – a book not possible without the epistemolog ical transformations that have taken place since the 1960s.[31] If there is still a place for social history, it is as a radically transformed practice, like Vernon's, for which the very name 'social history' may no longer be adequate. *Hunger: A Modern History* was praised on the back of its dust jacket by Geoff Eley, who spoke not about its contribution as a work of social history, but of its contribution to the history of the welfare state and of democracy and citizenship in twentieth-century Britain, 'a work of exciting originality'. Eley himself has recently published a personal and magisterial account of the transformation of historical practice during the past forty years, charting a journey, as he sees it, from 'optimism' about the promises of social history in the 1960s, to 'disappointment', to 'reflectiveness', to 'defiance', to borrow from his chapter titles. Attempting to rescue the best social historical practices from the past while recognising the profound transformations that have taken place in the wake of the cultural turn, Eley stresses the extent to which boundaries between different kinds of history have become blurred, encouraging individuals 'to move freely across the old distinctions between the social, the cultural, the political, the intellectual, and so forth, allowing new hybridities to form.'[32] The future should witness the appearance of many more hybrid products, further rendering the term 'social history' inadequate to describe the complexities of the best historical writing.

Gérard Noiriel

In this contribution I will begin by alluding to the analysis I have developed in a debate on the 'crisis' of social history that took place in France in the late 1990s. I will then present in outline the field of research that has been called 'socio-history', although lack of space prevents me from saying a great deal about the many empirical works that have been undertaken since the late 1980s in this area.[33]

Remarks on the 'crisis' of social history

The title of this chapter, 'Is there still a place for social history?' is informed by a view that many historians consider self-evident, that social history is indeed in 'crisis'. This view has been expounded in many different ways since the late 1980s, but I do not think that it has really been 'proved'. As I tried to show in my analysis of debates around the 'linguistic turn', there are two ways of arguing that a field of research is in decline.[34] The first is statistical. It consists of counting the number of articles and books published by researchers in order to quantify which sectors are expanding and which are in decline. The difficulty with this sort of accounting is that many works cut across a number of kinds of history. Those like myself who work on the history of immigration contribute at the same time to the development of economic, social, cultural and political history. For this reason such accounting is never very precise. That said, figures that we have for France suggest that the proportion of publications deriving from social history has not really declined over the past few decades.[35]

The second way of arguing that a field is in decline – and by far the most common way – is based on arguments drawn from theories of knowledge. In this case it is suggested that a field is in decline because it is no longer at the cutting-edge of research. It is said to have been 'overtaken' by new fields of enquiry, which use theoretical insights that come principally from philosophy. Dominick LaCapra's *Rethinking Intellectual History*, published in 1983, is a good example of this kind of approach. LaCapra argues that social history is in crisis because it has not woken from its 'dogmatic slumber', and that it persists in ignoring that reality is always textual because we can only reach it through the medium of documents. Mobilising the theories of Martin Heidegger and Jacques Derrida in support of his claims, he concludes that the discipline of history has to be totally 'refounded'.[36]

I have criticised this kind of argument by referring to the analysis of the philosopher Richard Rorty. According to Rorty, the 'textualists' are correct to argue that 'we cannot think without concepts or speak without words', but they are wrong to conclude that 'we cannot think or speak about what has been created by our thoughts or our words'.[37] In other words, to recognise that historians work on texts does not oblige us to conclude that textual criticism has a privileged access to knowledge. My aim in quoting Richard Rorty was not to fuel the ongoing struggle for pre-eminence that historians conduct by means of mobilising philosophers, but, on the contrary, to underline that we cannot settle debates among historians by relying on philosophers. In any case, that is what 'anti-foundationalists' such as Ludwig Wittgenstein, Richard Rorty, Jacques Bouveresse and Jacques Derrida have long argued, denying that philosophy can acts as a policeman or judge when it comes to theories of knowledge.

I have wondered why historians who are most concerned with innovation are fascinated by philosophy. I have concluded that it offers us the weapons we need to fight our internal struggles. What is at stake in these struggles is the definition of 'innovation'. To be recognised as authorities we must constantly convince other scholars that we have discovered something new. Real innovation, however, can only be recognised by specialists in the field concerned, that is, by a small number of people. Since the 1960s there has been a much greater division of labour in the world of historical research, leading to an extreme atomisation and fragmentation of research. As a result, the communities of experts, linking specialists who speak the same language, have become much smaller, even if they have become internationalised. This development has created a malaise in the discipline that has been well analysed by Peter Novick.[38] The politicisation of academic research and the higher profile of theoretical debates are, I think, both the expression and the consequence of this malaise.[39]

To begin with, I developed these arguments with a view to defending social history from criticisms that I did not think were justified. Subsequently, I wished to demonstrate that the success of social history in the past was explained by the same factors that have contributed to its recent fall from grace. Political conditions notably played a role in the emergence of social history. It was born in France at the end of the nineteenth century with the formation of the labour movement. It enjoyed a new success with the foundation of the *Annales* school of history in 1929, at a time of economic crisis and political extremism. The same thing happened after the Second World War and again after May 1968.

The privileged ties that social historians established with Marxism gave them an advantage when it came to theories of knowledge. In the case of France there were two stages in this process. The first occurred in the 1930s. In order to challenge the then dominant political history, the founders of the *Annales*, Lucien Febvre and Marc Bloch, used the criticism of their historical presuppositions that Durkheimian sociologists – notably François Simiand, the most Marxist of them – had developed at the beginning of the century. Lucien Febvre argued that political history served the ruling class because, while claiming to be impartial and objective, it simply adopted that class's vision of the world. To break free of these 'positivist' presuppositions, the historian had to refine a new line of questioning, with a critical distance on the passions and interests of his own time. This explains the importance of the 'problem history' for the founders of the *Annales*. It was not enough simply to go to the archives in order to be a good historian, he or she had to be clear about which problem they wanted to address.[40]

Only after the Second World War was the Marxist interpretation adopted by a new generation of social historians, in response to the political circumstances. The struggle with historical 'positivism' became more technical. Marxist historians, convinced that historical materialism unlocked the secret of 'laws of history', became involved in philosophical debates about the foundations of knowledge. They also – and above all – used Marx in their empirical work, constructing a framework of analysis which included all aspects of reality. This was the famous three-part or three-stage plan which organised so many theses between the 1950s and 1970s: first the economy, then society and finally politics. According to this plan the analysis of struggles for and exercise of political power was always left to the third part, alongside 'culture' and 'mentalities'. This framework of analysis enabled social historians to justify their pre-eminence, arguing, like Lucien Febvre in the 1930s, that social history was a 'total' history because everything 'in reality' was social.

The exceptional impact of social history between the 1950s and 1970s was also explained by the fact that historians who based their research on the Marxist interpretation were among the most original when it came to empirical research. The names of E. P. Thompson in Britain and Ernest Labrousse in France were fine examples of this marriage.

The factors which ensured the success of social history in the post-war decades nevertheless turned against it from the 1970s. By arguing that social history was total history, its proponents ended up by diluting their subject completely. Some of the more lucid social historians were already aware of this. For example, in the early 1970s Eric Hobsbawm pointed out that 'social history' was very difficult to define because of the multiple meanings of the term 'social'. He recognised that the fashion for social history was explained above all by its name, which had become overused in politics and that this had affected research.[41] Fifteen years later, Olivier Zunz drew attention to a problem of the same kind. Demonstrating the infinite widening of topics that came under social history, he feared that if things continued that way, social history would soon become 'whatever social historians chose to write'.[42]

Social historians thus made rods for their own backs which their adversaries then used to beat them with. The rivalry between generations of historians for recognition explained that young historians who emerged after May 1968 were keen to distance themselves from a social history which claimed to have a monopoly of historical innovation. What was particularly striking, however, was that the newcomers in turn took up the same arguments as their predecessors. As I said earlier, these partisans of the linguistic turn in history tried to refute the arguments of their rivals by arguing that the reality to which the historian had access was not social but textual. They found new weapons to attack 'positivism' in the philosophical currents that had been used to attack Marxism in the nineteenth century – what in Germany was called the 'philosophy of mind'. In France this new offensive was heralded by Paul Veyne's *Writing History*.[43] Rejecting the notion that history could be a true science, as Marxists maintained, Veyne argued that history was in fact only one kind of narrative, what he called 'la mise en intrigue' or 'emplotment'.[44]

Students of my generation who were immersed in these debates acquired an epistemological training that their predecessors did not have. Many of them, including myself, however, soon lost their theoretical illusions. We realised that – even if France was an extreme example – historical writing that was supposed to 'revolutionise history' by using the great philosophers of the moment, such as Foucault or Derrida, revolutionised nothing at all. We asked ourselves why this should be. The real reason was clear, although seldom declared in public. When they were asked privately about the epistemological works of Paul Veyne or Michel de Certeau, most French historians admitted that they 'didn't understand anything'. The avant-garde strategy adopted by these epistemological historians was thus to 'revolutionise' the expertise of a research community by speaking a foreign language to it, rather as in the old days country priests in France tried to persuade peasants that heaven existed by speaking Latin to them.

The failure of this approach encouraged a number of us to try something else. This is what lies behind the emergence of what in France is called 'socio-history'.

What is socio-history?

This field of research has been developed in the last fifteen years by historians, sociologists, anthropologists and political scientists who are disillusioned by politics, but also by all kinds of theoretical pretension. It is significant that the first books and articles defining socio-history came out about fifteen years after the publication of the first empirical works which appealed to it. The review *Genèses*, which we founded in 1991 as the first grouping of researchers practising socio-history, demonstrates that our aim was to create a new space in which researchers from different areas, working with a perspective that was both historical and sociological, would be able to come together to develop empirical research.[45] This strategy derived from the conviction that we could bring together different points of view and forge a common language, not through great theoretical debates but through practice.

Since one always has to look to philosophy to justify one's practice, I would say that socio-historians see their area of expertise as a 'play of language' in the sense of Ludwig Wittgenstein. Those who participate abide by the rules of the game. They have a common expertise which they develop by training and playing the game. Rather than defining the frontiers of their field precisely, socio-historians prefer to see it as a general field with shifting contours, bringing together research which has a 'family likeness'. To explain what socio-history is, it is important to give examples, urging those who wish to practise this play of language to use the toolbox it recommends.

Defining socio-history as a 'play of language' explains the importance that the socio-historian gives to the process of naming in the competition that sets researchers against each other in the struggle for innovation. The term 'socio-history' was chosen because it distinguishes the approach, both from traditional social history and from comparative historical sociology as practised by Charles Tilly in the United States and Jürgen Kocka in Germany. It also distinguishes the approach from micro-history, which nurtures strong ties with anthropology. Naming a field of enquiry is also to announce a brand, to raise a standard in order to give visibility to a group. An examination of the works undertaken under this brand name shows that many could equally have been claimed by social history or by historical sociology.

Rather than dividing up fields of research like 'territories' which correspond to 'slices' of reality, the socio-historian prefers a Weberian approach. Disciplines are seen as points of view onto reality, rather than reflections of it. This 'constructivist' perspective has been preferred because of the empirical advantages it affords. Interdisciplinarity can be seen as a convergence of expertises, as understood by researchers in the physical sciences. Undertaking socio-history requires a training in both history and sociology, but this in no way indicates that the field is only of interest to historians and sociologists. It has been enriched by researchers from all disciplines, and some of the most striking developments of socio-history in the last fifteen years have been in political science.[46] For this reason, frontier skirmishes between economic, political and cultural history make little sense to a socio-historian. Today, in France, there is a socio-history of the economic, of the political and of the cultural.[47]

Socio-historians could be criticised for promoting an approach which is eclectic and not very rigorous. Isn't the main innovation of socio-historians simply to call old-fashioned social history something else? After all, socio-historians are involved in the battle for recognition, of which I spoke earlier. To secure a visibility going beyond the small circle of specialists in one's field, it is necessary to demonstrate originality by using new terms, even if the content of the empirical research is not entirely new. But socio-history is not just about changing terms. Its originality is precisely its way of combining the approaches of history and sociology. The socio-historian's toolbox is the critical approach that was originally that of both those disciplines. I will develop this aspect now.

Against the reification of the social world

History and sociology both became scientific disciplines by criticising, in different ways, what may be called the 'reification' of the social world. History, as an autonomous academic discipline, emerged in Germany at the beginning of the nineteenth century, demonstrating that the 'things' that surround us (buildings, institutions, objects, archives) are the inert traces of human activity in the past. The historical method, of which the main lines were defined at this time, is based on a critical examination of those traces. Its aim was to rediscover flesh-and-blood individuals behind the inanimate world of objects they have left behind. Socio-history approaches this in its own way. It is particularly interested in the genesis or origin of the phenomena it studies. The socio-historian tries to illuminate the historical dimension of the world we live in, the better to understand how the past weighs on the present. This approach is also valid for early periods. In all human societies, the past conditions the present. Even if socio-history to date has been undertaken by historians of the period after 1789, its field of study is not limited in any way chronologically.

Sociology emerged at the end of the nineteenth century, developing a critique of another kind of reification, embodied in language, which consisted in seeing collective entities such as the Nation, the State or the Church as real people. The task of sociology was to deconstruct those entities in order to locate individuals and the relations they sustained between themselves – what one might call 'the social bond'. Socio-history has the same task, but is particularly interested in distance relations. Because of the invention of writing and money and technical progress, people can form ties between themselves which far outstrip the sphere of direct exchange, based on face-to-face communities. 'Invisible threads' today link millions of people who do not know each other. One of the principal aims of socio-history is to study these forms of interdependence and to show how they affect face-to-face relations.

We should add that sociology developed in Germany and France on the basis of another principle that socio-history has adopted, that of the conflictual nature of relations between individuals. The importance given to the social bond flows from the observation that social life is not a given. Rivalry and competition between individuals for wealth, power or honour have always been a central dimension of social relations. The socio-historian seeks to understand how the evolution of means of human action over long distances has transformed these relations of power. Power is seen as a 'cement' which permits individuals to establish bonds. It is not a question of criticising power relations but understanding concretely how they function. By combining the approaches of French Durkheimian sociology and German Weberian sociology we can define two broad perspectives.

The first perspective sees power from the point of view of social domination. The invention of writing, money and technological progress have played a decisive part in the development of the two great forms of domination that exist in the world today: economic domination (capitalism) and political domination (state power). The socio-historian, using the work of Max Weber and Norbert Elias, sees them as relations of interdependence over distance (mediated by bureaucracy), as social configurations bringing together actors who are joined by the same kind of economic activity (shareholders, employers, workers) and political activity (rulers and ruled). The second perspective on power relations uses the idea developed above all by Durkheim that social solidarity is based on constraint. Means of action over distance cannot simply be seen as forms of domination. They are also powerful means of collective action, thanks to which the weak and poor can organise themselves to defend their interests and ideals.

The toolbox of socio-historians is completed by the innovations developed by social sciences after the Second World War. One of the most important contributions of French critical thinkers of this period (like Gilles Deleuze, Jacques Derrida or Pierre Bourdieu) is their elaboration of a third dimension of power relations, a symbolic order which concerns language in particular. The shift from the spoken to the written word gives a symbolic power to those who control the means of communication over distance because they address a public, that is, a large number of scattered individuals who do not know each other. All public discourse traces a demarcation line between realities that are made visible to all by dint of being publicly expressed, and realities that remain invisible because they do not escape the sphere of 'private' language. Individuals who hold the privilege of defining the identities, problems and norms of the social world impose the conditions which must be observed by all those who wish to intervene in the public arena. That is why questions of naming, defining and categorisation are at the heart of the preoccupations of socio-history.[48]

In this way, if socio-history rejects the epistemological arguments used by the partisans of the linguistic turn in order to discredit social history, it recognises the importance of this current for the renewal of empirical research. Nevertheless, the socio-historian always sees language as a social relationship, linking he or she who speaks or writes with he or she who listens or reads. This explains the very great importance that socio-history gives to the reception of discourse.[49] The example of literature shows that writing can be a powerful means of distance action when it succeeds in playing on the emotions of readers, as in the case of the novel. The propensity of readers to identify with stories told to them is a symbolic way of decreasing the distance between the reader and the writer. This pattern is found in different forms in other fields. Very often, individuals interiorise the labels and symbols which defy the groups or categories to which they belong and which speak in their name. Conversely, when individuals are publicly designated in a negative or pejorative light, language can become a factor of stigmatisation and shame.[50]

To conclude this rapid presentation of the basic principles of socio-history, I would like to underline that it is not a theory of the social world, but rather a toolbox. Orientated towards the analysis of concrete empirical problems, the method of the socio-historian is to better understand the world we live in. The choice of tools and the way in which they are used always depends on the precise questions the research is asking. In the end, socio-history is a way of practising the social sciences which makes it possible to acquire 'tricks of the trade'. The community of expertise is defined by the fact that confronted by the same text, socio-historians would have the same reflexes, for example to explore its historical nature and to locate the individuals behind the collective entities.

The scholar and the politician

The last point I want to make concerns the relations between the scholar and the politician. Here again, socio-history follows the path of Norbert Elias.[51] Keen to produce findings that might be useful to those fighting for a better world, the socio-historian nevertheless seeks to maintain a distance from political activity, as this distance is a necessary condition of all scientific work. The civic purpose of socio-history is to produce understanding which helps to clarify the political and social issues of our time and helps citizens to develop their critical judgement, without ever speaking for them.

The socio-historian considers that the autonomy secured by academic communities at the end of the nineteenth century in Europe and North America has been a fundamental achievement of democracy, and one which must be preserved at any price. The 'positivist' historians of that period defended this achievement in philosophically naive language about the objectivity of knowledge. One of the main consequences of the entry of epistemological language into the language of the discipline has been to discredit this type of argument. Marxist historians led the way there, followed by feminist, postmodern and postcolonial historians. These criticisms of the objectivity of history are founded on fully justified observations. They have shown that until the middle of the twentieth century, the history of working people, women, immigrants or colonised peoples was ignored because academic posts were monopolised by men from the educated middle class. Not until researchers from these sectors were taken on by universities did these new research fields gain legitimacy.

The socio-historian, too, considers the traditional definition of objectivity to be redundant. That said, there can be no question of renouncing the ideal of truth held sacred by the world of science, for that would be to go backwards and to encourage confusion between history and memory. The objectivity of scientific research for Norbert Elias was based on the view that, unlike the artist, the scholar is subject to a collective discipline. In the natural sciences, the personal wishes of researchers, political ideals and passions are contained by institutionalised controls. Theories, instruments and specialised journals are so many objective factors which frame scientific activity. Thanks to this process the researcher can practise the 'emotional distancing' that defines the scholarly position. The best criterion to measure the degree of objectivity achieved by a scientific discipline is to measure the intensity of collective practices which bind members of the group.

One of the best ways to improve the objectivity of scientific work is to improve communication between researchers, encouraging free discussion and exchange of argument. The socio-history of cultural activity shows why such debates are rare. Writing introduces a relationship of interdependence between the writer and the reader. This relationship takes a particular form in the scholarly world because the readers are also the writers, and vice versa. To understand how scholarly texts are received, the socio-historian classifies them into two large groups. On the one hand, some reading is for appropriation, whereby the reader takes from the text only what is useful for his or her own writings. Other reading, by contrast, is to stimulate discussion. It is especially at this level that there is a lack of communication. Intellectual debates, particularly in France, observed Michel Foucault, are stuck in the polemics that characterise the world of politics.[52] The polemicist seeks to find a fact or opinion in the speech of his adversary, without paying any attention to his point of view or the coherence of his argument. He assumes a sovereign power in relation to his opponent, demolishing his speech without appeal and preparing the case against him. All that is required is to dig out quotes, making anyone say anything. To improve communication in the historical discipline, ways must be found to move from the polemical stage to the discussion stage. Experience shows that this is not always possible.

If socio-historians are serious about having an impact they must realise that the production of knowledge is not finished the moment they lay down their pen. They must follow the path of their discoveries from conception to ultimate destination. They must be able to present their discoveries in languages their target audiences can understand. Finally, they must mobilise to defend their scholarship publicly, for no one will do it for them.

Notes

1　Eric Hobsbawm, 'From social history to the history of society', in *On History* (New York, New Press, 1997), 79–80.

2　Harold Perkin, *The Making of a Social Historian* (London, Athena Press, 2002), 92–4. For an overview of the pre-1960s origins of social history, see Miles Taylor, 'The beginnings of modern British social history', *History Workshop Journal* 43 (1997), 155–76.

3　'Editorials', *History Workshop Journal* 1 (1976), 1.

4　Paul Cartledge, 'What is social history now?', in *What is History Now?*, ed. David Cannadine (Basingstoke, Palgrave Macmillan, 2002), 21.

5　David Harvey, *The Condition of Postmodernity: An Enquiry into the Origins of Cultural Change* (Oxford, Blackwell, 1989).

6　Lynn Hunt, ed., *The New Cultural History* (Berkeley, University of California Press, 1989), 22.

7　Perez Zagorin, 'Historiography and postmodernism: reconsiderations', *History and Theory* 29 (1990), 264, fn. 4 (Zagorin referred specifically to the work of Hayden White); F. R. Ankersmit, 'Historiography and postmodernism', *History and Theory* 28 (1989), 137–53.

8　Joyce Appleby, 'One good turn deserves another: moving beyond the linguistic; a response to David Harlan', *American Historical Review* 94 (1989), 1326; David Harlan, 'Intellectual history and the return of literature', *American Historical Review* 94 (1989), 581–609.

9　James Epstein, 'Understanding the cap of liberty: symbolic practice and social conflict in early nineteenth-century England', *Past & Present* 122 (1989), 75–118.

10　Patrick Joyce, 'The return of history: postmodernism and the politics of academic history in Britain', *Past*

& *Present* 158 (1998), 221.

11 See especially Peter Schöttler, 'Historians and discourse analysis', *History Workshop Journal* 27 (1989), 37–65.

12 Joan W. Scott, 'The evidence of experience', *Critical Inquiry* 17 (1991), 777, 779–80. See also Craig Ireland, 'The appeal to experience and its consequences: variations on a persistent Thompsonian theme', *Cultural Critique* 52 (2002), 87–107.

13 Gordon H. Chang, 'History and postmodernism', *Amerasia Journal* 21 (1995), 90.

14 Gareth Stedman Jones, 'Rethinking Chartism', in his *Languages of Class: Studies in English Working-Class History, 1832–1982* (Cambridge University Press, 1983); Carolyn Steedman, *Landscape for a Good Woman: A Story of Two Lives* (London, Virago, 1986); Patrick Joyce, *Visions of the People: Industrial England and the Question of Class, 1840–1914* (Cambridge University Press, 1991); Joyce, *Democratic Subjects: The Self and the Social in Nineteenth-Century England* (Cambridge University Press, 1994).

15 See David Mayfield and Susan Thorne, 'Social history and its discontents: Gareth Stedman Jones and the politics of language', *Social History* 17 (1992), 165–88; Patrick Joyce, 'The imaginary discontents of social history: a note of response', *Social History* 18 (1993), 81–6; James Vernon, 'Who's afraid of the "linguistic turn"? The politics of social history and its discontents', *Social History* 19 (1994), 81–97; Patrick Joyce, 'The end of social history', *Social History* 20 (January 1995), 73–91.

16 Victoria E. Bonnell and Lynn Hunt, eds., *Beyond the Cultural Turn: New Directions in the Study of Society and Culture* (Berkeley, University of California Press, 1999); Lynn Hunt, 'Where have all the theories gone?' *Perspectives* 40 (2002), available at www.historians.org/perspectives/issues/2002/0203

17 Alun Munslow, 'The postmodern in history: a response to Professor O'Brien', part of a debate, 'Discourse on Postmodernism and History', in the Institute's *Reviews in History*, available at www.history.ac.uk/discourse/index.html

18 Marcel van der Linden, 'Gaining ground', *Journal of Social History* 37 (2003), 69. See also Peter Stearns' introduction to the special issue, 'Social History Present and Future', 9–19.

19 Editorial, *Cultural and Social History* 1 (2004), 1.

20 'From Lord Briggs, the President of the Social History Society', *Cultural and Social History* 1 (2004), 2. One could argue that as early as his seminal *Victorian People* (1954), Briggs was most interested in what would become known, borrowing from the French *Annales* school, as the study of *mentalités* – in this instance, in the cultural logic of mid-Victorian Britain. For the complex relationship between these fields, see Paula S. Fass, 'Cultural history/social history: some reflections on a continuing dialogue', *Journal of Social History* 37 (2003), 39–46.

21 Penny Summerfield, 'Culture and composure: creating narratives of the gendered self in oral history interviews', *Cultural and Social History* 1 (2004), 65–93.

22 For community oral history projects and their work, see Chris Waters, 'Autobiography, nostalgia, and the practices of working-class selfhood', in George K. Behlmer and Fred M. Leventhal, eds., *Singular Continuities: Tradition, Nostalgia, and Identity in Modern Britain* (Stanford University Press, 2000), 178–95.

23 Andrew Davies, *Leisure, Gender and Poverty: Working-Class Culture in Salford and Manchester, 1900–1939* (Milton Keynes: Open University Press, 1992).

24 Reprinted in E. J. Hobsbawm, *Worlds of Labour: Further Studies in the History of Labour* (London, Weidenfeld & Nicolson,1984).

25 Andrew Davies, 'The Scottish Chicago? From 'hooligans' to 'gangsters' in inter-war Glasgow', *Cultural and Social History* 4 (2008), 511–27.

26 See David Reynolds, 'International history, the cultural turn and the diplomatic twitch', *Cultural and Social History* 3 (2006), 75–91, the responses by Patrick Finney and Antony Best, and Reynolds' reply, *Cultural and Social History* 3 (2006), 472–95.

27 See Vernon, 'Who's afraid of the "linguistic turn"?', 88ff.; Joyce, 'The end of social history', esp. part 3. For recent work on 'the social' as a site of governmentality, see Chris Otter, 'Making liberalism durable: vision and civility in the late Victorian city', *Social History* 27 (2002), 1–15.

28 John Burnett, *Plenty and Want: A Social History of Diet in England from 1815 to the Present Day* (London, Nelson, 1966); James Vernon, *Hunger: A Modern History* (Cambridge, Mass., Harvard University Press, 2007).

29 Burnett, x.

30 Vernon, ix.

31 Ibid. For a recent discussion of the shift from social to cultural history in the writing of the new imperial history, see Antoinette Burton, 'Thinking beyond the boundaries: empire, feminism and the domains of history', *Social History* 26 (2001), 60–71.

32 Geoff Eley, *A Crooked Line: From Cultural History to the History of Society* (Ann Arbor, University of

Michigan Press, 2005), 201.

33 For a presentation of empirical research on socio-history see Gérard Noiriel, *Introduction à la socio-histoire* (Paris, La Découverte, 2006)

34 Gérard Noiriel, *Sur la 'crise' de l'histoire* (Paris, Belin, 1996). I am summarising the principal themes of this book, which has been translated into Spanish, Japanese, Hungarian and Greek but not yet into English, for an English-speaking public.

35 Christophe Charle, 'Essai de bilan', in Christophe Charle, ed., *Histoire sociale, histoire globale?* (Paris, Maison des sciences de l'homme, 1993).

36 Dominick LaCapra, *Rethinking Intellectual History: Texts, Contexts, Language* (Ithaca, Cornell University Press, 1983).

37 Richard Rorty, *Consequences of Pragmatism* (University of Minnesota Press, 1982).

38 Peter Novick, *That Noble Dream. The 'Objectivity Question' and the American Historical Profession* (Cambridge University Press, 1988).

39 It is evident in historians' increasing use of terms such as 'new', 'post', 'beyond', and 'rethinking '.

40 Lucien Febvre, *Combats pour l'histoire* (Paris, A. Colin, 1953).

41 Hobsbawm, 'From social history to the history of society' (see note 1).

42 Olivier Zunz, *Reliving the Past. The Worlds of Social History* (Chapel Hill, University of North Carolina Press, 1985), 4.

43 Paul Veyne, *Comment on écrit l'histoire* (Paris, Le Seuil, 1971), translated as *Writing History: An Epistomological Essay* (Manchester University Press, 1984). See also Michel de Certeau, *L'écriture de l'histoire* (Paris, Gallimard, 1975), translated as *The Writing of History* (New York, Columbia University Press, 1988).

44 Paul Veyne, *Writing History*, Chapter 3.

45 *Genèses. Sciences sociales et histoire*, published by Belin, Paris. Belin also publishes the collection *Socio-histoires*, edited by Michel Offerlé and Gérard Noiriel.

46 For a general insight into this stream of research, cf. Yves Deloye and Bernard Voutat, eds., *Faire de la science politique. Pour une socio-histoire du politique* (Paris, Belin, 2002).

47 For recent examples of socio-historical research on economic questions, see Hélène Michel, *La cause des propriétaires. Etat et propriété en France, fin XIXe–XXe siècle* (Paris, Belin, 2006) and Gilles Laferté, *La Bourgogne et ses vins: image d'origine contrôlée* (Paris, Belin, 2006). A recent socio-historical work on the construction of public opinion is Nicolas Mariot, *Bains de foule. Les voyages présidentiels en province, 1880–2002* (Paris, Belin, 2006). On the politician's 'trade', see Michel Offerlé, ed., *La profession politique* (Paris, Belin, 1999). Antoine Lilti's *Le monde des salons. Sociabilité et mondanité à Paris au XVIII° siècle* (Paris, Fayard, 2005) is an excellent illustration of the contribution of socio-history to cultural issues.

48 See, in particular, Christian Topalov, *'Naissance' du chômeur 1880–1910* (Paris, Albin Michel, 1994) and Gérard Noiriel, ed., *L'identification. Genèse d'un travail d'Etat* (Paris, Belin, 2007).

49 On this, see Roger Chartier, *L'ordre des livres: lecteurs, auteurs et bibliothèques en Europe entre XIVe et XVIIe siècles* (Aix-en-Provence, Alinéa, 1992).

50 Gérard Noiriel, *Immigration, antisémitisme et racisme en France (XIXe–XXe siècle). Discours publics, humiliations privées* (Paris, Fayard, 2007).

51 Norbert Elias, *Engagement et distanciation* (Paris, Fayard, 1983), translated as *Involvement and Detachment* (Oxford, Basil Blackwell, 1987).

52 Michel Foucault, 'Polémique, politique et problématisation', in *Dits et écrits*, vol. 4 (Paris, Gallimard, 1994 [1984]).

2

Is economic history no longer fashionable?

Patricia Clavin and Michel Margairaz

Economic history has gone through a number of changes in the last hundred years. It emerged to investigate the challenges of industrialisation and economic depression. In a second phase, it was dazzled by the achievements of economic theory and endeavoured to become more scientific; this was the high point of cliometrics (the application of modern forms of statistical and macroeconomic analyses to history). At this point it parted company from mainstream history, which no longer 'understood' it. In recent years, however, there has been a convergence of economic history and mainstream history in new and exciting ways. Patricia Clavin and Michel Margairaz *demonstrate that economic history has become more open to social and cultural history, studying consumption as much as production, the management of businesses, the interplay of the market with other institutions and the 'invention' of economic categories such as unemployment. Equally, economic history has demonstrated its pioneering role in the development of new approaches in understanding globalism, transnationalism, migration and human rights, which augurs well for the approaches of economic historians to stimulate historical approaches across a range of fields.*

Patricia Clavin

From coal to cappuccino

The answer to the question posed in the heading of this chapter was an emphatic 'no', if two large-scale and richly-funded research schemes running in British universities in 2007 were anything to go by. Both collaborative projects, 'The Cultures of Consumption' and 'The Nature of Evidence: How Well Do Facts Travel?', were engaged with topics that were traditionally the preserve of economic historians. Within the huge 'Cultures of Consumption' programme, which comprised 26 discrete projects that looked at the changing dynamics of consumption, past and present, and the implications for the future, at least eight of the projects addressed issues historically in the field of economic history, including the history of Italian coffee, the history of water consumption, the role of the housewife in early modern England and the economics of horticulture in nineteenth-century America.

These projects, and others, remained faithful to the project brief in their sensitivity to consumption, exploring changes over time and across national and regional groups. The formulation of their research questions, the selection and exploration of evidence, and the conclusions drawn, demonstrated that this was not economic history, at least not in a form recognised by its nineteenth- and twentieth-century practitioners.[1] The commodity biographies that formed an essential part of the programme spent little time on the details of production and how this defined the importance of the commodity and its place in society's productive and communal relations. Production, in one of the programme's sub-projects, 'The Cappuccino Conquests', that traced the rise of the popularity of Italian coffees since the 1950s, was taken to mean the manufacture of symbolic meanings around these beverages. The work draws out how far cappuccinos, espressos and latte coffees were still seen as Italian, despite their large-scale appropriation by American multi-national coffee chains and the variety in their consumption. One of the headline findings of the project was that diversity continues in the global age of the twenty-first century: 'Drinking cultures remain diverse. In Italy, cappuccino is a morning drink, served in a 6oz. (diversity in weights and measures survive too it seems) cup ready to drink; in Britain it comes in 8oz. cups, to be sipped leisurely while with a friend at any time of the day; while in the United States people walk off with a 12oz. take-away mug.'[2] The old, important questions of economic history remained unaddressed: how many people were employed in the industry? What were its annual turnover and its global economic reach? How did the market for coffee continue to shape the economic relations between 'rich' and 'poor' people and countries in history? That coffee remained the world's foremost traded primary good remained unmentioned and perhaps undervalued in the formulation of this project.

Consumption, too, lay at the heart of a series of interrelated research questions posed by economic historians at the London School of Economics in 2004. The project examined not only whether and how facts travel, but what happens when they do: do they gain or lose status? The term 'facts' was broadly defined and taken to mean 'just those pieces of information that are privileged as being true among the community that uses them'.[3] The great advantage of this definition was that it allowed investigators to be agnostic about the 'truth' of the matter (the issue on which so much historical debate traditionally turned) and instead move on to a different set of questions, focused on the transfer of facts from one context to another: is information scrambled, and does this work for or against the facts? What types of mechanism enabled transit? Here, the question of how the facts were produced was integrated into the research design, and the project's preoccupation to integrate recent developments of cultural historical practice into the project's preoccupations was genuinely path-breaking. Particularly notable was its attempt to address long-established tensions in the field between medieval and early modern economic historians who argued that economic facts cannot be abstracted from their social and cultural contexts, and the new wave of modern economic history with its fancy for stylised facts.[4] This was cutting-edge research in all sorts of ways, but the project's formulation demonstrated that the primacy accorded to the production of goods and services, and to the social relations of production, so evident in earlier economic histories, has gone the way of the British manufacturing industries.

The golden age of economic history

The study of economic history in the UK was pioneered in the history department at Manchester University, where T. F. Tout created the department of economic history in 1890 and George Unwin was appointed as the first Professor of Economic History in the British Empire. (In this race, Harvard came second, appointing its first professor of economic history in 1892.) The location was no accident. The birthplace of Engels' *The Condition of the Working Class in England* (published in German in 1845 and in English in 1887), the school led the study of the Industrial Revolution, and its fortunes, in some ways, went on to mirror the rise and fall of the cotton industry in Lancashire, on which Manchester's prosperity depended. Unwin's achievements were significant. He helped to import the German tradition of research based on the use of original economic sources established by Gustav von Schmoller (1838–1917). Schmoller was part of what became known as the Younger School of Historical Economics, which, while abandoning the romanticism that infused Ranke's work and that of the founder of the Historical School of Ecomomics Wilhem Roscher, continued to represent its findings in descriptive terms. More importantly for the future of economic history, Schmoller understood economics in terms of the political economy, and continued to emphasise the importance of institutions. Unwin took this further by moving away from the nation state, the pre-eminent intellectual and practical structure in which German historians operated, and at the same time raising the criticism of political history to a new level by locating the well-springs of change within the actions of small voluntary groups in society, rather than with the state. Unwin then went on to establish a network of scholars who helped to forge the discipline's golden age in Britain from 1945 to 1975, notably T. S. Ashton, R. H. Tawney and Eileen Power. By then, however,

Manchester's own light was eclipsed by the emergence of powerful new competitors, notably in Cambridge and at the London School of Economics, and by the new methodology of economic history, which was shaped much more by the discipline's relationship to economics than to history.[5]

The challenge of economics

Given the powerful combination of institutional, political and intellectual pressures, it would have been unsurprising if British economic historians had not felt the need to start 'circling the wagons'. In intellectual and practical terms, the focus of leading practitioners of the discipline had been the need to stay abreast of new developments in economics rather than history. The hugely useful annual survey of periodical literature conducted by *The Economic History Review* lists only those articles published in other clearly denoted economic history journals – *Economic Affairs*, the *Journal of Monetary Economy*, the *British Journal of Industrial Relations* and *Accounting, Business and Financial History*. Neither *The Journal of Modern History*, the *Journal of Contemporary History*, nor *Contemporary European History*, for example, are included in the survey, although these journals, and others, all publish articles that bridge economic, political and cultural history. (The fact that only English-language publications are included is also revealing.) In common with journals in the social sciences, *The Economic History Review* advertised its performance in relation to journals in economics. It used a science citation index produced by the Institute of Scientific Information, which claimed to measure an article's 'impact factor', a methodology hitherto eschewed by other historical schools in the UK, which remained suspicious of the applicability of a methodology developed for articles in medicine and natural sciences.

The specialised nature of historical research and the fact that new ideas in history flicker slowly to life before they burn fiercely, made historians generally wary of the application of metrics to assess research quality. Indeed, the best examples of the limitation of 'impact factor' metrics were in the fields of economics and economic history itself, where it took thirty years, for example, for the work implications of John Nash's work in game theory to be appreciated.[6] In 2007, *The Economic History Review* was ranked 1st of 16 journals in the field of social history, and 98th out of 175 journals in economics.[7] To retain its intellectual credibility in economics, economic history had to keep up with practices adopted in economics, a preoccupation that also shaped the relationship between its sister-discipline business history and the social sciences of business studies or management.

As Nick Crafts put it, the challenge before the discipline was one of 'living with big neighbours'. Indeed, in the 1980s and 1990s, some of these big neighbours in economics produced among the most important and provocative studies in economic history, including Amartya Sen's *Poverty and Famine* and Partha Dasgupta's *Inquiry into Well Being and Destitution*.[8] In the last decade of the twentieth century, important theoretical developments on both sides were also helping to bring the two disciplines together once more. Key advances in mainstream economics, notably the discipline's recognition of imperfect competition and tools to make calculations based on imperfect or asymmetrical information, meant that economists were providing economic historians with theory that could be more satisfactorily applied to real historical situations.[9] Moreover, as economics became more attuned and comfortable with handling asymmetrical information, economists increasingly turned to historical data to explore contemporary policy issues, such as the study of corporate governance.[10]

These developments, of course, posed new challenges to economic and social historians, who had to stay abreast of the theoretical methodologies and the language used by the disciplines that currently dominated these discussions. In so doing, their language, methodology and, to a certain extent, the preoccupations of economic historians became increasingly impenetrable to historians in the political and cultural fields. Economic history also became increasingly divorced from social history, with the growing danger that economic historians were able only to speak to each other. For a time in the 1970s and 1980s, cliometrics – the application of modern forms of statistical and macroeconomic analyses to history – made the study of older economic models and ideas of economists seem not just old-fashioned but redundant. However, the challenges before the economies emerging from communism in central and eastern Europe, and before the wider world in the fields of development and environmental economics, in particular, meant that the history of economic thought and its corollary, the biographic study of economists, could never be consigned to an unfashionable past. The publication of Robert Skidelsky's final volume of his biography of Keynes secured a wide and enthusiastic readership in Britain and overseas, because it was an attractive and accessible way into the complexities of Keynes' thinking, and also because of contemporary economic problems. The stuttering performance of the Japanese economy and the deep recession gripping the American economy, together with George W. Bush's decision to spend his way out of it, revived an interest in Keynesian economics. (Milton Friedman's vigorous condemnation of George W. Bush's taste for government spending as 'crude Keynesianism' also did little to harm sales.)[11]

Intellectually, then, the discipline continued to thrive on a variety of fronts. The perception that economic history was dominated by an unhealthy obsession with quantification, which during the late 1970s was superseded by cliometrics, did not quite match the reality. The 'cliometric revolution', for example, made much less of an impact on the practice of economic history in Germany or France than it did in the United States and Britain. But there was a growing recognition that the language and concepts underpinning economic history were becoming less accessible to the wider historical community, and this wider community was becoming less interested in economic history.[12]

Economics moves closer to history

Part of the challenge before the discipline became how to incorporate economic history into the teaching and research agenda of 'mainstream' history. A good example of this was Nick Crafts' and Terence Mills' important research 'Was 19th century British growth steam-powered? The climacteric revisited', published in 2004. It demonstrated that, contrary to well-established accounts, steam-based mechanisation was still proceeding at a tremendous pace after the 1870s; in fact, it was more important to British industrialisation in the final decades of the nineteenth century than in the period before 1870.[13] This finding transformed the standard historical narrative of British steam-driven industrialisation that was confined primarily to the first half of the nineteenth century, a picture which permeated both the scholarly and popular imagination. This seminal article in mainstream economic history should have been included on undergraduate programmes on nineteenth-century history as a matter of course, but the word 'climacteric' in the title was enough to send many students and their teachers running for cover.

It was not impossible to incorporate cliometric research into mainstream interpretations. The work of Crafts and Harley on the British 'industrial revolution', published in the early and mid 1980s, helped to draw out how British industrial development differed substantially from other European countries, with only a small proportion of its labour force engaged in its highly productive agricultural sector. This liberated the majority of men and women to form a large, and not especially productive or dynamic, industrial sector.[14] But if history did not end with the collapse of the Iron Curtain in 1989, the idea that Marxist economics posed a direct challenge to capitalism did, and with it came the end of an ideologically motivated need to understand Marxist, and to some extent capitalist, economics. In the same way that consumption supplanted production as a subject of historical study, so history's consumers now largely shied away from economic history. Despite the challenges posed by economic inequality across the world and environmental economics, in the early twenty-first century there was much less a sense that the history of national, regional and international economies necessarily needed to be understood because they were important. The problem of communication was not new, but, as had been recognised before, the challenge needed to be tackled head-on.

In 1932, G. D. H. Cole, who was a serving member of Ramsay MacDonald's Economic Advisory Council and a tutor to Oxford undergraduates and adult education classes at the time, announced in language so evocative of the mores of education in the 1930s, in the best-selling *An Intelligent Man's Guide through World Chaos*:

> I believe the understanding of present-day economic problems is not really so hard a matter as it is often made out to be. Even the money problem, which frightens off so many potential enquirers is in fact largely a matter of plain commonsense; and most of it can be understood by anyone who is prepared to take a little trouble, if only it is presented without jargon. It may be difficult enough to decide what ought to be done about money; but there is no real reason why this vital problem should not be intelligently discussed by ordinary people.[15]

In 1932, of course, it was unnecessary to spell out why the history of the international economy was important.

In the twenty-first century, when it came to economic history, the topics for which students and general readers were 'prepared to take a little trouble' in Britain reflected the popularity of the history of the Third Reich and the Second World War among students in school and higher education, and among the general public. Adam Tooze's *The Wages of Destruction: The Making and Breaking of the Nazi Economy*, and Richard Overy's *Why the Allies Won*, were highly regarded and sold well, making light of their sophisticated economic underpinnings.[16] Beyond the institutions of higher education, however, economic history by stealth was abandoned as a necessary tactic by a number of school examination boards. They removed mainstream economic history topics from GSCE and A level exams, notably the origins of the Great Depression of the interwar period, because it is believed they have become too difficult for students to understand them. The trend was reinforced in controversial plans for revision of the A level syllabus announced in the autumn of 2007 by the examination board OCR, which sought to break free from the 'traditional pattern of teaching' focused on exploring particular periods – the Victorians, post-Second World War Britain, for example – in favour of a thematic approach that examines 'belief systems, controversies, and the significance of key figures'.[17]

The disappearance of economic history from the school syllabus was a reflection of the decline in the number of departments of economic and social history in the UK. Economic history departments in Birmingham and Manchester, for example, are no more, while in Scotland only Glasgow retains a distinct department of economic and social history.[18] For the most part, economic historians have been absorbed into so-called mainstream departments, with a rationale of promoting interdisciplinarity, though a significant element was also universities' drive to cut costs. Economies of scale were part of the reason (economic historians understood the principle, but were more aware than most of its some-times crudely deadening effect on productivity and creativity). The move away from distinctive programmes of economic and social history to economic and social history incorporated within the research and teaching of history also enabled universities to reduce funding for a subject traditionally taught in the more costly social science band to the 'cheaper' arts and humanities level. If cost-cutting partly lay behind economic history's move from the laboratory into the classroom, the trend was reinforced by institutional developments at school level, where the number of students studying a specific economic and social history A level was in dramatic decline, and after 1995 this also applied to the number of applications from single honours economic and social history graduates.

Concern over these developments prompted the Council of the Economic History Society in Britain to convene a standing conference of heads of depart-ments of economic/social history (quickly widened to include more junior representatives of the discipline), with the aim of strengthening the society's links to universities and colleges in the UK.[19] Although the Council recognised there was a 'perceived but not yet fully comprehended crisis in economic and social history in UK higher education – a crisis which was also occurring in Europe, Australia and Canada' – the role of the Research Assessment Exercise (RAE) in the funding of research in British universities was an additional pressure. Bringing greater recognition and cash into historical research, the structure of the RAE favoured concentration and specialisation. Economic historians knew, too, that incentives, especially financial ones, help to determine behaviour, and this was no less the case in the production and consumption of history. On a very simple level, it meant that even when economic history enjoyed an intellectual resurgence, as it did in the mid 1990s, there was no longer space in history departments to accommodate the change.

History moves closer to economics

If economic history's preoccupation with its relationship to economics to some degree led to a neglect of its relationship with history, it was a two-way street. The shift in historical methodology after 1990 also led history to neglect its relation-ship with economic history. Central debates in each field largely ran on parallel lines when there was rich potential for fruitful dialogue with each other. The challenge posed by the impact of cliometrics in economic history, for example, connects to the question of whether narratives and analyses should rely, either wholly or partially, on tools developed by economists to explain the economic present and to predict the future. This is a long-running methodological issue in economic history that would benefit from further engagement with work of cul-tural and social historians on how to write 'contemporary history', a term which some argued carries greater meaning when it offers sharp contrasts and ruptures, or with Reinhart Koselleck's distinctions between a 'present past, a present future and a present present'.[20]

The opportunities for fruitful dialogue between economic and cultural history remained rich and varied. The emphasis on measurement and measurability in economic history, for example, carried with it the implication that the views of economists of the past, in fact all non-numerate forms of contemporary opinion, were just that: opinion. As a result, cliometrics appeared dominant over, if not superior to, what appeared to be more old-fashioned economic history, notably the history of economic thought. But opinion was the stuff of history to cultural, social and political historians. Economic historians could have drawn more profitably on the innovative and sophisticated approaches that surfaced in cultural history in response to this challenge. Studies of economic growth and performance, especially those utilising cliometrics, tended to be dominated by a determination to judge economic efficacy. Efficacy became judgement based on efficiency, by the capacity of an economic system's capacity to produce, to maximise output and to satisfy demands. But as notions of efficacy shifted – a tendency that accelerated over time as environmental economics extended its reach – so these judgements became suspect. After all, economic efficacy itself was a construct. How it was constructed was worthy of careful attention. The fruits of such an approach were demonstrated in the work of Paul Johnson, for example, who demonstrated that the Victorian successful market economy was a legal and ideological construct much more than a natural self-regulating system (a conviction that continues to hold powerful sway today).[21] The work of historians on how well facts travel demonstrated that economic facts can be inscribed with a variety of meanings, and their validity can and should be challenged.

Indeed, contemporary economics increasingly moved away from the notion that the holy grail of economics lies in identifying the optimal policy. The growing and influential field of what became known as the 'new political economy' in economics was much less about grand issues of states versus markets, or democracy versus non-democracy. In the words of one of its leading practitioners, Tim Besley, 'debates about these issues very often end up being ill-focused and unanswerable.'[22] The key insight of this new approach was its determination to unpick carefully how institutional structure shaped the character and impact of economic and social policies. This recognition did not come with a blanket declaration that societies should be conservative in their capacity for government intervention, but was rather intended to help economists consider how institutional structures affect policy outcomes and to take this into account when advocating a particular course of economic action. As Larry Summers, Chief Economist of the World Bank, put it, the 'overwhelming lesson' of the 1990s was 'the transcendent importance of the quality of institutions and the closely-related questions of the efficacy of political administration. Well-executed policies that are 30 degrees off are much more effective than poorly-executed policies that are spot on.'[23]

The key feature of the new political economy was its determination to concentrate on specific examples and to eschew grand comparisons. It was a noteworthy development in the history of economic thought for these twenty-first-century economists, who deliberately eschewed the mission of their forebears – embodied vividly in figures as diverse as Adam Smith and Karl Marx – that the task of economists was to develop a theory of human interaction. The new political economists were refreshingly humble: 'what we [have] learn[t] is a complement with, rather than a substitute for, knowledge generated in other branches of the social sciences'.[24] Although the methodology was mathematical, the focus and careful approach to data and the explicitly interdisciplinary and 'micro' approach underpinning the new political economy was remarkably close in conception to the practice of many historians. There were echoes, here, for example, of how the debate between 'functionalists' and 'intentionalists' on the origins of the Holocaust were recast by the 'micro' studies of historians like Christopher Browning on *Reserve Police Battalion 101* and Jan Gross on *The Destruction of the Jewish Community in Jedwabne*.[25]

For all that economics and history were moving closer, it remained worth striving to retain one of the most invigorating features of old-fashioned economic history: the grand nature of its sweep, its enthusiasm for large-scale contrasts and comparisons, across continents and across centuries. Nor did the insights afforded by new political economy obscure the continued value afforded by the work of earlier practitioners, translated into the field by Charles Maier as the 'historical political economy'.[26] He argued that the reason that one economic policy was adopted in preference to another lay in analysing the political behaviour of conflicting interest groups to secure a particular economic policy. By the 1990s, the language of class conflict that shaped Maier's 1987 articulation was replaced by histories of interest group identity, with ethnic loyalties, feminism, and environmental and 'national security lobbies' all becoming important 'classes' of analysis.

Implicitly, cultural, political and social historians were drawing on a methodology long exploited by economic historians.[27] Indeed, historians exploring the key features of social and cultural change in the twentieth century in particular, were at the same time working their way back to economics. A striking example was Victoria de Grazia's exploration of the apparent triumph of American consumer society over Europe's bourgeois civilisation, which discussed traditional topics of economic and business history – production, marketing, consumption – through the prism of the gender, ideology and power issues evident in the relationships between consumer and producer. American economic hegemony, in this wonderfully colourful and evocative book, was a market empire forged out of American consumer culture and exported to Europe, through guile and skill.[28] Her bold argument did not entirely convince critics who argued that the taste for consumption was as much European as American, and that thrift was not only a virtue of the European bourgeoisie or the European left, but was practised in the USA too.[29]

If de Grazia's version of American Empire was as much resisted as irresistible, the hard power which underpinned the American twentieth century still needed to be understood. After all, it was the productive capacity, comparative efficiency, technological advances, financial resources and trading acumen that gave the USA goods and services to export, and the means to do so. The point finds an echo in Geoff Eley's pained call for historians to reconnect histories shaped by the 'cultural turn' to those informed by older social science methodologies in histories which recognised the 'interconnectedness of things'.[30] The model remained Emily Rosenberg's path-breaking study of American overseas loans, which offered hard numbers as to the amount and distribution of loans, but also explored the cultural assumptions which underpinned them, a story of manly virtue, racial destiny and professional enterprise that helped to reshape our understanding of American power in the twentieth century.[31]

The study of the historical political economy also bore a very strong resemblance to the vogue among social and cultural historians, in particular, to explore the transnational threads that wove different social groups together in their efforts to draw out the national as a 'bounded historical entity with imbricated structures and processes that connect' it to regions and potentially to every part of the world.[32] Much of the subject matter of economic history – the movement and exchange of money, goods, technology – was about connections, and these connections allow historians to reflect on, while at the same time go beyond, the confines of the nation. Economic history necessarily has always been global history. The national paradigm had never been an especially comfortable one for most types of economic analysis – and no economy is an island, however much governments might attempt economic isolation. Even the fiercely nationalist economy of Nazi Germany failed in its attempts for autarky, and recent studies of the German economy at war have drawn out the great degree to which the war effort relied upon economic and financial resources from the occupied territories, as well as access to a network of not entirely neutral powers. Economic history demonstrated that economic activity and actors frequently outpace and sometimes ultimately destroy the nation state, as when East German workers moved West in November 1989, effectively creating one economy that was cemented by the collapse of the GDR.

Economic history deserved to be not just fashionable but a constant field of enquiry, because of its global and international reach. It was also transnational before transnationalism was ever fashionable. Indeed, it is often forgotten that the first use of the term 'transnational' in the 1920s was in relation to economic phenomena. This was recognised by one of the leading economic historians of her generation, Susan Strange, whose career also reflected the not always acknowledged openness of economic history to female practitioners at a time when more established branches of history remained resolutely closed to women. Writing as early as 1976, Strange noted: 'many of the notions put forward in the last few years by those interested in it [transnationalism] are really only rediscoveries of truths very apparent to an older generations of writers.[33] Indeed, the newly unfashionable state-centred view of history had only ever formed one category in economic histories which embraced the study of regions, continents and the world.

Examples drawn from economic history also continued to provide a valuable counterpoint to the tendency to present transnational encounters in history to show a world becoming ever more enmeshed, and by implication more equal. Economic and financial motivations, as well as identity politics, helped to explain why some boundaries survive – financiers, ministers of finance and criminals, to name but a few, are all acutely aware of the profits to be made from exploiting different levels of taxation and prohibition that nation states impose.[34]

Sparing a thought for economic actors and phenomena also underlines some of the shortcomings in certain work on transnationalist phenomena to date. The contribution of transnational networks to the rise of regional identities and organisations in the modern world is little studied at present, and would seem an area ripe for growth in the twenty-first century. The little-studied history of the Economic and Financial Organisation of the League of Nations, the world's first international organisation explicitly dedicated to the promotion of economic co-ordination, revealed the large and varied array of knowledge-based networks of individuals (or epistemic communities) interested in economic and financial issues (including how to generate, interpret and disseminate statistics) in the interwar period, a period more usually identified with intense economic nationalism. These networks, comprising a dazzling array of different nationalities and political persuasions, shared and exchanged their ideas, skills and values across national boundaries, and brought together a desire to understand and, where possible, manage the international economy.[35] The social and professional networks of businessmen, financiers, economists and statisticians are ripe for interrogation by the new, more culturally orientated methodologies of transnationalism, holding the potential to offer new insights into why some networks hang together and others fall apart, and how the shared values of a transnational network can be transplanted or replicated in more anonymous mass societies.

Economic history was also well placed to respond to the challenges of 'cosmopolitanism', which was emerging as a major field of enquiry in sociology, anthropology, and political and social theory, in response to some of the tensions (or inadequacies) with conceptions of globalisation. Although cosmopolitanism in history, alongside some of the difficult conceptual issues, remained 'something awaiting realization', it had the potential to open a rich vein of research when it came to thinking about the past, helping historians to break free from old dualisms of domestic or foreign, national or international, in writing the history of the modern world.[36] Economic and business history, with its focus on the language and habits that forged connections, prompted information to be shared and goods of all kinds exchanged, is especially well suited to a cosmopolitan sensitivity. (In this context, the term 'multinational', as a prefix to financial and business organisations compared with social or communal groups that are assigned a multicultural or cosmopolitan identity, was worthy of interrogation.) Cosmopolitanism provided economic historians with a new, multifaceted connection to social, cultural and political history, given that peoples' and nations' experience of one another is mediated predominately through trade and finance.

As Marilyn Lake and Henry Reynolds have noted, cosmopolitanism was often evoked in the late nineteenth century in service of the free movement of peoples and goods, knowledge and ideas, and the notion of world citizenship. In their landmark study of the human rights 'from the margins' of the non-western world, Lake and Reynolds demonstrated the important role played by Chinese and Asiatic critiques of western liberalism when it came to the history of migration in the nineteenth century. Individual liberty and freedom of movement were heralded as universal rights, but ones which only Europeans could exercise.[37] Lake and Reynolds explored how increasing self-styled 'white men's countries' in North America, Australasia and South Africa worked together to exclude those they defined as non-white, in a series of actions that in turn provoked a long international struggle for racial equality. Their study drew out the significance of non-European critiques to racial discrimination, which formed the basis of modern articulations of human rights and offers an important challenge to histories that placed the evocation of human rights in the West.[38] But *Drawing the Global Colour Line* also demonstrates, often inadvertently, how the preoccupations and language of economics shaped the battles for the free movement and equality of treatment for men and women, as well as goods and services. Calls for a 'cosmopolitan level of profit' increasingly were set against complaints about cheap labour, low wages and unfair competition.[39] Economics helped critics of discrimination find a shared language and ideas to challenge the growing and varied discrimination ranged against them.

The campaign waged by the remarkable but not exceptional Lowe Kong Meng against the Australian Immigration Restriction Act of 1855, the first race-based immigration restriction in the world, was rich in the concepts and metaphors of economic history. Lowe Kong Meng was a British subject, a merchant who came to Victoria in search of gold, from the Sze Yap district near the port of Canton, long a centre of Arab, Malay, Siamese and European trade. Though his education and cosmopolitanism were of primary concern to Lake and Reynolds, Lowe Kong Meng had a strong command of contemporary economics as well as a fluent command of the English and French languages and of the classics of European literature. His anger at the rising levels of discrimination and violence meted out to Chinese migrants to Australia in the mid nineteenth century was born as much from the poor grasp of economics that this behaviour demonstrated as from the racial prejudice. The Chinese were condemned for being cheap migrant labourers who travelled without the financial obligation (and the ready market) of a family, thereby able to undercut 'local' white workers, Lowe Kong Meng told a Select Committee into Chinese Immigration in Victoria in 1857. Would 'any woman of average self-respect', he asked, 'expose herself to be chased through the country by a band of infuriated ruffians, and to see her children burnt to death, perhaps, in her husband's flaming tent? Treated as pariahs and outcasts by the people of this great, "free" country, the Chinamen in Victoria have hitherto had but scanty encouragement to invite their wives to accompany or follow them.'[40]

The debate about human rights in nineteenth-century Australia was a powerful reminder of economics' ability to be 'fashionable', if fashionable is taken to mean being capable of being shaped or moulded, brought into shape. Lowe Kong Meng's testimony also addressed issues regarding the rights of labour and migrants and questions of poverty and equality that strike at the heart of the contemporary history of the twenty-first century. It posed questions that remained important: Did the restriction of immigration discriminate against, or protect human rights? How should society square the challenges of economic development with the doctrine, if not the practice, of free trade? How could the world square environmental considerations with economic and social ones? The place of economics in history deserves to be both fashionable and refashioned to meet these challenges.

Michel Margairaz

To answer the question posed in the heading of this chapter I will not waste time considering how fashions are made in history, even though it is a good question. I will argue that economic history was fashionable from the 1950s to the 1970s and is no longer so, especially in France. I will nevertheless also argue that in recent years there have been a number of fruitful intersections of economics, economic history and mainstream history.

My contribution is organised around four points: the origins of economic history in Germany, the USA, the UK and France, and the peculiarity of French economic history; the first decline of economic history in the 1970s and 1980s; two paths of renewal of economic history and their limits; and finally, contemporary trends in a new economic history.

The origins of economic history and its French peculiarities

The two places where economic history was born in the 1890s were Germany and the USA. It is not fortuitous that economic history emerged as a discipline and in learned journals in the universities of Berlin, Strasbourg and Harvard at the same time as the construction of the nation state in their respective countries. Economic history was linked to the national and ideological ambitions of Germany and the USA. In Germany it was a reflection of national identity, even of nationalism itself. In the USA it was based on an economic interpretation of the American constitution, especially around the defence of property rights, or derived from a conception of the American frontier. In Britain, most works of economic history emphasised the early nature of British industrialisation. After the Second World War, during the cold war and the competition with the communist bloc, most works of economic history belonged to the American *consensus* school of history, which stressed the virtues of capitalism, especially in reducing social inequalities.

The development of economic history in France was late and relatively independent of these influences. Until the 1930s there was not a real school of economic history in France, but only some individuals, such as Levasseur and Hauser.[41] The main event – we all know – was the foundation in 1929 by Marc Bloch and Lucien Febvre of *Les annales d'histoire économique et sociale* (AHES), and more specifically for contemporary history, the domination of Camille Ernest Labrousse, who directed the Institut d'histoire économique et sociale (IHES) at the Sorbonne from 1945 to 1967. Labrousse constructed a model of economic and social history around his two theses, in law in 1933 and humanities in 1944.[42] This model was based on three principles: first, the use of statistical and historical series of prices or incomes; second, a concentration on economic trends (*conjoncture*), the fluctuations of growth or depression; and third, an a priori definition of the main social groups, such as farmers, workers, employers and managers, workers, and so on. It produced a quantified history in which preset and homogeneous social groups, such as workers and employers, defined collectively by their incomes, were subject to fluctuations of the economy according to the famous cycles of alternating phases of growth and depression worked out by Simiand and Kondratieff in the years between 1910 and 1930.

This economic history was conceived as part of social history and aspired to a total history in which the rhythm of change was provided by the unequal and fluctuating division of wealth between social groups. It had three major characteristics. First, it was deterministic and gave primacy to economic causation. For Labrousse, the economy preceded society, which in turn shaped political and mental phenomena, according to a quasi-pre-established hierarchy. Second, it had a fascination – Fernand Braudel would say after 1958 an obsession – with economic fluctuations. Third, it was particularly interested in pre-industrial crises, initially agricultural crises, in particular during the French Revolution and at the beginning of the nineteenth century. 'Economies have their structural crises', Labrousse was fond of saying. The classic convergence of this total history was the crisis of *Ancien Régime*, where a crisis of wheat price rises provoked social mobilisation and this, in turn, led to political revolutions in 1789, 1830 and 1848.[43]

This history, which dealt with facts which were quantitative and cyclical, had no interest in individual actors or even in individual events, except as the effects of economic conjuncture. The inspiration was both Marxist and structuralist, at a time when these currents dominated the intellectual landscape of the social sciences, but it was a rather ad hoc adaptation, even, some would say, a theoretical *bricolage*. This methodological and conceptual base generated a vast number of studies, under the uncontested intellectual leadership of Labrousse – Jean Bouvier spoke about 'the monopolistic Labroussian era' – who over a period of nearly thirty years supervised more than a hundred doctoral theses. This was a vast intellectual undertaking, made possible by a charisma that Labrousse shared with the pre-1914 socialist leader Jean Jaurès, and was crowned by a great collective synthesis, the eight volumes of the *Economic and Social History of France*, which he co-edited with Fernand Braudel in the 1970s.[44]

Curiously, this kind of economic and social history was undertaken outside of any relationship with economists, either French or non-French, whether those of the ISEA (Institut de statistiques économiques appliquées), directed by François Perroux and Jean Marczewski, who developed a 'quantitative history of the French economy' – a retrospective national accounting inspired by Keynes' works – or those who at the same time were developing the 'New Economic History' (NEH), or cliometrics, in the USA and the UK.

The decline of Labroussian economic history (1970s and 1980s)

Several factors combined to explain the decline of the Labroussian type of economic history. First, there were the ideological developments of the years 1975–89 and the questioning of Marxism. Second, there was a questioning of the total history of the *Annales* school, which resulted in a fragmentation of approaches, as evidenced by the analyses of Jean-Claude Perrot or Pierre Nora.[45] Third, there was the price of successes already obtained and the exhaustion of seams that had already been explored. Fourth, there was little interest in this model for the twentieth century. Fifth, there was the impact of the linguistic turn, which questioned, often in a radical manner, the 'given' nature of social and, in particular, statistical realities. Finally, there was the emergence of new historical approaches, such as the return of the event, of politics, the individual event and actor, the development of micro-history, and interest in marginal groups and forms of social mobility.

The ground was then occupied by other types of historical writing: historical demography, historical anthropology, the history of mentalities, then gender history, cultural history, and many others. Moreover, among the direct heirs to Labrousse, some historians wanted to establish the autonomy of social or urban history from economic history, and to explore the social groups of the modern age, such as new communities, social mobility and forms of sociability, independently of any pre-established hierarchy or categorisation.[46]

Even in Britain, where another kind of economic history developed, there were 5,000 members of the Economic History Society, and the *Economic History Review* was highly influential, but there was also a certain decline from the 1980s, as testified by David Coleman's *History and the Economic Past* (1987). This was undoubtedly accentuated by the autonomous existence of economic history in university departments, separated from departments of history on the one hand and economics on the other.

The New Economic History (cliometrics) and its limited impact

In the 1960s and 1970s there were two forms of renewal of economic history, starting in the United States and Britain. Only the second genuinely affected France. However, the limits to what they could achieve were fairly quickly established.

The New Economic History (NEH), or cliometrics, was the application of econometrics to history, in other words the development of retrospective econometrics. The author started from a theoretical economic model founded on algebraic functions which combined several variables. The model was tested using quantitative historical information drawn from time-series relating to the variables. Pioneer works were those of Robert Fogel, who in the 1960s published research on the role of the railways in the growth of the American economy in the nineteenth century. It made counterfactual assumptions about how the economy would have grown without the railways.[47] There were similar studies of the role of slavery in the economy of the American South in the nineteenth century, and of the steam engine on British economic growth in the eighteenth century.[48] These cliometric historians calculated the exact contribution of the selected variable – railway or steam engine – to the overall growth of the economy.

Despite its claims, the NEH provoked three kinds of criticism. To begin with, counterfactual history – asking such questions as 'What would American growth have been without…?' – went against the conventional approach of many historians. Indeed, the NEH was often produced by economists working in economics departments. Next, the NEH was attacked for not having enough critical distance on the quantitative statistical data it used. Finally, the NEH generally relied on neoclassical economic models, which assumed a priori that markets were perfect and that actors behaved in a rational and informed way.

These works nevertheless enjoyed significant success in Britain, Italy – where economic history was taught in economics departments – Spain and, from there, the Spanish-speaking world of Latin America. On the other hand, there were few echoes of the NEH in France, where there was a clear division between historians and economists, with the exception of some isolated works, such as those of Carré, Dubois and Malinvaud (1976) or Bourguignon and Lévy-Leboyer (1985).[49] Criticisms also multiplied in the USA during the 1980s, when the NEH current lost momentum.

Business history

Through the *Business History Review*, and under the influence of Chandler's work (1977), a series of studies of companies, especially of large ones, were published from the 1960s in developments in the USA, Britain, Germany and the Latin countries.[50] The trend appeared later in France – the review *Entreprises et histoire* was only founded in 1992 – mainly because of a long and reciprocal mistrust between researchers and the business world, and the difficulty of access to the private archives of companies. This sub-discipline has nevertheless developed in France over the last fifteen years, with the support of research foundations, public and private companies, history committees and specialised reviews in certain branches such as electricity, rail transport and aluminium.[51]

Despite the novelty of this micro-economic approach, a number of methodological and theoretical issues were raised by this historical movement. Three principal tendencies were noted. First, there was an overemphasis on the strictly internal history of the company, privileging the perspective of business leaders in the sources and in their own practices – in other words, a history *pro domo*. Second, there was a tendency to tell a success story, whereby, in a tautological and teleological way, the economic success or failure of the company was explained by pre-established criteria. Finally, the multiplication of company monographs produced a certain saturation and repetition, together with a lack of awareness of the meso-economic level – that of the branches of industry – or of the macro-economic implications.

Like the history of technology and innovation, which produced important works in the wake of those of David Landes, business history ran the risk of being limited to a descriptive approach, so long as it neglected such phenomena as dynamic networks of actors, market demand, and the social and cultural dimensions of consumption.[52]

Towards a social, cultural and political history of the economy

There has been a recent renewal of dialogue between economic history, social sciences and other fields of history, in both directions. Since the early 1990s, there have been promising forms of revival of economic history, as a result of interdisciplinary interaction with other social sciences, in particular political science, economics, sociology and law.[53] This has been articulated in key journals such as *Annales histoire, Sciences sociales, Genèses, Le mouvement social* and *La revue d'histoire moderne et contemporaine*. Four areas have been especially productive.

To begin with, the sociology of organisations has offered concepts and methods to renew the history of businesses, moving beyond the micro-economic study of the small firm to explore the history of management, research or training.[54] Second, following the linguistic turn, economists and economic historians have come to study the historical construction of statistical categories themselves, such as the 'invention of unemployment',[55] or that of social and economic categories, and even the development of statistical services, such as the Institut National de la Statistique et des Études Économiques (INSEE).[56] Third, based on the research of institutional economists, there have been historical works on various major social, economic and financial institutions, such as *Les conseils de prud hommes* or industrial relations tribunals, chambers of commerce, the Banque de France, the Caisse des Dépôts which oversees the financial sector, the economic and social ministries, or the Commissariat général au Plan which was in charge of French post-war planning. These institutions are studied not only as useful players correcting the imperfections of the market, but as organisations with their own structures, personnel, practices, traditions and cultures which also form part of a broader economic and also political, social and cultural framework.[57]

Finally, research by economists on game theory, and more especially the 'economics of conventions', has prompted historians to renew the history of economic actors. Understanding such actors as employers, employees, subcontractors and consumers through agreements which govern their relations with products and the market leads to defining companies and their dynamics in a new way.[58] By integrating the role of public services, research breaks down the opposition between the state and the market and analyses more complex configurations between private and public actors. In particular, the history of public economic services in France has brought together work in the disciplines of economics, politics and law.[59] This research has opened up new ways for the construction of a social, cultural and political history of the economy which, thanks to collaboration with other social sciences, is able to engage in dialogue between the disciplines and with other kinds of history beyond economic history.

Towards an economic history of society, culture and politics

On the other hand, it would seem difficult not to integrate the economic dimension into a renovated social, political or cultural history. How can we undertake the history of social and urban mobility, of migrations or of cultural production, without including consideration of changes in labour patterns, training, markets for products or money? In this way, recent work on the history of the book or of works of art explore the publishing or art market, or what might be called the 'cultural economy'.

Contemporary political history cannot ignore financial, economic or monetary questions, in at least three respects. As far as the history of state-building and political institutions is concerned, research on the development of the parliamentary system in France in the nineteenth century must address the important question of the control of public finances. Similarly, it is not possible to avoid the development, implementation and impact of the public economic policies when studying changes in the machinery of the state that took place in the twentieth century. In a broader sense, political decision-making in certain episodes of contemporary history cannot disregard the constraints, particularly material and financial, which limited the room for manoeuvre of the decision-makers. This might be applicable as much to the revolutionary period as to the Vichy period or the early years of the first Mitterrand presidency in 1981–84. Finally, some economic questions reconfigure the political landscape, such as the traditional antagonism between right and left. Questions of protectionism, public utility, planning or certain public policies appear largely cross-partisan and redefine political divisions to the point of recasting political cultures themselves. The long history of nationalisation in the twentieth century is one example. Again, when it comes to a periodisation of the twentieth century, a new contrast emerges between the second third of the twentieth century, from the 1930s to the 1970s, which was characterised by economic and social regulation, and the final third, from the 1980s, which was characterised by neoliberal deregulation.[60]

On the whole, it would appear that only a fossilised economic history would appear last of fashion. Indeed, questions raised by the renewal of economic history are of concern not only to economic historians but to the whole family of historians.

Notes

1   For an overview of the project, details of its principal findings and further publications, see www.consume.bbk.ac.uk
2   Ibid. 'Findings: 4½ lessons about consumption: a short overview of the Cultures of Consumption research programme', p. 1.
3   www.lse.ac.uk/collections/economicHistory/Research/facts/AboutTheProject.htm, 'A toolkit for travelling "facts"', Introduction p.1.
4   www.lse.ac.uk/collections/economicHistory/Research/facts/AboutTheProject.htm
5   Thanks to Theo Balderston for help here. See A. J. H. Latham, 'An interview with Dougals Farnie', *The Newsletter of the Cliometric Society* 21/2 (Fall 2006), 4–12.
6   R. J. Aumann, 'Game Theory', *The New Palgrave: A Dictionary of Economics* (London, Palgrave Macmillan, 1987), vol. 2, 460–82.
7   www.ehs.org.uk/journal/jnldefault.asp; 'Uses of research metrics in the arts and humanities: report of the expert group set up jointly by the Arts and Humanities Research Council and the Higher Education Funding Council for England, October 2006'; 'Peer Review: the challenges for the humanities and social sciences: report by the British Academy, September 2007'.
8   A. Sen, *Poverty and Famine. An Essay on Entitlement and Deprivation* (Oxford, Clarendon Press, 1981); P. Dasgupta, *An Inquiry into Well Being and Destitution* (Oxford, Clarendon Press, 1993).
9   A landmark book was by Antony B. Atkinson and Joseph E. Stiglitz, *Lectures on Public Economics* (New York, Mcgraw Hill, 1980). In economics, the problem of information asymmetry was explored largely though understanding business negotiations where one party had better information than the other (when an employer seeks to hire a new worker, all workers claim to be well trained, but some candidates in reality are better trained than others), and how to design strategies to combat this problem. Historians have long faced the challenge of not having all the information they would like to understand a problem. As economics provides creative ways of dealing with these gaps, the two disciplines came closer.
10 See, for example, T. Besley and M. Ghatak, 'Competition and incentives with motivated agents', *Centre for Economic Policy Research Discussion Paper*, No. 4641, September 2004.
11 R. Skidelsky, *John Maynard Keynes: Vol. 3, Fighting for Britain, 1937–1946* (London, Macmillan, 2000). In the USA the book was published under the subtitle *Fighting for Freedom,* and all three volumes were published in an abridged single volume in 2004.
12 See the fascinating debate in the German History section of H-Net between Albert Ritschl, Adam Tooze and Eli Rubin, based respectively in Germany, Britain and the United States. Each author offers an interesting justification for the continued utility of economic history to the study of modern Germany, while at the same time reflecting the different intellectual traditions of the countries in which they work. See www.h-net.org/~german/discuss/econ (forum discussion: 'Do we need a new economic history of Germany', June–July 2007, downloaded 5 October 2007). Also see the fascinating collected reflections on the discipline by some of the leading practitioners in the field collected by the Economic History Society to celebrate its 75th anniversary, in Pat Hudson, ed., *Living Economic and Social History* (Glasgow, Economic History Society, 2001).
13 N. F. R. Crafts, and T. C. Mills, 'Was 19th century British growth steam powered? The climacteric revisited', *Explorations in Economic History* 41 (2004), 156–71. This paper establishes that there are serious problems with the hypothesis that the Victorian climacteric was driven by the decline phase of steam as a General Purpose Technology. This is primarily because steam's contribution to industrial output and labour productivity growth was stronger after 1870 than before, and because the non-steam-intensive sectors exhibited an inverted U-shape in trend output growth through the nineteenth century, experiencing a marked slowdown between 1830 and the 1870s. Seeking to base an account of nineteenth-century British growth primarily on the implications of steam is thus misconceived.
14 C. K. Harley, 'British industrialisation before 1841: evidence of slower growth during the Industrial

Revolution', *Journal of Economic History* 42, 267–89; N. F. R. Crafts, *British Economic Growth during the Industrial Revolution* (Oxford, Clarendon Press, 1985).

15 G. D. H. Cole, *An Intelligent Man's Guide Through World Chaos* (London, Victor Gollancz, 1932). The book was reprinted five times in the space of four months. Although Cole's contribution to the interpretation of economics for the masses has been discredited because he failed to fully understand the Keynesian revolution, he wrote with a fluency and lucidity rarely matched by his peers. His related publications, with M. I. Cole, *The Condition of Britain* (London, Victor Gollancz, 1937) and *The Common People, 1746–1938* (London, Methuen, 1938), became classics of the emerging discipline of labour history – a subject which also has been in decline since 1990.

16 Adam Tooze, *The Wages of Destruction. The Making and Breaking of the Nazi Economy* (London, Penguin, Allen Lane, 2006); Richard Overy, *Why the Allies Won* (London, Pimlico Press, 1996).

17 Anushka Asthana, 'What links the British Empire, witch-hunts and the Wild West?', *The Observer*, Sunday 21 October 2007.

18 The department of economic and social history at the University of Edinburgh was incorporated into the new School of History, Classics and Archaeology in 2002.

19 www.ehs.org.uk/othercontent/StandingConferenceReport1998.doc

20 Koselleck goes on to distinguish between 'a past present with its own past past and past future, and a future present with its own future past and future future'. See R. Koselleck, 'Begriffsgechichtliche Anmerkungen zur "Zeitgeschichte"', in V. Conzemius, M. Greschat and H. Kocher, eds., *Die Zeit nach 1945 als Thema kirchlicher Zeitgeschichte* (Göttingen, PUB, 1988), 17–31, discussed in J. Caplan, 'Contemporary history: reflections from Britain and Germany', *History Workshop Journal* 63 (Spring 2007), 230–8; G. Donald Winch, 'The disputatious pair: economic history and the history of economics', paper presented to the Centre for Economics and History at the University of Cambridge, November 2001.

21 Paul Johnson, 'Market disciplines in Victorian Britain', working paper 6 (2005), available at www.lse.ac.uk/collections/economicHistory/Research/ facts/AbouttheProject.htm

22 T. Besley, 'The new political economy', Keynes Lecture, British Academy, 13 October 2004, available at http://econ.lse.ac.uk/staff/tbesley/papers/keyneslecturetext.pdf, p. 21.

23 Lawrence H. Summers, 'Development lessons from the 1990s', in Tim Besley and Roberto Zagha, eds., *Development Challenges in the 1990s: Leading Policy Makers Speak from Experience* (Washington DC, The World Bank, 2004).

24 Besley, 'The New Political Economy'.

25 C. Browning, *Ordinary Men: Reserve Police Battalion 101 and the Final Solution in Poland* (New York, HarperCollins, 1992); J. Gross, *Neighbors: The Destruction of the Jewish Community in Jedwabne, Poland* (Princeton University Press, 2001).

26 Charles Maier, *In Search of Stability: Explorations in Historical Political Economy* (Cambridge University Press, 1987), 2–3, 15–16.

27 See, for example, Michael Hogan's influential corporative analysis of *The Marshall Plan: America, Britain and the Reconstruction of Western Europe, 1947–1952* (Cambridge University Press, 1989), or Andrew Marrison's account of the fall of British Free trade in *British Business and Protection, 1903–1932* (Oxford, Clarendon Press, 1996).

28 V. de Grazia, *Irresistible Empire. America's Advance through 20th-Century Europe* (Cambridge, Mass., Belknap Press of Harvard University Press, 2005).

29 See National Thrift Committee of the Young Men's Christian Association, *Tenth Anniversary Report on the National Thrift Movement* (New York, National Thrift Committee, 1927).

30 Geoff Eley, *The Crooked Line: From Cultural History to the History of Society* (Ann Arbor, University of Michigan Press, 2005).

31 E. S. Rosenberg, *Financial Missionaries to the World. The Politics and Culture of Dollar Diplomacy, 1990–1930* (Cambridge, Mass., Harvard University Press, 1999).

32 T. Bender, ed., *Rethinking American History in a Global Age* (Berkeley, University of California Press, 2002), 11.

33 S. Strange, 'Transnational relations', *International Affairs* 52/3 (July 1976), 334; P. Clavin, 'Defining transnationalism', *Contemporary History* 14/4 (2005), 433–5. For a wonderful example of the recovered history of a pioneering female economic historian, see M. Berg, *A Woman In History: Eileen Power, 1889–1940* (Cambridge University Press, 1996).

34 The transnational dimension to the narcotic trade is long recognised. See N. Allen, *The Opium Trade* (Lowell, Harvard, 1853).

35 P. Clavin and J.-W. Wessels, 'Transnationalism and the League of Nations: understanding the work of its Economic and Financial Organisation', *Contemporary European History* 14/4 (2005), 465–92.

36 S. Pollock, H. Bhabha, C. Breckenridge and D. Chakrabarty, 'Cosmopolitanisms', *Public Culture* 12/3, 577–89. See also K. Appiah, *Cosmopolitanism: Ethics in a World of Strangers* (New York, W. W. Norton, 2006). I am indebted to the University of Sydney International Fellowship Programme and Professor Glenda Sluga for the opportunity to participate in an international conference on Cosmopolitanism in Sydney in August 2007.

37 I am greatly indebted to the authors for allowing me to read a draft of this book prior to publication. M. Lake and H. Reynolds, *Drawing the Global Colour Line: White Men's Countries and the International Challenge of Racial Equality* (Cambridge University Press, 2008).

38 See, for example, L. Hunt, *The French Revolution and Human Rights. A Brief Documentary History* (New York, Bedford/St. Martin's Press, 1996).

39 Charles Pearson, *Essays in Reform* (1867), 209, quoted by Marilyn Lake, 'Cosmpolitanism', paper presented to an ARC workshop on Cosmopolitanism, Sydney, 2 August 2007.

40 M. Lake and H. Reynolds, *Drawing the Global Colour Line,* 9–10.

41 Cf. Émile Levasseur, *Histoire des classes ouvrières en France depuis 1789 jusqu'à nos jours* (Paris, Hachette, 1867, 2 vols.).

42 Camille-Ernest Labrousse, *Esquisse du mouvement des prix et des revenus en France au XVIIIème siècle* (Paris, Dalloz, 1933, 2 vols.); *La crise de l'économie française à la fin de l'Ancien Régime et au début de la Révolution* (Paris, Presses universitaires de France, 1944, new printing Paris, PUF, 1990).

43 Camille-Ernest Labrousse, '1848–1830–1789 – Comment naissent les révolutions', *Congrès historique du centenaire de la révolution de 1848* (Paris, PUF, 1948), 1–20.

44 Fernand Braudel and Ernest Labrousse, eds., *Histoire économique et sociale de la France* (Paris, Presses universitaires de France, 1970–82, 8 vols.).

45 Jean-Claude Perrot, 'Rapports sociaux et villes au XVIIIe siècle', *Annales ESC* 23/2 (March–April 1968), 241–67; Jacques Le Goff and Pierre Nora, eds., *Faire de l'histoire* (Paris, Gallimard, 1974, 3 vols.).

46 Particularly Jean-Claude Perrot, Daniel Roche (for modern history), and Rolande Trempé and Yves Lequin (for contemporary history).

47 Robert W. Fogel, *Railroads and American Economic Growth. Essays in Econometric History* (Baltimore, Johns Hopkins University Press, 1964).

48 Robert W. Fogel and Stanley L. Engerman, *The Reinterpretation of American Economic History* (Boston, Little, Brown, 1971–74, 2 vols.); Ralph A. Andreano, *La Nouvelle Histoire Économique. Exposé de méthodologie* (Paris, Gallimard, 1974).

49 Jean-Jacques Carré, Paul Dubois and Edmond Malinvaud, *La croissance française. Un essai d'analyse économique causale de l'après-guerre* (Paris, Le Seuil, 1972, 2nd printing, 1977); François Bourguignon and Maurice Lévy-Leboyer, *L'économie française au XIXème siècle, analyse macro-économique* (Paris, Économica, 1985).

50 Alfred D. Chandler, Jr., *The Visible Hand. The Managerial Revolution in American Business* (Cambridge, Mass. and London, Belknap Press of Harvard University Press, 1977).

51 We may cite the Fondation EDF (for the history of electricity), the Association pour l'histoire des chemins de fer en France (AHICF), the Comité d'histoire économique et financière de la France (CHEFF), the Mission historique de la Banque de France, the Institut d'histoire de l'aluminium (IHA).

52 David Landes, *The Unbound Prometheus. Technological Change and Industrial Development in Western Europe from 1750 to the Present* (London, Cambridge University Press, 1969).

53 Carlos Barciela, Gérard Chastagnaret and Antonio Escudero, eds., *La historia económica en España y Francia (siglos XIX y XX)* (Alicante University, 2006).

54 Patrick Fridenson, 'Un nouvel objet: les organisations', *Annales économies, sociétés, civilisations* (Nov–Dec 1989).

55 Robert Salais, Nicolas Baverez and Bénédicte Reynaud, *L'invention du chômage. Histoire et transformation d'une catégorie en France des années 1890 aux années 1980* (Paris, PUF, 1986, 2nd printing, 1999).

56 INSEE, *Pour une histoire de la statistique* (Paris, INSEE, 1977), vol. 1; Alain Desrosières and Laurent Thévenot, *Les catégories socioprofessionnelles* (Paris, La Découverte, 1988).

57 Henry Rousso, ed., *De Monnet à Massé. Enjeux politiques et objectifs économiques dans le cadre des quatre premiers plans (1946–1965)* (Paris, Éditions du CNRS, 1986); Olivier Feiertag and Michel Margairaz, eds., *Politiques et pratiques des banques d'émission en Europe (XVII–XXèmes siècles). Le bicentenaire de la Banque de France dans la perspective de l'identité monétaire européenne* (Paris, Albin Michel, 2003).

58 Robert Salais and Michael Storper, *Les mondes de production. Enquête sur l'identité économique de la France* (Paris, Éditions de l'École des Hautes Études en Sciences Sociales (EHESS), 1993); André Orléan, *Analyse économique des conventions* (Paris, PUF, 1994).

59 Michel Margairaz and Olivier Dard, eds., 'Le service public, l'économie, la République (1780–1960)', *Revue d'histoire moderne et contemporaine*, 52–3 (July–Sept 2005).
60 Richard F. Kuisel, *Capitalism and the State in Modern France. Renovation and Economic Management in the Twentieth Century* (Cambridge, Mass. and London, Cambridge University Press, 1981).

3

What is cultural history now about?

Dominique Kalifa and Michael Kelly

Cultural history now dominates the historical scene. It has taken on the role of leading sector of the discipline that was previously held by economic and social history. Since the linguistic turn it has exercised a hegemony over other fields of history. The nature of cultural history is nevertheless still a matter for debate. Dominique Kalifa argues that cultural history cannot be confined to the history of cultural forms – art, music, film, literature – but is the social history of representation – how past societies have seen the world and how these perceptions have changed. He examines the examples of the cultural history of crime and of the press. Michael Kelly argues that huge contributions to cultural history are made outside history departments and that the study of art, music, film and literature in a social context has been revolutionised by the use of cultural theory. He goes on to explore how cultural history may be applied to a new understanding of the Liberation in France.

Dominique Kalifa[1]

The question posed in the chapter heading is a real challenge, because of the gap between the relative vagueness of the concept (What is culture? What is cultural history?) and its recent spread among contemporary French historians. Indeed it is this looseness, despite the epistemological problems it creates, which perhaps helps explain the success of the label 'cultural history'. This success makes any attempt to map the terrain completely extremely difficult. However, in the first part of this presentation, I will attempt to do this, sketching out the main issues brought up by those contemporary French historians who define themselves by and recognise themselves in the label 'cultural history'. In the second part, I will explore what cultural history is about today, in my view, from two examples taken from my own research, which, I hope, will raise more general questions for discussion.

Cultural history as 'the social history of representations'

What exactly do the French historians who recognise themselves under this label study? I will limit my remarks to 'official' cultural historians, excluding colleagues from other academic departments, such as cultural studies, civilisation, art, music or history of literature. My aim is obviously not to exclude what are often very relevant approaches, but to better understand the internal reconstruction that the 'cultural' has provoked in our profession. I said in my introduction that to map the terrain was difficult, but that does not mean that it is impossible. Three books have recently attempted such a mapping, each with different style, format and intention, but published in a remarkably short timeframe (September 2004, October 2004, and finally November 2005 – this last being the proceedings of a conference which took place in August 2004). One should note the unity of action here, since all three books have 'cultural history' in their titles. The first is *L'histoire culturelle*, by Pascal Ory, who has certainly been the most active pro-moter of a cultural history of the contemporary period. As early as 1981 he published the first essay on the topic and founded the first university research centre, together with the first association specialising in the field.[2] This is a short and incisive work, indeed it is something of a manifesto, and takes a vertical dive into what Ory sees as a question or an approach.[3] The second book, *Les enjeux de l'histoire culturelle* by Philippe Poirrier, offers a broader and more encom-passing analysis that surveys neighbouring territories – a historiographical overview – and is more a synthesis than a programme.[4] The third book, *L'histoire culturelle du contemporain*, brings together the proceedings of a week-long con-ference at the chateau of Cerisy–la–salle. It contains a wider range of essays (28 contributors, including myself), but the overall perspective is still cartographic, using juxtaposition, superposition or comparison to define its subject.[5] This offensive – three books on the same topic in just over a year! – is of course aston-ishing. One may interpret it as a sign of dynamism, even of imperialism. This is clear, for instance, in very annexationist bibliographies of these books. One might equally interpret it as an anxious attempt to assert its identity and ambi-tions, a concern which reveals a need for an institutional framework. It might even be read as a sign of exhaustion, a sort of death rattle concealing its episte-mological malaise by pronouncing and labelling. I will leave this open for discussion for the moment, and return to a reasoned analysis emerging from these three books, which will allow me to outline the historiographical perimeter of the field.

Two levels of analysis are visible here. The first one, a survey of the field, is generally consensual. The authors seem to agree on the main point, which is the definition of the subject. Cultural history, according to the three books, is 'the social history of representations'. It is social history in that it is focused on the collective, on contexts, on the mechanisms of production or the unequal distribution of goods. However, it is a history dedicated to the study of 'representations', defined as material forms of expression, or the forms of expression manifested through the senses, together with the practices that shape them. This history, according to these three books, is located in a long genealogy that makes its originality doubtful. The link with the history of 'mentalities' is explicitly made, so that homage is duly paid to the great ancestors of this tradition: Voltaire, Guizot, Lucien Febvre, Marc Bloch. The three books also agree on a few general or methodological principles. First, the need to widen the pool of sources ('from Goya to Chantal Goya', in the words of Pascal Ory), resolutely making use of classes of documents such as literature which had previously been rejected by historians because of their subjectivity. Second, the addition to the modern historical domain of many objects and practices previously seen as unworthy or illegitimate, such as those deriving from mass culture. Here we can record the combined influences of the early modern tradition of historical anthropology and of Anglo-American cultural studies. Third, a trend (though it is probably the dimension least agreed upon) toward a growing self-consciousness of historical methods, represented by the importation of new theoretical models or by what François Hartog has called 'the temptation of epistemology'.

Beyond agreement on these very general points there is profound disagreement about objects, practice and goals at a second level of analysis. A large majority of works claiming to belong to cultural history, or acknowledged as such, undertake what one may call, in short, the exploration of cultural fields. This is the history of cultural objects and of their social uses: books, media, films, theatre and other live shows and songs, their approach often limited to the mere description of their forms or their mode of production. This is also the history of cultural institutions and policies, of intellectuals and cultural mediators. Here I am simply quoting the chapter headings of the three works mentioned. It is also the history of ideas, of science or of cultural disciplines (art, literature, music, and so on). The annual programme of the Centre of Cultural History of Contemporary Societies of the University of Versailles, the only French research centre exclusively dedicated to cultural history, deals with the same themes: there are sessions on the history of the media, of publishing, of international cultural relationships, of photography, live entertainment, cinema and the writing of history.[6] Similar topics have been dealt with at past conferences: books, media, gastronomy, children, the press, censorship, George Sand, serials, Colette, the cultural relations of France and England, mass culture, and so on.

A substantial part of the work on cultural history is in fact about the history of culture, about its objects and practices. This is, of course, a very important field. We need to know the material, technical, economical and political constraints which shape forms of culture. Exploring different forms of cultural production, understanding as closely as possible the mechanisms of its circulation and of its social reception, are crucial historical tasks. This history is necessary, even indispensable, as has been demonstrated, for example, by path-breaking works on the history of publishing. To limit cultural history to these aspects of history would, however, mean reducing cultural history to a material, economic or social history of the phenomena of cultural production, which would singularly limit its ambitions. On a strictly epistemological level, such studies are related to a classic economic, social and political historiography. We can see clearly how little such an approach has contributed to the renewal of historiographical debate: the fields and approaches are broad but not new. The view of Christophe Prochasson is even harsher. 'One might say, a little brutally, that cultural history has sometimes been an emollient factor: it often resulted in lowering standards of the historiographical criteria of excellence in the name of a "cultural reading" of societies, offering generalizing and ill-founded interpretations without moving on from conventional issues or ever inventing new territories'.[7]

Within the field of cultural history there are nevertheless a few studies that do not consider the 'cultural' as a domain or as a stock of objects and practices, but as a perspective on and a way towards the whole of social reality, the culture of which would be, so to speak, the structuring expression. This particular cultural history is very close to what American scholars called in the 1980s the 'new cultural history'; it might be defined as an anthropological approach to societies. It is eager to restore perceptions, to explore the senses, values, beliefs, imagination; it examines the subjective or the symbolic dimension of experience. In a word, it considers any of the ways people feel, construct or understand the world around them. We are still left with a history of 'representations', but these are representations that do not remain at the material and figurative level of objects, images, prints, emblems, monuments, and so on – what I have proposed to call 'figurations'[8] – but representations that might be better called 'appreciations'. These would include categories for defining and comprehending the world, categories which are informed by sensorial systems and which in turn release sensations, feelings, emotions, desires and imagination. This project, naturally, is not new. It is what in the nineteenth century Guizot termed 'the moral state' of a society, and what the Goncourt brothers called 'the very accent of the soul of men who are not there anymore'. Indeed, it has always been one of the ambitions of history, even history of the most academic kind, which discovered these things long before 1980. 'Ideas, representations, errors of perspective have always been taken into account', wrote Antoine Prost and Jay Winter about the history of the First World War, and that remark could well be transferred to many other historical subjects.[9] In the last few years, however, the project has shifted through the choice of theoretical and methodological devices. These have relied less on geography, sociology or economics, and more on textual criticism, narratology or cultural anthropology. Even more, there has been a radical causal inversion of the system of representations so that it is no longer a function of economic, social or political factors, but a starting point, a prerequisite even, a dynamic whose construction is the very object of history. Here, cultural history demonstrates its capacity to reinvent problems and to suggest new paths for interpretation.

The history of the First World War, as it has been rewritten in the last fifteen years around the concept of 'culture of war', seen as a matrix for actions and behaviour, provides a good example of these new approaches. What was seen as 'incomprehensible' by previous generations – for instance, the plunge of a civilised and peaceful Europe into horror and brutality[10] – has now been opened up as understandable. Similarly, the works of Alain Corbin and his followers have turned the senses, emotions and depth of feelings into a privileged key to understanding the social world.[11]

Cultural histories of crime and the press

In the second part of this paper I would like to discuss two different examples taken from my own research work, which may demonstrate more explicitly the virtues of what can be a cultural history of the social field. The first is about the history of crime, which, one might argue, is not really a cultural subject. As a violent rupture of physical and corporal integrity, a brutal tearing of collective and social ties, and as an absolute transgression of norms, crime is an entirely social act. Nevertheless, how can the historian gain a better understanding of such an uncontrollable event? For, with a few exceptions, crime is an incomprehensible event. It is a sort of blank fact, the motives or circumstances of which are never obvious, a kind of blind spot, the site of an unspeakable story: hence the endless stream of representations it produces. 'One does not generally gain access to it directly', two sociologists of crime have written, 'but only through the reflection of society's reaction'.[12] Hence the disappointment of scholars who expected to find the 'truth' about crime by the study of objective sources. Neither judicial statistics, which measure the development of the 'litigious culture', hierarchies of what acts are punished and the turnover of courts, nor the police or judiciary or prison archives, which only give an account of the way a crime is reconstituted, nor the various treatises of penal philosophy, ever succeeded in defining the phenomenon of crime. Hence the very peculiar course of the historiography of modern crime from its inception in the early 1970s, seemingly beating around the bush and almost avoiding the core of the phenomenon. The history of prisons flourished, along with the history of criminal theories and that of penalties and penal institutions, but any analysis of transgressions themselves seemed to meet a dead-end.

Understanding the reality of the phenomenon of crime actually requires bringing together the totality of its intricate factors: systems of representations of the just and unjust that define transgressions, the social thresholds of tolerance that make transgressions more or less effective, the legal acts that inscribe transgressions in legal order, the types of repression that make them visible, together with the almost irreducible tangle of psychological, social or economic motives that drive a man or a woman to cross the line. The clues to this complex knot, as we can see, are mostly cultural. How can we make those clues work together? Investigation, as a concept, offers a possibility, provided that we can grasp the plurality of its forms and meanings. First comes the inquest, the judicial investigation, in which the various actors – police and detectives, prosecutors and judges, mayors, physicians, barristers, private investigators – enable us to cross-reference different views. Second, there is the social survey that emerges from the judicial investigation, through witnesses, and later, in the twentieth century, through social workers. Third, there is the journalistic investigation, operating by means of news items and news reports, gossip columns and articles about the courts, that reveals the crime to public awareness, gives it visibility and spins it into a social, or even a political, event, and gives rise in its wake to a whole world of literary and cinematographic fiction.

From the first testimonies or topographic reports carried out by policemen, to the many judicial, journalistic and literary reconstitutions, together with forensic reports or lawyers' arguments, the investigation is thus the process which permits the representation of the crime. It is what turns a previously incomprehensible event into a speakable, readable and socially controllable reality. To analyse concurrently the multiple investigations and investigators, the procedures they use, the constraints and motivations weighing on them, the representations they produce, seems to constitute an excellent way to grasp the whole of the cultural processes that makes crime a social reality. Such an analytical overview, taking all the actors involved in the judicial operation into account, is a project I undertook in a work co-authored with Jean-Claude Farcy and Jean-Noël Luc, *L'enquête judiciaire au XIXe siècle*.[13] A similar analysis was undertaken on a micro-historical scale by Philippe Artières and myself in our book on the case of Henri Vidal, the killer of two young women in 1901 near Nice.[14] Our idea was to take into account the whole 'file' of the investigation and of Vidal's trial, the whole collection of reports and representations related to the crime. That meant looking at those representations dramatised by the penny press, which had made itself the spokesman of social awareness, served up in broadsheets, chapbooks and gallows sheets. It also meant reading the accounts of the actors of the judicial system, detectives, judges, lawyers and the penal staff, whose voices also transmit the voices of those they have interviewed: parents, neighbours, witnesses, victims. There are also the accounts of the numerous experts, physicians, psychiatrists, criminologists, graphologists, and so on, who piled onto the 'woman killer' a huge amount of knowledge, most of it published in books or in newspapers. Finally, it meant reading the account of the criminal himself, Henri Vidal, who spontaneously or 'under duress', filled up over fourteen notebooks with notes, sketches, drafts and recollections, from which he later drafted a 60-page memoir.

Thus, from Vidal's crimes emerges a huge and polyphonic text, in which convergences as well as discords and contradictions compose the social tale of that crime and its reception. It is this prism, in all its vastness and diversity, which we have attempted to grasp. Keen to read simultaneously stories and speeches that had been produced and published together, and keen to restore the dynamic that then constructed the social figure of the criminal, we chose the genre of documentary montage, so that we could reconstruct the criminal's biography in much the same way as had been done gradually by the society of the belle époque when it uncovered and appropriated Vidal's crimes and character. This seems to me a good example of what can be called a cultural history of crime, that profoundly social event.

A very different example can be drawn from a joint work carried out, with the collaboration of a literary team, on the history of the French press during the nineteenth century.[15] One might imagine that, by studying the newspaper, we are returning to the world of cultural objects. But that is not the case. Although part of our work is indeed dedicated to updating the material, technical, social and economic history of nineteenth-century newspapers, the main thrust of the project is very different. It stems from the following hypothesis: because of the manner of its production, because of the importance of circulation and because of the new rhythms it imposes on the ordinary flow of things, the growth and generalisation of periodical writing and reading – mostly daily – tends to modify social, economic, political and cultural activities as a whole. It changes all perceptions and representations of the world, which are shaped by the flow of the media and a culture of periodicity. The progressive involvement of the different layers of society in a sphere organised by the principle of periodical writing and reading ultimately constitutes a major anthropological change, which is at the very source of our media modernity. The point is, in a way, to answer Henri Berr's question of 1934, in his foreword to Georges Weil's study of newspapers: 'The progress of the press is startlingly clear. But what about progress through the press?'[16] The question is thus to understand how the newspaper, through its various uses, shapes the social world, polishing or refracting it, altering or constructing it. The press was one factor in the construction of social identities during the nineteenth century. Jeremy Popkin has shown the leading role played by Lyon's newspapers during the uprising of 1831–34 in the definition of bourgeois, working-class or feminist identities that had yet to define themselves.[17]

Our approach, however, also affects the movements, the activities or the behaviours of individuals. Literary scholars have shown how newspapers played a creative role in the making of nineteenth-century literature, demonstrating how the press was the melting pot of aesthetic innovation, modifying discourse, encouraging new forms that changed the whole field of literary creation, including poetry – privileging brevity, the visual over the spoken, together with irony. Rapid and wide popularisation also affected developments in the fine arts and in scientific invention, not only in matters of expression, but also on the exercise of scientific activity itself. For instance, Fabien Locher has demonstrated how weather forecast experiments by the Observatoire de Paris had to take into account, as early as the 1860s, the publication of forecast bulletins in the newspapers.[18] Politics itself was affected. The generalisation of news written, published and read daily was undoubtedly a factor that transformed the functioning of Parliament, the strategies of actors in the political game, and the behaviour of voters. Returning to the matter of crime, we can see how much the gradual construction through the nineteenth century of 'public safety' as a national and political issue owed to the workings of the media. This new cultural history of the press is not therefore limited to a study of the forms and the practices associated with it. It aims to understand the 'work' or the social action of the newspaper, the collective experiences that were fashioned by uses to which the press was put.

I am uncertain whether the many French historians who specialise in cultural history will recognise themselves in these two examples. It does not really matter, because my work has no normative function whatsoever, and I am not convinced of the absolute usefulness of declaring a position, which may have the effect of needlessly hardening positions. However, as Bernard Lahire noted, the return to empirical research work often brings with it 'pacifying virtues'.[19]

Conclusion

In conclusion I would like to stress how much, whatever their uncertainties and weaknesses, the body of works identified by the expression 'cultural history' has, in my view, contributed to three major advances. The first is related to the realm of sources, where in the last twenty years there has been a decisive shift and multiplying effect. On the one hand, as I said before, we have seen the continuing expansion of the range of sources, the use of material that was regarded, only yesterday, as unable to tell the truth of history, without any legitimacy other than its existence as traces of the past, whatever their nature. On the other hand, we have seen a critical evaluation of the very nature of each source, a more intimate relation with archives, now seen not so much as a means to the past as an object in itself, not so much for what it can say about the world, as for what it actually says about itself. We have seen a closer attention to systems of representation, a consideration of how these systems have been set up and preserved, a closer look at the language and words codifying sources, and at the aims and views which shape the rhetoric of the description and structure the world view of the source. These operations are certainly part of the historian's traditional task of source criticism, but they were improved by Foucault's project of *The Archaeology of Knowledge* (*L'archéologie du savoir*), and they seem to me today to be at the very heart of the practice of history, namely consideration of the archive, its origins, its limits and its social uses.

The second breakthrough is the steady widening of the spectrum of our understanding of the social world. Not only has the spectrum of what is studied never ceased to grow, but modes of exploration have been enriched by a shift to understanding long underestimated social divisions, such as gender or age. Our study of society has also been strengthened by greater attention to perceptions, representations, the play of memory and the sensorial environment of the actors of history, while the individual construction of social identities has become a major concern. Reconstructing the world of these historical actors has also been complicated by the reconstitution of what Alain Corbin calls their 'time architecture': in short, their perception and use of time. A denser and more fragmented social world is taking shape under the historian's pen. This close attention of the infinite plurality of actors and representations does not entail a denial of wider and more panoramic readings such as those concerned with defining the thresholds of collective sensitivity, or the matrix around which the systems of representation are organised. The notion of a social imagination seems to me to articulate this relationship and this dialectic between individual and social constructions of the world.

The last advance is of a methodological order. These advances derive from a growing self-consciousness of historical interpretation: an interest in other theoretical models, prominence given to ways in which objects are constructed rather than taken as given, and a taste for experimentation. The triumphant overarching analysis of the omniscient historian has lost its splendour. The relationship of historians to historical writing has also been modified: we are more aware of the distinct natures of the text and of the historical account; it is understood that the historian can employ narrative – even rhetorical – resources (which naturally affects questions of causation). It is agreed that historical narrative itself can be studied as a literary form, and the idea that the historian can link the narration of his or her investigation with the exposition of their results – a method long banished from the conventions of historical writing – is no longer seen as a scandal. This does not entail questioning the limits of what we can know or the truth of historical discourse; rather it improves historical writing by a mastery of its forms of expression.

No doubt many of these developments have not waited for cultural history to assert themselves, nor of course can their effects be limited to this one field. However, what we have called cultural history, in its various forms, has never ceased to accompany these changes. This is why, despite its weaknesses or its contradictions, cultural history can still constitute a standard-bearer.

Michael Kelly

This question is particularly challenging, both because of the broad and unstable nature of the two concepts it combines, and because it may be addressed to a wide range of scholars who will approach it from different perspectives. Any answer to the question will therefore be partial and provisional: a contribution to dialogue rather than an authoritative conclusion. I will offer a partial and provisional view, looking in the first part at the range of perspectives from which responses may come within the broader community that now sees itself as engaging with cultural history. In the second part, I will offer a view of what some kinds of cultural history are about, drawing on two examples taken from my own research.

Perspectives on cultural history

'Culture' and 'history' are both broad concepts which are continuing to expand. This is now reaching the point where it is difficult to identify any account of the past that is not in some respects cultural, or any cultural activity that is not in some respects historical. But the combined term 'cultural history' does suggest an activity that is distinct, by contrast with other terms of the same type, combining the same noun with different adjectives or the same adjective with different nouns. In this sense, cultural history is different from political history, economic history or military history, and different from cultural theory, cultural criticism or cultural anthropology. Cultural history has had long and complex relationships with all of these neighbouring activities, and more. Standing at the confluence of cultural concerns and approaches to history, it is challenged and enriched by both. The challenges have been expressed in a number of debates about, for example, whether there is really a distinction between cultural history and social history, or whether cultural history is really different from cultural studies. The enrichment has often flowed from reflections on the role of theories or methods developed in other domains, and their application to historical issues. The 'cultural turn' and the 'linguistic turn' are well established examples of this process.[20]

The interaction between domains, to mutual benefit, has produced one of the most interesting developments of recent years: the encounter between scholars who might be regarded as 'official' historians, to use Dominique Kalifa's useful phrase, and colleagues from other academic areas, who could perhaps be termed 'unofficial' historians. The encounter is particularly interesting because it throws light on the question of history as a discipline. Pierre Bourdieu, analysing the social structure of academic life in *Homo Academicus* (1984), takes up Immanuel Kant's suggestion that disciplines are a combination of 'temporal' and 'cognitive' factors.[21] These factors correspond broadly to the social and intellectual dimensions of academic activity. On this reading, the distinction between 'official' and 'unofficial' historians is primarily a social distinction, rooted in institutional structures. It identifies the particular (social) status of scholars, primarily in terms of their career trajectory and the departments or sections in which they work. Their status is also shaped by the committees and panels which scrutinise their professional careers in various ways: for appointments and promotions, for evaluation of their teaching and research, and for the award of grants and fellowships, among other things.

Whatever their status, historians are also distinguished by their intellectual 'stance'. This distinguishes them cognitively from each other, by reference to what they study and how they study it. They will, for example, choose to study a particular country or region, focusing on a given period, such as contemporary France. They will adopt characteristic methods of study and theoretical frameworks with which to approach their subject. And they will choose the ways in which they disseminate their findings, from particular journals or publishers to broadcast and online media.

The relationship between social status and intellectual stance is therefore a fairly loose one, enabling historians of similar status to have markedly different intellectual stances, and vice versa. This relationship has become more complex with the increasing emergence of collaborative projects which bring together scholars from several disciplines to elucidate a set of issues, both in teaching and in research. It is also made more complex by the growing number of encounters between historians from different countries, leading them to understand that each of them divides the academic domain in subtly different ways. In the French context, history has traditionally been closely linked with geography, and both parts of 'histoire-géo' may typically be taught by the same teacher in a French lycée. Conversely, in the British context, history is more likely to be found in arts and humanities groupings, with natural affinities to languages, literature and philosophy.

Unofficial cultural historians

Where Dominique Kalifa focuses on 'official' historians, who may be found in history departments, I shall focus on the 'unofficial' cultural historians in the English-speaking world. They are based in other academic departments, such as art, music, literature, languages, area studies and cultural studies. In the first instance, their interest is in the history of culture, and in many cases their social role has been to provide a historical background for the study of how a particular cultural domain operates, in order to support either analysis or performance.

As an example, historians of music will often expect to contribute insights to a wider group of musicologists, studying composition, performance, reception and other aspects of music. The work of music historians and other musicologists will in turn inform the production and reproduction of music in the present. But a historian of music will also be able to contribute insights to the wider group of historians, studying art, literature and other cultural activities in their social context at particular times and places. Robert Morgan's work exemplifies this, analysing the development of modern music in relation to the social, economic and political context of the twentieth century.[22] Keith Negus offers a similar analysis of recent popular music, relating it to the activities of large corporations as well as to the wider cultural trends of the period.[23] Daniel Leech-Wilkinson offers a more complex view in his book on the modern invention of medieval music, which focuses as much on the ideologies and tastes of the contemporary period as on the Middle Ages.[24] All three build bridges between music and history that encourage scholars to cross in both directions.

Historians of a particular country often find themselves in a similar position, in which their work has strong connections with that of scholars studying other aspects of the country. So historians of France, for example, find their work in strong demand from scholars focusing on other aspects of French studies: language, linguistics, literary and cultural studies, or social and political studies. 'Official' historians of France within the British university system have frequently taken this into consideration, and there is extensive discussion of cultural dimensions in the works of the late Douglas Johnson, Roderick Kedward and Colin Jones.[25] They are joined by a large number of 'unofficial' historians in departments of political science, geography, sociology and area studies, for example. Such historians are found especially in languages departments, where their historical research is aimed both at enhancing an understanding of the country concerned, and at informing the work of theorists and critics of culture. Frequently, their historical analysis is linked to particular thematic areas, such as women's studies, for example. Contemporary scholars whose work is located in this category include Siân Reynolds, who has worked extensively on gender and politics, especially in the interwar period; Hanna Diamond, who has focused on the role of women in occupied France; or the late Claire Duchen, who charted the developing social and political condition of women in post-war France.[26] Their work is valued both as a dimension of mainstream historical studies and as an illuminating context for the texts and artefacts which were produced during the period in question, and which are still read or studied for their cultural value in the present day.

An important link between 'official' and 'unofficial' historians of France lies in the bond of solidarity engendered by their proficiency in the French language and their experience of contemporary French culture. A similar bond exists between scholars of other countries in which most of the archival material and large numbers of studies are only available in a foreign language. But French is the second language most widely spoken by scholars in Britain, and is valued for the access it provides to sources and archives that would be inaccessible to a monolingual English scholar. Scholars who are able to read the material in the original will often find themselves consulting the same sources as colleagues from a variety of other disciplinary backgrounds. This is particularly true in the contemporary period. For example, Marcel Ophüls' film *Le chagrin et la pitié* (1971) has been studied from many standpoints, from the history of the Second World War, and the history of France of the 1970s, to political science, cinema history and film criticism.

Film history has been a particularly fertile field of enquiry, especially in twentieth-century history. In part this is because the reach and impact of film has been understood by many different regimes, which have turned to cinema to represent or promote their social and political objectives. In part, the historical importance of film has sprung from its importance as a record of life and events in the past century, an increasingly important factor as the dissemination of historical research is taken up by broadcast media. Pam Cook's classic, *The Cinema Book*, played a pioneering role, combining contemporary film studies with history of cinema.[27] In a more recent book, she examines debates about the role of cinema in mediating history, through strategies of memory and nostalgia.[28] Lester Friedman has edited several volumes that explore the interaction between cinema and politics in 1970s America and 1980s Britain.[29] And James Chapman has undertaken detailed analyses of the relationship between cinema and contemporaneous cultural identities in such diverse genres as historical films and James Bond movies.[30] In recent years these kinds of approaches have been developed in relation to French cinema by British scholars such as Susan Hayward and Phil Powrie.[31] Most recently, a *French Cinema Book* has been produced by Michael Temple and Michael Witt, as part of a series, currently including British and German cinema.[32]

There has typically been little contact between historians of a particular cultural area (such as art) with those of another (such as philosophy), or between these and 'official' historians. In part, this was because the history of a cultural area is closely bound up with other disciplines proper to that area. So an art historian requires substantial knowledge in the domain of fine art in order to be able to understand the composition and meaning of an artefact, or the skills and technology that have been used in its production. It may not be surprising, then, that an art historian's work will often focus on the changing conceptions and practices in the world of art, making relatively weak connections with the historical changes in other cultural areas or in the broader social context. In recent years, art historians have made stronger links with the wider historical field. This has been inspired by the discovery of Walter Benjamin's work on literature and art in the nineteenth century.[33] It has been taken up by T. J. Clarke, who presents art in close interaction with the major changes of its age;[34] by Thomas Crow, who examines the interaction between art and politics in the twentieth century and before;[35] and by Dana Arnold, who connects architectural history to the development of broader cultural identities.[36]

The history of philosophy and the history of ideas have traditionally been identified with departments of philosophy and literature, with the primary aim of providing historical contexts to the development of their respective disciplines rather than making a contribution to broader historical understanding. The most striking attempt to overcome this historical segregation was probably the work of Bertrand Russell. His many pamphlets are now documents of historical interest in their own right, but his much reprinted *History of Western Philosophy* (1946) remains one of the most ambitious attempts to connect the history of philosophy with broader historical contexts and with the debates of his own era.[37] These attempts have been continued by philosophers of the stature of Richard Rorty and Quentin Skinner,[38] but have largely failed to engage the interest of scholars outside their own discipline. The historians of ideas have been more successful in creating meaningful exchanges with other disciplines, including the 'official' historians. Scholars of the medieval, early modern and nineteenth centuries have been particularly successful over many years in integrating the literary expression of ideas with broader historical issues. Arthur Lovejoy's *Great Chain of Being* (1936) and Peter Gay's *Enlightenment* (1966) are classics in this genre.[39] For the twentieth century, this has been more difficult, since literary studies of more recent ideas have often been too close to their subjects to provide dispassionate accounts. There are exceptions, however, and Stefan Collini's *Absent Minds* (2006) has largely escaped advocacy and hostile polemic to provide a historically rooted analysis of British intellectuals in the twentieth century.[40]

The history of literature has for the most part served the study of literary texts, by setting them in the context of longer-term literary traditions. This is the scope of Denis Hollier's classic survey in the genre,[41] though David Coward's more recent survey has located its subjects more explicitly in historical contexts.[42] Studies of particular writers have frequently explored aspects of the social setting that would permit a richer reading of their texts. This is the stock-in-trade of the 'l'homme et l'œuvre' approach. Literary history has at times stepped outside this framework to explore a social context in greater depth, illuminated by the writer's perspective. This happens particularly where a writer has explicitly claimed to represent the society of his or her time. Balzac is the *locus classicus* of this kind of writer. More recently, literary approaches have been mobilised by scholars to illuminate important moments in France's history. In Britain, Margaret Atack's studies of literature during the Occupation period and during the events of May 1968 exemplify this approach, as does Philip Dine's study of literary representations of the Algerian crisis.[43] Leading American scholars have similarly woven literary and socio-political themes to capture the cultural complexion of France during its recent history. Fredric Jameson's works on narrative as a socially symbolic act, and on the cultural logic of late capitalism have been influential in this respect.[44] The use of literary sources to illuminate social issues was an important factor in the development of cultural studies *à l'anglais*. Raymond Williams' pioneering studies of the British literary tradition in its social context connected with the concerns of sociologists, social theorists and historians to spark the interdisciplinary configuration of cultural studies.[45] While the link between literature and society has provided opportunities for scholars to engage in political comment of a direct or indirect nature, it has also created an opening for the insights of linguistics, cultural studies and critical theory to inform historical research.

The reconstruction of identity

Taking two examples from my own work on the immediate post-war period in France, I should like to suggest some of the things that cultural history can now be about, bringing to bear the analytical methods of different cultural domains to illuminate the broader social context.[46] A first example concerns the ways in which French cultural elites were mobilised by the provisional government to support the reconstruction of the country in 1944. Alongside the physical and political damage caused by the events of the war and occupation, France experienced serious damage to its sense of national identity. The idea of identity is a key concept in most areas of cultural study, and the gravity of damage to national identity in particular is shown by its consequences in the more recent cases of Yugoslavia and Iraq. Reconstructing national identity in post-conflict France was fraught with difficulty. In their heyday, both the Third Republic and the État français of Vichy were able to embody the nation in the symbols of the state: flag, uniforms, ceremonies, the person of the head of state, and similar representations. The provisional government of de Gaulle found it a more difficult task in the immediate circumstances of the end of the war. They were obliged to turn to a range of other symbolic systems in support of the state symbols, in order to represent the nation adequately. The state therefore undertook a major work of what Claude Lévi-Strauss called 'bricolage',[47] and called on the entire spectrum of identities to give weight and gravity to the cultural restoration of the national identity. It drew many of its resources from the religious domain.

As Benedict Anderson points out, since the eighteenth century, the institutions of nationhood have assumed many of the functions of religion, constructing themselves sacramentally as entire cultural systems.[48] The principal function of national systems of cultural representation, he argues, is that of making sense of the inevitabilities of human life, among which death and suffering are perhaps the most irreducible. The situation of France in 1944 brought this crucial function into sharp focus, as the scale of death and suffering loomed darkly over the country, and the capacity of the nation to imagine itself as a community was stretched almost to the limit. The experience of death haunts the period after 1944. Death and suffering figure prominently in its narratives and images. For example, it is visible in the painting of Picasso and the sculpture of Giacometti; the films of Marcel Carné: *Les enfants du paradis* and *Les portes de la nuit*; the plays of Jean-Paul Sartre and Albert Camus: *Huis clos, Morts sans sépulture, Le malentendu, Caligula*; the novels of Simone de Beauvoir: *Tous les hommes sont mortels, Le sang des autres*; the poetry of Éluard and Aragon; or the songs of Edith Piaf and Juliette Gréco.[49] Coincidentally, the high points of the Paris theatre season of 1944–45 were T. S. Eliot's *Murder in the Cathedral* and Strindberg's *Dance of Death*, both directed by Jean Vilar.

It is striking how far religious themes are interwoven with the rebuilding of the nation in texts and images. One of the most striking wall-posters distributed around Paris at the moment of the insurrection and eventual liberation of the capital was by Paul Colin, dated 17 August 1944. It depicts Marianne, symbol of the Republic in her Phrygian bonnet, standing and shielding her eyes as she looks into the distance.[50] She may be shielding her eyes from the heat of a blazing building or from the rays of the sunrise. Printed in colours suggesting the French tricolor, she wears a tunic patterned in a way that suggests the shells of ruined buildings, and her hands are scarred in a way that recalls the stigmata of Christ crucified. The symbolism is simple and immediate, but also rich and complex. At the immediate level, it presents, as Colin's fellow affichiste Raymond Gid says, 'a tricolor image, with a cloud-free blue sky' in which 'France, with her hands crucified until only yesterday, lifts her gaze beyond her ruins towards the future'.[51] This is an inspiring image to mobilise the population to rise up against the occupying forces, and no doubt was not read or intended in any other way. However, it conceals further implications that emerge on closer reading. The conjunction of Marianne and Christ is unusual, not least because of the traditional enmity and *de jure* separation between the Roman Catholic Church and the secular Republic. However, these were heady days of reconciliation, and Colin's 'bricolage' no doubt helped to encourage the process. The implicit transgression of gender distinctions is not wholly unprecedented, and Joan of Arc is an obvious association, but the tradition of women exhibiting Christ's stigmata is rather specific to Catholic spiritualism, whereas Marianne initially appears as France crucified; there are therefore residual echoes of her merely simulating the signs of the Passion.

Calling up the connotations of Christ after His physical death and Resurrection, passing on to a higher plane, the poster may also suggest that the new France would be significantly different from the old, a point which would resonate with both the internal Resistance movements and de Gaulle's Free French. Ruined buildings appear on the tunic like an image on a shroud, suggesting the extent of the physical destruction incurred. But at this time, such images also carried the suppressed point that a large part of the destruction was actually carried out by France's allies, who may therefore be complicit in the crucifixion. As in much of the French iconography of the period, as distinct from the Allied equivalent, the poster does not otherwise identify either enemies or allies. Colin's poster is in one sense highly specific to its moment, the beginning of the week in which Paris was liberated. Appropriately, Marianne has just emerged from the tomb and is looking around, perhaps a little bewildered at the confused action which awaits her, and of which she is a symbol. She would not belong in the earlier period of preparation for liberation, nor to the later period of consolidation of the nation state. But in another sense the poster is emblematic of a much longer period. The symbols of the state and of religion are assembled together in an attempt to give meaning and purpose to destruction and death. What emerges from the ruins is hope, which is directed towards a newly reconstructed France, rooted in universality and transcendence. Death, though real, is conquered in the imagined symbols of the nation.

The humanist synthesis

Alongside the integration of religious themes and images in France's identity, the process of reconstruction was strongly assisted in 1944 by the adoption of a common ideology, which expressed the shared values of the state, incorporating but not confined to religious beliefs. In the aftermath of many conflicts, religious movements have been adopted as a common framework of beliefs and values around which a nation can unite. In France, this occurred after the defeat of 1940, when the Vichy regime mobilised Catholic piety in support of its National Revolution. But with the collapse of that regime, the credibility of Catholicism was severely damaged, and the French political and intellectual elites had to look elsewhere for a unifying ideological framework: that is, a set of beliefs that would be effective in achieving the desired social effects. It was not easy for the French political and intellectual elites to manage the aftermath of a near civil war, or to construct a viable political system from the wide spectrum of competing forces who claimed the right to a place in the new order. They had an urgent need for a common framework of agreed values, within which the issues could be debated and resolved. Neither the Church, nor the State, nor any other social institution could offer a value system that was sufficiently inclusive for the purpose. Over a period of a few weeks in late 1944, a tentative process of conceptual 'bricolage' produced a viable version of humanism. It rapidly emerged as the common framework of discussion, and all the main forces agreed to work within it. In this sense, humanism played a crucial ideological role in rebuilding unity and a sense of common purpose at the end of the war.

Pierre Bourdieu's notion of the 'rules of the game' is useful for understanding how this came about.[52] He suggests that any field of activity is structured by a set of rules which are accepted, usually implicitly, by all the participants. The rules determine what actions are legitimated and how a participant or group of participants may gain ascendancy within the field. In France in 1945, the field of ideas acquired a new set of rules, or at least an extensively revised set of underlying values. These values defined what could be said or thought, and how writers and thinkers might gain recognition. They were presented explicitly as a framework of humanism.

Humanism in the French sense is a somewhat eclectic notion, which has proven to be more persuasive the less closely it is analysed, and most persuasive of all when it is taken as an unstated assumption. In this it bears some resemblance to the force of gravitation, which is not strong enough to be observed in small-scale interactions but exerts a bonding effect on a large scale. Normally, humanism is not clearly visible in the detail of intellectual debate, but functions nevertheless to hold the cultural field together. In France in the immediate postwar period, when the cultural field was radically disrupted, the French political and intellectual elite expounded humanism explicitly, finding in it a consensual means of rebuilding a measure of cultural unity. Like much of the 'new' thinking of the time, its elements were largely to be found in earlier debates, from which a fragile and provisional synthesis began to emerge in the 1930s. The circumstances in which the war ended then provided the environment in which the elements could be brought together and could flourish.

The humanist voice articulates a concept of Man, or Humanity, as the touchstone by which projects and achievements must be judged, possibly referring also to a transcendental dimension. It focuses on the individual or the human person, possessing a sense of identity as a subject with purpose, meaning and value, nourished by personal freedom. It is engaged in building a future society against the dangers of alienation, oppression and inequality. It values literary, artistic and intellectual culture against barbarism in its various forms, and seeks to ensure that it is passed on to succeeding generations. Humanists respect Science and its power for good or ill, recognising that the benefits of progress come at a price. They also wish to learn from and influence the future course of History, hoping to learn from the catastrophe of war and prepare an era of peace and progress for all humanity.

While these themes do not comprise a comprehensive list of humanist concerns, they provide a broad profile of humanist tones in what Roland Barthes called the 'voice of knowledge' (*la voix de la science*), the cultural codes which convey an important strand of meaning in any text, and refer to the bodies of knowledge or wisdom they invoke implicitly or explicitly.[53]

The extent of the post-war humanist upsurge can be seen in the plethora of books published with some variant of '*l'homme*' or '*l'humanisme*' in their title. A handful of such books in 1945 was followed by three times as many the following year.[54] The post-war humanist hegemony was a product of the ideological conditions prevailing in the summer of 1944, dominated by the need for an inclusive frame of reference to which all parts of the nation could relate. At its heart was the humanist vision articulated by the Resistance, with which social democrats and Christian democrats could feel at home, and to which other forces, particularly communists and nationalists, could broadly subscribe. Once this vision was publicly proclaimed, it carried both conviction and legitimacy in the absence of an articulated alternative. On the other side of the ideological divide, the supporters of collaboration degenerated into an increasingly destructive and self-destructive rhetoric, amply reflected in the deeds of their military and paramilitary wings. Vichy, reduced to a rump, split into diehards and opportunists. The opportunists, a substantial majority, fled for the most part under the copious skirts of Mother Church. There they joined the *attentistes*, who had adopted a wait-and-see attitude, and 'workers of the eleventh hour', who had joined the fight for national liberation at the last moment. They found that Christian humanism had kept a foot in both camps and offered a very convenient lifeline. Hence, at the end of the war, very little ideological adjustment was required, and the blossoming discourse of Man was echoed by humanists of every ilk, eagerly seizing their opportunity.

In this way, and with surprising unanimity, post-war French humanism served as a bonding agent for the bruised and divided French nation, enabling it to reconstruct national unity within a broad ideological consensus. There was no broader basis available for consensus than humanism, since it ostensibly excluded no major strand of opinion and identity, other than those who had supported Nazism during the period of occupation, but who were now constrained to silence. Humanism became, in effect, the conceptual form of French universalism. Its hegemony was built on an alliance of social democracy and Christian democracy, the dominant political forces, but was sufficiently general and ecumenical that all of the major movements in post-war France could find some link or ancestor that enabled them to identify with it.

Inevitably, there were problems inherent in the situation, which may be summed up as the repression of difference. It was not only that the collaborationist Right were excluded; it was also that in rallying to humanism, many other groups, including existentialists, Marxists and Catholics, were obliged to abandon or diminish significant aspects of their own intellectual and cultural past, which were critical of humanism. Post-war humanism was also quite unblushing in its assumption that the model of Man was a certain idea of the white French male, leaving little space for those who, by virtue of their gender, race, class, religion or other difference, could not be assimilated to the dominant model. The excluded groups for the most part accepted the humanist hegemony as a necessity of the moment. Some internalised it and became its strongest advocates, while others lapsed into resentful acquiescence, paying minimal lip service to it. The result was an ideological framework that held sway in France for a generation, encountering serious challenge only with the return of the repressed differences and the collapse of the Fourth Republic in the late 1950s.

Conclusions

These examples suggest two main conclusions. The first is that cultural identities and frameworks of values play an important role in the history of a period. It is not necessary to argue, as does Bernard-Henri Lévy, that the cultural domain was inflated to substitute for the lack of material prosperity in the austere post-war years.[55] But it is nonetheless valuable to highlight the role that cultural factors played in the difficult transition from 'les années noires' to 'les trente glorieuses'. Second, these examples show how the understanding of identities and ideologies is enhanced by the theoretical approaches and analytical techniques developed in the disciplines of culture. Taken together, these conclusions provide a basis for asserting the value of continued dialogue between 'official' and 'unofficial' cultural historians.

Notes

1   For her reading, her advice and her personal assistance during the conference, I am deeply grateful to Jann Matlock.
2   Pascal Ory, 'Pour une histoire culturelle de la France contemporaine', *Bulletin du centre d'histoire de la France contemporaine* 2 (1981), 5–32, updated and extended in 'L'Histoire culturelle de la France contemporaine. Questions et questionnement', *Vingtième siècle. Revue d'histoire* (1987), 67–82. The Centre d'histoire culturelle des sociétés contemporaines was founded in 1992 at the University of Versailles-Saint-Quentin-en-Yvelines, and the Association pour le développement de l'histoire culturelle was set up in 1998.
3   Pascal Ory, 'Que-sais-je?' in *L'histoire culturelle* (Paris, Puf, 2004).
4   Philippe Poirrier, *Les enjeux de l'histoire culturelle* (Paris, Le Seuil, 2004).
5   Laurent Martin and Sylvain Venayre, eds, *L'histoire culturelle du contemporain* (Le Paris, Nouveau Monde, 2005).
6   Centre d'histoire culturelle des sociétés contemporaines, Programme 2004–2005, Université de Versailles-Saint-Quentin-en-Yvelines, 96.

7 Christophe Prochasson, 'La guerre en ses cultures', in Jean-Jacques Becker, ed., *Histoire culturelle de la Grande Guerre* (Paris, A. Colin, 2005), 255–6.

8 Dominique Kalifa, 'L'histoire culturelle contre l'histoire sociale?', in Martin and Venayre, *L'histoire culturelle*, 78–9.

9 Antoine Prost and Jay Winter, *Penser la Grande Guerre. Un essai d'historiographie* (Paris, Le Seuil, 2004), 49.

10 Jean-Baptiste Duroselle, *La Grande Guerre des Français. L'incompréhensible* (Paris, Le Perrin, 1995).

11 See Dominique Kalifa, 'L'expérience, le désir et l'histoire. Alain Corbin, ou le "tournant culturel" silencieux', *French Politics, Culture & Society* 22/2, (2004), 14–25; also Anne-Emmanuelle Demartini and Dominique Kalifa, eds., *Imaginaire et sensibilités au XIXe siècle* (Paris, Créaphis, 2005).

12 Bernard Laffargue and Philippe Robert, *L'image de la justice criminelle dans la société. Le système pénal vu par ses clients* (Paris, SEPC, 1977), 10.

13 Jean-Claude Farcy, Dominique Kalifa and Jean-Noël Luc, eds., *L'enquête judiciaire en Europe au XIXe siècle: acteurs, imaginaire, pratiques* (Paris, Créaphis, 2007). See also my essay, 'Criminal investigators at the fin de siècle', *Yale French Studies*, 108 (2005), 36–47.

14 Philippe Artières and Dominique Kalifa, *Vidal le tueur de femmes: une biographie sociale* (Paris, Perrin, 2001).

15 See, for a first approach, Dominique Kalifa and Alain Vaillant, 'Pour une histoire culturelle et littéraire de la presse française au XIXe siècle', *Le temps des médias. Revue d'histoire* 2 (2004), 197–214. See also Marie-Ève Therénty and Alain Vaillant, *1836. L'an I de l'ère médiatique* (Paris, Nouveau Monde éditions, 2001) and *Presse et plume. Journalisme et littérature au XIXe siècle* (Paris, Nouveau Monde éditions, 2004).

16 Foreword to Georges Weil, *Le journal. Origines, évolution et rôle de la presse périodique* (Paris, La Renaissance du Livre, 1934), XVII.

17 Jeremy D. Popkin, *Press, Revolution and Social Identity in France, 1830–1835* (Pennsylvania, Penn State University Press, 2002).

18 Fabien Locher, 'Le nombre et le temps: la météorologie en France (1830–1880)', (history thesis, EHESS, 2004).

19 Bernard Lahire, 'Remarques sociologiques sur le *linguistic turn*', *Politix* 27 (1994), 192.

20 These developments are discussed in some detail in the Introduction.

21 Pierre Bourdieu, *Homo Academicus*, trans. Peter Collier (Cambridge, Polity, 1988). Originally published in French (Paris, Minuit, 1984).

22 Robert P. Morgan, ed., *Modern Times: From World War I to the Present*, 1st North American edn, *Music and Society* (Englewood Cliffs, NJ, Prentice Hall, 1994).

23 Keith Negus, *Music Genres and Corporate Cultures* (London and New York, Routledge, 1999).

24 Daniel Leech-Wilkinson, *The Modern Invention of Medieval Music* (Cambridge University Press, 2002).

25 Douglas W. J. Johnson and Madeleine Johnson, *The Age of Illusion: Art and Politics in France, 1918–1940* (London, Thames & Hudson, 1987); H. R. Kedward and Nancy Wood, eds., *The Liberation of France. Image and Event*, Berg French Studies (Oxford, Berg, 1995); Colin Jones, *Paris: Biography of a City* (London, Allen Lane, 2004).

26 Siân Reynolds, *France between the Wars: Gender and Politics* (London, Taylor and Francis, 1996); Hanna Diamond, *Fleeing Hitler: France 1940* (Oxford University Press, 2007); Claire Duchen, *Women's Rights and Women's Lives in France 1944–1968* (London, Routledge, 1994).

27 Pam Cook, ed., *The Cinema Book* (London, BFI Publishing, 1985); the third edition was published in 2007.

28 Pam Cook, *Screening the Past: Memory and Nostalgia in Cinema* (London and New York, Routledge, 2005).

29 Lester D. Friedman, *American Cinema of the 1970s: Themes and Variations*, *Screen Decades* (New Brunswick, NJ, Rutgers University Press, 2007) and *British Cinema and Thatcherism: Fires Were Started* (London, UCL Press, 1993).

30 James Chapman, *Licence to Thrill: A Cultural History of the James Bond Films* (New York, Columbia University Press, 2000), and *Past and Present: National Identity and the British Historical Film Cinema & Society* (London, I. B. Tauris & Co, 2005).

31 Susan Hayward, *French National Cinema* (London, Routledge, 1993); Phil Powrie, *French Cinema in the 1980s: Nostalgia and the Crisis of Masculinity* (Oxford, Clarendon Press, 1997).

32 Michael Temple and Michael Witt, eds., *The French Cinema Book* (London, BFI Publishing, 2004); Robert Murphy, ed., *The British Cinema Book*, 2nd edn. (London: BFI Publishing, 2001); Tim Bergfelder, Erica Carter and Deniz Göktürk, eds., *The German Cinema Book* (London, BFI Publishing, 2002).

33 See his essay on 'The work of art in the age of mechanical reproduction' in Walter Benjamin, *Illuminations*, 2nd edn. (London, Fontana, 1992); and *Charles Baudelaire: A Lyric Poet in the Era of High*

Capitalism, trans. Harry Zohn (London, New Left Books, 1973).

34 See T. J. Clark, *Farewell to an Idea: Episodes from a History of Modernism* (New Haven, Yale University Press, 2001); also Retort et al., *Afflicted Powers: Capital and Spectacle in a New Age of War* (London, Verso, 2005).

35 Thomas E. Crow, *Modern Art in the Common Culture* (New Haven and London, Yale University Press, 1996), and *The Rise of the Sixties: American and European Art in the Era of Dissent, Perspectives* (London, Weidenfeld & Nicolson, 1996).

36 Dana Arnold, ed., *The Metropolis and its Image: Constructing Identities for London 1750–1950* (Oxford, Blackwell, 1999), and Dana Arnold, *Cultural Identities and the Aesthetics of Britishness 1750–1950* (Manchester University Press, 2004).

37 Bertrand Russell, *A History of Western Philosophy and its Connection with Political and Social Circumstances from the Earliest Times to the Present Day* (London, George Allen and Unwin, 1946).

38 Richard Rorty, *The Linguistic Turn: Recent Essays in Philosophical Method* (University of Chicago Press, 1992); Richard Rorty, Quentin Skinner and J. B. Schneewind, *Philosophy in History: Essays on the Historiography of Geography, Ideas in Context, 1* (Cambridge University Press, 1984).

39 Arthur O. Lovejoy, *The Great Chain of Being: A Study of the History of an Idea: The William James Lectures Delivered at Harvard University, 1933* (Cambridge, Mass., Harvard University Press, 1998); Peter Gay, *The Enlightenment: An Interpretation: The Rise of Modern Paganism* (New York, W. W. Norton, 1966).

40 Stefan Collini, *Absent Minds: Intellectuals in Britain* (Oxford University Press, 2006).

41 Denis Hollier and R. Howard Bloch, eds., *A New History of French Literature* (Cambridge, Mass., Harvard University Press, 1989).

42 David Coward, *A History of French Literature from Chanson De Geste to Cinema* (Oxford, Blackwell, 2004).

43 Margaret Atack, *Literature and the French Resistance: Cultural Politics and Narrative Forms 1940–1950* (Manchester University Press, 1989), and Margaret Atack, *May 68 in French Fiction and Film* (Oxford University Press, 1999); Philip Dine, *Images of the Algerian War. French Fiction and Film 1954–1992* (Oxford, Clarendon Press, 1994).

44 Fredric Jameson, *The Political Unconscious: Narrative as a Socially Symbolic Act* (New York, Routledge, 1981), and *Postmodernism: Or, the Cultural Logic of Late Capitalism* (London, Verso, 1991).

45 Raymond Williams, *Culture and Society: Coleridge to Orwell* (London, Chatto and Windus, 1958), and *The Long Revolution* (London, Chatto & Windus, 1961).

46 The following examples are drawn from Michael Kelly, *The Cultural and Intellectual Rebuilding of France after the Second World War* (London, Palgrave Macmillan, 2004).

47 'Bricolage' is a term originally used for amateur 'do-it-yourself' manual building work. Claude Lévi-Strauss introduced it as a concept in cultural anthropology, using it to describe the use of available materials to create artefacts with new cultural meanings. See Claude Lévi-Strauss, *La pensée sauvage* (Paris, Plon, 1962).

48 Benedict Anderson, *Imagined Communities. Reflections on the Origin and Spread of Nationalism*, 2nd revised edn. (London, Verso, 1991).

49 Anne Bony, *Les Années 40, Collection Couleur Du Xxe Siècle* (Paris, Editions du regard, 1985); Pontus Hulten, ed., *Paris–Paris 1937–1957* (Paris, Centre Georges Pompidou, 1981); Frances Morris, ed., *Paris Post War: Art and Existentialism 1945–55* (London, Tate Gallery, 1993).

50 Hulten, *Paris–Paris 1937–1957*, 455.

51 Ibid., 454.

52 See Pierre Bourdieu, *The Logic of Practice* (Cambridge, Polity Press, 1990).

53 Roland Barthes, *S/Z, Tel Quel* (Paris, Le Seuil, 1970), 24–8.

54 The following titles were published in 1945: Paul Alpert, *Économie humaniste*; Léon Blum, *A l'échelle humaine*; Pierre Bourgelin, *L'homme et le temps*; Jacques Maritain, *Les droits de l'homme et la loi naturelle*; Jean Mouroux, *Le sens chrétien de l'homme*. A longer list appeared in 1946: André Ulmann, *L'humanisme du XXe siècle*; Luc Sommerhausen, *L'humanisme agissant de Karl Marx*; Louis Aragon, *L'homme communiste*; Jacques Rennes, *Du marxisme à l'humanisme*; Fernand Robert, *L'humanisme: essai de définition*; Georges Friedmann, *Machine et humanisme*; Georges Izard, *L'homme est révolutionnaire*; Daniel Perrot, *Style d'homme*; André Lang, *L'homme libre, ce prisonnier*; André George et al., *Les grand appels de l'homme*; Simone de Beauvoir, *Tous les hommes sont mortels*; Nicolas Berdiaeff, *De l'esclavage et de la liberté de l'homme*; Edward Montier, *Les jeunes devant l'humanisme intégral*; Louis de Lavareille, *Humanisme et prière*; Charles Moeller, *Humanisme et sainteté*; Xavier de Virieu, *Perspectives d'humanisme militaire*; Jean-Paul Sartre, *L'existentialism est un humanisme*.

55 Bernard-Henri Lévy, *Les aventures de la liberté* (Paris, Grasset, 1991).

4

What future for gender history?

Ruth Harris and Laura Lee Downs

In 1987 the American historian Joan Scott announced that gender was 'a useful category of historical analysis'. This inaugurated a shift from women's history, as a history of women's lives, to gender history, which considered gender as a cultural rather than a biological category, a product of discourse rather than experience, and used gender distinctions as a means to explore ways in which past societies were organised into public and private spheres. Ruth Harris and Laura Lee Downs *describe how the Anglo-American academic world was taken by storm, although in France, where feminist studies were considered 'sectarian', universities were slower to react. In recent years there has been a shift away from seeing gender simply as a product of discourse. The importance of subjective experience and the female body has once again been recognised; there has been a new emphasis on the material, family, religious and political context in which women's aspirations were conceived, and struggles for sexual, social, religious and political identity took place. This has reopened the debate about the division between public and private spheres, together with central questions about republicanism, Catholicism and fascism.*

Ruth Harris

Is gender dead?

In 2001 Joan Scott revised her earlier pronouncements on gender[1] in an article entitled 'Millennial fantasies: the future of "gender" in the 21st century'.[2] In it, she jettisoned the term entirely on the grounds that it had become interchangeable with the earlier label of 'sexual difference'. More seriously, she recognised the flaw in her earlier dismissal of the corporeal, and invoked psychoanalytic theory to re-emphasise the role of the culture-body link. She also admitted to being at a loss about how to attack the conceptual reductions of the biomedical sciences and their growing hegemony in America for analysing human behaviour and sexual identity.

This article marks the end of the line for the Scottian notion of 'gender' as a dominant strand in historical theorising. So perhaps it is proper to recall its impact now that the underpinnings of the concept have been largely abandoned by its chief advocate. It is also important to examine whether the concept has any historical 'fuel' left in it. I will suggest that it does, and that there is a wealth of historical studies yet to be done, which engage with 'gender' and with women's and family history more particularly.

I hope readers will excuse me for discussing myself in this brief account. I realised as I began to write that the history of the concept of gender was central to my adult intellectual life; from the moment I became a professional historian I was engaged with these debates, and I cannot separate myself from the retelling of the story.

Scott's article '"Gender": a useful category of historical analysis', published in the *American Historical Review* some twenty years ago, inaugurated the centrality of the concept among feminist historians in the Anglo-Saxon world. I remember joining a gathering of faculty members involved in the Women's Studies programme at Smith College, my first permanent academic post, to discuss it; the room buzzed with a sense of occasion, and the prospect of talking about it brought together some of the most intellectually engaged academics at the college from across the social sciences and the humanities. Although American myself, I had only recently returned to the United States after several years in Oxford, and I think I was one of the few people in the room uneasy about Scott's programmatic statement. The meeting was not so much a debate, more the coronation of a new orthodoxy, and I felt even then that my doubt and scepticism was positively ungrateful, if not nascently heretical.

There was much in the piece that was hard to quarrel with, especially its central conviction that 'gender' was a relational category that helped to define culture. But from the outset there were historiographical and theoretical assertions that worried me. The first was the critique of women's history, Scott's conviction that unearthing new documentation about the lives of women was somehow both theoretically inadequate and historically naive. She asserted that, at its worst, such work was nothing more than '*herstories*' that threatened to ghettoise women's history from mainstream historical enquiry.[3] Infatuated with the conceptual promise offered by postmodernism – from Foucault, through Derrida, to Lacan – she maintained that women's historians must embrace the theoretical reflections of the 'linguistic turn' as the only way of furthering feminist history.

The discussion turned on the importance of close textual readings to decipher the omnipresence and power of 'gender systems'. But there was a marked contrast between her grandiose aspirations and the conceptually modest, historical proposals which ended the article. She advocated the examination of gender in the discourse of the French Revolution as well as Nazi and fascist regimes. What was striking was how readily she accepted the categories and periodisation of conventional *political* history, rejecting in a stroke the study of material culture – be it Marxist or *Annalist* in style – in which patterns of social evolution, often continuous rather than disruptive, stand outside the textbook dates of revolution and regime change. The hope was that an analysis of gender in conjunction with class and race would open up a new, transformative dimension to historical investigation. She did not worry that such presentist concerns and categories might transfer awkwardly to the study of the past.

In her assertion that gender was culturally constructed, she also ignored the corporeal reality of the body, and its centrality in the construction of gender identity. Denise Riley, theorist and poet, even wrote a book entitled *Am I that name?*, which suggested that 'man' and 'woman' were nothing more than discursive fictions.[4] As someone who had worked seriously in the history of medicine and science, I understood and sympathised with the attempt to cut the feminist debate away from the biological moorings that made 'anatomy destiny'; gender, by focusing on culture, seemed to belie the biological determinism that still hemmed in feminist demands for emancipation and equality.

Gender studies produced a wealth of work investigating the *discourses* surrounding the body, rather than the body itself. Following Foucault, historians explored the biomedical and legal 'discourses' that managed the insane, the criminal and the diseased. But in ridding the philosophical arena of the 'subject', postmodernist theorists relegated the history of experience – of both individuals and groups – to an unknowable region. It was seen as almost philosophically naive to attempt to recover or historically imagine that experience, or to discuss the intersection of the psychological and the physical. In retrospect – and of course this may merely be a self-justificatory reading of my own intellectual history – the unease with such a programme helped to reset my own historical compass. In this sense, and in common with others who wrote on women in history in the same period, I owe much to the linguistic turn, even in my growing rejection of it.

My doctoral work was on criminal insanity in France, and it examined the biomedical as well as legal discourses surrounding the transformation in criminological discourse during the *fin de siècle*, as well as paying attention to the language of honour and melodrama that characterised the *criminels passionnels* of that era.[5] In this work, I was indebted to Foucault, to the historiography of social management, and to the literary-critical style that pervaded work on the human sciences in the 1980s.

During the next decade I worked on the history of Lourdes, and realised how crucial were the visionary Bernadette's physical transformation during her ecstasies and especially the existential experience that pilgrims related about their cures. I rejected those who urged me to do a 'semiotic' interpretation of such phenomena, and decided it was possible not merely to recount the discourses that surrounded the 'miracles', but to offer some account of the subjective experience associated with physical transformation. Although I do not believe personally in divine intervention, I think there is little doubt that there are 'cures' at Lourdes, and that their history was vital to my study.[6]

There was another problem, however, with Joan Scott's radical social constructivism: she used Lacanian theories which underscored the induction of the subject into the phallic *symbolic* order, an approach which privileged, once again, the discursive shaping of the individual.[7] In contrast, Kleinian and feminist psychoanalysis in England stressed the significance of the body–culture dynamic to the development of gender identity. Both the pleasurable and aggressive dimensions of sucking, evacuating and masturbating were all seen as central to how individuals came to identify themselves as feminine or masculine. This process of 'individuation' was anything but a disembodied one.[8]

Although I remain troubled by certain dimensions of psychoanalytic theory, Lyndal Roper's remarkable *Oedipus and the Devil*, with its unflinching concentration on the intersection between the body and mind, on fantasy and the unconscious psychic dimensions of life in early-modern Germany, was a revelation.[9] Using Freudian and Kleinian theories, she analysed the interpersonal and larger cultural dynamics of witchcraft accusations. She condemned the 'flight from the body' associated with the linguistic turn, and focused on the central emotions of envy and the desire to inflict pain. Her later *Witch Craze* not only examined the 'discourse' of torture, but forced the reader to imagine the physical reality and consequences of extracting confessions from 'witches'.[10]

Scott's notion of gender, therefore, was being undermined long before she published her 2001 article, and it is easy, in retrospect, to assert the foolhardiness of her endeavour. Nonetheless, and despite my criticisms, it is evident that 'gender studies' produced a rich harvest. Gender and women's history did transform the way mainstream history was imagined and interpreted. Whether it is the examination of maternalist imagery in understanding saintliness in the medieval world,[11] or women's role in salon culture in the eighteenth century,[12] or visions of masculinity and codes of honour and visions of war and peace,[13] or the relations between gender and fascism in the twentieth century,[14] gender remains a powerful tool for thinking about the past.

New approaches to women's lives and gender

In the Anglo-American world, gender history is even an accepted part of the undergraduate curriculum, evidence of a generational shift in which the young accept that both gender and women's history form part of their intellectual formation. Precisely because of this great success, however, gender sometimes loses its analytical edge, especially when used with race and class in a mantric fashion. But for every formulaic regurgitation, there are works of verve, imagination and scholarship that remain indebted to gender. Suzanne Desan's recent *Family on Trial* takes issue with Joan Landes and the first generation of gender historians who asserted that the French Revolution was primarily about the invention of domesticity. What Desan shows instead is the extent to which revolutionary ideology challenged patriarchal power, especially in the *tribunaux de famille*, where women achieved remarkable success in divorce and inheritance disputes. Using a mixed social and cultural approach, sensitive to the dynamics of place and material expectations, she shows how the family and state were engaged in a mutual refashioning, and how vital considerations of both gender and family were in creating the new state and its politics.[15]

Desan made me realise, once again, how good history and serious scholarship is enhanced by a gender and feminist approach. Nor is she the only example; early women's history among Anglo-American historians of France focused on the rise of feminism, and the many distinctive models of emancipation it offered. Some acknowledged the way the anti-clerical Republican political model or the fear of demographic decline explained feminism's relative weakness.[16] But they did not engage with the central spiritual, social and familial preoccupations which meant many women were unconvinced by what they saw as the atomistic model of Republican citizenship in contrast to the vocational and spiritual activism offered by the Roman Catholic Church. Women often identified with models of subordination and suffering, not with the contractual vision of a secular society.[17] Although as historical subjects they assail our emancipatory sensibilities, it is worth studying their very different moral claims, spiritual hopes and subjective experience.

Indeed, some of the most interesting new work that I know focuses on those aspects of gender history that question the very political agenda that animated feminist politics in the first place. Caroline Ford, now working on Muslim women in France, has written on the issue of headscarves in France. Although she has yet to explore in print the views of Muslim women – due to difficulties of access and of interpretation – she has shown the profound similarity between the nineteenth-century anti-clerical critique of nuns' habits and that of the vituperative assault on Muslim headscarves articulated by the defenders of laicité.[18] In this work she suggests the importance of a historical legacy of intolerant (enlightenment) republicanism that unconsciously – and often reflexively – infuses current political debate.

Issues of this kind – in France and around the world – force us to question our emotional response to practices that are difficult for us to appreciate, let alone comprehend. Lynn Thomas' article on clitorodectomy in Kenya in 1956 shows how women underwent hard labour to defend their right to practise infibulation. Since the ban on such practices, adolescent girls have shown their determination in breaking the law in order to excise each other; rather than victims, they see themselves as agents in struggle against the 'foreign', universalist arguments of sexual oppression.[19] And, while there is no doubt that men dominated women in Kenyan family and community relations, it is nonetheless wrong to suggest that they practised clitoridectomy just to conform to patriarchal dictates.

In a similar vein, Lata Mani's *The Debate on Sati in Colonial India* examines the controversy surrounding widow burning – or Suttee – in the subcontinent of the early nineteenth century. Rather than merely rehearsing the British colonial vision of this 'inhumane' practice, Mani examines the debate among literate (male) Indians during the Bengali renaissance. And, instead of using the position of Calcutta intellectuals to show up either their conservative or reformist pro-clivities, she shows that both sides in the struggle saw themselves as champions of tradition. Those who sought to abolish Suttee recalled a golden age of pure Hinduism based on the most ancient texts before the 'contaminating' intrusion of Islamic ritualism and dogmatism. They challenged Suttee because it defied the spirit of Hinduism, which required the lifelong rigour of a selfless existence, not a moment of self-immolation. They also maintained that women who leapt into the flames did so out of fear of the cruelty they would experience at the hands of their deceased husband's family, who wanted to reappropriate their son's property.[20]

Brahmins and Pundits in the other camp saw Suttee as a privilege, as less painful than the sorrow of loss, and as a means of controlling the transgressive sexual impulses of women now free from the marital state. They too cited scripture to support their case in favour of custom. Although fascinating, the details of this struggle – and the fact that the East India Company and British Hindu Scholars upheld the anti-camp – are insignificant in comparison to Mani's larger point. In this debate the women–religion couplet was central to articulating a whole range of political positions, and, as she perspicaciously insists, the widow herself remained marginal to a male political debate. No one in the anti-camp sought to ameliorate the social conditions of widowhood or to investigate the impact of the custom among upper-caste women.

I could elaborate on such studies – for example, on gender relations and machismo in Sandinista Nicaragua,[21] or the impact of redemptive ideologies of masculinity on the elaboration of revolutionary ideology of Castro or Che Guevara.[22] There is a growing, remarkable body of work on gender, labour and globalisation that examines in particular female garment workers in China, and their role in transforming the lives of their families as well as the world's economy.[23] The latter suggests the continuing importance, not only of gender, but of what many would see as a rather old-fashioned emphasis on women's labour history and on material culture.

Indeed, I would like to end my contribution by briefly pointing out that what was derided as '*herstories*' has increasingly come back into vogue. The lure of the discursive lives on, but not at the expense of the gritty, and invaluable, historical excavation of the material reality of women's lives across country and class. Olwen Hufton's *The Prospect Before Her*, published in 1995, offered an unusual comparative sweep from 1500 to 1800, by examining the lives of girls and women from the perspective of the life-cycle.[24] We learned about the religious discourse surrounding women, certainly, but what caused such a stir was her picture of the often harsh reality of life. She was able to imagine and convey the rigours of women carrying water from wells, a country girl's hopeless struggle to accumulate a dowry by breaking the cocoons of silkworms in a Lyonnese factory, women trying to find a clean place to make the lace that would enable a family to survive. Increasingly, historians are returning to the importance of kinship, objects and money in understanding the psychology of the past. We do need to know how nineteenth-century Galician women turned over their babies to their mothers, placed puppies on their breasts and used their milk to earn enough as wetnurses in Madrid to return home in order to buy a dairy cow. Or to know, as Silvia Evangelisti has shown, how convent cells were inherited in Renaissance Italy and became the focus of massive legal disputes in which religious congregations and great patrician families intervened.[25] Gender plays a role in these studies, but they are principally inspired by an undying interest in the lives of women in the past.

There are still basic questions of fact, let alone interpretation, that require historical investigation. When did women become seen as primarily responsible for children? How did class identity vary for women and men? A recent manuscript article by Selina Todd on domestic service in England shows how central having a maid was to middle-class identity.[26] Indeed, the attachment to such service meant that, in comparison with the USA, the market in labour-saving domestic appliances appeared much later, so tightly did English middle-class women hold on to their charwomen.

Nor are these the only innovative studies. There remain remarkable possibilities in thinking about the intersections between culture and biology. Culture, it seems, prefers binary oppositions, a fact which the pioneering work of Lévi-Strauss and the linguistic turn emphasised. But biology, we know, prefers diversity, with growing research showing how many people experience a 'middle sex' that falls outside the norm.[27] Years ago, Michel Foucault worked on the tragic fate of the hermaphrodite, Herculine Barbin, who saw herself as a woman but was categorised by the 'experts' as a man.[28] There is still much that can be done to untangle these middle regions of experience, as Lotte Van der Pol has begun to do in her studies of cross-dressing in early-modern Holland.[29] Indeed, I believe that the best way of challenging the reductionist allure of biomedicine which so worries Joan Scott is to insist on the complicating intersections between culture and biology in the elaboration of sexual identities and gendered illness, and to do so without fear of transgressing the taboos of political correctness.

Finally, gender has been used almost always descriptively, as another binary opposition in the linguistic grid so central to textual dissection. But such work often sidesteps its importance for historical causation. Suzanne Desan shows how important it might be in political transformation, while Hufton suggests its centrality to continuity and discontinuity in the labour market. Such approaches will continue to bring the study of gender into the mainstream of historical and social analysis, without marginalising experience, and enable it to continue as a 'useful historical category' for some time to come.

Laura Lee Downs

French history without gender

In 2004, I announced rather optimistically in the conclusion to *Writing Gender History* that over the remarkably short period of time separating the birth of second-wave feminist history (*c.* 1970) from the early twenty-first century, scholars had come to agree that 'it is no longer possible to write history – whether of the military, political, economic, social or intellectual varieties – without taking gender into account'.[30] Two years later, Siân Reynolds quite rightly pointed out that this assessment, while perhaps justified in the Anglo-American context, could by no means be offered with such confidence in the French academic world.[31] This is not to say that gender has no place in French research of the early twenty-first century. It is, rather, to say that its future seems less obviously assured in an academic environment that has upheld a certain notion of scholarly objectivity/disinterest and (equally important) of republican neutrality, by rigorously excluding all forms of scholarship that are seen to be driven by 'sectarian' political militancy. By focusing on the conditions of women and men, grasped in all their individual particularity, feminist scholarship threatens the republican ideal of the abstract, sexless citizen, or so the academy's staunchest defenders would have it.

If full-scale frontal attacks on feminist 'sectarianism' are increasingly rare these days, the far more effective tactic of simply ignoring work on women and gender continues to limit the reach of such scholarship within the academy. Hence, several of the most widely read and eagerly debated reflections on the state of the discipline published over the last decade or so – *Les formes de l'expérience: une autre histoire sociale*; *L'histoire et le métier de l'historien en France 1945–1995*; *Jeux d'échelles: la micro-analyse à l'expérience* – all manage to say absolutely nothing about either women or gender.[32] While feminist scholars have continued to publish much excellent work that is, moreover, read by a fairly broad public outside the academy, gender as a category of historical analysis has had as yet precious little impact on mainstream scholarship in France.

In light of the powerful institutional forces that continue to array themselves against it, the outlook for gender history in France might seem bleak indeed. However, certain developments over the past several years suggest that this structural impasse might gradually be giving way; that despite formidable obstacles, gender may well ultimately make its way in France. Should this in fact occur, it will doubtless happen along a very individual path, one that is shaped by the way in which particular elements of this Anglo-American scholarly tradition are being selectively borrowed and put into practice by a younger generation of historians in France.

But the recent movement in favour of gender studies in France will bear fruit, I believe, not only because of shifts in the institutional balance of forces (shifts whose long-term outcome is difficult to predict), but also, and more importantly, because French academics, however sceptical of 'partisan' histories, will find themselves increasingly drawn by the analytic power of gender. As feminist historians have long been aware, gender is a tool of historical analysis that, when wielded alongside others (class, race/ethnicity, religion, nation/region) can render intelligible phenomena that are otherwise condemned to remain obscure, hidden and unreadable. For gender is a relational concept, one that allows us to consider simultaneously the social, symbolic and psychic aspects of sexual difference.[33] By underscoring the constructed, shifting and precarious nature of sexual identities, gender allows us to explore the powerful impact of culture on subjectivity, the multiple femininities and masculinities that have taken shape in various historical contexts, the various ways that ideas of gender difference have intersected with political or economic structures to shape divisions of labour and power while lending the imprimatur of nature's authority to such divisions by shrouding what is, after all, a human arrangement in the garb of biological (hence ineluctable) destiny. Finally, gender, with its attentiveness to the role of language in shaping subjectivity, its far-reaching critique of traditional notions of agency, its insistence that notions of sexual difference are key in constructing hierarchies of power, has revealed its force as a tool of critical thinking, one that allows us to interrogate some of the discipline's most cherished categories of analysis. It is this latter quality that may, in the end, recommend it most highly to the sceptics.

In this 'post-feminist' age, some feminist scholars have been tempted to regard gender as a concept that has lost its critical edge; a notion that has been rendered utterly banal through overuse, or, conversely, a notion that, in its failure to theorise race, sexuality and nationality/ethnicity as integral elements of women's identities, shows itself to be 'not a useful enough' category of analysis.[34] Tracing the twisted tale of France's relationship to gender, complete with a revisiting of gender's virtues as a tool of critical reflection, may help us to think our way past the sense that gender is a tired, increasingly irrelevant concept whose day has already gone. I would therefore like to open this article with a brief outline of the obstacles, past and present, that have limited the reach of France's own vibrant tradition of women's and gender history, while containing the impact of any foreign imports in this domain. I will then turn to a more detailed discussion of gender's capacity to function as a tool of critical analysis. Finally, I will close with a few remarks on the ways that the sands appear to be shifting on the present-day academic landscape in France.

As recently as the spring of 2007, Françoise Thébaud (one of France's pre-eminent scholars and activists in the fields of women's and gender history) remarked, 'in France we do not say "feminist scholarship" or "feminist history" because to do so would appear to disqualify the research and its author. Feminist history is considered a point of view, a militant discourse, not a scientific one. Moreover,' she continued, 'the use of the word "*genre*", which is translated from the English "gender," is very recent and has only been adopted in the past five or six years.'[35] The reasons for this dreary scenario are not hard to identify, for the very different structures that govern academic life in France, notably a highly centralised university system where faculty are recruited via a single, national exam, the *agrégation*, that is organised by discipline, makes for a rigidly disciplinary cursus that prevents those interdisciplinary encounters that have been so vital in the conceptualisation of women's and gender history. This ultra-centralised and highly traditional structure (traditional in the sense of upholding disciplinary boundaries) has also made it well-nigh impossible for women's and gender studies to find a real toehold in the universities. If women constitute one-third of the teaching faculty in French universities, and 23 per cent of full professors, only *five* professors have been recruited to teach women's history since 1984.[36] It will come as no surprise to hear, then, that there are no programmes or departments in women's and gender studies, and only a very few courses (nearly always elective) being offered by individuals at just a few universities (10 out of a total of 87).[37]

The failure of women's and gender history to make much of a dent in the institutional structures of French academia is owing in part to the particular importance of history to Republican politics. Indeed, since the founding of the Third Republic in the last decades of the nineteenth century, history has stood at the centre of that civic education that, dispensed in elementary schools all over the country, constitutes the cultural underpinning of democracy in France. As such, it has proved especially resistant to the intrusions of identity politics in academic dress, for such politics are seen to dissolve the national community as embodied by the French Republic.[38] Here, individuals in their socially-neutral incarnation as citizens are meant to meet on the strictly neutral ground of the Republic, encumbered neither by the weighty carapace of sex, nor that of race/ethnicity, nor – crucially – that of religion.

The cultural politics of French republicanism would seem to imply that there is little space indeed for women's and gender history inside the official institutions of the Republic. Nonetheless, Professor Thébaud paints a cautiously optimistic portrait of the current situation in France, claiming that it is less 'serious' than 'paradoxical'.[39] Though more or less consigned to the margins of the formal academic world, research and publication in this domain are sustained by a broad societal interest in the issues raised by gender historians, lending women's and gender history real intellectual, if not institutional legitimacy. Hence, the widely popular five-volume series on the *History of Women,* edited by Georges Duby and Michelle Perrot, sold over 20,000 copies in France, while scholars in women's and gender history are constantly solicited for free lectures by associations, groups and local councils. If the institutionalisation of women's and gender history remains minimal, French strategies of diffusion across civil society are less complicated and more efficient than in the USA or the UK, thanks to a more unified publishing structure that produces for both university readerships and the broader reading public.[40]

Moreover, there is reason to believe that we can look forward to a different balance of forces in the near future, as a number of structural factors are conspiring to loosen the deadlock of the dinosaurs in French universities. Most notable among them is the increasing centrality of European funding, and of programmes favouring student mobility, in the research-and-teaching lives of each of Europe's component nations. Gender, therefore, numbers among the priorities in Brussels-funded research, while the circulation of students via Marie-Curie and Erasmus programmes means that French students encounter gender in other, less deadlocked European contexts and happily transport it back into their classes and seminars in France. Even the not-very-demand-sensitive French system has been forced to respond by paying more attention to gender. A second factor, very difficult to interpret at this early stage, is the imminent reform of French universities. This may end up making them more demand-sensitive, and hence more open to gender, given the broad public interest in these questions.

Before pursuing further the question of what changes can be observed on the ground in present-day France, I would like to discuss in greater depth gender's potential as a tool of critique; one that allows historians to reflect critically on the categories of analysis by which they habitually organise their work. I have written elsewhere on the ways in which gender reshapes our understanding of class, race, religion, subjectivity and the public/private distinctions through which modern, western, liberal societies have organised social and political life in the context of

British, German, American, and colonial African and Indian history.[41] Here I would like to extend that reflection by exploring in some detail the ways in which gender is allowing French historians to rethink their tools of analysis in a couple of key areas of research, namely, religion, politics and the analysis of extreme right-wing movements.[42] In so doing, I hope to demonstrate that there is good reason to believe that gender has a bright future in French historical research. Equally important, however, analysing the reception and deployment of gender in present-day France may help us to see our way past the uneasy 'post-feminist' sense that gender may have outlived its usefulness as a category of analysis.

Towards a gendered history of Catholic political mobilisations: France–Italy, 1901–1930

At the end of November 2007, a young historian, Magali della Sudda, defended her dissertation on the 'para political' activity of the avowedly apolitical throngs of women (tens of thousands in Italy, and nearly two million in France) who joined the Catholic and 'feminine' leagues in France and Italy during the first 30 years of the twentieth century.[43] *A Women's Conservative Political Movement before Universal Suffrage in France and Italy* introduces us to the hitherto ill-explored world of female Catholic activism in early twentieth-century France and Italy. It is a world populated by Catholic women of the upper bourgeoisie and the aristocracy, women who demanded and militated actively for a specifically feminine way of belonging to the nation, all the while refusing to accept the right to vote, which they saw as divisive of family solidarity and, moreover, threatening to sully women's pure hands with the vile, masculine business of politics. In this paradoxically anti-political political engagement hides the untold history of certain forms of women's political activity that would emerge in the immediate aftermath of the Second World War, when newly enfranchised French and Italian women voted massively for the conservative Catholic people's parties. As Dr della Sudda convincingly demonstrates, this outcome was immanent in the long-term political socialisation of Catholic women by these mass associations, initially organised for the very different purpose of mobilising women against the secular state and in defence of Catholic institutions, notably Catholic schools.

Dr della Sudda thus obliges us to reconsider the range and forms of public and political activism carved out by women who themselves vigorously denied any feminist, or indeed any political ambitions. Overtly committed to the notion that the destinies of the two sexes were rigorously distinct, the women of the French *Ligue patriotique des femmes* (LPDF) and the Italian *Unione tra le donne cattoliche d'Italia* (UDCI) nonetheless hurled themselves into the public arena in the first decade of the twentieth century in order to defend religion against the assaults of a rapidly secularising state. Inspired by the conviction that the institutions of the Church were the sole guarantee of a healthily structured civil society, the hundreds of thousands of women mobilised by these mass organisations strode into the breach left by fathers, husbands and brothers who were too often themselves won over to the secularist cause (or at best insufficiently militant in the face of the secularist threat), defending the role of the Church in strategic sectors such as education, health and welfare, while campaigning actively in support of Catholic candidates to national office.

In order to pursue her comparative study of the precise mechanisms whereby hundreds of thousands of women (and, in France, two million) were politicised on the Catholic right, Dr della Sudda conceptualised her doctoral research at the confluence of several disciplines, notably sociology, history and political science. The dissertation thus combines political and religious history with the history of women and gender in order to create a narrative that moves outward from women's political activity in the strictest sense (fund-raising for Catholic candidates, reviewing electoral lists in the hope of striking from them the names of as many anticlerical voters as possible) toward broader forms of social action undertaken in the hope of attracting members from the popular classes. By showing in detail how League activists were able to transfer competencies acquired in the realm of social and religious action into the realm of politics, and so move easily from one sphere to the other, Dr della Sudda underscores the extreme porosity of the frontiers between politics, religion and social action in this era of religious 'wars' between secularising anticlericals and staunch defenders of the Church. Finally, *A Women's Conservative Political Movement* broadens the concept of social citizenship by emphasising how League militants did not content themselves with simply demanding that the State accord social rights to women (such as protection for mothers), but took concrete action to construct the basis of such rights in a 'para-political' space outside the state and squarely within civil society, by organising assistance to young mothers, workshops for unemployed women workers and consumers' associations. Militants in the LPDF and UDCI thus contributed to reconfiguring the fields of social action and social assistance in France and Italy even as they crossed continually back and forth across the boundaries that, in theory, separated social and religious activity from economic and political activity (their workshops were all highly profitable ventures, for example).

Throughout the thesis, Dr della Sudda approaches the UDCI and LPDF as organisations that, wittingly or not, furthered the political education of Catholic women. The author is careful to define education in its broadest sense: helping women to make the connection between party political choices and the issues closest to their hearts (notably the promotion of Catholic primary and secondary schools against the Republic's secularising onslaught), training them in the effective use of both the pen and the public tribune, and honing their sense that only through collective action could the role of the Church in structuring social life and institutions be preserved and defended. In this fashion she is able to sustain one of her most audacious claims, namely, that the leagues constituted a form of political socialisation that allows us to understand the massively conservative vote of French and Italian women in the first post-war elections in which they were permitted to participate.

Rejecting political scientists' ahistoric claim that this vote represented a kind of eternally feminine conservative political instinct, Dr della Sudda is able to document precise processes of political socialisation on the Catholic right that unfolded at the heart of these leagues, which constituted the two most massive feminine organisations in pre-women's suffrage Italy and France. Moreover, by posing the question of women's political mobilisation as women *and* as right-wing Catholics, Dr della Sudda's research invites historians of religion to reconsider the tools they use for understanding the political mobilisations of Catholics in twentieth-century Europe. For in France, such historians have all too often tended to distinguish in their analyses those actions undertaken by the faithful in their incarnation as members of a believing community from those undertaken in their incarnation as women or men. Only the latter are seen to be influenced by the variable of gender. Dr della Sudda, by contrast, introduces us to activists for whom their engagement in the militantly political defence of the Church *and* in a range of specifically feminine religious and devotional activities were two sides of the same coin. By examining the lives of individual militants, she is able to construct a kind of collective biography that demonstrates conclusively that no visible barrier separated the former activity from the latter in the lives of individual militants. Rather than distinguishing their political activity in defence of the Church from specifically feminine forms of devotion, then, Dr della Sudda argues that the two kinds of activity existed in continuity with one another, shaping the lives of individual militants for whom their identities as women and as Catholics were inseverable. Constituted in a space that straddled the notional frontier separating religion from politics in this age of sharp religious/secularist strife, the identities 'Catholic' and 'woman' constituted but one seamless subjectivity, one will, one source of politico-religious activity/activism that was engaged in both the public political realm and that of private devotion.

Magali della Sudda's thesis thus concludes with the bold claim that religious action of any kind cannot be adequately analysed in the absence of gender, for the Church itself was so wedded to notions of absolute gender difference that such difference is central to understanding the new forms of grass-roots activism that Pope Leo XIII's 1891 call to fight secularism by 'going to the people' called into life. In other words, the categories of analysis deployed by those historians and political scientists who seek to understand Catholic activism in early twentieth-century France and Italy must inevitably miss their mark so long as they are not inflected by that male–female distinction that the Church itself so highly valorised.

Permit me to offer a second example, drawn from my own research on the women's social action groups of a mass movement/political party on the extreme right of interwar French politics, the Croix de feu. These women engaged in highly politicised strategies of social assistance, targeting impoverished working-class districts in the hope that the Croix de feu movement might widen its political appeal beyond the middle- and lower-middle classes. If the hope of broadened support ultimately proved vain, the extensive network of movement social centres and *colonies de vacances* created by these militants set in motion a full-scale socialisation of politics within the Croix de feu that, as we shall see, casts into question political history's conventional distinction between a harshly masculine realm of politics and the altogether warmer and fuzzier women's world of social work. Once again, and in a slightly different key, gender analysis helps us to complicate, if not recast altogether the categories that organise historical research.

To conquer the 'milieux of hatred': women's social action groups and the politicisation of social work in the Croix de feu movement, 1930–1939

The study of interwar politics in France has long been bedevilled by the debate between those who believe that France produced home-grown fascists in the 1930s, and those who maintain that, thanks to the solidity of Republican democracy, 1930s France remained 'allergic' to fascism.[44] Colonel François de La Rocque's extreme right-wing Croix de feu movement constitutes a central piece in the dossier, for this league of decorated war veterans turned political party attracted far more members than any of its fellow travellers on the right. Indeed, after its (forced) conversion from extra-parliamentary league to more electorally oriented political party, in 1936, the Croix de feu, rebaptised the Parti social français, swiftly expanded to become what was doubtless the largest party in France before the Second World War.

The controversy over the fascist or not fascist nature of interwar France's extreme right-wing leagues first joined some 25 years ago, and continues to swirl ever more tightly around La Rocque's integral nationalist movement.[45] For if scholars can demonstrate that the Croix de feu was fascist, then victory goes to those who claim that France had a significant fascist movement. If not, then it must be conceded that fascism, however visible/demonstrable it might have been in the other, far smaller circles of the extreme right, remained a minority phenomenon. So long as historians continue to disagree over what, precisely, defines fascism, the debate seems condemned to circle wearily without end, unresolved and unresolvable; this despite the fact that participants show signs of tiring of a debate that many find 'sterile', of limited interest (how interesting is it to spend all one's research force on an effort of classification?), and perhaps beside the point altogether.[46]

A rapid look at the archives of the Croix de feu/Parti Social Français (CF/PSF) confirms that the fascist/not fascist debate is indeed a sorry way to spend one's time, especially when considered alongside the host of intriguing questions about interwar French politics and society that can be explored by consulting these papers for something other than evidence for and against members' fascist tendencies.[47] One fascinating arena of research opened up by these papers concerns the immense social action network established by the Colonel in 1934–35 as the key to his new, 'social' strategy of political conquest, a network that was run almost entirely by movement women. For no sooner did this league of decorated veterans open its doors to broader categories of society in the early 1930s, than hundreds of thousands of people (ultimately a million or more) came flooding into party locals all over the country and in Algeria, among them some 400,000 women.[48]

Now much contemporary political history turns on a heuristic division of public space into a feminised social sphere and a masculinised realm of politics. But the La Rocque archives reveal a rather different and altogether more complex picture. For, far from being a means of channelling movement women's energies away from politics and towards more benevolent and gender-appropriate activities, the women's social action groups were harnessed to, and participated actively in, the progressive 'socialisation' of Croix de feu political action. This social turn was inaugurated by La Rocque's announcement in 1935 that, henceforth, the Croix de feu would seek to draw that working-class support that had hitherto eluded it via a 'social penetration' of the impoverished 'red belt' around Paris.[49]

The social action groups thus constituted the principal engine of La Rocque's new soft-power strategy adopted as a complement (and ultimately, alternative) to the violent street politics pursued throughout the mid 1930s by the Croix de feu's paramilitary leagues. These latter spent most of their time in street brawls with similarly inclined communist youth, ratcheting up the sense of public disorder and insecurity to the point where, in June of 1936, Léon Blum's freshly elected Popular Front government decided to restore order in the streets by dissolving all paramilitary leagues, the Croix de feu included. La Rocque then swiftly transformed his movement (which had hitherto been notably ambivalent about electoral politics and democracy more broadly) into a political party, the Parti social français (PSF). From this moment forward, the much-vaunted 'social penetration' of France's working-class suburbs took on heightened significance, as winning the allegiance of disaffected poor, unemployed and working-class voters became one of the PSF's explicit goals. 'Be it a question of the ascension of our ideas to power, of the penetration of peasant and working-class milieux or, in a less elevated field of action, of the electoral campaign, this social action is the *sine qua non* of our success ...[it] is currently, and until you receive orders otherwise, the essential factor in our movement', wrote La Rocque in a secret memo to his recalcitrant local section *chefs*. Discomfited by the rapid ascension of relatively autonomous women's social action groups in their midst, these men had to be reminded that their movement's pre-eminent goal – increasing CF/PSF influence ('rayonnement') – depended above all on the women's efficient and *professional* social work mission to the poorest neighbourhoods of Paris's infamous 'red zone', a vast shanty town that had grown up, higgledy-piggledy on the ex-military zone just beyond the city's fortifications.[50]

La Rocque was fascinated – and convinced – by Marshal Lyautey's doctrine of social pacification, first put into practice in the Moroccan Protectorate at the turn of the twentieth century.[51] If the Colonel remained unpersuaded by Lyautey's assertion that the civic and social education of the masses should be placed in the hands of the military, believing, on the contrary, that such education had to remain in the hands of families, teachers and other civilian experts, one can nonetheless see in the modalities of the CF/PSF campaign to 'reconquer' the 'savage' populations of the zone the imprint of Lyautey's larger vision, in which an unbending commitment to national defence was joined to the secular (i.e. non-confessional) *encadrement* of the population.[52] The notion that the zone populations had to be drawn (back) toward love of the French nation via an acculturating 'mission', impregnated with the militaristic values of hierarchy and obedience, was given concrete form by the women who ran the movement's vast network of social centres and *colonies de vacances*. Indeed, these women conceived of themselves as the civilian equivalents of Lyautey's famous officers, imbued with a social mission vis-à-vis the untutored mass of children. In the militarised organisation of Croix de feu social centres and *colonies de vacances*, these children took on the role of Lyautey's ordinary foot soldiers; culturally impoverished beings whose physical and moral regeneration would be assured by the movement's social work 'officers'.

The strongest imprint of Lyautey's doctrines can be seen in the CF/PSF movement's insistence that all social work be performed by trained professionals, women who possessed the technical expertise that would enable them to distinguish the deserving poor from 'les professionnels de la mendicité'. Their technical qualification would not only cover movement social centres from a legal standpoint, it would also reassure their clients, guaranteeing a certain 'technical prestige' with working-class women and men, who were justifiably suspicious of the arbitrary whims that governed plain, old-fashioned charity.[53] La Rocque's application of Lyautey's doctrines thus opened an unexpected route by which the women of CF/PSF social action were able to carve out careers for themselves at a time when women's attainment of professional autonomy was neither a simple nor self-evident process. Moreover, the Colonel's transposition of Lyautey's methods onto metropolitan soil allowed these women to assume the front-line soldier's mantle, prime source of transcendant value in CF/PSF circles, in this case by adopting, and adapting, the 'rôle social de l'officier' in their mission to the red zone.

In the campaign for the hearts and allegiance of poor and working-class voters, CF/PSF social centres had a key role to play, winning such families away from the communist 'menace' one by one, by appealing to them at their very base, that is, by looking after their children: 'In a word, we must diagnose misery, follow and counsel those families who suffer from it, prepare the atmosphere of [national] reconciliation, and so prepare the ground in which the recruitment to the Croix-de-Feu will be developed by other means', announced Mme de Gérus, head of the Croix de feu social action network in a brief résumé of their work that might – and should – recall the highly politicised social-work strategies employed at the time by European communist parties, and today by groups like Hamas. But her words also reveal how blurry the line between political and social action (gendered male and female, respectively) had become with the advent of La Rocque's strategy of social penetration.[54] Movement social workers thus appropriated for themselves the Croix de feu's mystique of the First World War veteran, which took on a whole new significance on the battlefields of Paris's redoubtable 'red belt'. Mme de Gérus's text thus goes on to vaunt the unswerving courage of movement social workers, ever 'calm and smiling' in the face of the 'wild hostility' that hung like a fog over the zone. Indeed, de Gérus cast these valiant women as 'our front-line soldiers of peace', persevering in their mission, undeterred by the 'knives and revolvers, the threats of death' that awaited them each day as they opened the doors of their neighbourhood social centres. Penetrating deep into the hostile territory of these 'milieux of hatred', CF/PSF social workers militarised the vocabulary of social work by transposing it onto an imaginary battlefield structured by the precepts of right-wing social Catholicism: 'With his immeasurable love of the people, our Chef has transmitted to us the mission of making the national flag fly over the citadels of communism', wrote Mme de Gérus in the autumn of 1935. 'We give ourselves over to this peaceful battle with the serene tenacity that such a mission demands. We carry the orders of the 1,500,000 Dead of 1914–1918. From this comes a supernatural power against which all other powers fail'.[55]

Mme de Gérus's report draws our attention to the importance of the hierarchical, if not downright militarised structure of command that the women of the *Bureau social* imposed on their organisation. It also points to the importance of military metaphors and the mystique of the glorious war dead, heroically fallen in battle, in shaping women's conception of the nature and value of the work they did. Finally, the extensive documentation on daily life in CF/PSF social centres and *colonies de vacances* underscores the extent to which Movement social provisions were saturated by the militarised hierarchies and integral nationalist fervour that crystallised the essence of the Croix de feu movement. Indeed, the social services aimed at children (which constituted the very heart of CF/PSF social action, reaching some 15,000 children in the summer of 1937 alone) can fairly be characterised as constituting prefigurative child communities, in which the values and sociability preached by movement militants (discipline, hierarchy, unity, love of France) were meant to be lived by the children in their day-to-day life together.[56]

The women's social action groups thus cast into question the conventional, hermetic distinction between a feminised realm of social work and the masculine world of politics that has long organised narratives of political history. For as we have seen, these groups politicised movement social work in all its dimensions. At the same time, La Rocque's decision to emphasise the strategy of social penetration 'socialised' CF/PSF politics to the extent that the political wing of the movement would ultimately find itself marginalised in the various configurations of power that succeeded themselves with dizzying rapidity after the defeat in 1940. The women's social action groups, by contrast, managed to hang on, and even flourish, throughout the war and immediate post-war eras, thanks to the support of CF/PSF sympathiser and fellow traveller Robert Garric. As the head of Pétain's *Secours National*, Garric directed substantial sums to the women's social action groups (rebaptised the 'Artisans du Devoir Patriotique') long after the political wing of the movement had been dissolved along with all other political parties, in January of 1941.

The gendered analysis of La Rocque's large and strange organisation, at once social and paramilitary, thus reveals a 'socialisation' of politics, and a politicisation of social work that complicates the simple binary 'le social = women/le politique = men' that has mindlessly structured too much research in the field. One can only hope that French scholars, weary of the tired old 'fascist-or-not-fascist' debate, will turn their eyes outward toward the fruitful reconfiguration of their object that gendered analyses can deliver.[57]

By way of a conclusion

When I first came to the EHESS in the spring of 1997, as a recently tenured Associate Professor on a faculty exchange with the University of Michigan, a number of my senior colleagues in Paris were extremely interested in the public debate I had had with Joan Scott four years earlier;[58] not because they were particularly interested in gender (though a few of them were), but because of the way it encapsulated so many of the arguments that animated the famous 'theory wars' of the period 1988–94, when everyone was taking, or studiously avoiding and angrily protesting, cultural and linguistic turns.[59] No such wars had ever broken out in France, where the concept of *mentalités* had always allowed for more easy exchange between social and cultural history.[60] Rather, the 1990s in France were characterised by a series of 'quiet exchanges' between social and cultural history around such innovative approaches as that of micro-history, or the new, 'cultural' approach to the history of war.[61] Scholars in France were thus genuinely baffled by the violence of the exchanges in the USA and the UK, and sought illuminating perspectives on their incomprehensible fury wherever they could find them.

When I returned five years later to the EHESS, freshly elected to the rank of *directeur d'études* (full professor), I offered the school's first seminar on gender history. About 20 doctoral students attended. All save one were women; all felt that France was desperately backward in this realm, and brought an impassioned engagement to the seminar. This enthusiasm was combined with a profound ignorance of what had been done in this field over the past 35 years, not only in the Anglo-American world, but by French feminist scholars as well.

Just a year or two later, gender seminars began to spring up here and there on the university landscape in France. And in 2005, the editor of the journal *Enquête*, sociologist Irène Théry, asked permission to translate my article 'If woman is just an empty category' (first round in the exchange with Joan Scott) for publication. She had of course read the piece in 1997, along with my other senior colleagues at the EHESS. Only eight years later did it suddenly seem urgent that it be made available in French; no longer (as in 1997) because of the way it represented a particular, contested moment in American intellectual history, but because of what it had to say about the evolution of women's and gender history in the Anglo-American world of the 1970s, 1980s and early 1990s. For by 2004–5, an interesting thing was happening in France: Judith Butler's work was being seized upon with tremendous enthusiasm by students interested in queer theory.[62] Without passing by much (if any) of the earlier work in women's and gender history on which such theory reposes (including Joan Scott's important 'Gender: a useful category of analysis'), these students were discovering gender in its most radically constructivist, Butlerian guise.[63] French scholars who have been tilling away in France's women's and gender history field for the past 20 years or more have not always been terribly pleased by this development, in which queer theory seems to have left women's and gender history in the dust. Hence the recent interest in my 1993 article, which advances a certain number of arguments in favour of a more socially grounded approach to gender history. But the rearguard actions of those who have been active in the field for a generation or more are unlikely to block the upsurge of interest in Butler's ideas, which has, since the first translations of her work (in 2005–7), begun to spill over to reach a broader reading public.

I think the timing of this sudden passion for Judith Butler and queer theory more generally has a number of causes, including the increasing social and political visibility of gay people, and especially gay men, in France, and, consequently, of studies in sexuality in the academy. But the single most important reason for Butler's eager reception in the early twenty-first century is doubtless linked to the vital role that her work has played in the latest replay of an ongoing internal political struggle over the place of identity politics in the Republic. Hence, Butler's work first attracted widespread attention in 2003–4, during the most recent round of debate over the Muslim headscarf, and over the famous 'Loi Stasi' of February 2004, intended to reinforce the regime of strict neutrality by banning visible symbols of religious identity in public schools and lycées throughout France.[64] All sectors of society, feminist included, were divided over the question of young girls and women wearing headscarves in these, the most sacred spaces of the Republic. While some older feminists defended the Républican notion of *laïcité* as instantiated by the Stasi law, many in the generations that are now in their teens, twenties, thirties and forties found the republican model too rigid on this issue.[65] And some in this latter camp found arguments for their side in Judith Butler's philosophical reflections on identity and politics.

It is hard to tell where this latest wave of interest in gender and sexuality will lead. But animated in part by the excitement over Butler's work, the gender studies field appears suddenly to be exploding in France. Thanks in some measure to European incentives, but also to the massive enthusiasm of students, new master's programmes on gender and sexuality (or specialisations in gender and sexuality within existing programmes) are being created all across the university landscape, in what appears to be that rarest of developments in France's hierarchical university world, a trend that is fuelled from below, by student enthusiasm and demand rather than by the dictates of professors. If a comparable welling-up from below in the 1970s found scant institutional expression in the 1980s and 1990s, there is reason to believe that this may all change in the very near future. For, unlike the case of the 1970s, 1980s and 1990s, the current groundswell is encountering a solid structure of institutions, programmes, journals and associations put in place over the past ten to fifteen years by the previous generation of feminist scholars: journals such as the *Cahiers du genre, Travail, genre et sociétés* and especially *Clio HFS*; the feminist history archive at the University of Angers, which complements the revamped and revivified collections of the Bibliothèque Marguérite Durand; research networks like Mnémosyne (subtitled 'The Association for the Development of Research in the History of Women and Gender'), the National Association for Feminist Studies (ANEF), and Inter-university and Interdisciplinary Network on Gender (RING); the vast and very active EFiGIES network of doctoral students interested in gender. Perhaps most important, in terms of assuring a broad transmission of these questions across French society, was the installation of the Aspasie centre in the University of Lyon's teacher-training institute, dedicated to promoting the equality of boys and girls, men and women, at the heart of the national educational system.[66]

The structural environment for women's and gender studies in France is thus undergoing a rapid and positive evolution, thanks to the new structures and incentives put in place by Europe, the creation of regional gender institutes like the Institut Emilie Châtelet (2006) and the promised reform of French universities (which may or may not finish by making the curriculum more responsive to student demand). But more open and receptive structures alone cannot guarantee the success of the fledgling sub-discipline. Gender history's ultimate success will rise or fall on its capacity to deliver the intellectual goods not only to its own specialists but to a range of scholars across the field. And I think that this, too, is beginning to happen as scholars outside of gender studies begin to read some of the excellent and innovative work on gender and find in this literature tools for a critical rethinking of the concepts and categories that organise historical research.

Notes

1   Joan W. Scott, '"Gender": a useful category of historical analysis', *American Historical Review* 91 (1986), 1053–75.
2   Joan W. Scott, 'Millennial fantasies: the future of "gender" in the 21st Century', in Claudia Honegger and Caroline Arni, eds, *Gender-die Tüken einer Kategorie* (Zurich, 2001) 19–37.
3   Judith Bennett's 'Feminism and history', *Gender and History* 1 (1989), 251–72, was one of the earlier statements in defence of examining women's social, economic and political positions in 'patriarchal' societies in the past. She has developed these ideas in her *History Matters: Patriarchy and the Challenges of Feminism* (Philadelphia, University of Pennsylvania Press, 2006). Other scholars worried about the abstracting power of 'discourse' in the study of relations between the sexes include Catherine Hall, in 'Politics, post-structuralism and feminist history', *Gender and History* 3 (1991), 204–10.
4   Denise Riley, *'Am I that Name?' Feminism and the Category of 'Women' in History* (London, Palgrave Macmillan, 1981).
5   This became my book, *Murders and Madness: Medicine, Law and Society in the Fin de Siècle* (Oxford, Clarendon Press, 1989).
6   Ruth Harris, *Lourdes: Body and Spirit in the Secular Age* (Harmondsworth, Allen Lane, 1999).
7   For the classic account of the transformation of psychoanalysis by French theorists, see Elisabeth Roudinesco, *Jacques Lacan & Co: A History of Psychoanalysis in France, 1925–1985,* trans. Jeffrey Mehlman, (London, Free Association Books, 1990).
8   See, above all, the remarkable, *Love, Guilt and Reparation and Other Works, 1921–45* (London, Virago, 1991).
9   Lyndal Roper, *Oedipus and the Devil: Witchcraft, Religion and Sexuality in Early Modern Europe* (New York, Routledge, 1994).
10 Lyndal Roper, *Witch Craze: Terror and Fantasy in Baroque Germany* (New Haven and London, Yale University Press, 2004).
11 Among a host of excellent works, see Caroline Walker Bynum, *Holy Feast and Holy Fast: Religious Significance of Food to Mediaeval Women* (Berkeley, University of California Press, 1987), and *Fragmentation and Redemption: Essays on Gender and the Human Body in Mediaeval Religion* (New York, Zone Books, 1991).

12 See for example, Joan Landes, *Women and the Public Sphere in the Age of the French Revolution* (Ithaca, Cornell University Press, 1988).

13 Robert Nye, *Masculinity and Male Codes of Honor in Modern France* (Oxford University Press, 1993); and 'Western masculinities in war and peace', *American Historical Review* 112 (2007), 417–38 provides an excellent bibliography in the footnotes.

14 Dagmar Herzog, *Sexuality and German Fascism* (Oxford and New York, Berghahn Books, 2004)

15 Suzanne Desan, *The Family on Trial in Revolutionary France* (Berkeley, University of California Press, 2006).

16 The work in this field is excellent and diverse, and seeks to explain the relative 'timidity' of French feminism. See, for example, P. K. Bidelman, *Pariahs Stand Up! The Founding of the Liberal Feminist Movement in France 1858–1889* (Westport, Conn., Greenwood Press, 1982); Charles Sowerwine, *Sisters or Citizens? Women and Socialism in France since 1876* (Cambridge University Press, 1984). For the extent of the suffrage movement, see Steven C. Hause and Anne R. Kenny, *Women's Suffrage and Social Politics in the French Third Republic* (Princeton University Press, 1984). For a good survey of French Feminism, see L. Klegman and F. Rochefort, *L'égalité en marche* (Paris, Editions des Femmes, 1989). See also J. Waelti-Walters and Steven C. Hause, *Feminisms of the Belle Epoque: A Historical and Literary Anthology* (Lincoln, University of Nebraska Press, 1994). See Karen Offen's classic article for the importance of 'familialism' in the French feminist tradition: 'Depopulation, nationalism and feminism in the *fin de siècle*', *American Historical Review* 89 (1984), 648–76.

17 For more on this, see my *Lourdes: Body and Spirit in the Secular Age*. For the enormous influx of women into the feminine orders, see Claude Langlois, *Le Catholicisme au féminin: Les congrégations françaises à supérieure générale au XIXe siècle* (Paris, Le Cerf 1984); Yvonne Turin, *Femmes et religieuses: Le féminisme 'en religion'* (Paris, 1989); Jacques Léonard, 'Femmes, religion et médecine: Les religieuses qui soignent en France au XIXe siècle', *Annales, ESC* 32 (1977), 887–907; Odile Arnold, *Le corps et l'âme: la vie des religieuses au XIXe siècle* (Paris, Le Seuil, 1984). Nor was this sensibility confined to Catholic women who took orders; see also James McMillan, 'Religion and gender in modern France: some reflections', in Frank Tallett and Nicholas Atkin, *Religion, Society and Politics in France since 1789* (London, Hambledon Continuum, 1991), and Steven C. Hause and A. Kenny, 'The development of the Catholic women's suffrage movement in France 1896–1922', *Catholic Historical Review* 68 (1981), 11–30. As these selections show, Catholic women, such as Marie Maugeret, supported the suffrage in an attempt to defend the Church and reform the Republic, and were hence viewed warily by their anticlerical sisters. Finally, the more recent work of Richard D. E. Burton, especially his *Holy Tears, Holy Blood: Women, Catholicism and the Culture of Suffering in France, 1840–1909* (New York, Cornell University Press, 2004), shows how redemption was seen in sacrificial terms.

18 Caroline Ford, 'Between the public and the private: Islam, laïcité, and the veil in modern France', unpublished paper, cited with permission of the author.

19 Lynn M. Thomas, 'Imperial concerns and "women's affairs": state efforts to regulate clitoridectomy and eradicate abortion in Meru, Kenya, c. 1910–1950,' *Journal of African History* 39 (1998), 121–45. See also her recently published *Politics of the Womb: Women, Reproduction, and the State in Kenya* (Berkeley, University of California Press, 2003).

20 Lata Mani, *The Debate on Sati in Colonial India,* (Berkeley, University of California Press, 1998).

21 Roger N. Lancaster, *Life Is Hard: Machismo, Danger, and the Intimacy of Power in Nicaragua* (Berkeley, University of California Press, 1992).

22 María Josefina Saldaña-Portillo, 'The authorized subjects of revolution: Ernesto "Che" Guevara and Mario Payeras,' in Saldaña-Portillo, *The Revolutionary Imagination in the Americas* (Durham, NC, Duke University Press, 2003), 63–108, 299–303.

23 Ching Kwan Lee, *Gender and the South China Miracle: Two Worlds of Factory Women* (Berkeley, University of California Press, 1998), and Jane Collins, *Threads: Gender, Labor and Power in the Global Apparel Industry* (Chicago University Press, 2003).

24 Olwen Hufton, *The Prospect before Her: A History of Women in Western Europe, 1500–1800* (London, HarperCollins, 1995); for a more programmatic vision, see Hufton's 'Femmes/hommes: une question subversive', in *Passés recomposés: champs et chantiers de l'histoire* (Paris, 1995), Jean Boutier and Dominique Julia, eds., 235–42.

25 Silvia Evangelisti, 'Rooms to share: convent cells and social relations in early-modern Italy', in *The Art of Survival: Gender and History in Europe, 1450–2000* (Past & Present Supplement 1, Oxford, 2005), 55–71.

26 Selina Todd, 'Domestic servants and social relations in England, 1900–1950', *Past & Present* (forthcoming).

27 'Middle sex', documentary by Antony Thomas, first transmitted in May 2005 on Channel 4.

28 Michel Foucault, ed., *Herculine Barbin: Being the Recently Discovered Memoirs of a Nineteenth-century*

Hermaphrodite, trans. Richard McDougall (Brighton, Harvester Press, 1980).

29 Lotte Van der Pol with Rudolf Dekker, *Vrouwen in mannenkleren. De geschiedenis van een tegendraadse traditie* (Amsterdam, 1989).

30 Laura Lee Downs, *Writing Gender History* (London, Hodder Arnold, 2004), 185.

31 Siân Reynolds, review of Downs, *Writing Gender History*, *Clio HSF* 23 (2006).

32 Bernard Lepetit, ed., *Les formes de l'expérience: une autre histoire sociale* (Paris, Albin Michel, 1995); François Bédarida, ed., *L'histoire et le métier de l'historien en France 1945–1995* (Paris, Maison des sciences de l'homme, 1995); Jacques Revel, ed., *Jeux d'échelles. La micro-analyse à l'expérience* (Paris, Le Seuil, 1996).

33 Joan Scott, 'Gender: a useful category of analysis', in Scott, *Gender and the Politics of History* (New York, Columbia University Press, 1988).

34 Joan Scott, 'Feminism's history', *Journal of Women's History* 16/2 (spring 2004), 22. See also Scott's introduction to the second edition of her *Gender and the Politics of History* (New York, Columbia University Press, 1999).

35 François Thébaud, 'Writing women's and gender history in France: a national narrative?', *Journal of Women's History* 19/1 (spring 2007), 167–72, 167. The persistent cold-shouldering of women's and gender history in France suggests that no one is fooled by feminist scholars' avoidance of the term 'feminist history'. For a more in-depth exploration of these issues, see F. Thébaud's excellent survey, *Écrire l'histoire des femmes et du genre* (Saint-Cloud, ENS Editions, 2007).

36 Thébaud, 'Writing women's and gender history in France', 169. Three of these were assistant professors (recruited in 1984, 1991 and 1993), and two were full professors (recruited in 1998 and 2001).

37 Thébaud, *Écrire l'histoire des femmes*, 97–8, which also underscores 1) the fact that prestigious disciplines like history remain highly masculine, and 2) the fact that women's and gender historians have, in consequence, been split between those who follow the radically anti-institutionalist strategy preached by the MLF (Antoinette Foucq et al.) and those who, like Arlette Farge, are concerned that the separatist strategy of constituting women's and gender studies departments will merely lead to the constitution of an intellectual ghetto, 'tolerated but devalorised and without influence on the discipline'. French historians of women and gender have thus pursued a strategy of 'entrisme', entering institutions and exploring all possible middle roads between separatism and complete assimilation, 'admittedly without much success, but it's not clear that the opposite strategy would have worked better, given the French context…' (98). See also Michelle Perrot, 'Où en est en France l'histoire des femmes?', *French Politics, Culture and Society* 12/1.

38 French sociologists and anthropologists have both shown far more interest in deploying gender as an axis of analysis than have their colleagues in history.

39 Thébaud, *Écrire l'histoire des femmes*.

40 Ibid., 169, 168.

41 Downs, *Writing Gender History*.

42 Though I've chosen to confine my discussion to religion and politics (an eternally 'hot' topic in French history), gender is also proving its mettle in recent work on immigration, colonialism and transnationalism, to name but a few other 'hot' topics in contemporary French history where scholars are deploying gender alongside other tools of analysis.

43 Magali della Sudda, *Une activité politique féminine conservatrice avant le droit de suffrage en France et en Italie. Socio-histoire de la politisation des femmes catholiques au sein de la Ligue Patriotique des Françaises (1902–1933) et de l'Unione tra le donne cattoliche d'Italia (1909–1919)* (doctoral thesis, EHESS, 2007).

44 Serge Berstein, 'La France allergique au fascisme', *Vingtième siècle: revue d'histoire* 2 (April 1984), 84–94. While many other names could be cited on both sides of the controversy, Robert Soucy has led the charge in asserting that France did produce its own brand of fascism: *French Fascism: The Second Wave* (New Haven, Yale University Press, 1995).

45 In some ways, this goes back to the mid 1930s, when the Popular Front government first tarred the Croix de feu with the label 'fascist'.

46 Political sociologist Michael Dobry thus points out that the question of whether such movements were fascist or not 'does not constitute the sole, or even the principal, research question', in *Le mythe de l'allergie française au fascisme* (Paris, Albin Michel, 2003), 67; while Brian Jenkins asserts that the ongoing debate is condemned to remain sterile so long as there is no consensus among historians around a precise definition of fascism: Jenkins, ed., *France in the Era of Fascism: Essays on the French Authoritarian Right* (New York, Berghahn Books, 2005), 213–15.

47 Happily, a number of younger historians are beginning to do just that, notably Kevin Passmore, but also Sean Kennedy, Albert Kéchichian, Cheryl Kroos and Daniella Sarnoff.

48 Daniella Sarnoff, Cheryl Kroos and Kevin Passmore have all looked at various aspects of women's involvement in the Croix de feu movement, with Sarnoff and Kroos focusing more particularly on the civic education of women, and the implications of their involvement for understanding the place of women and gender in fascist and extreme right-wing movements. While Passmore has analysed more closely the dynamics of women's involvement in the social-work side of the movement as well, no one has yet explored the day-to-day functioning of this immense social service network, nor placed it in the context of other, extra-state social service initiatives in interwar France, nor reflected on the implications that this massive investment of still vote-less women, in an enterprise that was animated by right-wing social Catholic values, would have for the political orientation of these women after 1945. See Sarnoff and Kroos in Passmore, ed., *Women, Gender and Fascism in Europe 1919–1945* (Manchester University Press, 2003); and Passmore, 'Planting the tricolor in the citadels of communism. Women's social action in the Croix de Feu and Parti social français,' *Journal of Modern History* 71 (December 1999), 814–51.

49 The red belt included working-class cities, structured by socialist and communist municipal power, and the utterly unstructured shanty-towns of the recently demilitarised 'zone' that lay in the shadow of the city's fortifications.

50 Archives Nationales (AN) 451 AP 93, Président général des Croix de feu, mémorandum 'Mouvement Croix de feu', 2 January 1936, 10 pages, 9–10. Social action thus demanded 'l'emploi presque exclusif de femmes, et de femmes professionnellement qualifiées. Les fruits de cette splendide besogne sont recueillis sous forme d'un rayonnement augmenté de nos Associations'. Ibid. Document destiné aux seuls yeux des chefs de section 'elle ne doit, en aucun cas, circuler'. Ibid.

51 La Rocque had served two tours of duty under Maréchal Lyautey in the Moroccan Protectorate (in 1913–16, 1925–26) His interest in those doctrines was such that, after returning to Paris, he participated in meetings on social action organised by the Maréchal in his Paris apartment.

52 Indeed, the very idea that the goal of social action was 'réconciliation' was first articulated by Lyautey in his famous article 'Le rôle social de l'officier', *La revue des deux mondes* (1891). See also Colonel de la Rocque, 'La cavalerie', *La revue hebdomadaire*, 12 (23 March 1912). In September of 1934, La Rocque published in the pages of *Le flambeau* an article which affirmed his intention to apply in the metropole the method of pacification he had first learned in Morocco from Lyautey. La Rocque, *Le flambeau* (Sept. 1934), 2.

53 AN 451 AP/172, Préval à Frandaz, 19 October 1937, 3. *Surintendantes d'usine* were particularly well-paid professionals, earning up to 30,000 F per year, the equivalent of a male engineer's salary.

54 AN 451 AP 93, Section féminine, 'L'assistance social dans les groupes féminins', *s.d.*, 1.

55 AN 451 AP/87, Section féminine, Rapport sur les camps de vacances de l'été 1935, p 3–4. 'Une hostilité farouche, renforcée, planait donc sur la zone. Les affiches, les tracts, les appels au meurtre contre les Croix de feu et leur chef surexcitaient les malheureux. Révolvers, couteaux, menaçaient à leur entrée nos Assistantes, calmes, souriantes… Ce sont dans la paix nos soldats des premières lignes'.

56 In this respect, the *colonies de vacances* of the CF/PSF participated in the broader trends of the interwar *colonie* movement, studded at it was with self-consciously prefigurative colonies, both on the left (the socialist 'children's republics') and in Catholic milieux (Père Fillère's famous 'cités paroissiales de Dieu'). For more on the colonies of the Croix de feu, see Downs, 'To re-unite the national family in the folds of the tricolour: gender and the social politics of working-class childhood on the extreme right, 1930–39', forthcoming in the *Journal of Modern History*, special issue on European childhood. On the prefigurative child communities of communists and Catholics, see Downs, *Childhood in the Promised Land: Working-class Movements and the Colonies de Vacances in France, 1880–1960* (Durham, NC, Duke University Press, 2002).

57 Kevin Passmore's work on the French Right has also shown how gender analysis helps to transcend a number of the 'too-simple oppositions' that have structured much of the recent work on fascism as a 'political religion'. Passmore, 'The gendered genealogy of political religions theory', forthcoming in *Gender & History*, special 20th anniversary issue.

58 'If "woman" is just an empty category, then why am I afraid to walk alone at night? Identity politics meets the postmodern subject', *Comparative Studies in Society and History* (April, 1993), 414–37. See also L. Downs, 'Reply to Joan Scott' in the same issue, 444–58.

59 These were mainly men of the old school, for the ranks of *directeur d'études* (full professor) at the EHESS boasted precious few women at the time. When I was elected *directeur d'études*, in 2001, women made up about 10 per cent of the corps. In six years this has progressed hardly at all: I think we may be up to 13 or 14 per cent at the time of writing (2008) – at the *maître de conferences* (assistant professor) level, women make up about one-third of the corps, as they do in universities. The EHESS is a very elite school, and hence more masculine. As we have seen, the situation in the universities is a bit less drastic, with women making up nearly a quarter of the rank of full professors.

60 See Downs, *Writing Gender History*, for a more thorough discussion of this point.

61 Thébaud, 'Writing women's and gender history in France', 169.

62 To my knowledge, six of Butler's books have been translated to date, including several that have played a key role in gender/queer studies in the USA, Great Britain and France: *Trouble dans le genre: le féminisme et la subversion de l'identité*, preface by Eric Fassin (Paris, La Découverte, 2006); *Défaire le genre* (Paris, Editions, 2006); *Le récit de soi* (Paris, PUF, 2007); *Le pouvoir des mots* (Paris, Editions Amsterdam, 2004); *La vie psychique de pouvoir* (Paris, Léo Scheer, 2002); *Vie précaire: les pouvoirs de deuil et de violence après le onze septembre* (Paris, Editions Amsterdam, 2006). Her entire oeuvre is available in English as well at the *Bibliothèque nationale*.

63 I refer in particular to Butler's conception of subjects' self-construction via the 'performance' of already existing scripts. See *Gender Trouble* (1990), in which the author argues that identities and differences are not the outcome of a groups' 'objective' location in social, political and economic hierarchies. Rather, such identities are discursively constructed by individuals who 'perform' those identities (including gender) through pre-existing cultural processes. Butler later modified this position to amplify the agency of individual actors (*Bodies that Matter*, 1993), to argue that, while discursively constructed, subjects nonetheless possess critical capacities (which are also culturally constructed) that allow them to engage in novel actions and even 'rewrite' the scripts, thereby re-signifying their own subject positions.

64 See Françoise Gaspard and Farhad Khosrokhavar, *Le foulard et la République* (Paris, La Découverte, 1995); and Florence Rochefort, 'Foulard, genre et laïcité en 1989', *Vingtième siècle. Revue d'histoire* 75 (July–Sept 2000), 145–56 for useful discussions of earlier rounds in this debate.

65 The older generation thus supports a Republic that showed every sign of being prepared to exclude them forever from formal political activity on the ground of ineradicable sexual difference.

66 See Thébaud, *Écrire l'histoire des femmes et du genre* for a fuller discussion of these developments.

5

Has history again become a branch of literature?

Robert Gildea and Jean-Frédéric Schaub

In the nineteenth century history was conceived very much as a branch of literature. A historical school then developed, beginning with Ranke in Germany, that insisted on a hard-headed approach requiring the critical study of primary sources left behind by churches and states. In the twentieth century claims were made that history was a social science, using quantitative methods to lay bare social reality and postulating laws of social change. In the 1970s it was pointed out to historians that when they wrote history they subconsciously adopted narrative models from literature: comedy, tragedy, romance and satire. During the linguistic turn it was claimed that the primary sources they used were not 'windows onto reality', but texts elaborately constructed according to the conventions of the institution that produced them and with viewpoints shaped by the culture in which they were located. Robert Gildea argues that these challenges have allowed historians to experiment with different forms of historical narrative in their own writing. Jean-Frédéric Schaub argues that historians must now learn from the techniques of literary criticism, showing how fiction is put together, in order to extract the maximum meaning from their primary sources. Both conclude, in the end, that history is not just a branch of literature.

Robert Gildea

History is commonly regarded as one of two things: past events, and accounts of those events. One requires a critical interrogation of the documentary evidence left by the past; the other refers to narratives which refer to that evidence but are constructed to make the past intelligible and meaningful. As narratives, such accounts may overlap with works of literature which also reconstruct the past. In the nineteenth century there developed a school of critical history which required that historians adhere to the historical record in their accounts of the past, a requirement that was not incumbent on novelists or playwrights, who were free to dramatise and to simplify. This requirement was intended to prevent historians making use of the past for their own moral, religious or political purposes. In the early twentieth century there were attempts to remove history from the realm of the arts and to make it into a science. This sacrificed the agency of individuals to the working out of historical laws, reduced political events to the status of side effects of deeper economic and social developments, and prioritised what could be counted over what could not. 'Narrative history' became a term of condescension in the mouths of historians who saw themselves as social scientists. More recently there has been a revival of history as a narrative form and experimentation with different forms of narrative. With the linguistic turn it has been suggested that there is no such thing as historical reality, only texts representing it, and that each historical account is as valid as any other. Political correctness indeed gave greater credence to accounts by victims over accounts by perpetrators. So has history, once again, become a branch of literature?

Romantic history

Paris is in the streets; – rushing, foaming like some Venice wine-glass into which you had dropped poison ... the multitude flows on, welling through every street; the tocsin furiously pealing, all drums beating the *générale*: the Suburb Saint-Antoine rolling hitherward wholly, as one man... On, then, all Frenchmen, that have hearts in your bodies! Roar with all your throats, ye Sons of Liberty ... Smite, thou Louis Tournay, Cartwright of the Marais, old soldier of the Regiment Dauphiné; smite at the Outer Drawbridge chain, though the fiery hail whistles round thee! Never, over knave or felloe, did thy axe strike such a stroke. Down with it man, down with it to Orcus: let the whole accursed Edifice sink thither, and Tyranny be swallowed up for ever! ... At every street-barricade, there whirls simmering a minor whirlpool, – strengthening the barricade, since God knows what is coming; and all minor whirlpools play distractedly into that grand Fire-Maelstrom which is lashing round the Bastille.[1]

As a whirlpool of boiling waters has a centre point, so, all this raging circled round Defarge's wine shop, and every human drop in the caldron had a tendency to be sucked towards the vortex ... 'Come, then!', cried Defarge, in a resounding voice, 'Patriots and friends, we are ready! The Bastille!' With a roar that sounded as if all the breath in France had been shaped into the detested word, the living sea rose, wave on wave, depth on depth, and overflowed the city to that point. Alarm-bells ringing, drums beating, the sea raging and thundering on its new beach, the attack began … still the deep ditch, and the single drawbridge, and the massive stone walls, and the eight towers, and still Defarge of the wine-shop at his gun, grown doubly hot by the service of Four fierce hours … it had been as much as they could do to hear each other, even then: so tremendous was the noise of the living ocean, in its irruption into the Fortress, and its inundation of the courts and passages and staircases … more like dry waterfalls than staircases'.[2]

These two nineteenth-century texts deal with the same historical event: the storming of the Bastille by the people of Paris on 14 July 1789. One is a work of history, the other of literature. Both use a metaphor of the sea, with its roaring waves and whirlpools, to describe the crowd. Both intensify the atmosphere with the din of church bells sounding the alarm and beating drums. Both focus on the crossing of the drawbridge and the surge into the fortress prison that stood between the working-class Faubourg Saint-Antoine and the centre of Paris. The first has a reference to Orcus, a god of the underworld in Greek myth, and is cast more as an epic, drawing out the general truth of a struggle between liberty and tyranny, and suggests the hand of God behind human actions.[3] It is more mannered and grandiose in its literary conventions. And yet this is a work of history, Thomas Carlyle's *The French Revolution* (1837). The second text is from Charles Dickens' *A Tale of Two Cities* (1859), and it is striking that Dickens borrowed from Carlyle not only the imagery of the crowd, but an overall structure of the novel that followed the 'rising sea' and 'rising fire' of the Revolution to the Guillotine, the title of the third and final part of Carlyle's *Revolution* and the final scene of self-sacrifice of Dickens' English hero, Sidney Carton.

In between these two works, its first volume published in 1847, appeared *The History of the French Revolution* by Jules Michelet. 'This subject is an ocean', he wrote to his son-in-law.[4] Whereas Carlyle and Dickens saw the crowd as a storm-tossed ocean, Michelet solidified the ocean of the Revolution in the People and made it his hero. The People were not vicious, but the bearers of a new religion, that of liberty. The taking of the Bastille by the People was an 'act of faith'. The Revolution was not a cataclysm but a resurrection, the defeat of monarchical tyranny and persecution by the old Catholic religion, and the self-realisation of the People in a fraternal *patrie* of free and equal citizens. For those who lived through the Revolution, said Michelet, only the 14th of July was the day of the whole people. 'May this great day', he said, 'therefore remain one of the great feasts of the human race, not only for being the first day of deliverance, but also for being the highest in concord'. The first celebration of the fall of the Bastille took place a year later, when delegations from all over France travelled to Paris for the Fête de la Fédération. 'In the villages', wrote Michelet, 'there was no longer rich or poor, noble or commoner; food was shared, meals were eaten together. Social divisions and discord disappeared. Enemies were reconciled, opposing sects fraternised, believers and *philosophes*, Protestants and Catholics'.[5] This was a supreme work of history, based on five years' research in the archives, but Michelet used few quotations and added no footnotes. 'What gives authority to the account', he wrote in his preface to the 1868 edition of the work, 'is its drive and coherence rather than a multitude of little bibliographical curiosities'. That quality, together with the literary greatness of the work, were acknowledged by Victor Hugo, who wrote a letter to Michelet which praised 'your moral authority and your literary power. I shake your hand'.[6]

Critical history

In Germany, meanwhile, the principles of a much more critical history were being laid down by Leopold Ranke. Rather than being inspired by literature, he was horrified by the lack of historical accuracy in Sir Walter Scott's historical novel *Quentin Durward*, in which the portrayal of Louis XI of France bore no relation to the fifteenth-century chronicles of Philippe de Comynes. In his introduction to his *History of the Latin and Teutonic Nations* (1824), Ranke said that 'history has had assigned to it the office of judging the past and of instructing the present for the benefit of future ages. To such high offices the present work does not presume; it seeks only to show what actually happened [*wie es eigentlich gewesen*]'.[7] On the strength of this work, Ranke was appointed professor at the University of Berlin, and was then given three years' leave to undertake research in the archives of Vienna, Venice and Rome. There he perfected the discipline of the critical evaluation of sources, taking account of the intellectual background, ideas, interests and agenda of the writer, and privileging archival sources which were written as close to the people and events they described as possible. 'No poeticising, no fantasising', he demanded.[8]

Source criticism was one thing, however, and writing history another. 'A strict presentation of the facts, contingent and unattractive as they may be, is the highest law', continued Ranke in his introduction to his *History of the Latin and Teutonic Nations*. 'A second, for me, is the development of the unity and progress of the events ... I have preferred to discuss in detail each people, each power and each individual only at the time when they played an important or leading role'.[9] Writing history required a stage on which the struggles of individuals, powers and peoples were played out, and a script from which they spoke. This imposed a process of selection, including some events and developments, excluding others. Ranke's *History of the Popes* (1834–36), for example, explored the emancipation of the Papacy from the power of the Holy Roman Emperor, and then the spiritual decline and corruption of the Church as the Papacy became a secular power like any other. He traced the spiritual regeneration of Christianity outside the Catholic Church, with Luther and the Protestant Reformation, and the Reformation's link to Protestant states, such as Prussia and England, which fought back against the Papacy, Holy Roman Empire and Catholic Spain.[10] In his *History of Prussia* (1847–48), he followed the emergence of Prussia as a great power after Frederick II's conquest of Silesia from Austria in 1740, and its transition from a Protestant power to an agent of the Enlightenment.[11] In his essay on the Great Powers, moreover, Ranke analysed the attempt of France to impose itself as a universal monarchy under Louis XIV and as a universal republic in the 1790s, frustrated by the cooperation of Prussia and Britain to achieve a balance of power.[12] For all his critical theory and insistence on objectivity, it is difficult not to see in Ranke's works a grand narrative of the rise of Protestant Europe at the expense of the Counter-Reformation, the rise of nation states at the expense of the Holy Roman Empire, and the achievement of a self-righting balance of power between Teutonic and Latin powers. The historian Friedrich Meinecke, in a lecture delivered in 1936, argued that Ranke saw political history not as brutal power politics but the working out of some 'spiritual reality', indeed 'the thoughts of God'.[13]

Ranke's critical method spread to Britain and France, but the insistence on source criticism and objectivity never disposed of the next stage, which was to assemble reliable facts into a coherent and meaningful narrative. Lord Acton trained as a historian in Germany before becoming one the founders of the *English Historical Review* in 1886, and was appointed Regius Professor of Modern History at Cambridge in 1895. In his inaugural lecture he called Ranke 'my own master'. He told the story of Ranke's anger at Sir Walter Scott's taking liberties with the historical record, and his decision to 'follow, without swerving … the lead of his authorities. He decided effectually to repress the poet, the patriot, to banish himself from his books, and to write nothing that would gratify his own feelings or disclose his private convictions'.[14] Acton directed the production of *The Cambridge Modern History*, which was to be based on the mass of historical documents now made available in the official publications of European countries. It would be written by over a hundred authors, who, as he told them in a letter to contributors in 1898, would have to maintain a strict impartiality, so that 'nobody can tell, without examining the list of authors, where the Bishop of Oxford laid down his pen, and whether Fairburn or Gasquet, Liebermann or Harrison took it up'.[15]

Impartial history, of course, did not exclude the need for narrative drive, for Acton as much as Ranke. 'We have to describe the ruling currents, to interpret the sovereign forces, that still govern and divine the world', Acton told his contributors, urging them to produce a 'universal history … which is not a rope of sand but a continuous development'.[16] Establishing a grand narrative, naturally, implied a process of selection. The first volume of *The Cambridge*

Modern History, devoted to the Renaissance, published in 1904, two years after Acton's death, gave a large amount of space to Italy, at the centre of the Renaissance. On the other hand, it said nothing about Scandinavian countries, which 'needed the Reformation to bring them into the circle of general European politics', nor about Russia, which 'remained, as yet, inert'.[17] This lopsidedness, which was excusable from the point of view of narrative, was however compounded by lapses of impartiality. Acton himself, in his lectures on the French Revolution, given in Cambridge in 1895–99, for example, described Robespierre as 'the most hateful character in the forefront of history since Machiavelli reduced to a code the wickedness of man'.[18]

The French opposite number of Acton was Charles Seignobos, a lecturer at the Sorbonne who in 1898 co-authored an *Introduction to the Study of History*. He announced that 'history is written with documents. Documents are the traces which have been left by the thoughts and actions of men of former times'. These documents were to be subjected to rigorous source criticism, to 'discover what in a document may be regarded as true'. 'Historical facts', he continued, 'are derived from the critical analysis of documents', and the task of the historian was to build up a database of incontrovertible facts. This done, the work of 'historical construction' could take place, inventing a narrative account to relate and explain the facts. Influential individuals and political events would play a crucial role in this narrative.[19] Ironically, just as Acton did not observe his own rules of impartiality, Seignobos did not follow his rules of devotion to original documents in his *Political History of Contemporary Europe* (1897). So great was the mass of documents for the nineteenth century, he pleaded, that he could study only secondary monographs, not primary sources. He did not use footnotes, but provided a bibliography, and did not engage in historiographical debate. Concentrating on political events, he constructed his history around a European overview, nation states and chronology, but in the end concluded that 'three accidents decided the evolution of contemporary Europe' – the agitation of small groups of revolutionaries in 1830 and 1848, and the war of 1870, which was the 'personal responsibility of Bismarck'.[20] For Seignobos, the actions of individuals would always get the better of structures and trends.

Scientific history

The naivety of this kind of political history was subjected in the early twentieth century to the challenge of economics and sociology, but also demography and geography, for the prize of leading discipline in the social sciences. The discipline of history was forced to change, and there was a reaction against the 'history of events', which was purely political and prioritised individual agency. History became more quantitative, more deterministic, and even offered itself as a laboratory in which hypotheses could be tested.

The world economic depression after 1929 stimulated economic history, which sought to place the depression in a long-term historical context of boom and slump by a quantitative examination of prices and wages. The economic historian François Simiand proposed a model of an expanding economy characterised by rising prices and wages in a Phase A, such as 1730–1820, 1850–80 and 1900–28, and a Phase B of a contracting economy, with falling prices and wages, as in 1650–1730, 1820–50, 1880–1900 and from 1928.[21] Simiand's method was taken up by Marxist historians such as Ernest Labrousse, who undertook a more detailed study of prices and wages in eighteenth-century France, distinguishing long-term trends, shorter cyclical variations and seasonal crises. These quantitative methods, privileging the long term over what Simiand called *l'histoire événémentielle*, were linked to the historical approach of the *Annales* school of history, established in 1929 by Lucien Febvre and Marc Bloch, which set the individual within the context of much broader structures – that of the environment, physical and human geography, social class and collective mentalities – which shaped the behaviour and thoughts of individuals and without which they could not be understood.[22] At the opposite extreme of a history of medieval kings and battles, Marc Bloch's *Feudal Society* (1939–40) explored the deep structures of 'links of dependency between men' under the feudal system, how they were governed and their world view.[23] In *The Mediterranean and the Mediterranean World in the Age of Philip II*, first published in 1946, Fernand Braudel attacked the old-school history of events as 'surface disturbances, the crests of foam that the tides of history carry on their strong backs'.[24] He established the mountains, plains, sea-coasts, climate and seasons of the Mediterranean as the broadest envelopes conditioning human activity, before placing under his microscope such processes as migration and transhumance, trade by land and sea, urbanisation, and the formation of social classes and empires.

'Tomorrow's historian will have to be able to programme a computer in order to survive', wrote Emmanuel Le Roy Ladurie in May 1968.[25] He was responding to the challenge of the 'New Economic History' in Britain and, above all, the United States in the 1960s. Using statistical models and computers, 'cliometrics', as it became known, used history as a laboratory in which theories could be tested. In *Railroads and American Economic Growth*, Robert Fogel ran a historical experiment in which the railways were never built and cargoes were carried by river and canal. He calculated that the impact of railways on American GNP by 1890 was a mere 6.3 per cent.[26] In their study of Southern antebellum slavery, *Time on the Cross*, Robert Fogel and Stanley Engerman argued that slavery had been more efficient than free agriculture and free industrial labour, and that 'the typical slave fieldhand received about 90% of the income he produced'. They prefaced their work by saying that 'Today the findings and methods of the new economic history are routinely taught at the graduate level at Harvard, Yale, Chicago, the University of California and other leading universities which together produce most of the PhDs in the field'.[27]

Even the ascendancy of scientific history did not mean the elimination of history as narrative. The price and wage fluctuations established by Simiand and Labrousse could not escape the pull of that great historical event, the French Revolution. 'I am happy to point out', said fellow Marxist historian George Lefebvre in 1937, 'that M. Labrousse finishes by emphasising the coincidence that I myself noted between the *journée* of 14 July and the highest point of the eighteenth-century price rise'.[28] Scientific history was harnessed to explain events, not to eliminate them, and in 1939 Lefebvre himself published a book entitled *Quatre-vingt-neuf*.[29] Marc Bloch had just published his *Feudal Society* when war broke out and he was mobilised. He analysed the collapse of France in the 1940s both as a historian and as a participant in a shattering historical event in his *Strange Defeat*, and his involvement with the French Resistance led to his death in 1944. In spite of his emphasis on structures and trends, Braudel devoted the third and final part of his *Mediterranean* to 'Events, politics and people' – to events such as the Battle of Lepanto in 1571 and the St Bartholomew's Day Massacre of 1572. His work ended with the death in 1598 of Philip II, 'a monarch sitting at the centre, the intersection of the endless reports which combined to weave the great web of the Spanish Empire and the world'.[30] Even cliometric history was not without its literary dimension. The counterfactual history it invented, seeking to understand what *did* happen by imagining what *might* have happened, was described by one reviewer in 1966 as 'a new branch of literature, quite unlike what has hitherto passed as historical knowledge and somewhat more analogous to science fiction'.[31]

The return of literary history

The offensive of scientific history, which had gathered momentum in the interwar period and reached a climax in the 1960s, began to lose momentum in the 1970s. Literary history made a comeback in a number of ways. First, literary critics pointed out to historians that their histories were constructed as narratives around a choice of plots. Second, historians themselves became more aware that primary historical sources were themselves crafted as narratives. Third, they gained a sense that questions of power divided different narratives and that narratives were constructed differently by different cultures.

In 1973, Hayden White, Professor of Comparative Literature at Stanford University, announced that all historical works, except perhaps 'the monograph or the archival report', have a 'deep structural content which is generally poetic and specifically linguistic in nature', which provides unity and intelligibility.[32] Early historical accounts such as annals were mere lists of dates randomly recording battles and plagues; they had no central subject such as a king or state. Chronicles had such a central subject but no beginning, middle or end which afforded a moral or dramatic dimension to the story. Full-bodied histories, and notably the great histories of the nineteenth century, were constructed, consciously or unconsciously, around plots which were drawn from the great literary genres: comedy, tragedy, romance and irony or satire.[33] He argued that no historical account was intrinsically comic, tragic, romantic or ironic, but that the same event, such as the French Revolution, could be emplotted in different ways. Meanwhile, Ranke's histories were plotted as comedies, not because of any jokes, but because his narratives ended with a reconciliation of conflicts between churches and states and between great powers.[34]

This challenge to historians to shift their gaze away from sources and to become much more self-critical about how they constructed their narratives coincided with a decline in confidence in scientific history, whether Marxist, *Annales*-inspired or cliometric. In a key article on 'The revival of narrative', Lawrence Stone argued that economic determinism had not been able to displace the agency of individuals and groups, and that there was 'a revival of recognition that political and military power, the use of brute force, is a historical force'. Equally, there was a loss of faith in quantitative history, as *Time on the Cross* since Fogel and Engerman had analysed the material conditions of slaves through a computer, but had nothing to say about the psychological effects of slavery. New narratives would be different from the old, said Stone, centred more on the microcosm or 'bottom-up', but narratives they would be.[35]

Stone paid tribute to the vogue among historians of anthropology rather than economics, and anthropologists were demonstrating that there could be no overarching, impartial historical narrative because history-telling was shaped by the culture of the community that told the story. In *Vision of the Vanquished*, first published in 1971, anthropologist and historian Nathan Wachtel explored the Spanish Conquest of Peru in the sixteenth century not from the point of view of Pisarro and his *conquistadores*, but from that of the Incas, showing how the Incas' myths persuaded them to see the Spaniards initially as gods, to be offered gold, except that the 'gods' then resorted to plunder and destruction.[36] Similarly, anthropologist Marshall Sahlins explained the killing of Captain Cook in Hawaii in 1779 in terms of the myths of the Pacific islanders. The first and second times of his arrival coincided with the islanders' new year, when they expected the return of a god bringing fertility, but the third time he landed, to refit after a storm, the new year was past and Cook was seen as a usurper and killed. 'Different cultural orders', argued Sahlins, 'have their own modes of historical action, consciousness and determination, their own historical practice'.[37]

Meanwhile, some historians were arguing that primary sources were not 'the traces of past facts', or some unmediated window onto the historical past. Letters, reports, even accounts were drawn up according to set styles and conventions, so that the historian had less to worry about the 'bias' of the author of the document they were reading than about the formal nature of that document. In *Fiction in the Archives* (1987), for example, Natalie Zemon Davis examined highly crafted letters of remission written by condemned individuals to the king, requesting pardon as 'one of the best sources of relatively uninterrupted narrative from the lips of the lower orders in sixteenth-century France'.[38] In his history of *The Footnote*, Anthony Grafton pointed out that Ranke took documents such as Venetian ambassadors' reports to their Senate 'as transparent windows on past states and events rather than as colourful reconstructions of them', and as objective ambassadors those who 'wrote within rigid conventions, had not seen or heard everything that they reported, and often wished to convince their own audience of a personal theory rather than simply to tell what happened'.[39]

This new awareness of the narrative devices embedded in both historical accounts and primary sources encouraged some historians to appreciate the close relationship of history and literature, and to experiment themselves with different forms of narrative. Natalie Davis, reading the account of a sixteenth-century judge about a man who pretended to be the husband of a peasant woman whose man had left for the wars and not returned in order to secure home and property, recorded that 'I thought, "This must become a film". Rarely does a historian find so perfect a narrative structure of events of the past or one with such dramatic appeal'. She discovered that a film was in fact being made of this story and became its historical adviser. The set became 'my own historical laboratory, generating not proofs but historical possibilities'. She became sceptical, however, that for dramatic effect the film was 'departing from the historical record', and determined to return to the archives to write her own historical account of *The Return of Martin Guerre*.[40]

Narrative history, for so long regarded as anti-scientific, began to make a comeback. Among the mass of histories that greeted the bicentenary of the French Revolution in 1989, Simon Schama's *Citizens* explored the tensions between liberty and patriotism, and the question of revolutionary violence. Since the Revolution, he argued, was 'much more the product of human agency than structural conditioning, chronology seems indispensable in making its complicated twists and turns intelligible. So *Citizens* returns, then, to the form of the nineteenth-century chronicles, allowing different issues and interests to shape the flow of the story as they arise, year after year, month after month'. Schama said that he had been influenced less by Hayden White than by Richard Cobb, who taught him to see the Revolution 'not as a march of abstractions and ideologies but as a human event of complicated and often tragic outcomes'. If, however, it followed one of Hayden White's plots, it might well have been tragedy, a story of dreams of liberty and equality gone mad and tipping into mob lynching, the Terror and the guillotine. Schama's last image was of the revolutionary Théroigne de Mérincourt, sitting naked in an asylum, 'a logical destination for the compulsions of revolutionary idealism'.[41] Two years later, Schama published *Dead Certainties*, which wove together two very different narratives, one concerning the death of General James Wolfe at Quebec during the Seven Years War in 1759, the other a murder in Boston in 1849. The link turns out to be the nephew of the murdered man, who undertook research into the death of Wolfe. 'In its original Greek sense the word *historia* meant an inquiry', concluded Schama, but 'to have an inquiry, whether into the construction of a legend or the execution of a crime, is surely to require the telling of stories'.[42]

There was not necessarily a contradiction between a more playful use of narrative form and what J. H. Hexter called 'fidelity to records'. 'The standard of judgement of a fictive work does not depend on its compatibility with external reality', he argued, but 'the standard of judgement of a historical work is ultimately extrinsic. Its authenticity, validity and truth depend on the effectiveness with which it communicates knowledge (not misunderstanding) of the actual past, congruent with the surviving record'.[43] Sanctions for historians who were deemed to be careless, if not dishonest, in this respect could be very serious. In 1982 a young American historian, David Abraham, was taken to task by senior members of the profession for the inexactitude of his use of sources for *The Collapse of the Weimar Republic* (1981). In particular it was said that he mistranslated or misinterpreted documents to suggest a closer link between German big business and the Nazi party during the latter's rise to power than the evidence allowed. In part this was a criticism of Abraham's Marxist model of historiography, supposed to be 'scientific', but in fact seeking evidence for a neo-Marxist theory for which Nazism and fascism were the political wing of capitalism in crisis. In part it was a turf war between older historians and an ambitious young historian up for tenure at Princeton. The polemic, however, was fought out over the question of fidelity to the record, and Abrahams was denied tenure as a historian. He retrained as an academic lawyer.[44]

The cosy world in which historians dug up new primary sources or pored over old ones, and wrote their monographs and surveys on the back of them, however, came under frontal attack in the 1990s from the linguistic turn. This, as we have seen, argued that texts were not windows onto the world but media that constructed the world. Indeed, there was no external reality beyond the text. 'There is nothing outside the text', proclaimed Jacques Derrida.[45] To historians brandishing references and footnotes, Roland Barthes retorted that these referred not to some external reality, but simply to other sources. History was dead and gone; it could not be summoned up as evidence except as what it left in textual sources. The queues of footnotes were not reality, only a 'reality effect'.[46] Once this had been established it was no longer possible, it was asserted, to write objective history, upon which everyone could agree. Following the linguistic turn, any historical account was as valid as any other – cultural relativism – and indeed that which posed as 'official history', written by academics from the top universities, but in fact distorted by their white, male, middle-class, imperialist backgrounds, was undoubtedly less valid than accounts written by the victims of history – workers, women and ethnic minorities. Curiously, the politics and moral judgements that had been excluded from historical writing in the nineteenth century were making a comeback.

In many ways the linguistic turn freed up historical writing. The notion that history could and should be written from a multiplicity of voices rather than the synthetic voice of the omniscient historian-narrator had already been advocated by anthropologists who presented historical accounts as culturally specific. Richard Price's *Alabi's World* (1990), which took its name from the chief of the Saramakas, a people of Surinam descended from African slaves who had fought for freedom in the eighteenth century, was written in four voices, set out in the book in four different typefaces. The first was that of the Dutch colonial administrators of the colony, the second that of the missionaries, the Moravian Brethren from Saxony, and the third that of the Saramankas, based on their oral tradition. The fourth was that of the historian, no longer omniscient, plundering the narratives of others to construct his own, but now only one voice among others. Natalie Zemon Davis's *Women at the Margins: Three Seventeenth-Century Lives*, reconstructed from their own writings (and drawings) the lives of a German-Jewish merchant woman, a French Catholic nun who went to North America, and a Protestant Dutch entomologist who travelled to Surinam. All owed much to their religious identity and their craft skills, but each 'forged a sense of herself' individually, and away from the centres of power and learning in Europe.[47]

The option of writing history from a multitude of viewpoints was reinforced by the emergence of the history of memory and oral history. Pierre Nora constructed his *Lieux de mémoire* as symbols, texts and commemorations that together represented a single French Republic and a single French nation. By the time he reached the third volume in 1992, however, he was obliged to acknowledge that French Protestants had different memories from French Catholics, revolutionaries from counter-revolutionaries, Gaullists from communists from Vichyists. Nora's history of collective memory was a history of representations, not of oral testimony, and involved no oral history. Oral history created a whole new range of sources, either as recordings, or as transcripts and translated transcripts. These sources are by definition multiple voices. The historian may well wish to focus on the oral testimony of a particular group, such as working-class British women, Australian war veterans, Italian victims of a Second World War massacre, or French youths who became militants in 1968, but the basic unit will be an interview with a single individual with their own particular life history and experience. The challenge for the historian is to weave a coherent analysis from a multiplicity of individual accounts, each of which has its truth to tell. One way for the Second World War is to explore the tension between the official version of events and the wartime experiences of individuals; another is to register the 'divided memory' of those who resisted fascism and those who survived collective reprisals administered by occupying forces in response to resistance attacks; while a third exposes the 'repressed memory' of people unable to come to terms with traumatic events; but general conclusions will always be based on patterns emerging from samples of individual interviews.[48]

Simon Schama's 2005 book, *Rough Crossings*, was adapted for the theatre and went on tour in Britain in 2007, marking the 200th anniversary there of the abolition of slavery. Telling the story of the British sponsorship of slave emancipation during the American War of Independence from the point of view of two British abolitionists who went on to found the free black settlement of Sierra Leone, and an ex-slave reluctant to accept white rule in Africa, it made use of local colour, narrative drive and changing voices.[49] 'I didn't want to get in his way', said Schama of the director Philip Goold. 'It's absolutely his work. It gets absolutely to core truths of character as well as the essence of the history, but has the poetic licence to embroider.'[50] Whether the poetry got the better of the history is another matter. One critic called the play 'a bit of a history lesson', while *The Stage* picked up 'the unshakeable air of theatre-for-schools, the sort of thing that should be accompanied by a teacher's guide and list of discussion topics'.[51]

Historians have come a long way in the last thirty years. They see documents such as Inquisition records or police reports no longer as 'windows onto the world', but as representations of it, crafted according to certain conventions. They are open to a far wider variety of sources than those produced by the state or church, including letters, diaries, memoirs, with a high degree of subjectivity built into them. They are attuned to hear a multiplicity of voices, divided by class and gender, generation and race, and while maintaining their critical distance are less likely to assume the role of the omniscient historian. They are sensitive to narrative play and fictional devices, often under pressure from publishers and agents to develop plots and characters in order to build a bridge from the 'academic' to the 'general' reader. And yet history remains resolutely different from fiction. It holds firm to the idea that it is about a 'real' past, as evidenced by the documentary traces it has left behind, and as declared in the footnote. 'The culturally contingent and eminently fallible footnote', writes Grafton, 'offers the only guarantee we have that statements about the past derive from identifiable sources. And that is the only ground we have to trust them'.[52]

Jean-Frédéric Schaub

History and literary criticism

Historians are both readers and writers. Far from being an innate skill of scholars, reading requires a careful training. My purpose here is not to privilege cultural studies based on fictional texts over historical work based on archival materials.[53] However, the historian can learn from literary criticism at a basic methodological, if not technical, level. The techniques that define tropes, levels of language, the relationships between writing and meaning, and intertextuality, may be compared with the most technical skills of palaeography perfected by historians.[54] One of the most famous metaphors chosen by Gérard Genette in order to explain his method towards reading literary texts, is that of the palimpsest, a notion that comes from the science of material palaeography.[55] In other words, historians owe a great deal to literary scholars in their understanding of how to read archives, printed material and even images.

As writers, historians need to be aware of the mechanisms, tropes and conventional codes that they derive from reading literature and also from other kinds of texts. These are very basic reasons why history has never ceased to be a branch of literature. In the world of texts, it is both impossible and vain to draw a clear-cut distinction between those which reflect reality and those which are purely fictional. On the one hand, historians may decide to use literary works as sources for their research. And why should they consider that the narrative of a courtier paid to compose chronicles for princes is less fictional than a novel? On the other hand, they may take seriously the ambitions of great writers, particularly during the nineteenth century, to be historians. Many of these explicitly saw themselves as historians when describing contemporary or past societies: Honoré de Balzac, Sir Walter Scott, Alessandro Manzoni, Benito Pérez Galdós, Camilo de Castelo Branco, August Strindberg, and so on. The novels written by these authors may provide insights that are hardly available within the framework of scientific historical research. A book like Balzac's *Les paysans* develops a socio-historical analysis that historians cannot easily achieve. It is a brilliant narrative about local notables, informal power, kinship woven throughout the whole country, and the dependence of the higher authorities on locally grounded social networks. In a sense, this novel may be taken as a methodological lesson for every specialist in the social history of political power. The same can be said about Sir Arthur Conan Doyle's technique of using small clues to access a larger reality, according to a famous essay by Carlo Ginzburg.[56] Coming from the other direction, literary critics may also have a good deal to say about historians. For example, Roland Barthes, a major scholar in literary studies and semiotics, wrote a seminal and very influential book about Jules Michelet, the father of

French historical national narrative.[57]

Professional historians, of course, subscribe to their own professional code. One of these rules is that they have to distinguish legitimate sources, generally archival materials, from less legitimate sources, narratives written (or drawn) with a specific audience in mind. The central opposition here is not that between fiction and non-fiction, but between written (or visual) documents which are produced for specific audiences, and documents produced for practical reasons, evidence for further discussions or internal memoranda. However, written archives derived from institutional organisations, such as the State or the Church, do incorporate legal culture, theological background and fictional imagination, precisely because the writers of these documents were educated and were themselves readers.[58] We must remember that fiction was of major importance in legal expertise and reasoning, and in theological treatises as well. Law, faith and fiction are not disconnected: all three are key elements of the global background of those who wrote the public and private papers that historians consider as 'hard' sources for their research.[59]

A novel as history

When historians decide to study a fictional text or a series of fictions, their research may follow several strategies. To take a novel as a source among other kinds of documents is perhaps the least exciting way to make literature part of a historical approach. To take a novel as a historical phenomenon may be much more creative. Recently, I published a study of Aphra Behn's *Oroonoko*.[60] Aphra Behn, a seventeenth-century English Catholic lady and playwright, was briefly married to a Dutch or German merchant, and was a spy for the Court of Charles II in Holland. My study is a historical essay, based upon the analysis of a novel. This is a twilight text, in which three endings, textual and contextual, cannot be separated. The story tells of the death in Amazonia of an African prince who has been sold to a slave-trader; it was written in 1688 on the eve of the Glorious Revolution and the downfall of the Stuarts; Aphra Behn, a faithful supporter of James II, died a few months later. In a very short period of time, therefore, the black hero, the author and the dynasty she supported meet their end. The martyrdom of the African prince is a clear metaphor of the suffering of the Stuarts.

One of the characters in the story is the author herself, as a twenty-year-old girl. In presenting herself as an eyewitness of the story, Behn asserts that the events are real. Certainly the slave-trade system is seriously and consistently described in her narrative. Does that imply that historians could use this text as a primary source for historical research on the slave trade in the late seventeenth century? The reality of Behn's travel to Amazonia is highly probable, but still not proved. She never went to Africa. But her novel bears witness to the circulation of important texts. A careful investigation of the textual sources of her creation, however traditional it may appear as a method, sheds new light on the English involvement in the global European expansion from the fifteenth century. Within Behn's narrative may be found elements derived from a wide range of previous texts, whether in English, French, Spanish or Italian.

Oroonoko offers a good example of the diversity of resources available for thinking about the Atlantic system in late seventeenth-century London literate milieux. The tone of the book is one of uncertainty and anxiety. It suggests the instability of cultural identities. Aphra Behn creates a fragmented world, in which the self and the other cannot be clearly separated. She expresses a feeling of internal weakness in the ongoing European domination of the world. The seriousness of her information about the Atlantic slave trade cannot be used as direct evidence for the history of slavery, but it is evidence of how central the question was for a London writer during the Restoration. In this case, historical research focuses on the writing of a piece of literary fiction as a cultural, political and social episode within the general evolution of English (or even European) society in the early modern period. Such an approach requires historians to be familiar with the critical tools that may be applied to the literary sources they deal with. Without such expertise in literary analysis, historians may risk, for instance, seeing as oddities that need to be historically explained elements that are simply the internal mechanisms of the text.

Challenges to scientific history

The writing of history and the production of knowledge that supports the claim of history to be scientific in character have been confronted by several challenges in respect of their relationship to texts. The first challenge came from the methods and concepts evolved by literary criticism, which insisted on the primacy of language in the way in which the world is constructed or represented. This claim was scarcely new. Historians have always grappled with the textual nature of the phenomena they observe and with the diversity of ways of making sense of that textuality. According to Hayden White, from the 1970s the historian is taken into a universe of representations whose sheer linguistic and semiotic density prevents any attempt to describe the social realities lying beyond them.[61]

The very idea that historical narrative is nothing but a hidden fictional plot is a seductive hypothesis. It may be a useful tool for accessing non-explicit meanings in documents and books. At the beginning of the professionalisation of historical research, the dominant model was the nineteenth-century novel. In earlier times, the Bible, the epic and perhaps drama were the structural matrices from which most chronicles of the past and present were generated.[62] In a similar way, semiotics is certainly extremely useful in understanding communication, exchanges, the creation and transformation of rules, in the evolution of any society. This is particularly evident in exploring processes of politicisation. However, the general conception that social life is only a text may be just an elegant formula, an assertion that requires no demonstration.[63]

If all historians have to go on is texts, organised according to certain conventions, then they may be able to incorporate imaginary facts into their analysis, as phenomena whose relevance is equal to any other, supposedly real, facts about life in society.[64] In doing, this, they reflect on how phenomena are represented in different ways, and narratives are structured about both the individual and collective past. In their interpretations they have to weigh the competing claims of different kinds of text, a task which requires detailed local studies to be undertaken, and to find a way to give prominence to the greatest possible number of configurations, which vary according to time and place.

Simply to acknowledge the role of textuality in the construction of the subject matter of historical investigation does not necessarily open the door to a cultural relativism. On the contrary, it restores as the subject of historical research old social phenomena that are usually taken for granted, and thus remain unarchived in the ordinary discourse of historical narrative. This is especially true in the case of subject matter of cultural history, as Dominique Kalifa shows in this volume, where the history of phenomena and the history of categories that describe them are permanently embedded.[65]

This leads us to the second challenge thrown down to historians, which derives from the analysis of their discourse as narrative and of their system of verification as a sort of theatre.[66] Historians are skilled in the practice of suggesting the coherence and connectedness of evidence, in spite of the fragmentary nature of available sources. If such a practice is criticised, biography is moved from the status of an obvious genre to a complicated subject.[67] In spite of the apparent unity of an individual's life as historical field, its coherence is only an illusion of stability, for this field is as artificial as any other. In addition, biographies are often dependent on literary models, from the religious confessions to the eighteenth- and nineteenth-century individualistic novel.

The critical analysis of regimes of historicity, which have succeeded one another and from time to time have co-existed, suggests different ways of writing history. It could be argued that historians are equipped with the theoretical tools that enable them not to give in to the temptation of a relativism that is as much ideological as methodological.[68] Can we nevertheless avoid questioning the relationship between historical writing and narrative? Historians and experts in textual and discourse analysis need to examine the rhetorical models that underpin narrative writing. It must be recognised that non-continuous narrative is an asset rather than a difficulty, both in literary fiction and in historical research.

Historians are involved with the textual character of the traces of the past at many levels. They reflect upon the semiotic entanglement in which historical actors get involved as they relate to their own social world. They also reflect on their own writing codes as well as those of the past. The necessary answer to the challenge of textuality cannot be found in a clear-cut assertion that all historians have the same disciplinary identity. Do scholars whose work relies upon archival materials really have better access to the reality of past societies than those who only deal with literary sources? This is the wrong question. It is infinitely more fruitful to produce series of detailed responses, which accept that different historical approaches will have different rules of research.

However, historians cannot give a simple answer to questions raised by the primacy of language. Procedures of verification in history, which are constructed by analogy with experimentation in the natural sciences, cannot ignore what specialists in literary and linguistic domains have suggested about ways in which fiction is produced. There has been a powerful renewal of scientific interest in the technical identification of fictional strategies. It has used methods from the study of cognition, giving rise to innovative interdisciplinary results.[69] What is distinctive about fiction can provide historians with the potentially decisive analytical tool in the search for an adequate way of handling the textual materials they construct into sources of knowledge.

In this way, the expectations of historians and literary scholars may be seen to converge. Modes in which fiction is constructed are shaped by historical period, as even the most formal approaches to fiction must accept. Observable variations in modes of reading and writing strategies send us back, for some explanations, to the cultural systems in which they occur. This leads us to a socio-historical analysis. Both research on the formal structures of texts and the willingness of historians to shed light on social variations have become the elements of a new methodological approach.[70] Formal and cognitive identification techniques of analysing fictional discourse can become crucial to a historical approach, which is concerned with both the discursive and historical nature of its sources.[71] The underlying mechanisms by which historical discourse generates continuity, causality and purpose can be effectively explored in this way.

The poverty of grand narrative

The civic dimension, one might say 'ritual', to which the writing of history is subject in democratic political regimes has recently become quite shaken up. We may consider, for instance, the impact of the construction of Europe on existing modes of historical writing.[72] In most countries, massive transfers of sovereignty and new territorial organisation, scarcely imaginable only a half a century ago, have already changed the dominant framework of historical enquiry.[73] There has been a great deal of academic soul-searching about how to write national histories, from the melancholy inventory of sites of national memory to questioning whether the nation is the most suitable framework for asking historical questions, from the adoption of an anthropological approach to a wider understanding of our own past, to a recognition of the gaps that separate us decisively from the previous states of European societies.[74] In spite of the confusion brought about by the relationship between history and memory, historians have been asked to say precisely which kinds of chronological, cultural and institutional framing are most useful to get away from illusions of identity and continuity in writing a nation's history.[75]

A commemorative fever gripped many countries from the end of the 1970s. Celebrations included the bicentenary of the French Revolution, the fifth centenary of Luther's birth, the fifth centenary of the great Spanish and Portuguese discoveries, the anniversaries of Charles V's birth and Philip II's death, and the thousandth anniversary of the baptism of Clovis, to name but a few. This fever coincided with a high tide of methodological scepticism, especially damaging among historians, and has only served to widen the gap between history as a subject for study, and history as a tool of identity, unity and legitimacy in our societies. These commemorations have stimulated a return to the practice of monumental writing, which endowed historical writing with a quasi-constitutional function in the nineteenth century, when the invention of national history was used to generate a sense of national belonging.[76] Historians contributed in this way to the construction of national sovereignty. Communion around great collective events was intended to strengthen civic ties in societies where the original social contracts seemed to have weakened or to have been forgotten. Since then the fervour for apology for the misdeeds of nations may have an atomising effect in the opposite direction. It is much too early to tell.

The political function served by the wave of memorial ceremonies has become the subject of historical and cultural analysis in its own right. Yet one must also measure their effects on the writing of history, especially its tendency to legitimise certain grand historical narratives that lay the foundation of both cultural identity and political coherence. In this context, it is uncertain whether the scepticism or relativism much dreaded in certain academic milieux has modified in any profound sense existing forms of historical writing. These modes are usually based on a rigorous examination of texts regarded as sources, on an assumption of continuity of national history, and on a reconstruction of causes which is most consonant with contemporary common sense.[77]

In the 1980s, the French Centre National de la Recherche Scientifique (CNRS) launched a colossal research programme, 'Genesis of the Modern State', which was later taken up by the European Science Foundation programme under the barely modified title of 'Origins of the Modern State'. The results of this project were disappointing, notably because of the difficulty of breaking away from an entrenched institutional history.[78] It was too much to ask for the revision of categories derived from contemporary constitutions and institutions in order to reconstitute much older processes of politicisation in European societies.[79] The only real successes that political history registered came from the importation of two hermeneutic approaches, each of a noticeably different construction.

On the one hand, the work of intellectual historians such as John Pocock, Quentin Skinner and the contributors to the Ideas in Context series has achieved the most thorough reconstitution of the intertextual space in which the texts and political theories develop. A study of these texts' horizon of pertinence helps us to understand how they were received, interpreted and debated by the audiences and actors of the period. Reinhardt Koselleck's project to establish a historical dictionary of concepts supplied another spectrum of critical tools to political historians.[80] Within French scholarship, Paul Bénichou's outstanding four-volume work on French Romanticism has been a wonderful achievement for literary scholars and historians alike.[81] On the other hand, legal historians such as Pietro Costa, Bartolomé Clavero[82] and António Manuel Hespanha,[83] have reconstituted systems of legal dogma based on both textual traditions and theories of interpretation. They have established everything that distinguishes these legal conventions from current ones, and above all from political ideologies.

Historians have reaped considerable benefits from the work of practitioners of textual and literary analysis. Here are some examples: theories and research on the audiences of literary works and theories of public space in the political order;[84] the release from the 'authorialness' of the writer and the emergence of the individual as subject to the law;[85] the role of the monarchy in the regulation of academic style and the birth of the great corpus of the State.[86] Furthermore, we need to understand the political and cultural contexts that give meaning to the construction of (national) histories of literature. There is no doubt that collective investment in the cult of late, great writers (Goethe, Hugo, Zola, Scott, Manzoni, d'Amicis, Ibsen, Sôseki) still plays a large role in the development of a sense of national citizenship, for the construction of national pride is as important as the enforcement of constitutional law. It may also be useful to compare the diverse itineraries of history and literature in various countries, for it may not be that all societies have the same conception of the national importance of their national literary anthology.

Working with cultural difference

To escape from still powerful simplifications, historians rightly wish to free themselves from questions of identity. The easiest way to avoid the temptation of identity is to recognise that the subjectivity of the historian-author cannot reach back through personal memory more than two or three generations. Once this threshold has been passed, the claim that we can recover certain – no longer valid – conditions of the societies that preceded our own can be described as a sort of partisan recreation which lacks any scientific credibility.

The notion of 'otherness' has given the historians relative immunity from contemporary power politics when they study societies that are not their own. This brings us back to our starting point: such a critical distance may not be achieved without a sharp critique of what is implicit in historical writing, whether in its pedagogical, ceremonial or scientific versions. Here, the techniques of formal narrative analysis of how the past is narrated have a strategic role to play.

Finally, historians, philosophers and literary specialists must be willing to respond as one to the denunciation of European human sciences formulated by a number of colleagues from the former colonies. An ambition to 'provincialise' Europe has recently been voiced by Dipesh Chakrabarty.[87] His manifesto asserts that the universalist and self-centred model of colonialist Europe has never been the subject of criticism from Europe itself. This requires that non-Europeans turn their backs on European academic milieux, particularly those which attempt to understand historical and cultural societies outside Europe. Historians, sociologists and other European specialists of human and social sciences could see themselves divested of their authority because they are rooted in a system that is at the same time domineering and self-referential, to the point of not being aware of its own singularity.

There are several possible responses to this charge. It is easy to show that European authors first raised the question of the diversity of civilisations. The very concept of civilisation, from its birth in the middle of the seventeenth century, had two opposite meanings: a big narrative of a unified conception of humankind, and a tool available for describing the diversity of human cultures. Four series of scholarships, at least, made compatible such a double meaning: philosophical criticism from Diderot and Nietzsche onwards, philological and linguistic enquiries, the comparative studies of narrative forms and historical research. This made possible, although only possible, setting aside notions of superiority or advance of one civilisation over another. Historians and literary specialists point out that a new awareness of social and cultural difference was the fruit of philosophical and cultural work that was specifically European.[88]

We can thus gauge the extent to which the historian's conscious turn towards the textual character of his sources, the primacy of language over social and normative institutions, can only be enriched by collaboration with the work of literary scholars, especially when it comes to the relationship between historical narrative and fiction. Our aim has been to bring to light the promise of such interdisciplinary collaboration.

Conclusion

If one tries to ascertain to what extent history is still (or has become again) a branch of literature, the question of the intellectual relationship between historians and other scholars is central. There is no doubt that critical approaches to texts, the conscious ordering of knowledge and skills, and attempts to understand meaning are the three main indications that history is both a scientific discipline and a liberal art. As a consequence, there is no contradiction between the recognition of its dependence on literary traditions and its status as social science. History, then, may be presented as a backbone of a system in which the humanities and social sciences are interconnected. This has implications of real importance, especially when one bears in mind the need to develop comparative studies. To do so, historians need to facilitate communication between scholars in history departments and the historians belonging to area studies departments, whose main orientation is frequently in linguistics and literature. Literature reminds us how difficult is it to be readers and writers at the same time. This is a problem every scholar has confronted, at least once, most probably every day.

Notes

1   Thomas Carlyle, *The French Revolution* (Oxford University Press, 1989 [1837]), 188–200.
2   Charles Dickens, *A Tale of two Cities* (London, Penguin, 1985 [1859]), 244–7.
3   Mark Cumming, *A Disemprisoned Epic. Form and Vision in Carlyle's French Revolution* (Philadelphia, University of Pennsylvania Press, 1988), 52, 63–5, 85, 112–13.
4   Jules Michelet to Alfred Dumesnil, 28 July 1846, in Michelet, *Correspondance Générale* V (1846–48) (Paris, Honoré Champion, 1996), 163.
5   Jules Michelet, *Histoire de la Révolution Française* (Paris, Robert Laffont, 1979 [1847]), 144–5, 330. See also Lionel Gossman, *Between History and Literature* (Cambridge, Mass. and London, Harvard University Press, 1990), 167–205.
6   Victor Hugo to Jules Michelet, 30 Nov. 1847, in Michelet, *Correspondance Générale* V, 456.
7   Cited in Leopold Ranke, *The Secret of World History. Selected Writings on the Art and Science of History*, ed. Roger Wines (New York, Fordham University Press, 1981), 58.
8   Ranke, *Zur Kritik neuerer Geschichtschreiber* (Leipzig and Berlin, 1824), 28, cited by Felix Gilbert, *History, Politics or Culture? Reflections on Ranke and Burckhardt* (Princeton University Press, 1990), 20.
9   Cited in Leopold Ranke, *The Secret of World History*, 58.
10 Leopold Ranke, *The History of the Popes, their Church and State in the Sixteenth and Seventeenth Centuries* (London, 1843).
11 Leopold Ranke, *Memoirs of the House of Brandenburg and History of Prussia during the Seventeenth and Eighteenth centuries* (3 vols., London, 1849).
12 Leopold Ranke, 'The Great Powers' [1833], in Theodore von Laue, *Leopold von Ranke. The Formative Years* (Princeton University Press, 1950), 181–218.
13 Friedrich Meinecke, 'Leopold von Ranke', in *Historicism* (London, Routledge and Kegan Paul, 1972), 499–500. See also Georg G. Iggers, *The German Conception of History* (Middletown, Conn., Wesleyan University Press, 1968), 63–81.
14 Lord Acton, Inaugural lecture on the study of history, 11 June 1895, in *Lectures in Modern History* (London, Macmillan, 1906), 11, 19.
15 Lord Acton, 'Letter to Contributors to the Cambridge History', 12 March 1898, in *Lectures in Modern*

History, 315–18.

16 Ibid., 317.

17 *The Cambridge Modern History*, planned by the late Lord Acton. *I. The Renaissance* (Cambridge University Press, 1904), vii.

18 Lord Acton, *Lectures on the French Revolution* (London, Macmillan, 1910), 300.

19 Charles-Victor Langlois and Charles Seignobos, *Introduction to the Study of History* (London, Duckworth, 1898), 17, 141, 211.

20 Charles Seignobos, *Histoire politique de l'Europe contemporaine. Evolution des parties et des formes politiques* (Paris, A. Colin, 1897), v–ix, 805.

21 See, for example, François Simiand, *Les fluctuations économiques à longue durée et la crise mondiale* (Paris, Alcan, 1932).

22 Charles-Olivier Carbonnell and Georges Livet, *Au berceau des Annales. Le milieu strasbourgeois, l'histoire en France au début du XX siècle* (Toulouse, Presses de l'Institut d'Études Politiques de Toulouse, 1983).

23 Marc Bloch, *La Société Féodale* (2 vols., Paris, Albin Michel, 1939–40).

24 Fernand Braudel, *The Mediterranean and the Mediterranean World in the Age of Philip II* (New York, Harper & Row, 1972), 21.

25 Emmanuel Le Roy Ladurie, *Le nouvel observateur*, 8 May 1968, reprinted in *The Territory of the Historian* (Hassocks, Harvester Press, 1979), 6.

26 Robert Fogel, *Railroads and American Economic Growth* (Baltimore, Johns Hopkins University Press, 1964).

27 Robert William Fogel and Stanley L. Engerman, *Time on the Cross. The Economics of American Negro Slavery* (Boston and Toronto, Little, Brown, 1974), 5–7.

28 Georges Lefebvre, 'Le mouvement des prix et la Révolution Française', *Annales d'histoire économique et sociale* 44 (1937), 167.

29 George Lefebvre, *Quatre-vingt-neuf* (Paris, Maison du livre français, 1939), translated as *The Coming of the French Revolution* (Princeton University Press, 1947).

30 Braudel, *The Mediterranean*, II, 1236.

31 Charlotte Erikson, review of Fogel, *Railroads and American Economic Growth* in *Economica* 33 (1966), 107.

32 Hayden White, *Metahistory. The Historical Imagination in Nineteenth Century Europe* (Baltimore and London, Johns Hopkins University Press, 1973), ix.

33 Hayden White, 'The value of narrativity in the representation of reality', *Critical Inquiry* 7 (1980), 5–27, reprinted in Hayden White, *The Content of Form. Narrative Discourse and Historical Representation* (Baltimore and London, Johns Hopkins University Press, 1987), ch. 1.

34 Hayden White, *Metahistory*, 149–264.

35 Lawrence Stone, 'The revival of narrative: reflections on a new old history', *Past & Present* 85 (1979), 3–24.

36 Nathan Wachtel, *Vision of the Vanquished. The Spanish Conquest of Peru seen through Indian Eyes, 1530–1570* (Hassocks, Harvester Press, 1977).

37 Marshall Sahlins, *Islands of History* (University of Chicago Press, 1985), 34.

38 Natalie Zemon Davis, *Fiction in the Archives: Pardon Tales and their Tellers in Sixteenth-Century France* (Cambridge, Polity Press, 1987), 5.

39 Anthony Grafton, *The Footnote. A Curious History* (London, Faber and Faber, 2003), 60.

40 Natalie Zemon Davis, *The Return of Martin Guerre* (Cambridge, Mass. and London, Harvard University Press, 1983), vii–viii.

41 Simon Schama, *Citizens. A Chronicle of the French Revolution* (London, Folio Society, 2004), I, xiv, 841.

42 Simon Schama, *Dead Certainties (Unwarranted Speculations)* (London, Granta Books, 1991), 325.

43 J. H. Hexter, 'Rhetoric in history', in *Doing History* (London, Allen & Unwin, 1971), 47–8.

44 David Abraham, *The Collapse of the Weimar Republic* (Princeton University Press, 1981, 2nd edition 1986). See reviews by Henry Turner, *Political Science Quarterly* 97 (1982–83), 739–41, by Tim Mason, *American Historical Review* 87 (1982), 1122–3, by Charles Meier, *Journal of Modern History* 56 (1984), 89–95, and debates between Turner, Mason and Abraham in *American Historical Review* 88 (1983), 1142–9 and between Gerald Feldman and Turner, *Central European History* 17 (1984), 169–293.

45 Jacques Derrida, *Of Grammatology* (Baltimore, Johns Hopkins University Press, 1997), 158–9.

46 Barthes, 'Le discours de l'histoire' and 'L'effet du reel', in *Le bruissement de la langue* (Paris, Le Seuil, 1984), translated as 'The discourse of history' and 'The reality effect', in *The Rustle of Language* (Oxford, Blackwell, 1986), 127–48.

47 Natalie Zemon Davis's *Women at the Margins: Three Seventeenth-Century Lives* (Cambridge, Mass. and London, Harvard University Press, 1995).

48 Alistair Thomson, *Anzac Memories: Living with the Legend* (Melbourne and Oxford, Oxford University Press, 1994); Alessandro Portelli, 'The massacre of Civitella Val di Chiana (Tuscany, June 29, 1944): Myth and politics, mourning and common sense', in his *The Battle of Valle Giulia. Oral History and the Art of Dialogue* (Madison, University of Wisconsin Press, 1997), 140–60 ; Michelle Mouton and Helena Pohlandt-McCormick, 'Boundary crossings: oral history of Nazi Germany and Apartheid South Africa', *History Workshop Journal* 48 (1999), 41–63.

49 Simon Schama, *Rough Crossings. Britain, the Slaves and the American Revolution* (London, BBC Books, 2003).

50 *The Daily Telegraph*, 12 Sept. 2007.

51 www.musicomh.com/theatre/rough-crossings_0907.htm; www.thestage.co.uk/reviews/review.php/18363/rough-crossings

52 Grafton, *The Footnote*, 233.

53 Arlette Farge, *Le goût de l'archive* (Paris, Le Seuil, 1989).

54 D. F. MacKenzie, *Bibliography and the Sociology of Texts* (London, British Library, 1986); Fernando Bouza, *Corre manuscrito. Una historia cultural del Siglo de Oro* (Madrid, Marcial Pons, 2001); Roger Chartier, *Inscrire et effacer. Culture écrite et littérature (XIe–XVIIIe siècle)* (Paris, Gallimard-Seuil, Hautes Études series, 2005).

55 Gérard Genette, *Palimpsestes* (Paris, Le Seuil, 1982).

56 Carlo Ginzburg, 'Clues: the roots of an evidential paradigm', in Ginzburg, *Myths, Emblems, Clues* (London, Hutchinson, 1990), 96–125.

57 Roland Barthes, *Michelet* (Paris, Le Seuil, 1954).

58 Carlos Petit, *Pasiones del jurista. Amor, memoria, melancolía, imaginación* (Madrid, Centro de Estudios Políticos y Constitucionales, 1997).

59 Paolo Grossi, *L'ordine giuridico medievale* (Rome, Laterza, 2001).

60 Jean-Frédéric Schaub, *Oroonoko, prince et esclave. Roman de l'incertitude coloniale* (Paris, Le Seuil, 2008).

61 Hayden White, *The Historical Imagination in Nineteenth-Century Europe* (Baltimore and London, Johns Hopkins University Press, 1973).

62 David Quint, *Epic and Empire. Politics and Generic Form from Virgil to Milton* (Princeton University Press, 1993).

63 Arlette Farge and Jacques Revel, *Logiques de la foule. L'affaire des enlèvements d'enfants, Paris 1750* (Paris, Hachette, 1988); Michèle Fogel, *Les cérémonies de l'information dans la France du XVIe siècle au XVIIIe siècle* (Paris, Fayard, 1989); Gérard Sabatier, *Versailles ou la figure du roi* (Paris, Albin Michel, 1999).

64 Gabrielle Spiegel, *The Past as Text: The Theory and Practice of Medieval Historiography* (Baltimore, Johns Hopkins University Press, 1997); Stephen Greenblatt, *Marvelous Possessions. The Wonder of the New World* (University of Chicago Press, 1991); Denis Crouzet, *Les guerriers de Dieu. La violence au temps des troubles de religion (vers 1525–vers 1610)* (Seyssel, Champ Vallon, 2005).

65 Michael Werner and Bénédicte Zimmermann, 'Penser l'histoire croisée: entre empirie et réflexivité', *Annales. Histoires sciences sociales* 1 (2003), 7–36. See above, pp. 47–56.

66 Paul Ricœur, *Temps et récit* (3 vols., Paris, Le Seuil, 1983, 1984, 1985).1. L'intrigue et le récit historique; 2. La configuration dans le récit de fiction; 3. Le temps raconté.

67 Pierre Bourdieu, 'L'illusion biographique', *Actes de la recherche en sciences sociales*, 62–63 (1986), 69–72; Sabina Loriga, 'La biographie comme problème', in Jacques Revel, ed., *Jeux d'échelles. La micro-analyse à l'expérience* (Paris, Seuil-Gallimard, 1996); Sabina Loriga, 'Tolstoï dans le scepticisme de l'histoire', *Esprit* (June 2005), 6–25.

68 Joyce Appleby, Lynn Hunt and Margaret Jacob, *Telling the Truth about History* (London, W. W. Norton, 1995); Roger Chartier, *Au bord de la falaise. L'histoire entre certitudes et inquiétudes* (Paris, Albin Michel, 1998).

69 Jean-Marie Schaeffer, *Pourquoi la fiction?* (Paris, Le Seuil, Poétique series, 1999).

70 Alain Boureau, 'La compétence inductive. Un modèle d'analyse des représentations rares', in Bernard Lepetit, ed., *Les formes de l'expérience. Une autre histoire sociale* (Paris, Albin Michel, 1995) 23–38.

71 Jean-Claude Passeron, *Le raisonnement sociologique* (Paris, Nathan, 1991).

72 Marcello Verga, *Storie di Europa. Secoli XVIII–XXI* (Rome, Carocci, 2004).

73 Juan Sisinio Pérez Garzón, *La gestión de la memoria. La historia de España al servicio del poder* (Barcelona, Crítica, 2000).

74 Alain Guerreau, *L'avenir d'un passé incertain. Quelle histoire du Moyen Âge au XXIe siècle?* (Paris, Le Seuil, 2001).

75 Pierre Nora, 'Entre mémoire et histoire, la problématique des lieux de mémoire', introduction to *Les lieux*

de mémoire, vol. I, La République (Paris, Gallimard, 1984).

76 François Hartog and Jacques Revel, eds., *Les usages politiques du passé* (Paris, Editions de l'EHESS, Enquête series, 2001).

77 Steven Englund, 'The ghost of nation past', *Journal of Modern History* 64 (1992), 299–320.

78 Jean-Frédéric Schaub, 'Le temps et l'État: vers un nouveau régime historiographique de l'Ancien Régime français', *Quaderni fiorentini per la storia del pensiero giuridico moderno* 25 (1996).

79 Robert Descimon and Alain Guéry, 'Un État des temps modernes?', in André Burguière and Jacques Revel, eds., *Histoire de la France. La longue durée de l'État*, vol. ed. Jacques Le Goff (Paris, Le Seuil, 2000), 209–534; Angela de Benedictis, *Politica, governo e istituzioni nell'Europa moderna* (Bologna, Il Mulino, 2001).

80 Javier Fernández Sebastián, *Diccionario político y social del siglo XIX español* (Madrid, Alianza, 2003).

81 Paul Bénichou, *Le sacre de l'écrivain 1750–1830: essai sur l'avènement d'un pouvoir spirituel laïque dans la France moderne* (Paris, Gallimard, 1996 [1973]); Paul Bénichou, *Le temps des prophètes: doctrines de l'âge romantique* (Paris, Gallimard, 1977); Paul Bénichou, Les mages romantiques (Paris, Gallimard, 1988); Paul Bénichou, L'école du désenchantement. Sainte-Beuve, Nodier, Musset, Nerval, Gautier (Paris, Gallimard, 1992).

82 Bartolomé Clavero, *Razón de estado, razón de individuo, razón de historia* (Madrid, Centro de Estudios Políticos y Constitucionales, 1991); Bartolomé Clavero, *La grâce du don. Anthropologie catholique de l'économie moderne* (Paris, Albin Michel, 1996).

83 António Manuel Hespanha, *La gracia del derecho. Economía de la cultura en la Edad Moderna* (Madrid, Centro de Estudios Políticos y Constitucionales, 1993).

84 Hélène Merlin-Kajman, *Public et littérature en France au XVIIe siècle* (Paris, Les Belles Lettres, 1994).

85 Michel Foucault, *Naissance de la bio-politique* (Paris, Le Seuil-Gallimard, Hautes Études series, 2004); Christian Jouhaud, *Les pouvoirs de la littérature. Histoire d'un paradoxe* (Paris, Gallimard, 2000).

86 Hélène Merlin-Kajman, *L'excentricité académique. Littérature, histoire, société* (Paris, Les Belles Lettres, 2001).

87 Dipesh Chakrabarty, *Provincializing Europe. Postcolonial Thought and Historical Difference* (Princeton University Press, 2000).

88 Jean Starobinski, 'Le mot civilisation', *Le remède dans le mal. Critique de l'artifice à l'âge des Lumières* (Paris, Gallimard, 1989), 11–59.

6

How should historians deal with extreme political change and political violence?

David Andress and Sophie Wahnich

For a long time political history was marginalised as 'the history of political events', a narrative of kings and queens, battles and peace treaties. In recent years it has made a comeback, exploring new and difficult subjects such as political violence, drawing on the insights of other disciplines such as anthropology, philosophy and psychoanalysis. Here the French Revolution is taken as a case study. David Andress *explores the shift from Marxist historians who regarded political violence as an unproblematic feature of the revolutionary process, to historians who judged the use of violence to discredit all revolution. He traces the emergence of a more sophisticated understanding of violence, which takes into account political culture and the reality of counter-revolution with which revolutionaries were confronted.* Sophie Wahnich *investigates the psychic as well as the social forces behind extreme political change, the hopes and fears of French revolutionaries, stranded in a no-man's-land between past and future. She shows how the revolutionaries elaborated rules governing political violence and did their best to install a new free and equal political order without recourse to violence.*

David Andress

Violence: for and against

In asking how historians should approach this thorny issue, an evident starting point is to explore how they have done so. Taking the French Revolution as our case study, a survey of writings over the last generation shows that attitudes have turned from accepting revolutionary violence, to starkly rejecting it, and finally towards much more complex reflections on its causes. Prior to the bicentenary of the revolution in 1989, Anglophone writers on the topic tended to take one of three paths. The first, perhaps the most original in formulation, and the most international, both in focus and personnel, was that of the 'Atlantic Revolution'. In this view, put forward most notably by R. R. Palmer's two-volume *The Age of Democratic Revolutions*, what had happened in France needed to be seen in the light of the American Revolution, and also in a wider sphere of modernising upheaval that brought to birth the individualistic, capitalistic societies of the West.[1] It is no criticism of this view to note that, in its way, much like the sociological structural-functionalism of the same era, this was a cold war response to the overarching claims of Marxism for a particular class-based interpretation of revolutionary history. The hegemony of Marxist, class-based interpretations is visible, for example, in the French counterpart of Palmer, Jacques Godechot, whose *France and the Atlantic Revolution of the Eighteenth Century* states matter-of-factly that 'The revolution in France did not in fact begin with a popular uprising or even with a riot instigated by the bourgeoisie, but with a revolt of the aristocracy'. This accepts without question the canonical interpretation given by Georges Lefebvre in 1939, that there had been a series of distinct, class-based 'revolutions' in 1787–89, adding up to the one great 'French Revolution'.[2]

The second path, opened by Alfred Cobban in a series of lectures later published in 1964 as *The Social Interpretation of the French Revolution*, became in time a major challenge to the Marxist 'orthodoxy'.[3] In itself sometimes little more than a set of sweeping claims, but later reinforced by major empirical scholarship, this anglophone 'revisionism' countered the claims of Marxism about revolution as the tool of a rising bourgeoisie with two key evidence-based points: first, that the personnel of the revolution tended to come far more from the legal and administrative sectors than from the supposedly dynamic and formerly suppressed capitalist class of merchants and traders; and second, that at the heart of French society was not the decisive chasm between a 'feudal' nobility and a repressed bourgeoisie, but rather a zone of fusion, where nobility was relatively easily purchased by wealth, and where industrial investment was as likely to be carried out by dukes and marquises as by commoner entrepreneurs. In short, revisionism argued, the dramatic structural conflict posed by Marxism as the driving force of revolutionary change did not exist.[4]

Without an easy overarching explanation for the upheaval of the revolution, and its violence, historians could reach in one of two directions. The first represents the third major pre-1989 path of writing: to turn to the provinces, and under the auspices of the eccentrically brilliant Oxford scholar Richard Cobb, to immerse oneself in the archival records of a particular place, revealing the rich and often grimy texture of pre-revolutionary and revolutionary life. Cobb's own books, appearing through the 1960s and early 1970s, represented a notably individual view of revolutionary violence.[5] Fascinated by low-life and underworlds, verging almost on the voyeuristic in his attention to sordid recitals of assaults, murders and other crimes of passion, opportunity and premeditation, Cobb showed, first, that the great transformations of revolution often meant nothing, or no more than additional hardship, to those who lived down among the people; and second, that some at least of those who rose to greater prominence on the tide of violent revolution knew or cared little for its supposed ideals. Seen with dispassionate eyes, such men were little better than the 'blood-drinkers' their counter-revolutionary enemies had always painted them as.

Those who followed in Cobb's wake were rarely as cynical. Some, such as Alan Forrest, married the concern for archival detail and provincial realities with a stern evaluation of the merits of revolutionary philanthropy, producing in *The French Revolution and the Poor* an unvarnished vision of the suffering caused by upheaval to those who most needed the support of society.[6] In this Forrest was following the equally pioneering work of Olwen Hufton, who had unearthed the hidden world of poverty in the eighteenth century, and was to go on to press the claims of women for historical attention – especially when they, to the scorn and detestation of male revolutionaries, rejected political slogans in favour of older verities and pressing material concerns.[7] Other 'Cobbists' included Colin Lucas, whose work on *The Structure of the Terror* illustrated the complex dynamic between local allegiances and adherence to the violent demands of revolutionary authority. Echoing Cobb in its clear-eyed portrait of brutality, but also with a more refined analytical sensibility regarding underlying structures and local anthropologies, Lucas's work showed that one could make systematic observations without needing a 'system' à la Marxism within which to insert them.[8]

While the Cobbist turn dug deep into social realities and local political interactions, a final pre-bicentenary turn brought both cultural and political structures into new focus. Lynn Hunt, in *Politics, Culture and Class in the French Revolution*, produced a remarkable Janus-faced work, at once a political sociology, and a reading of signs and texts in the emergent frame of 'new cultural history'.[9] Moving away from the quest for causal explanation towards a 'reading' of the events and their implications, Hunt noted the drives towards linguistic innovation at the heart of revolutionary discourse, as well as their equally strong tendencies to demonise and exclude. Alongside this, and in some respects almost unconnected to it, Hunt also performed a statistical analysis of local elites through the revolutionary years, depicting in concrete terms the rise to power of a new bourgeois stratum, and thus calling into question some of the 'debunking' aspects of the Anglo-American revisionism of previous decades.

At the bicentenary of the revolution in 1989, there can be no doubt that Simon Schama's *Citizens*, with its unalloyed contention that 'In some depressingly inevitable sense, violence *was* the French Revolution', altered the focus of attention dramatically.[10] Schama provided a reactionary populist account, in which disreputable elements of the urban population, driven on by discontented intellectuals fetishizing violence from their own resentments, destroyed a golden age of aristocratic refinement, governmental moderation and rational economic reform. Such a view, with its exaggerations, was nonetheless also in tune with a more intellectually rigorous publication of the same time. Keith Michael Baker, in *Inventing the French Revolution*, pieced together key elements of the philosophical thought and political responses of the generation that made the revolution of 1789, asserting that, through the choices made at the very start of the revolution, such men were essentially 'opting for the Terror.'[11]

While previous forms of 'revisionism' were motivated by the shortcomings of an increasing schematic Marxist account, and by a worthy drive to reclaim underused archival sources, these new modes, coming as they did at the point of collapse of the Soviet Union's empire in east-central Europe, and coinciding with the apotheosis in France of François Furet's essentially pessimistic interpretation of the deadly power of revolutionary discourse, seem almost overtly to be ideological products.[12] The suggestion that flowed from them was that the injection of revolutionary violence into a body-politic was, at best, a mistake of gargantuan proportions, and, at worst, a symptom of the vileness of the mob, best extruded from judgement of affairs of state.[13] In the world-historical moment of the late 1980s and early 1990s, perhaps best summed up in Francis Fukuyama's famous pronouncement that the fall of the USSR marked 'the end of history', the undying triumph of liberal-capitalist propertied order, an attention to violence generated from intrasocietal conflicts as a wholly negative phenomenon was, one might say, entirely predictable.[14]

Violence in context

In the face of this apparent global triumph, there have been very few voices willing to resuscitate the cool acceptance of the Terror that marked classical Marxist accounts. Where efforts have been made to revive the value of Marx's insights, they have taken the route, with George Comninel, of reinterpreting Marx's model of the structural preconditions of revolution, or more recently, with Henry Heller, of simply reasserting a view of the significance of the capitalist bourgeoisie to the structural changes of the revolution, and sliding over more difficult causal questions.[15] However, while the most recent generation of revolutionists have avoided head-on confrontation with the question of violence, many have taken paths around this central impasse which ultimately sketch out a new route onwards.

Some attempts to skirt round violence have been less than successful. Patrice Higonnet's study of the ideology of revolutionary Jacobinism was so concerned to raise his protagonists above the imputation that their ideas were merely bloodthirsty, that he was forced to palm off those aspects of their thought, rather unconvincingly, on to 'inherited social atavisms', the consequence of 'long habits of absolutist politics and intolerant religion'.[16] Others, who have moved further away into reconsiderations of the dynamics of events in both the short and longer terms, have developed more telling analyses. One of the most productive avenues has been to turn aside from the events of the revolution itself, and indeed from the supposed 'revolutionaries' among the lower classes, and to reappraise the nobility. At first glance, much of this work would seem to be following a classic 'revisionist' pattern of saving the nobility from charges of blanket privilege, economic backwardness and political and cultural disengagement, but the deeper structure of noble identity thus revealed points towards telling criticisms of their basic attitudes, and a re-evaluation of just how much was at stake in 1789.

Rafe Blaufarb and Jay Smith, in overlapping works on the military nobility of France before and during the revolution, establish a series of key points: the officer-class was not immune to the claims of merit; they were highly conscious of the damaging effects of unalloyed privilege; and they were heavily engaged in professional discussions over structural reforms.[17] But, and this is the key point, the 'merit' reformers advocated was essentially that of the humble provincial noble, whose aptitude for leadership was bred in the bone; the 'privilege' they were averse to was that of haughty courtiers short-cutting the promotions system, and, even worse, that of the recently ennobled buying themselves precedence over ancient families. The 'reforms' such men sought, couched in the language of 'careers, talent, merit', to echo Blaufarb's title, were a fundamental endorsement of the unique and privileged relationship of the nobility to the crown, and a repudiation in advance of the revolutionary claims to overturn such connections in the name of equality. Even more recently, Jay Smith has highlighted the extent to which the nobility had for decades before the Revolution embraced an overt language of 'patriotism' – the very warp and weft of revolutionary sentiments in 1789 – but had used it, in large part, to advance their claims for special treatment by the state.[18]

In such assessments, the classic 'revisionist' view of the nobility's forward-thinking butts up against such men's ardent concerns to continue to justify their own privileges against any attack from below. Elements of this have been clear in some historians' writing for some time: as early as 1991, Gail Bossenga highlighted in a local study of Lille how elites consistently bewailed the privilege of those 'above' them, while fighting furiously to resist any pretensions to equality from those 'below'.[19] Michael Kwass, drawing on in-depth study of taxation in Normandy, shows a similar pattern: while nobles and other privileged groups paid considerable taxes in the eighteenth century, contrary to old stereotypes, they did so grudgingly, at far lower levels than the 'unprivileged', and at the cost of continual pleas and negotiations with local authorities for exceptions, exemptions and special treatment.[20]

But are we not, in talking of taxation and service, moving away from the problem of violence? Not really. Violence for the Marxist paradigm was 'de-problematised' by making it part of an inevitable larger conflict, a passage to a predetermined future – one could not blame violent revolutionaries (indeed one ought to applaud them), because they were enacting their role in a fight choreographed by History itself, and they were on the side of truth, justice and freedom. What all the various strands of 'revisionism' did was to strip away this notion of a two-sided contest: without a reactionary aristocracy, firmly distinguished socially and economically from the rising classes, the violence of revolution came to seem ever more absurd and excessive, until the nadir was reached with Schama's pronouncements that made violence the goal of revolutionary activity, rather than its consequence.

In the new 'post-revisionist' world, the wicked aristocrats are back, and as it turns out, more scheming than ever.[21] Recent work has reinforced the active presence of the counter-revolutionary émigrés, or emigrated nobles, from early in the cycle of revolutionary violence.[22] Other studies have shown how vigorous was the 'counter-enlightenment' of conservative and reactionary thinkers that resisted the reforming philosophies of the age.[23] Turning to the heart of political practice, while John Hardman has shown convincingly that politics under Louis XVI was a subtle and complex affair, his researches also reinforce a classic narrative of personal manipulation and factional malice, subsumed by more structural accounts earlier in the twentieth century.[24] Hardman shows particularly clearly how personal influences, most notably those of the queen herself, and a breakdown of some of the restraining structures of conciliar governance, facilitated the decline into 'pre-revolutionary' conditions, while also fostering rising hostility to reform at the very heart of the state.

More damningly still, Munro Price's sympathetic treatment of Louis, Marie Antoinette and their closest advisers shows how intransigent they were, faced with a revolution they never stopped understanding as illegitimate rebellion. Whether taking the advice of Louis's reactionary brother Artois, and botching the attempt to quash the revolutionaries in July 1789 by going too far, too fast, thus provoking the storming of the Bastille, or caballing behind the scenes through the drafting of the new constitution to disown the whole document, the royal couple were always set on what came to be identified as 'counter-revolution'. Fleeing in June 1791, recaptured, playing on the blind optimism of revolutionary politicians desperate to have a king as a stabilising figurehead, swearing a perjured oath to be faithful to the constitution in September 1791, and already plotting means to lead the country to armed confrontation and a supposed restoration of royal powers (and noble privilege), Louis and Marie Antoinette were dead set against accommodation to what had befallen 'their' realm. With the queen taking a vigorously active role, sufficient to justify almost all the revolutionaries' suspicions against her, if not their cruel sexual slanders, the couple's ultimate fate, while tragic, also comes to seem tragically inevitable.[25]

Timothy Tackett, who over a substantial career has focused consistently on the attitudes cultivating division in revolutionary France, has in his more recent books shown keenly how the active presence of anti-revolutionary forces propelled conflict forward.[26] In his landmark study of the psychological dynamics of the National Assembly of 1789–91, the 'aristocratic' party are an ever-present menace in the minds of 'patriots'.[27] While a 'Schama-ist' reading might be tempted to dismiss this as paranoia, Tackett shows how nobles' own writings confirm the reactionary intentions of some among the most powerful (while others of the elite, true to the findings of old-school revisionism, were among the most zealous advocates of reform). Aristocrats caballed from the earliest days of the Estates General in May 1789, working to seduce the waverers in their own ranks with flattery and alarmist prognostications. The shocking events of July seemed to throw reformers and conservatives together temporarily, but by the end of the year, despite the massive structural changes that the National Assembly had already implanted, it was with a sense of themselves as an embattled minority that radicals formed the first of a nationwide network of 'Jacobin Clubs'. In his book *When the King Took Flight*, Tackett shows how decisive were the king's own actions in trying to escape the country in June 1791 in turning mainstream political opinion against him, unleashing a first wave of republican agitation, and virtually guaranteeing the impossibility of making the constitutional monarchy implemented a few months later into a stable regime.[28] Covering some of the same ground, but focusing on the enormous efforts of revolutionaries in 1789–91 to produce such a stable order, Michael Fitzsimmons illustrates the multiple and overlapping spheres in which pre-existing differences stoked new conflicts, and bold initiatives crumbled under the onslaught of events.[29]

Works such as these, which dive repeatedly into the heart of the complex construction of revolutionary politics, with its almost day-by-day challenges and confrontations, shifting allegiances and drumbeat of fear and suspicion on all sides, make generalisations about the causes and responsibilities for violence increasingly difficult. One such attempt is that of Arno Mayer, who follows theorists of earlier generations in trying to equate the French experience with later revolutions, in this case the archetype of twentieth-century upheaval, Russia in 1917. The difficulty of this kind of work is that it must be in the end quite unhistorical. To equate two societies, collapsing under quite different circumstances in revolution 130 years apart – one under the conscious shadow of the other, as perpetuated by Marxist theory and practice – requires a degree of abstraction quite alien to real specific insights. Thus Mayer offers chapters on 'Violence', 'Terror' and 'Vengeance', replete with citations from theorists from Machiavelli and Hobbes to Weber, Schmitt and Arendt, setting up a framework into which partial narratives of some aspects of revolutionary experience can be inserted. Ending with visions of the 'externalisation' of the French Revolution (into Napoleon), and the 'internalisation' of the Russian (into Stalin), the whole is redolent far more of preconception than of real historical insight.[30]

The move away from anglophone generalisations about French revolutionary violence, even in comparison to francophone historians, is tellingly visible in a special number of the bilingual journal *Historical Reflections/Réflexions historiques* produced in 2003. In French, Haim Burstin was prepared to address 'a phenomenology of revolutionary violence', while Patrice Gueniffey offered a discussion of the Terror in its widest contours: 'exceptional circumstances, ideology and revolutionary dynamic'.[31] In English, on the other hand, Ted Margadant offered a piece on the limitations and ambivalences of royal summary justice during the crisis of 1789, and Timothy Tackett rehearsed some of his views on the turning point of the flight to Varennes.[32] The exception that proves the rule is a piece by Howard Brown on 'Echoes of the Terror'[33], which is explicitly concerned with the longer-term structural survival of 'terrorist' methods and commitment to strong state-directed public order in the decade after 1794. Brown's work, more recently consolidated into a book-length study, *Ending the French Revolution*, is almost unique for anglophone writers in consciously exploring the power of conceptual rethinking to illuminate understanding of revolutionary politics.[34] Working as he does on the later 1790s and beyond, the violence of the Terror is an unavoidable background in Brown's work, which perhaps assists him in more clearly considering the terms in which the men and women of the day dealt with what, for them, was a shattering immediate past. As familiar with the theorists of violence as is Mayer, Brown confines his use of their insights to closely structured case studies, and draws up a new balance sheet of the impact of revolutionary violence, driving the steady formation of a 'security state' in which initial 'liberal authoritarianism', holding the ring against extremists of left and right, gives way in time to authoritarianism *tout court*, as dictatorship comes to be accepted as the only apparent route out of endless cycles of upheaval.

If we are here attempting to use the French Revolution as a case study, and to learn something genuinely useful for wider study from its upheavals, then a pairing of Brown's insights with several other recent publications may be a fruitful end point. Stuart Carroll, a specialist in the brutal complexities of early modern aristocratic codes of honour, recently edited a collection on *Cultures of Violence*.[35] The authors demonstrate that, in circumstances of both apparent stability and radical disorder, violence has rules, both explicit and implicit, and that it represents a fundamental part of cultural experience. Two other recent books, one ranging widely across the early modern period, and one focusing closely on the revolution itself, have drawn attention to the central role of conspiratorial thinking in promoting violent political solutions.[36] While critiques of revolutionary violence have often focused on the 'paranoia' displayed by leaders of the Terror – and their ineradicable belief in nefarious plotting, producing a never-ending stream of new 'traitors' at the heart of the republican body politic, is undeniable – wider study shows how such thinking was never far from the surface on all sides at this historical juncture.

In sum, anglophone writing on the French Revolution has now reached a point of genuine subtlety in its perceptions of the background to violent upheaval. No amount of such subtlety is ever going to resolve questions of whether different forms of violence are 'justified' in different circumstances. These are topics for moral philosophy (or partisan assertion), and society's assumptions about such issues are contradictory at best – Maximilien Robespierre, responsible for thousands of deaths, is routinely depicted as an inhuman monster, while Napoleon Bonaparte, who had a far more personal responsibility for conflicts that killed millions, is one of history's 'Great Men'.[37] However, it is undoubtedly the case that we are now in a position to 'unbundle' all the very different violences of the French Revolution – popular insurrections, factional strife, counter-revolutionary reaction, national defence, mutual incrimination, common criminality and opportunism, and, above all, fear-driven pre-emption of perceived threats – and see the tragic canvas of the 1790s as a concentration of many traits which, sadly, have disfigured almost all efforts to build a polity on the foundations of lasting justice.

Sophie Wahnich

To begin with, we must clarify what we mean by 'extreme political change'. 'Extreme' may refer both to the manner of change – rapid or intense – and to the importance of what is at stake politically. To use the term 'extreme' is on the one hand to signify that the change concerns the foundations and structures of politics, that it entails a radical transformation of society, and that it constitutes an event that is irreversible and definitive. Extreme political change is in fact a 'revolution' in the modern sense of the word.[38] We would have to speak of extreme phenomena which occur in exceptional situations. On the other hand, 'extreme' refers to the manner or means of change. This suggests that there is a 'technology'[39] to control what is extreme about the change, which may not in fact work out. Here, 'extreme' signifies departure from established rituals and processes, actions which are at the frontiers of politics, in an indeterminate zone between the political and non-political, which revolutionaries called 'the silence of the laws' or 'anarchy'. In this case, political violence cannot be separated from passions aroused before and after that violence. Extreme political change is thus change which, as it unfolds, explodes and subsides, releases political passions and emotions.

I will therefore suggest three types of answers to the initial question posed in the heading of this chapter. The historian may analyse extreme political change first by investigating the specific quality of the moment in which extreme political change occurs; second, by investigating the dynamics of passions that are aroused by that political change and which may require seeking answers from other disciplines, such as literature or anthropology; and third, by exploring the multiple manifestations of political violence in those passionate dynamics.

The specific quality of the moment when extreme political change occurs

A powerful dynamic

At moments of extreme political transformation powerful forces are at work. A number of forces come together at a specific moment and produce an event, that of extreme political change. What are these forces? First of all, these are social forces which are mobilised for a specific purpose. In 1788, the French Estates General was summoned in order to remedy the State's finances. However, the election and meeting of the Estates General set in motion other forces which overtook that limited purpose. In particular, electors were invited to draft grievance registers (*cahiers de doléances*). This process created a new dynamic connected to these social forces, that of the 'hope principle', a dynamic of projected expectations, of articulated and unarticulated desires.[40] They were psychic forces at the intersection of the culture of eighteenth-century Enlightenment and rapid politicisation, which together created a new horizon of collective expectations. Timothy Tackett has shown how this horizon of collective expectations made the deputies of the Estates General conscious of their strength and power.[41] According to the Marxist historian Georges Lefebvre, the revolution was characterised by two fundamental psychic mechanisms: hope and fear. This fear was a fear of repression by the State, fear that the revolution might be driven back, or else that it would spin out of control.[42]

In order to control these two contradictory psychic forces, those of action and reaction, stimulated and thwarted expectations, French revolutionaries had a powerful tool: the effervescence of language. This in itself was a dynamic process which increased the momentum of change as well as slowed it down, both intensified and pacified it. That effervescence was visible in all sorts of written material: newspapers, pamphlets, petitions that succeeded in making a grievance political, turning pain into words, transforming the plaintive voice into the demand. This linguistic effervescence was also oral, rhetorical and deliberative, manifest in places where words were articulated in a public sphere, such as political societies, district assemblies or the National Assembly. This linguistic effervescence elaborated immediate expectations and experiences so as to make the revolutionary project particularly fluid.

How is it possible to understand these dynamics, to grasp their social, psychic and linguistic complexity? By comparing sources, of course, but also by establishing a minute chronology, which is the only way to pin down the acceleration of actions and reactions, and the fluidity of a situation. The approach must be intensive rather than extensive. Does this mean reverting to the practice of positivist, political history? No, for time is not, as Walter Benjamin says, 'uniform and empty', but on the contrary, made denser by the cumulative intensification of lived experiences.[43] It requires, on one hand, what Antoine de Baecque has called a 'thick source', and on the other, working on the source that has been artificially rarified but intensely scrutinised.[44] Such a source must be examined like a photograph, every plane of which is clear-cut, for the historian must freeze short lapses of time. The surface is thickened by a deep understanding of the political culture and ways of thinking of those who experienced those short but intense moments. Such a photograph is not unlike the anthropologist's 'thick description'.[45] The historian describes the brief moments lived through by actors who have accumulated and embodied experiences and expectations from much longer time periods.

One example will serve. The petition 'relative to the agitation in this part of the city' delivered on 23 January 1792 by a deputation of the Paris Faubourg St Marceau can be analysed as one of these rare sources which reveal this compression of experiences and expectations into a short time. It asked the Assembly to take cognizance of the two psychic mechanisms of the revolution, the citizens' hope and fear. The fear was about the shortage of food, but as always in the revolutionary period, the question of hungry stomachs was linked to the question of good governance and rights. The petitioners were afraid of the eternal return of tyrants or tyranny of which the lack of food was only a symptom.

> Don't tell us that the increase in sugar prices is due to revolt in the colonies. It is due to hoarding by bad citizens. Churches, tennis courts and other public places have been filled with sugar by hoarders. You tell us that the constitution guarantees free trade. But the constitution also says, 'Liberty is doing what does not harm others'. Isn't hoarding a necessity harming others?[46]

The petitioners were questioning the explanation given by the authorities for the disappearance of sugar from the markets. They suggested another but were not heard. This refusal of the authorities was all the more unacceptable because some natural representatives of the people were suspected of being 'sugar merchants'.

'How scandalous to see a former magistrate and member of the Constituant Assembly declare himself chief of the hoarders'.[47] The accusation recalls the denunciation of the 'famine plot' of 1789, but the target has shifted.[48] No longer is it the king who has been accused of betraying his role as father of his people by trading in grain, but a magistrate and lawmaker who has betrayed his role as protector of the people by becoming a sugar merchant. The political culture and panic are deep-seated, and the Assembly was forced to act as arbitrator between the people of Paris and the municipality. It obliged the mayor of Paris, Pétion, to abandon the view of the Jacobin Club, according to which to fight for coffee with sugar, often the only thing consumed before 2pm, was to fight for a 'sweet', and to take the petitioners seriously.

Complex notions of historical change

The changes taking place in the actors' present is thus saturated with accumulated expectations and experiences.[49] Ideologies have often been described as following one another, so that, for example, the *Ancien Régime*'s obsession with honour was succeeded by the revolution's passion for equality, but it could be argued that often they are cumulative rather than successive. Revolutionaries learned new things which contradicted old ways of thinking, but was that enough to be rid of them? This revolution and hostility to revolution co-existed in the minds of revolutionary actors who remained attached to ways of thinking, feeling and seeing that seemed obsolete to many of their contemporaries. In 1792, for example, Marat deplored the fact that patriots should declare their support for war. They left for war moved by a sense of honour forged by the expectation of equality, and by a love for the homeland born of the revolutionary experience of laws that protected the good life. Making war as a patriot thus meant declaring the coming of equality twice over: once as instituted by the laws, and once instituted by sharing the honour of fighting to defend those laws. For Marat, however, those patriots needed to be wary of an executive power that betrayed its promises and oaths, and to oppose a war that would lead them to their deaths.[50]

To speak of cumulative experiences is to question the sudden break in historical time that has been proposed as the classic notion of revolution in modern times.[51] The writer and politician Chateaubriand described people during the revolution as swimming between two river banks, that of the world as it was, according to their experience, and that of the world as it might be, according to their expectations.[52] Experiences acquired before and during the revolution became obsolete, although for many people they remained meaningful. They lost their capacity to see that what they were doing was entirely conditioned by their experience. Thus a member of the Limoges ruling directory thought that it was still possible to threaten and debase people who killed a non-juring (counter-revolutionary) priest in July 1792 in the name of the fatherland in danger. He wanted to erect a monument condemning the authors of this atrocity, but suffered the consequences of his tardiness to learn the new rules when his home became the target of popular insults. His viewpoint was no longer contemporary.

By contrast, those who were already on the other shore sometimes lost their sense of the situation because of the strength of their expectations, so that they took their desires for reality. In Lyon, for example, when the meeting of the Estates General was announced, ordinary people thought they had got what they hoped for by this triumph: the abolition of city tolls on food and drink. Early in July 1789 they brought barrels of wine into the city to celebrate without paying the tolls and threw the toll registers into the Rhône. This premature gesture was ferociously punished, for they had not understood that their geographical distance from the epicentre of revolution in Paris was also a distance in time. The revolutionary power that they anticipated had not yet arrived in Lyon. The bloody repression of these riots concretised this 'not yet'. This 'not yet', as well as the 'no longer', underlines the political difficulty actors had in comprehending extreme political change, in reformulating their experiences in light of change. Such an upsetting of experiences was faced both by revolutionaries and counter-revolutionaries, who constantly found themselves out of step. The image of the swimmer between two shores, taken up from Chateaubriand by François Hartog, perfectly expresses this uncertainty.

There was, however, an even greater and more extreme loss of temporal points of reference, when neither experience nor expectations could help the actors. Those were moments of revolutionary enthusiasm, when radical decisions were taken. Some individuals lost their minds, such as the member of the Constituent Assembly who could not come to terms with the fact that in a moment of hubris he had sworn the Tennis Court Oath not to go home until a constitution was enacted.[53] Such moments of hasty decision could tear through even the revolutionary horizon of expectations. Should one then speak of a time when the revolution became unhinged?

The revolution unhinged

If the hinges are, on the one hand, the horizon of expectations, and on the other, the field of experience, then the revolutionary moment – of which actors have no experience and know that on the other bank their expectations are not necessarily awaiting them – is indeed 'unhinged time'. This expression is used by Nicole Loraux, and borrowed from Jean-Max Gaudillière, who was in turn inspired by Shakespeare's *Hamlet*.[54] In a similar way, Jacques Rancière speaks of 'achrony'. In each case there is the idea of a classical, historical temporality being suspended in favour of another sort of time. Nicole Loraux speaks of a time that 'does not depend on the time carried by history', a time 'that must be invented, if only to describe things which at certain periods are imagined before they occur, by anticipation as it were'.[55] This time makes space for utopia and forgets that politics is 'by definition about conflict'. In these moments outside normal historical temporality, there is a 'censored memory' of political conflict and 'the muted workings of desire'. It is a time of the unconscious and of passions. She proposes a history of the repetitive and of analogy, in which the passions are 'generators of repetition'.[56]

These repetitive analogies can be seen even in such a short period as the ten revolutionary years. We might then see certain processes not in their superb contextual uniqueness, but as patterns that allow us to grasp what is repetitive about this time. How did the massacres of revolutionary times come about? What were the dynamics at work? Could they be prevented or stopped? We are in fact rerunning the political debate engaged in by the revolutionaries themselves when they were confronted by extreme events. We must revisit the revolutionaries' political debate about what to do in the face of the extreme: heads cut off, the Glacière massacre at Avignon in October 1791 or the September massacres in Paris in 1792. To focus on the specifics of times of extreme political change therefore also means concentrating on such times when political passions come to the fore.

Interdisciplinary alliances to understand the dynamics of political passion

Describing extreme political change implies isolating those moments of excess, when political passions boil over. However, striving to be a rational and scientific discipline, history has long neglected the subject of passions.[57] In order to understand the role of passion in history, the historian must learn from other, allied disciplines.

Literature
A first way to do this is for history to resume where it left off in the nineteenth century, as a field of literature. To describe extreme political change requires history to make an alliance with literature or the literary representation of history. We have already mentioned Chateaubriand, but, as Jacques Rancière has shown, Michelet too used the present tense in order to make us empathise with what the actors of the time felt and lived through. Such, for example, were those 'village patriots, who, like young, inexperienced lovers simply repeat the stereotypes of love which should not so much be quoted as made visible'.[58] However, for the purpose of understanding extreme political change, the most eloquent example seems to me to be Victor Hugo. His literary representation of extreme political passions allows us to understand theory in the body of history. Claude Lefort, for example, argued that exercise of terror was a constraint imposed on

oneself, that it had to be desired in the same way that one desired liberty. This self-imposed constraint is at the heart of Victor Hugo's novel *1793*. In it the former priest, but now committed revolutionary, Cimourdain decides that the ex-noble Gauvain must die for having spared the royalist Lantenac, who saved two republican children from a fire. And yet Cimourdin loves Gauvain like a son. The self-imposed constraint is linked to the dilemma of public virtue pitted against private love, the dilemma of having to choose between a sentiment of political humanity and a feeling of natural humanity.[59] Public virtue carries a consequence. Cimourdain does not recover from his dedication to the revolution, and dies spiritually at the same time as Gauvain. Hugo's attempt to understand the complexity of feelings experienced by the various characters caught between public and private life is a lesson for all who need to reflect on political passions in a time of extreme political change.

Philosophy and psychoanalysis

Earlier periods took more seriously the role of passions in the social and political arenas than did the nineteenth and twentieth centuries. Aristotle, Plato, Spinoza, Hobbes, Locke, Hume and Shaftesbury thought about the way they worked, how they linked together, their impact and their moral function. If, as Nicole Loraux suggests, this time of passions is a time of repetition, it must be investigated in the very heart of the revolutionary process, but also in other comparable historical periods, when passions and emotions set to work. I will address two questions: what is anger, and when is it legitimate?

In the case of kings, heroes and gods, Aristotle analysed anger as serving to repair an offense or insult.[60] But anger also regulates relations between individuals when reciprocal expectations are not satisfied and when, for instance, there is a feeling of ingratitude. This anger is linked to a sense of honour and self-respect, but also to courage. A person who never gives way to anger is thus cowardly. In the end, anger is a generous passion, for one never feels anger for oneself alone. Anger may be provoked by an offence inflicted on a friend or ally. Its purpose is to re-establish justice. That said, this anger must be assuaged according to rules of intensity and duration. Passions are legitimate, but must not be boundless.

Aristotle's approach thus leads us to analyse more carefully certain revolutionary declarations when anger was vented, as in this proclamation in Marseilles in June 1792:

> The day of the people's anger has come. This people which has long been wounded or chained and is sick of warding off blows is now in turn ready to strike back … This generous lion is today incensed and will wake from its slumber to hurl itself against the pack of its enemies.[61]

The political paradigm of anger is the same. The people has been offended and decides to respond with anger. That anger is connected with generosity, and the forthcoming battle will indeed restore justice. Far from being an uncontrolled passion, anger becomes a moral stance whose narrative structure is clear: offence, anger, generous combat, justice restored.

Another passion is enthusiasm, which was analysed in all its ambivalence by Shaftesbury.[62] On the one hand, enthusiasm is synonymous with fanaticism and produces a powerful rage or fury; on the other, it is also solidly anchored in the 'good foundation of a visionary spirit'. If it produces anger, this comes from the violence of the sentiment of sociability and not from men's hostility to one another. It is no longer a question of protecting the state and religion from enthusiasm, but of understanding how they mobilise it, and of considering the ambivalence of enthusiasm as a human factor which can be regulated.

All this is not very far from the Freudian theory of mass identification.[63] What turns enthusiasm into fury is the love between individuals. That is one way of linking up with psychoanalysis and the famous 'desiring moment' of Nicole Loraux. Like Aristotle and Shaftesbury, Freud does not give us all the answers, but he provides useful concepts that must be applied with discretion.

Anthropology

The alliance with anthropology is similar to the preceding ones, although perhaps more familiar to historians. For our purposes it enables us to understand the way in which political and symbolic processes are institutionalised in extreme situations. For anthropologists, vengeance is understood not as a vengeful impulse, but institutionalises debts of honour and blood between two antagonistic groups which are nevertheless committed to restoring group unity. Vengeance is thus considered as a form of justice in a particular social situation.[64] Revenge is a political mechanism which permits society torn apart by strife to be repaired once again. The anthropological interpretation makes it possible to understand how the term revenge was used by revolutionaries. For to speak of revenge means to speak of justice and honour, which are the very foundation on which a society may be rebuilt in co-operation with one's adversaries.

Equally, anthropology is a discipline which, perhaps more than others, deals with the domain of the 'exceptional' or extreme. It invites us to rethink the exceptional or extreme violence of periods of very rapid political change. Violence, in the anthropological context, has often been given a sacred function. The ritual killing of a monarch, separated from the other members of society in African kingdoms, is supposed to guarantee the vitality of the group, to refound it on a regular basis.[65] Extreme violence, like revenge, permits the founding or refounding of the social body. As Robespierre said at the king's trial, 'Louis must die so that the fatherland may live'.[66]

Such an approach, however, which anthropologises politics and uses anachronism, albeit in a controlled way, seems to deny the specifically political attempt of subjectification at work in these periods. In these 'islands of immobility' of human as well as political passions, we must not lose sight of the political changes which found a new society. We must understand ways in which passions are made legitimate and made to work, especially when they are linked with violence.

Extreme political change and the question of political violence

We need to understand political violence at work as inseparable from passions, but to grasp the subjective meaning of the political in this passionate thinking. This is crucial because, without a doubt, violence could lead to forsaking the political, something that the revolutionaries themselves feared and denounced. Certain extreme phenomena, such as the Glacière massacres and the September massacres, were vigorously debated and analysed not as acts of violence per se, but in order to understand the conditions in which these acts of extreme violence took place. We must be particularly attentive to these debates among revolutionaries if we wish to understand ways in which they hoped to found a new society in new ways, by recourse to violence if necessary. What sort of violence are we speaking about?

The legislative violence of language and the law, the physical violence of the executive and military

In situations of extreme political change, violence is first and foremost aimed at the law, using political pressure. The Tennis Court Oath and the renaming of the Estates General the 'Constituent National Assembly', were of this order. This juridical and linguistic violence supposed that language could be used to produce a radical institutional revolution. It asserted that a group of men and its declarations embodied the whole of the new projected society and had a right to act in its name. It meant claiming power (*kratos*) over the whole – whether the power of the people or the power of an aristocracy or a tyrant. It was an explicit declaration of war on those who refused them that power. Against this declaration there was a counter-declaration and an opposing power or reaction on the part of those who still disposed of executive violence. Thus, against the violence of a law that asserted a new conception of just and unjust, the violence of the executive was asserted, seeking to undo this juridico-linguistic violence by all possible means, including by 'the force of bayonets'. Indeed, for the revolutionary actors, championing 'the will of the people' against 'the force of bayonets' was the confrontation of two kinds of political violence. Extreme political change is extreme precisely because it sets the symbolic violence of a new law against the physical executive and military violence used to defend the old law. The Tennis Court Oath was not a wordplay but a declaration of war. If one deputy was driven mad by it, it was because nobody knew, nobody could know, where that war would lead the country; nobody knew how it could be controlled. That is where the unheard-of nature of revolution and the extremity of political change lay.

The breakdown of law-making bodies and the repressed memory of political conflict

The succession of violent actions and reactions replayed this assertion of the will of the people in search of irreversible gains. The revolutionary experience, however, highlighted the immense difficulty in making the people's will and democracy prevail. The emergence of the sovereignty of the people was repeatedly suppressed. In 1789 the taking of the Bastille, the Great Fear and the October days forced the king to ratify the abolition of privileges and the Declaration of the Rights of Man and the Citizen. The work of the Constituent Assembly, however, was to limit that victory by a voting system which confined the vote to taxpayers, by the imposition of martial law and the introduction of economic liberalism. It was an attempt to obliterate the memory of conflict, the memory that politics is by nature conflict. The improbable union of the nation, which was constantly reaffirmed in the face of injustice, blocked off the possibility of acknowledging the people's will as a conflictual will that required answering. When in times of crisis the revolutionaries reasserted the principles of 1789 by demanding that the fatherland be declared in danger (*la patrie en danger*), they were following rules of revolutionary rhetorical art: requiring a symbolic violence that might spare them from insurrectional violence. They demanded a law that would permit them to take up arms to defend the *patrie*. They demanded a law that would honour them fully as citizens. This law was refused by the politicians who attempted to incriminate them. At this point, insurrection was organised against deficient politicians who were incapable of voting laws that could regulate and appease the people's anger, and the people no longer asked for the blessing of the law.

Uncertainty at the heart of political violence

Insurrection was imagined and carried off like a quasi 'velvet revolution'. The aim was to make a show of force without causing any harm. Because they were political, the revolutionaries were keen to limit violence, did not wish it, and declared it must only be a last resort, when political means were finally exhausted. Using violence was only legitimate when all other solutions had failed. At this point revolutionaries were forced into violence. However, the exercise of violence always opened the door to uncertainty.

Describing extreme political change involves exploring the lurch into uncertainty that recourse to violence entailed. Insurrection meant that ordinary laws were suspended in favour of the laws of war or the laws of nature, which would reinstate new laws after victory had been recognised. Problems arose when the politicians failed to recognise this victory, the Legislative Assembly demanding criminal proceedings for crimes committed when the monarchy was overthrown on 10 August 1792, and then requiring the incoming Convention parliament to try the king for breaking his oath.

Violence might then become radicalised, for insurrection ushered in what the revolutionaries called 'the silence of the laws' that might turn the people into an executioner. This people-executor was not a criminal people, but the people driven to violence without mediation in order to establish definitively the advent of its sovereignty. Do we now need to refer to a sacred sphere, as described by Giorgio Agamben, a place without any laws, human or divine?[67] This notion of a sacred sphere blurs the distinction made by Walter Benjamin between mythical violence, which is arbitrary, and divine violence, which is intended to re-establish justice.[68] Of course, no one can infallibly decide what is just or fair. Uncertainty once again prevails. Walter Benjamin's main point, however, is that all violence, however extreme, is inseparable from the political project that underpins it. Even in the sacred sphere, violence remains political. It is not a way out of political conflict.

Can violence which articulates revenge spontaneously found a new political order? None of the revolutionaries thought so; they felt rather that physical violence carried the risk of destroying society as a whole. Liberty was not licence. Insurrection by a free people should not inflict physical harm or bloodshed. That is why they feared such violence, which they sometimes discredited by using the term 'anarchy'. They hoped to be able to do without it and discussed its dangers. Robespierre, for instance, as early as November 1791, attacked the Girondins for leading the people towards insurgency by their enthusiasm for war, and urged suspicion of the executive power.

> Suspicion, you say, is a dreadful state of mind! But much less dreadful than the stupid trust that has caused all our problems and suffering and is leading us to the edge of the precipice. If we are betrayed, said a patriot deputy whom I oppose, the people will be there. No doubt, but you cannot ignore the fact that you are propounding a rare, uncertain, and extreme remedy. The people was also there when, in all free countries, despite all its rights and all its power, clever men put it to sleep for a moment and then chained it for centuries. It was there too, when, last July [17 July 1791, the Champ de Mars massacre[69]] its blood ran unavenged in the very heart of this capital city, and by whose order?

Yes, the people are there but, you, representatives of the people, are you not there also? What are you doing, if instead of foreseeing and countering the plans of the people's oppressors, you know only how to abandon them to their terrible right of insurrection?[70]

In this debate, Robespierre declares that it is up to the people's representatives to be suspicious of the executive, in order to spare the people the extremely dangerous alternative of resorting to insurrection. He goes even further, asking the representatives to act themselves in the name of the people, and to protect them from the consequences of such an insurrection, which may indeed be terrible.

This speech of Robespierre opens up a whole field for research. In times of extreme political change, insurrection must be thought about, but also pulled back from violence. It is necessary to dissociate extreme political change from violence, and imagine revolution that spares the need for violence. It was the dearest wish of the revolutionaries not to act like tyrants. The historian of revolution must take account of this wish.

Notes

1 R. R. Palmer, *The Age of the Democratic Revolution: A Political History of Europe and America, 1760–1800, vol.1: The Challenge, vol. 2: The Struggle* (Princeton University Press, 1959, 1964).
2 Jacques Godechot, *France and the Atlantic Revolution of the Eighteenth Century, 1770–1799*, trans. Herbert H. Brown (New York, Free Press, 1965), 75; Georges Lefebvre, *The Coming of the French Revolution*, trans. R. R. Palmer (Princeton University Press, 1947).
3 Alfred Cobban, *The Social Interpretation of the French Revolution* (Cambridge University Press, 1964).
4 The history of the revisionists' rise was documented by William Doyle, *Origins of the French Revolution* (Oxford University Press, 1980, updated in subsequent editions, 1988, 1999).
5 Richard Cobb, *Terreur et subsistances, 1793–1795* (Paris, Clavreuil, 1965); *A Second Identity: Essays on France and French History* (Oxford University Press, 1969); *The Police and the People: French Popular Protest, 1789–1820* (Oxford, Clarendon Press, 1970); *Reactions to the French Revolution* (Oxford University Press, 1972); and the belated translation of his 1961 masterwork, *The People's Armies: The Armées Révolutionnaires, Instrument of the Terror in the Departments, April 1793 to Floral Year II*, trans. Marianne Elliott (New Haven, Conn., Yale University Press, 1987).
6 Alan Forrest, *The French Revolution and the Poor* (Oxford, Blackwell, 1981), following on from *Society and Politics in Revolutionary Bordeaux* (Oxford University Press, 1975).
7 Olwen H. Hufton, *The Poor of Eighteenth-century France, 1750–1789* (Oxford, Clarendon Press, 1974); *Women and the Limits of Citizenship in the French Revolution* (University of Toronto Press, 1992).
8 Colin Lucas, *The Structure of the Terror: The Example of Javogues and the Loire* (Oxford University Press, 1973). Lucas also made a notable contribution to 'revisionism' on the nature of the so-called revolutionary bourgeoisie; see his 'Nobles, bourgeois and the origins of the French Revolution', orig. pub. in *Past & Present* 60 (1973), reprinted in D. Johnson, ed., *French Society and the Revolution* (Cambridge University Press, 1976), 88–131.
9 Lynn Hunt, *Politics, Culture, and Class in the French Revolution* (Berkeley, University of California Press, 1984). See more widely Lynn Hunt, ed., *The New Cultural History* (Berkeley, University of California Press, 1989).
10 Simon Schama, *Citizens: A Chronicle of the French Revolution* (New York, Viking, 1989), xv.
11 Keith Michael Baker, *Inventing the French Revolution: Essays on French Political Culture in the Eighteenth*

Century (Cambridge University Press, 1990).

12 Furet's 1978 *Penser la Révolution française* had been translated three years later: *Interpreting the French Revolution*, trans. Elborg Forster (Cambridge University Press, 1981); but it was only with the bicentenary and the production of *A Critical Dictionary of the French Revolution,* trans. Arthur Goldhammer, ed. François Furet and Mona Ozouf (Cambridge, Mass., Belknap Press of Harvard University Press, 1989) that Furet's rising interpretive dominance became evident.

13 A set of more subtle and varied interpretations was also produced in 1989 and after, in the four volumes of *The French Revolution and the Creation of Modern Political Culture*, published by Pergamon Press under the editorship of Keith M. Baker, Colin Lucas and François Furet. While lacking the polemical force of more headline productions, these, however, did focus attention on the version of 'political culture' favoured by Baker, namely that of the thinkers of the elite, downplaying a minority of contributions which tried to extend a more 'new cultural history' perspective of wider anthropological notions of culture.

14 Francis Fukuyama, *The End of History and the Last Man* (Harmondsworth, Penguin, 1992).

15 George C. Comninel, *Rethinking the French Revolution: Marxism and the Revisionist Challenge* (London, Verso, 1987); Henry Heller, *The Bourgeois Revolution in France, 1789–1815* (New York, Berghahn Books, 2006).

16 Patrice Higonnet, *Goodness Beyond Virtue: Jacobins during the French Revolution* (Cambridge, Mass., Harvard University Press, 1998), 3, 182.

17 Rafe Blaufarb, *The French Army, 750–1820: Careers, Talent, Merit* (Manchester University Press, 2002), esp. chs. 1, 2; Jay M. Smith, *The Culture of Merit: Nobility, Royal Service, and the Making of Absolute Monarchy in France, 1600–1789* (Ann Arbor, University of Michigan Press, 1996).

18 Jay M. Smith, *Nobility Reimagined: The Patriotic Nation in Eighteenth-century France* (Ithaca, Cornell University Press, 2005).

19 Gail Bossenga, *The Politics of Privilege: Old Regime and Revolution in Lille* (Cambridge University Press, 1991).

20 Michael Kwass, *Privilege and the Politics of Taxation in Eighteenth-century France: Liberté, Égalité, Fiscalité* (Cambridge University Press, 2000).

21 For an example of an ardent bourgeois individual's struggle with the abuse of privilege in the economic sphere of the late eighteenth century, see the vigorous case study by Gwynne Lewis, *The Advent of Modern Capitalism in France, 1770–1840: The Contribution of Pierre-François Tubeuf* (Oxford, Clarendon Press, 1993). For a very recent and wider meditation on the same theme, see Jeff Horn, *The Path Not Taken: French Industrialization in the Age of Revolution, 1750–1830* (Cambridge, Mass., MIT Press, 2006).

22 Kirsty Carpenter and Philip Mansel, eds., *The French Émigrés in Europe and the Struggle Against Revolution, 1789–1814* (Basingstoke, Macmillan, 1999). For the specifically British role in stoking royalist subversion, though largely after the worst of the Terror, see Elizabeth Sparrow, *Secret Service: British Agents in France, 1792–1815* (Woodbridge, Boydell Press, 1999).

23 Darrin M. McMahon, *Enemies of the Enlightenment: The French Counter-enlightenment and the Making of Modernity* (Oxford University Press, 2001).

24 John Hardman, *French Politics 1774–1789: From the Accession of Louis XVI to the Fall of the Bastille* (London, Longman, 1995).

25 Munro Price, *The Fall of the French Monarchy: Louis XVI, Marie Antoinette and the Baron De Breteuil* (Basingstoke, Macmillan, 2002). On the 'myth' of Marie Antoinette, see Dena Goodman, ed., *Marie Antoinette: Writings on the Body of a Queen* (London, Routledge, 2003).

26 Earlier works include Timothy Tackett, *Priest and Parish in Eighteenth-century France: A Social and Political Study of the Curés in a Diocese of Dauphiné, 1750–1791* (Princeton University Press, 1977); and *Religion, Revolution and Regional Culture in Eighteenth-century France: The Ecclesiastical Oath of 1791* (Princeton University Press, 1986).

27 Timothy Tackett, *Becoming a Revolutionary: The Deputies of the French National Assembly and the Emergence of a Revolutionary Culture (1789–1790)* (Princeton University Press, 1996).

28 Timothy Tackett, *When the King Took Flight* (Cambridge, Mass., Harvard University Press, 2003).

29 Michael P. Fitzsimmons, *The Remaking of France: The National Assembly and the Constitution of 1791* (Cambridge University Press, 1994); and *The Night the Old Regime Ended: August 4, 1789, and the French Revolution* (University Park, Penn, Penn State University Press, 2003) – four of the latter's five chapters take the story of this event's reverberations through the following several years.

30 Arno J. Mayer, *The Furies: Violence and Terror in the French and Russian Revolutions* (Princeton University Press, 2000); see Carla Hesse, 'Revolutionary historiography after the cold war: Arno Mayer's "Furies" in the French context', *Journal of Modern History* 73 (2001), 897–907. For another (among many) efforts

to be both general and meaningful about 'violence', see John Keane, *Reflections on Violence* (London, Verso, 1996), and Keane, *Violence and Democracy* (Cambridge University Press, 2004).

31 Haim Burstin, 'Pour une phénoménologie de la violence révolutionnaire: réflexions autour du cas parisien', *Historical Reflections/Réflexions historiques* 29 (2003), 389–407; Patrice Gueniffey, 'La Terreur: circonstances exceptionnelles, idéologie et dynamique révolutionnaire', ibid., 433–50.

32 Ted W. Margadant, 'Summary justice and the crisis of the Old Regime in 1789', ibid., 495–528; Timothy Tackett, 'The flight to Varennes and the coming of the Terror', ibid., 469–93.

33 Howard G. Brown, 'Echoes of the Terror', ibid., 529–58.

34 Howard G. Brown, *Ending the French Revolution: Violence, Justice and Repression from the Terror to Napoleon* (Charlottesville, University of Virginia Press, 2006).

35 Stuart Carroll, ed., *Cultures of Violence: Interpersonal Violence in Historical Perspective* (Basingstoke, Palgrave Macmillan, 2007). Carroll's own book, *Blood and Violence in Early Modern France* (Oxford, Clarendon Press, 2006), is an emphatic demonstration that revolutions are not required to fill a social space with conflict.

36 Barry Coward and Julian Swann, eds., *Conspiracies and Conspiracy Theory in Early Modern Europe: From the Waldensians to the French Revolution* (London, Ashgate, 2004); Peter R. Campbell, Thomas E. Kaiser and Marisa Linton, eds., *Conspiracy in the French Revolution* (Manchester University Press, 2007).

37 Two recent biographies: Steven Englund, *Napoleon, A Political Life* (Cambridge, Mass., Harvard University Press, 2004); Ruth Scurr, *Fatal Purity: Robespierre and the French Revolution* (London, Metropolitan Books, 2006).

38 Reinhardt Koselleck, *Le futur passé, pour une sémantique des temps historiques* (Paris, Editions EHESS, 1990).

39 In Foucault's sense of the term.

40 Ernst Bloch, *Le principe espérance* (3 vols., Paris, Gallimard, 1976, 1982, 1991).

41 Timothy Tackett, *Becoming a Revolutionary. The Deputies of the French National Assembly and the Emergence of a Revolutionary Political Culture* (Princeton University Press, 1996).

42 Georges Lefebvre, *La Grande Peur de 1789* [1932], followed by 'Les foules révolutionnaires [1934], presented by Jacques Revel (Paris, Armand Colin, 1988). English edition: *The Great Fear of 1789. Rural Panic in Revolutionary France*, presented by George Rudé (New York, Pantheon Books, 1973).

43 Walter Benjamin, *Œuvres complètes* (Paris, Gallimard, 2000), Thèses sur le concept d'histoire (vol. 2).

44 Walter Benjamin, *Œuvres complètes* (Paris, Gallimard, 2000), Thèses sur le concept d'histoire (vol. 2).

45 Clifford Geertz, *The Interpretation of Cultures* (New York, Basic Books, 1973).

46 *Le Moniteur* 11, 198.

47 *Le Moniteur* 11, 198.

48 Steven Kaplan, *The Famine Plot Persuasion in Eighteenth-century France* (Philadelphia, American Philosophical Society, 1982).

49 Bernard Lepetit, *Les formes de l'expérience* (Paris, Albin Michel, 1995), especially his article on the present of history, 273–99.

50 Sophie Wahnich, *La longue patience du peuple, 1792, naissance de la première République* (Paris, Payot, 2008).

51 Reinhardt Koselleck, *Le futur passé*.

52 The expression of Chateaubriand is taken up by François Hartog, *Régimes d'historicité, présentismes et expérience du temps* (Paris, Le Seuil, 2003).

53 Scene described by Albert Mathiez, *Les grandes journées de la Constituante* (1st edn, Paris, Hachette, 1913), republished by Les éditions de la passion, 1989, 21.

54 Nicole Loraux, 'Éloge de l'anachronisme en histoire', Le Genre humain (1993), republished in *CLIO EspaceTemps* (2005), 128.

55 Nicole Loraux, 'Éloge de l'anachronisme en histoire', 128.

56 Nicole Loraux, 'Éloge de l'anachronisme en histoire', 137–8.

57 As explained by Jacques Rancière in *Les mots de l'histoire* (Paris, Le Seuil, 1992).

58 Jacques Rancière, *Les mots de l'histoire*, p. 94.

59 Sophie Wahnich, 'De l'économie émotive de la Terreur', *Annales, Histoire sciences sociales* (2002), 889–913.

60 I am referring to a paper by Giulia Sissa at a workshop on political passions in September 2005 (EHESS-Laios, UCLA, University of Montreal).

61 *Archives parlementaires*, 45, 397.

62 Shaftesbury, *Lettre sur l'enthousiasme*, presented by Claire Crignon de Oliveira (Paris, Livre de poche, 2002).

63 Sigmund Freud, *Psychologie des foules et analyse du moi* [*Group Psychology and the Analysis of the*

Ego]. We are using this 1921 edition in the 1981 French edition, edited by André Bourguignon, *Essais de psychanalyse* (Paris, Petite Bibliothèque Payot, 1981).

64 Raymond Verdier, *La vengeance, études d'ethnologie, d'histoire et de philosophie* (Paris, Editions Cujas, 1980).

65 Marc Abélès, *L'échec en politique* (Belval, Circé, 2005).

66 Speech of Robespierre at the Trial of the King, 28 December 1792.

67 Giorgio Agamben, *Homo sacer, le pouvoir souverain et la vie nue* (Paris, Le Seuil, 1997).

68 Walter Benjamin, *Œuvres complètes*, (Paris, Gallimard, 2000), especially 'Critique de la violence' (vol. 1).

69 See the works of David Andress, especially *Massacre at the Champ de mars, Popular Dissent and Political Culture in the French Revolution* (London, Royal Historical Society, 2000).

70 Robespierre, *Œuvres de Maximilien Robespierre* (Paris, Publications de la société des études robespierristes, Phénix éditions, 2000), vol. VIII, 58–9, 18 December 1791.

7

Where does colonial history end?

Martin Evans and Raphaëlle Branche

Once the poor relation of the history syllabus, colonial history is now at the forefront of historical controversy. Riots in the communities of immigrant origin in French cities, and debates over how to teach colonial history, have brought home that empire is no longer 'out there' and 'over', but here and now. European national histories which attempted to tell a story of peaceful decolonisation have come up against the accounts of former colonial societies, now nation states, highlighting imperial violence and telling their own heroic national histories of liberation. Narratives of empire bringing prosperity and civilisation to the world have been attacked by post-colonial thinkers who have exposed the reality of capitalist exploitation and racial discrimination, so that the benefits of empire can no longer be taught in schools. Commemoration of the colonial experience has revealed deep fractures not only between colonisers and colonised, but between resisters and collaborators, and between men and women. Martin Evans *and* Raphaëlle Branche *examine ways in which these developments have created challenges and opportunities for contemporary historians of the French empire. The colonial experience is no longer dead and gone, but illuminates questions of relations with former colonies and populations from former colonies, brings the past into the present, makes colonial history part of national history and national identity. Colonial history is being recast in the context of transnational and global ties, and in a comparative perspective examining imperial structures existing not only over the last 150 years, but over the last two millennia.*

Martin Evans

The empire strikes back

University syllabuses must grant the place that it deserves to the history of France's presence overseas, particularly in North Africa. School courses must … recognise the positive role played by the French presence overseas, particularly in North Africa, and must accord the prominent position that they merit to the history and sacrifices of members of the French armed forces.

(Article Four 23 February 2005 Law)

On 23 February 2005, the French National Assembly passed a private bill, drawn up by the conservative *Union pour un mouvement populaire* (UMP) deputy Christian Vanneste, on France's overseas civilising mission during the colonial period. For Vanneste, on the right of the party and well known for his outspoken views on homosexuality and the death penalty for terrorists, the law reflected his belief in the need to end self-flagellation. In his opinion, France's colonial past must be reassessed in a renewed light. Feelings of pride had to replace those of guilt, shame and embarrassment.[1]

On these grounds, Article One of the law stipulated that there must be recognition of the country's 'debt to the women and men who participated in the work carried out by France in its former departments in Algeria, Morocco, Tunisia and Indochina and in all the territories formerly under French sovereignty'.[2] Article Two formally linked the repatriated populations from North Africa, the disappeared and the civilian dead to the annual homage rendered to the soldiers killed in North Africa on 5 December, describing them as 'victims of massacres or exactions committed during the Algerian War'. Article Three announced the future establishment of a government-supported foundation dedicated to the memory of the Algerian war and those who fought in Tunisia and Morocco.[3] Article Four decreed that France's overseas civilising mission must be taught in schools and universities in a positive fashion.

The new law, but in particular Article Four, provoked a condemnatory response from many of the country's leading historians. Hundreds, drawn largely from the left, signed a petition launched in the pages of *Le monde* on 25 March 2005, entitled 'Colonisation: no to the teaching of an official history', led by Claude Liauzu, emeritus professor at Paris VII and a distinguished specialist of colonialism.[4] They rejected the law on the grounds that it represented government interference and an end to analytical debate. The protest against the 23 February law was linked to a wider debate about the role of professional history in society. A further petition, published in *Libération* on 13 December 2005, and signed by some of the most prestigious members of the profession, including Jean-Jacques Becker, Marc Ferro, Pierre Nora, Mona Ozouf and René Rémond, saw Vanneste's initiative as just one example of how historical research was being prescribed by the law.[5] Such moves, they warned, were unworthy of a democratic system. Professional historians must not be ciphers. They need to be free to pose awkward questions. History is not memory culture. Nor is it national remembrance or the law, even if the discipline draws on all three to recreate the past.

Abroad, the law produced a fierce polemic between France and Algeria. The Algerian President Abdelaziz Bouteflika, who had been pressing the French government for an apology for colonialism, proclaimed his revulsion at the law. In this spirit he set out to expose the hypocrisy of the French civilising mission at a conference to mark the sixtieth anniversary of the repression in Sétif, where in May 1945 a nationalist uprising against French rule was ferociously repressed, leading to the death of thousands of Algerians.[6] Just at the moment when huge numbers of Algerians were giving their lives in the liberation of Europe from Nazism, Bouteflika told his audience, the French were carrying out a massacre of unspeakable horror.[7] Conveniently forgetting the vast human rights abuses carried out by the Algerian regime since independence in 1962, Bouteflika readily assumed the mantle of victim. Attacking France as a country in denial about the colonial past, he made an explicit link between the Holocaust and colonialism.

Elsewhere in November 2005, large-scale public protests were provoked by the visit of Nicolas Sarkozy, then Minister of the Interior and, as President of the UMP, a fervent supporter of the 23 February law, to the overseas departments of Martinique and Guadeloupe. The law was also condemned by Ségolène Royal, leading Socialist Party politician and soon-to-be presidential candidate for the May 2007 election; Aimé Césaire, the veteran French Caribbean intellectual; and the 'natives of the Republic', a new movement that aimed to confront discrimination against French citizens of African or Caribbean descent.[8] This debate was then fuelled still further by the riots in deprived urban areas during autumn 2005, the worst civil disturbances since 1968, which many commentators linked to the after-effects of colonialism.[9] In this charged atmosphere, President Jacques Chirac too made plain his opposition, stating categorically:

> In a Republic there is no official history. It is not up to the law to write history. Writing history is the business of historians.[10]

For this reason, in defiance of his own UMP majority, he asked the Constitutional Council to rescind Article Four at the start of 2006.

Politicians and petitions, apologies and anniversaries, anger and accusation: what does the controversy over the 23 February law reveal about the place of colonial history within France? First, it shows that this is a history which is being written within a highly politicised context, not just in terms of the ongoing issue of Franco-Algerian relations, but also the continuing debate about immigration, social exclusion and national identity. It underlines too the transnational nature of colonial and post-colonial history. The reason that the law produced an acrimonious response beyond the boundaries of the French nation state is because colonialism is not just about the history of France. It is also about the histories of the former colonies. This was felt most acutely in Algeria, where anger at colonialism is a cornerstone of official discourse and permeates all levels of politics.[11]

On this contested terrain, historians were determined to assert their independence. Through petitions, a long-established method of expression among French intellectuals, they wished to draw a line in the sand. They wanted to differentiate their own discipline from the law or memory culture, and the fact that these interventions had such a public impact is testament to the way in which colonial history and its legacy has moved to the centre stage. It is a major historical controversy not just within the profession, but society at large. Thus Benjamin Stora and Gilbert Meynier, both historians of the Algerian war, have a high profile within public life.[12] Their views are regularly sought by the print and broadcast media, as France grapples with the unravelling effects of colonialism.

Of course, this specifically French twist to the rethinking of empire cannot be divorced from the generalised reconsideration within the Anglo-Saxon world. There too, imperialism has moved from the margins to the mainstream, through the work of David Cannadine, Linda Colley, Niall Ferguson, Catherine Hall and Stephen Howe.[13]

In part this new focus is attributable to the emergence of post-colonial studies as an academic discipline in the wake of Edward Said's path-breaking book *Orientalism* in 1978.[14] It was here that Said, based in the English Department at Columbia University in the United States, mapped out the ways in which western scholars, administrators, explorers, painters and novelists viewed the Orient as the 'other', in a way that was racialist, patronising and ideologically motivated. Accordingly, he argued, Orientalism became a mode of thought for dominating the non-European world. It opened the way for the construction of whole fields of knowledge, including ethnography and anthropology, as well as history, whose starting point was the assumption that the Orient was trapped at an inferior stage of development.

Within France, post-colonialism is still largely unknown. It is only now beginning to have an impact on a younger generation of historians such as Sylvie Thénault, who feel that French academia is lagging behind in theoretical terms. In the Anglo-Saxon world, however, Orientalism has been one of the major debates of the late twentieth and early twenty-first centuries whose influence has been felt well beyond the confines of academia, principally because it raises the question of the relationship between the historical nature of seeing and political power. Said himself was Palestinian and he wished to contextualise Israeli Zionism as a product of a nineteenth-century imperialist mindset that looked down upon the Muslim world as inherently inferior. Moreover, it is a debate that has straddled disciplinary boundaries. From the beginning, the radicalism of post-colonial studies was its heterogeneity. By analysing perceptions and images and linking these to one of the central issues to imperialist conquest, namely who has the right to own the annexed landscape, post-colonial scholars like Rasheed Araeen, Homi Bhabha, Gayatri Spivak and Robert Young were engaging with history in the broadest sense of the term.[15] The crux of their argument was that the structures of power derived from nineteenth-century imperialism remain the major determinant of the contemporary world, and that to be properly understood, all factors, whether race, class, economics, gender, sexuality or the nation state, must be analysed in the context of their relations with the colonial past. By any token it was an ambitious research agenda that has affected not just academics in traditional history departments, but also art historians, historical geographers and cultural studies researchers.

Yet if post-colonialism is one aspect of the present preoccupation with empire, the other is the current debate over the global political order. The post-September 11 debate about whether the USA's present actions should be analysed in imperialist terms means that writing about empires has commanded widespread attention. Not a week goes by in the US press without some consideration of the imperial phenomenon, and here historians have been at the epicentre of the arguments. Niall Ferguson, for example, has argued in terms of the positive side of September 11. Why? Because it stopped the USA being an empire in denial.[16] It obliged the USA to face up to the fact that empire is a reality of the contemporary world and that, like the British Empire in the nineteenth century, the American equivalent must be a force for good in the twenty-first. Of course, Ferguson recognises that British imperial conquest was brutal. But this, he maintains, must be balanced against the positive legacy whereby empire opened up the world to free market capitalism, democracy and the rule of law. In this way, Ferguson does not wish to rehabilitate imperialism per se. Instead, he wishes to underline the unique virtues of the British Empire, a superior model to all the other European competitors whose values now reside with the USA.

Surveying this imperial moment, Stephen Howe has underlined the way in which this has produced a 'lessons of history' approach to the study of past empires.[17] History is trawled for political and strategic usage. It is used to shine a light on the present dilemmas, which means that books like Judith Herrin's *Byzantium: The Surprising Life of a Medieval Empire*, examining how the Byzantine imperial system managed to endure 1,000 years, are read in a different way than pre-September 11 and will command a much wider audience.[18] In particular, this search for parallels has led to a preoccupation with the British experience. This is seen as the most illuminating comparison with the present US dilemmas, and the resultant literature has charted not only the whys of Britain's retreat from empire, but also how, in the case of Kenya, this process produced human rights abuses on a vast scale.[19]

Making sense of this vogue for empire, Linda Colley calls on historians to go beyond the British and European empires of the nineteenth century.[20] What is required is a more comprehensive approach because, Colley argues, empire has been one of the most enduring, versatile and ubiquitous forms of political organisation. We need a genuinely global history of empire that integrates the huge range of imperial designs across the ages. In setting out the parameters of this project, Colley calls too for a methodology that is relentlessly wide-ranging, eclectic, comparative and pluralistic in approaches.[21] In this vein she takes issue with Edward Said, who, in one of his last articles, argued that it was immoral to concentrate on imperialists because it ignored the 'suffering and dispossession' of the colonised.[22] In Colley's opinion this is too limiting. Why should one preclude the other? Surely a detailed, sensitive analysis of the multiple ways European empires affected colonised societies must be accompanied by a consideration of the imperialist perspective. This is vital, Colley feels, if we want to build a complete picture of the variegated relationships and understand the vulnerabilities and contingencies of empires.

National narratives

Howe's notion of an imperial moment demonstrates that history writing cannot be divorced from the contemporary political context. Thus the marginality of empire within France after the end of the Algerian war in 1962 must be understood as a product of the assertion of the nation state. Within de Gaulle's brave new world, decolonisation was retrospectively constructed as an uncomplicated linear process. The hesitations, divisions and complexities were deliberately forgotten as decolonisation came to stand for a skilfully managed process. Through it, the nation state had cast off the burden of colonialism and embraced the realities of the mid twentieth century. In de Gaulle's post-1962 world of nation states, colonies were out and a resolutely hexagonal France in, and this meant that the empire became a focus of official forgetting. The imperial phenomenon was considered a minor aspect of national history. But, ironically, this was just at the moment when the reordering of space entailed by decolonisation meant that, arguably, France became a nation state for the first time. Only now could France, divested of the complications of empire, define itself in terms of a singular citizenry in a single territory.

On the colonised side, the nation state was no less entrenched. For all the talk of pan-Africanism and Third World non-alignment within the newly independent countries, the nation state was seen as pathway to modernity. By transcending tribal differences, invented, it was claimed, as instruments of imperial rule, the nation state was held up as a force for unity and strength; the basis of a new world that would act together through equality and partnership. Decolonisation was presented as the movement from empire to the nation state which was inevitable once national self-determination was accepted as a universal, rather than just a European, right. Consequently, concepts of space and interaction were flattened out as independence was conjured up as a self-evidently desirable goal shared by all subjects.

Within these newly independent states, the recovery of the national past went hand in hand with the assertion of political sovereignty. The practice of history, often written in difficult circumstances, conditioned by lack of resources and tight censorship, was about righting the wrongs of colonialism. It was about the restoration of an authentic national identity stolen by empire. It was about the construction of heroic narratives to legitimise post-independence regimes. The past became a morality play which, as Frederick Cooper has underlined, made history into little more than an inventory of the horrors of colonialism, where nothing was said about complicity or collaboration.[23]

On the French side in the 1960s and 1970s, such anticolonial nationalism instilled feelings of post-colonial guilt that contributed even more to the amnesia surrounding empire. Significantly too, it reinforced the idea that colonial history properly belonged to the realm of foreign relations. As a result, historians tended to treat subjects such as the scramble for Africa or decolonisation as episodes in France's external history.

Fractured narratives: beyond amnesia and hagiography

In 1987 and 1988, Charles-Robert Ageron and Jean-Pierre Rioux at the *Institut d'Histoire du Temps Present* (IHTP), at that time the leading contemporary research institute in France, were behind a determined attempt to open up the Algerian war as legitimate object for research. Their intention was to assert historical professionalism over a period that now, given the distance at that time of nearly thirty years since the end of the conflict, was seen to be leaving politics and entering the realm of history. Through three major conferences in Paris, the IHTP brought together historians and eyewitnesses.[24] Explicitly, the aim was to understand the conflict in a more detached and objective manner, as well as to map out the future agendas for research.

The approach of the thirtieth anniversary stimulated further historical reflection within both the profession and the media at large. Early in 1992 there was a rush of exhibitions, films and documentaries on differing aspects of the conflict, and a major international conference at the Sorbonne.[25] The previous autumn, Benjamin Stora's four-part series, *Les années algériennes*, was screened on French television.[26] Based upon 58 filmed interviews, the intention was to give everybody a voice. No aspect was taboo. No perspective was ignored. All, ranging from soldiers and settlers through to Algerian nationalists, were interviewed as Stora sought to present the Algerian war in all its complexity.

In understanding the Algerian war thus, the ever-present point of comparison was the Occupation period, whose complex memory had been meticulously dissected by Henry Rousso in his 1987 book *The Vichy Syndrome*. Specifically, Rousso's concepts of repression, the collective unconscious and fracturing moments were hugely influential in framing the way in which historians approached the Algerian War. As with Vichy, Algeria was seen to be at the centre of a 'syndrome' whose painful aftermath was only too evident with the rise of Jean-Marie Le Pen's National Front since the mid 1980s.[27] This meant that for the likes of Stora, as well as Pascal Blanchard, Nicolas Bancel, Jean-Luc Einaudi, Claude Liauzu and Sandrine Lemaire, history writing was a therapeutic process.[28] It was about breaking down amnesia within wider society. It was about getting France as a whole to come to terms with a difficult past. Equally, it was history writing which wished to demonstrate that colonialism was not peripheral to French history. On the contrary, the 'colonial syndrome' was key to understanding issues of racism and immigration in contemporary politics.

If the notion of taboo was one context for history writing, the other was a new generation of researchers entering the profession. Sylvie Thénault and Raphaëlle Branche completed their PhDs on the Algerian war in 1999 and 2000 respectively. Branche worked on French army and torture, while Thénault examined the workings of the justice system, and both applied rigorous historical methods to the archives. The two PhDs were subsequently published, and together their work pointed to another crucial dimension of this new context for research: the opening up of official archives.[29] Under the 30-year rule, declassified documents were now being released, although, given the sensitive nature of the subject, the flow of material was restricted. This meant that much of the 1990s was about the fight for unfettered access in the name of openness. Only on this basis, historians argued, could the Algerian war finally emerge as an object to be analysed. This pressure, along with renewed controversy over torture during the Algerian war, led the then prime minister, socialist Lionel Jospin, to send out an official circular on 13 April 2001 to all government departments, aiming to facilitate greater speed and transparency.[30] It was a significant victory. One, as Raphaëlle Branche has argued, that demonstrated a new willingness at the highest level to confront France's Algerian past.[31] Consequently, conditions in the archives improved, although there were continued demands for a simplification of procedures. In particular, historians called for the creation of a single overall body to process requests for special dispensation to work on classified documents.

Within the former colonies too there was a shift. In Algeria, anti-government rioting in October 1988 led to a breakdown of the heroic narrative of the war of liberation. In the eyes of many younger Algerians, born after independence, this official memory had become a cynical veneer which, by continually blaming any problems on the legacy of colonialism, was a way of keeping a corrupt elite in power.[32] Such hostility was emblematic of a general crisis in post-colonial Africa that has, John Parker and Richard Rathbone have emphasised, transformed the relationship to history.[33] If in the 1960s history was about correcting colonialism, now history must speak to a troubled present. It is about comprehending the roots of contemporary problems marked by stalled development, dictatorship and repression.

This shift was also shaped by the recognition that these states are no longer young. As countries approach their fiftieth or even sixtieth anniversaries of independence, a sufficient block of time has elapsed for historians to analyse. They now have the necessary perspective to explore, for example, the connections between post-colonial, colonial and pre-colonial periods, and within this reassessment triumphant anticolonial nationalism was seen as too simplistic. By eschewing complexity and ambiguity, it had produced a highly sanitised version of the past. New history writing, then, was about breaking away from hagiography. It was about recovering histories which were marginalised by the grand narratives of anticolonial national liberation.

Pluralistic histories

This desire to dispel amnesia and hagiography within the wider society has produced a new climate where the keyword is pluralism. More than ever, historians of French colonialism are willing to employ a variety of methodological approaches that go beyond monocausal explanations. Thus, previously the dominant historical controversy has been about the relationship between imperialism and capitalism. Too often there was a top-down approach. Imperial history has been thought of solely in terms of European rivalry, high diplomacy and military feats. Now, however, the emphasis is on a complex and variegated history. It is a history that wishes to move beyond a mode of analysis that treats coloniser and colonised as two indiscriminate blocs; one that wants to analyse how colonialism and decolonisation drew in a range of French, African, American, Asian, Caribbean and Pacific actors whose aims were multiple, shifting and evolving. Finally, it is an approach that is interdisciplinary. Of course, the economy is still vital, but it must now be linked to considerations of politics, culture, sociology and memory.

Such pluralism is testament to the ongoing impact of post-colonial studies. For Said, colonialism was a complicated web of economics, politics and culture. Similarly, by setting out to empower the 'other' and deconstruct Enlightenment notions of progress and civilisation, revealing how such notions were central to imperialist domination, Said wanted to challenge the very basic ideas about how objects of historical analysis are conceived. For him, it was no longer possible simply to analyse the past in Africa and Asia through a narrow Eurocentric framework. If new and more fully rounded objects of enquiry were to emerge, questions of power, knowledge and politics had to be addressed head-on.

These arguments had a huge impact on English literature departments in Britain and North America, which became the driving force behind the emergence of post-colonial studies as a separate field during the 1980s and 1990s. Likewise within French departments it led to a major rethink of notions of France and the wider francophone world among literature and area studies specialists.[34] In contrast, some historians have been fiercely critical. For Bernard Porter, one of the leading experts on British Empire, the language used by post-colonialists is impenetrable. Worse still, their lack of historical training means that many of their conclusions are wrong.[35] John Mackenzie, another recognised expert on the British Empire, also called into question Said's historical credentials.[36] In Mackenzie's view there is little attempt to anchor his work in the empirical depth of the imperial experience, with the result that Said's work, like much of post-colonialism, suffers from vagueness and oversimplification. If Said can be called a historian at all, Mackenzie characterises him as one who is trapped by a simplistic Whiggish approach to history – in other words, a presentation of the past as the inexorable march of progress, in this case one where scholars can break free from an imperialist mindset and approach the study of the Orient in ways that are not manipulative.

Others, however, took the view that historians had much to learn from the post-colonial turn. In the USA, Frederick Cooper sees Said's contribution as crucial because of the way in which he shook up historians' complacency about the European boundaries of their field.[37] By showing how certain visions of African, Asian and Caribbean societies are deeply woven into canonical European literature, he was reordering notions of time and space. Colonisation was no longer out there, in exotic places, but in the heart of European culture. Cooper admits that in *Orientalism* Said was criticised for presenting a reductive view of the colonised 'other'. But in his subsequent book published in 1993, *Culture and Imperialism*, Cooper argues that Said restored the balance.[38] There, Said emphasised not the stark separation of European and indigenous discourses, but the efforts of colonised intellectuals to work between them and to develop cross-cutting languages of liberation.

For Cooper, such insights are critical. They have allowed historians to rethink the nature of empire and dissent as space-crossing notions.[39] So the anti-slavery revolt in Haiti, one that began in 1791 and ended with independence in 1804, was not that of a community against external aggression. It was a struggle in which insurgents and counter-insurgents were operating on an ocean-crossing, culturally and politically differentiated space, defined by the imperial nature of French polity. The Haitian leaders closely followed debates in revolutionary France, drawing upon them to put forward the claim that all people within the political and moral space of empire had the right to citizenship.

In the same way, 150 years later, the Senegalese political leader Leopold Senghor sought to transform the French Empire into a federal system which insisted that all French people of Africa, Asia, the Americas and the Pacific should have equal rights before the law.[40] Labour and political movements in French West Africa in the 1940s and 1950s seized on the language of post-war French imperialism – in a moment when France needed more than ever for colonies to be orderly, productive and legitimate – and turned it into demands for equality of wages, benefits and, ultimately, standard of living among all people whom the government asserted to be French. This logic of equivalence – backed by well-organised protest movements and in the context of worldwide debates over self-determination – presented the French government with a dilemma: how to convince its metropolitan citizens to pay for this welfare colonialism. Ultimately, the new Fifth Republic, in place since 1958, baulked at such a cost, and in explaining the unravelling of the French Empire this cold calculus is just as important as the liberation struggles in Indochina and Algeria. No less significantly, in Cooper's opinion, it shows that the national conception of France was born of the same process that gave rise to nation states in North and sub-Saharan Africa.

Pluralism and a willingness to engage with post-colonial studies are also at the heart of Robert Aldrich's research. Within a range of books and articles he has dissected the French Empire from a variety of angles.[41] He has not only analysed the economic dimension, but the cultural and social ones, too. He has paid close attention to representations in photography, painting and film, as well as issues of violence and memory. The cumulative impact is an impressive corpus of work that is highly nuanced; an attentiveness to difference and variation that is also at the core of Tony Chafer's research on French West Africa, Nicola Cooper's on Indochina, and Martin O'Shaughnessy's on colonial film history.[42]

Collectively what is significant about all this work is the desire to move colonial history out of a ghetto. Colonialism and post-colonialism are not an exotic diversion from the main narrative. They are fundamental, and this in turn has had an impact on mainstream studies of France. For example, in the case Roderick Kedward's highly successful general history, *La vie en bleu*, published in 2005, the question of empire is seen to be central to the issue of French identity since 1900.[43]

Future agendas

In paradigmatic terms, empire has returned. It has entered the mainstream and become a past that is permanently present, one of the contexts in which French history has to be analysed and understood. Given this status, what are the future research agendas?

In the first instance, there is the ongoing desire to assert the independence of the historical profession. Invariably this is couched in language unfamiliar to the Anglo-Saxon tradition, which tends to see history as a subject belonging to arts and humanities. Consequently, the starting point for a major international conference on Franco-Algerian history in Lyon in June 2006 was the need to be rigorous, systematic and, above all, scientific in approach, in order to confront historical lacunae.[44] By bringing historians from Algeria, France and beyond, the conference wanted to break away from amnesia, nostalgia or official memory to recreate the past on its own terms. In working thus it also explicitly rejected Article Two of the 23 February 2005 law, which, by talking about the French 'disappeared', ignored the suffering inflicted upon Algerians. Proper history, the conference organisers warned, cannot be selective.

Allied to this is the continuing call for a history that is much less singular and far more plural. History from above must be complemented by history from below, and here oral history has been particularly important. Both Claire Mauss-Copeaux and Natalya Vince, working respectively on French conscripts and the participation of Algerian women in the national liberation struggle, have used personal testimony as a way into understanding the complexities of experiences, choices and perspectives on the ground.[45] Oral history, too, has been used to recover alternative perspectives, drowned out by the weight of official memory. Ryme Seferdjeli has explored the experiences of pro-French Algerian Muslim women, and her work underlines the great strengths of a history that is less deterministic; one that wishes to explore counterfactual scenarios or recover lost voices in order to deepen our understanding about what actually happened.[46] Furthermore, by focusing on how specifically the French sought to win over Algerian women through welfare provision, her research points to a history that is finely tuned to the complexities of gender, class and locality. In the same way, the project set up in 2003 under the auspices of the IHTP by Raphaëlle Branche and Sylvie Thénault is also highly significant.[47] Working together with a network of 40 local researchers throughout France, the intention is to explore the impact of the Algerian war in each metropolitan department from the bottom up. It wants to reorientate understandings through the assertion of micro-history that will break away from oversimplified grand narratives.

However, this emphasis on the specific and the local must be combined with Cooper's richly suggestive ideas about space. For imperial rulers from the Roman Empire through the Ottoman and Austro-Hungarian Empires to the French Community and the British Commonwealth, governing an imperial polity produced a different set of structures and a different way of imagining political space than did a nation state. Empires must not be reduced to national polities projecting their power overseas. National space and colonial space were intertwined, and this produced a whole set of tensions which were crucial to the eventual unravelling of the French Empire.

Taken together, therefore, such a pluralistic transnational framework will open up the field in a number of significant ways. It will allow us to calibrate the different phases of empire more precisely. Thus, was the post-1945 French Union a significantly new development from the policies of both the Third Republic and Vichy? Did it approach the dilemmas and possibilities of empire in a different manner? Did it see empire in terms of limited rule or the realisation of a universal political culture? On these questions, Martin Thomas's book on the 1930s has already been richly suggestive.[48] He shows how, away from the grand political rhetoric, thinly stretched colonial bureaucracies were confronted with the perennial problem of rule. They had to deliver ad hoc arrangements on a shoestring budget and this meant giving local allies a stake in the imperial whole.

This pluralistic and transnational approach will also facilitate comparative work. In the past there has been too little dialogue between historians of different parts of the French Empire. Yet we need to know much more about how the different parts interacted. To what extent, for instance, did knowledge of rule on the ground in Algeria in the 1830s and 1840s establish a template for all subsequent colonial experiences? Moreover, we need to compare local responses. Is it possible, for example, to talk about common patterns of accommodation or opposition? What about the cross-fertilisation of ideas between the various anti-colonial nationalisms? No less important, this framework will permit us to put colonialism and decolonisation into an international diplomatic context. Building upon the insights of Irwin Wall and Martin Shipway, it will allow us to understand how the end of the French Empire was determined by relations with Washington, the NATO alliance and the United Nations.[49]

Finally, to return to Linda Colley at the beginning of this chapter, this framework will enable us to put France into a broader agenda of the global history of empire. If a fuller version of the story of French colonialism and decolonisation is to be told, it must be measured against empires past and present.[50] Equally, it must also be put alongside the two powers with wide reach and an ambivalent sense of themselves as imperial powers: the USA and, after 1917, the Soviet Union. Only in this way can historians come to conclusions about what was specific and what was generic about the French Empire as an imperial phenomenon.

So, to the question of whether colonial history is finished, the obvious response is 'no', because all history is unfinished. The emergence of new generations of researchers, the potential for fresh documentary evidence, greater distance, fresh theoretical models: together these factors make every period subject to constant revision. That said, given the train of contemporary events both within France and beyond, this is a particularly rich and productive moment for colonial history.

Raphaëlle Branche

In November 2005, French Prime Minister Dominique de Villepin decided to use the state of emergency law to deal with the urban riots that had been going on since October. These riots were mainly in the suburbs of the great cities, especially in neighbourhoods where immigrants, and particularly people born into the former French Empire, or their children, were living. Poor neighbourhoods were simply described by most of the media and French people as *les quartiers*, an expression which suggests the existence of a frontier between 'them' and 'us'.

It is specifically in that context that the prime minister chose to use a law which was linked by history to the last colonial war France had to fight: the French-Algerian war.[51] In 1955, the emergency was prompted by a rebellion that spread through Algeria. What was the similarity with the emergency of 2005? Some people could not help thinking that it had something to do with the population targeted by the law, that is, immigrants and their children, particularly of Arab or African and West Indian origins.[52]

This political decision also confirmed for some people of such origins that they were right to call themselves, in a polemical manifesto, 'indigènes de la République' or 'natives of the Republic'.[53] The connection between colonial discrimination and contemporary discrimination against African or Caribbean people was stressed. Colonial history, they said, was not over at all, since the colonial roots of discrimination were considered to be the main cause of the troubles. Were they talking about post-colonialism? It did not really matter. The main point was that France had been an empire founded on discrimination and racism, yet this had not been acknowledged by the state or even by the French people in general.

The 'indigènes de la République' wanted to denounce a political and social situation. Their movement, however, may be considered as part of a much more general phenomenon challenging the French state about its colonial past.[54] This was clear from the beginning of the 1990s, with the demonstrations of the children of *harkis* – Algerian auxiliaries of the French army during the Algerian war – demanding an improvement of their fathers' situation and a clearer recognition of their difficult past. It gained intensity from 1999, when the French Parliament voted a law acknowledging that the Algerian war had not been merely 'maintaining order' in what was technically part of metropolitan France, but an 'Algerian war'. Since then, each year, there have been claims for compensation and for a symbolic recognition in respect of France's colonial past.[55] Two laws in particular were passed: the law of 2001 on slavery as a crime against humanity, and the law of 2005 on people repatriated from Algeria after Algerian independence in 1962, namely French settlers and *harkis*, which included an Article Four which required French schools to teach 'the positive role of colonisation'.[56]

Since 1999, it appears that the colonial past is not over at all. Indeed, it has even become a very present theme in French society – and not only in the media. This concern, of course, has an impact on historians of France's colonial past. Do they share this post-colonial obsession? What do they do with the questions that French society, or parts of it, is asking of the State about the past? To answer these questions, we must make a detour and explore colonial history from the beginning of the post-colonial period, and consider whether decolonisation has inaugurated a new era of academic studies. I will begin with some general remarks about colonial history as a field in France and then focus briefly on the historiography of French Algeria.

Colonial history in perspective

First of all, one should keep in mind that colonial history is not really a specific field in French academic research.[57] Always on the periphery of academic studies during the colonial period, colonial studies were strongly linked with colonial administration and the question of how to deal with indigenous populations. Colonial history was not a major field of research, and that was certainly an important difference between France and the UK.

After the decolonisation period, colonial studies suffered a kind of disgrace: they were considered to have been part of the colonial project and indeed of colonial ideology.[58] Colonial history was the story of victorious conquests, of the struggle between civilisation and barbarism, and indigenous peoples were supposed not to have anything that could be considered as history. In a later period, colonial history was a little more subtle: some historians were genuine critics of French policies and well aware of the seeds of wrath sown by decades of inequality.

The second characteristic of this field is that it is divided. The first line of division is chronological: specialists of the first French empire in the eighteenth century and specialists of the second one in the nineteenth and twentieth centuries do not work together. They do not generally study the same countries, and the academic division in France between early modern historians and modern historians makes it even more difficult for them to work together. Yet these periods have themes in common. Slavery, for example, is a common topic of study for the two empires. This link, however, has been largely invisible until today, for two reasons: first, because of the idea that the French Revolution gave birth to a new idea of man which excluded slavery, and second, because of the way the second colonial empire was built, closely tied to the republican idea of the equality of man. The truth is nevertheless that slavery continued throughout the nineteenth century in some French colonial territories, and, above all, that the law was twisted so that the French way of life in the colonies, which was based on inequality – for example, on forced labour imposed on the indigenous populations – was not considered to contradict the French idea of equality. These factors of discrimination – slavery being the strongest of course – are one of the most dynamic themes of research today.

The second line of division is geographical. This is partly a legacy of the administrative divisions of the French Empire. Indochina specialists meet colleagues working on South East Asia much more than they meet colleagues working on Africa. Black Africa specialists do not really know specialists from the Maghreb. But the inherited division is not the only reason. Specialists from Tunisia or Morocco, for example, may feel closer to specialists of French Algeria, whereas from the mid nineteenth century, Algeria was composed of French departments and these two territories were added much later to the French Empire as protectorates. Morocco was considered to be quite different from Tunisia, and Algeria was used at that time as a counter-example by the French colonisers in Morocco such as Lyautey, who thought that Algeria was a bad example of colonial conquest and administration and strove to do better.

A quick survey of academic journals confirms this. The French journal for overseas history, *La revue française d'histoire d'outre-mer*, recently renamed *Outremers*, is a single vehicle for a colonial history which overrides these divisions. But the journal is an old one, and has great difficulty finding a public. A new journal was founded a few years ago called *Afrique & histoire*, dealing mostly with Black Africa, but not excluding North African countries. The journal's main purpose was to study Africa in the long term, deliberately ignoring the academic divisions into periods of time. *Afrique & histoire* intended to promote the history of Africa in general and to contradict the colonial view of Africa as the continent without a history. Unfortunately, the journal's last issue was in October 2006.

These divisions between chronological periods or territories have consequences on the way colonial history has been and continues to be written. Let us take two examples: a source and a theme. The source is oral history. Historians of Black Africa do not feel uncomfortable using oral testimonies. Oral history also belongs to the way African historians themselves explored their own country's past in the aftermath of independence. Oral history was considered as more than a useful source: indeed its legitimacy was that it could be used against the coloniser to promote an unexplored past. This post-colonial attitude is still common nowadays. On the other hand, historians of North Africa have not been very keen on oral history at the beginning and are still not using it as systematically as historians of Black Africa. This is perhaps because official history has largely dominated in Algeria since the end of the war, and has concentrated on the history of the war of independence.[59]

The theme is women's history, and, later on, gender history. While this is quite an old field of research for the specialist of Black Africa, women's history has not really been studied in the context of Morocco, Tunisia or Algeria, which have been dominated by a political history of nationalism. Only a few recent studies have adopted a gender approach.[60]

Parallel to this slow and limited rethinking, a few authors have acquired popularity by stressing the racism of the French Empire and the French Republic. They have stressed the colonisers' negative image of the colonised people, the violation of indigenous culture by the French (especially with regard to women) and, lately, the enduring process of discrimination inherited from the colonial period.[61] In their view, French society has suffered from a 'colonial fracture'.[62] Their work is mainly based on images of empire and lacks the complexity of the social and political background.[63] Most of all, however, they have preferred to ignore facts which contradict their view. The response they have had in the media had two contradictory effects. On the one hand, they have furnished arguments to some post-colonial militants such as the 'indigènes de la République'. On the other hand, they have undermined the post-colonial approach by irritating most of the academics, at a time when no important book on post-colonialism has been translated into French, which is of great relevance for teaching.[64] This double effect is quite devastating at the moment.

The case of French Algeria

French Algeria is an emblematic case because Algeria was France's biggest colony, the most important territory as far as national identity, emotional involvement and dramatic events are concerned. It is emblematic, too, because of the extreme sensitivity of French society about this subject over the last few years. France's colonial past was mostly seen through Algerian spectacles: what was said to be colonial heritage was in fact the Algerian heritage.

Following the traditional colonial historians, a few historians trained towards the end of the French imperial moment suggested new perspectives on Algerian history. First of all, they focused on the Algerian population or on relations between French and Algerian people from the nineteenth to the beginning of the twentieth century. André Nouschi studied the population of the eastern part of Algeria, the less colonised part of the territory. He studied their standard of living and explored the way in which colonisation inflicted poverty and sometimes destroyed social and economic structures.[65] Annie Rey-Goldzeiguer studied the short period of the second French Empire in the 1860s, and the consolidation of a French Algeria based on discrimination and on the exclusion of the majority of the native part (except for the Jews). She showed how Emperor Napoleon III nevertheless tried to promote a policy of friendship and self-respect between communities.[66] Lastly, Charles-Robert Ageron explored the way French Algeria was constructed by the Third Republic, although his purpose was to try to tell the story from the point of view of Algerians as well as from the different French lobbies and groups involved in these very specific French departments.[67]

This was the generation that linked forerunners of the colonial period, and the youngest generation which has deliberately chosen to study more recent and political subjects. They did a very important job, but they did not have a large following of graduates studying colonial Algeria. That is one of the reasons why so many structures still have to be set up in colonial history.

The most recent generation of historians has chosen much more political subjects, focusing on the twentieth century and the rise of indigenous nationalism.[68] Some very important aspects of contemporary Algeria were examined, but the main purpose was to understand how French colonialism broke down. Social, cultural and economic aspects were subordinated to this issue. For example, they argued that Algerian nationalism could not be understood if Algerian migration to France, mostly from a Kabyle background, was not studied. These migrated to France after the First World War and constituted the first framework for Algerian nationalist ideas. Workers' organisations, on the one hand, and the network of cafés and hostels, on the other, gave this modern nationalism its context. By the same token, to study Algerian migration it was necessary to understand Algerian nationalism, for migration was not a purely social or economic entity.[69]

Things have changed considerably since 1992, because the opening of the public archives on the Algerian war has stimulated much new work on the war and, beyond that, on the colonial period. Many subjects, such as immigration[70] or even nationalism,[71] have been revisited. Sociology and anthropology have helped historians to reconsider the past, especially in terms of agency. Collective actors such as trade unions, the scout movement and football teams have been brought into focus, and a social history of colonial Algeria is now possible because of the availability of the French archives. Of course, large gaps exist and many documents which remained in Algeria are not very easy to locate today. Overall, however, there is a vast range of new materials and new perspectives on French Algeria. Foreign researchers are heavily involved, and part of the international community which gathers in Aix-en-Provence every summer is there not to listen to the opera festival, but to go to the Overseas archives. French historians are less numerous than overseas scholars, but we may anticipate that a new generation of colonial historians is on its way.

Apart from new subjects based on new archives and the renewal of the colonial themes, one of the main issues for colonial historians may be the role the colonial past played in French national history. Never central to national identity, colonial identity was nevertheless part of it. The denial of this role is still a constant in French teaching. In 2005, many historians fought against the law presenting colonisation as something positive to teach to school students. They succeeded, in part. Article Four of the law of 23 February 2005 was abolished by President Jacques Chirac in January 2006. It would be too optimistic, however, to assume that these historians attempted to promote a wider reflection on colonial history and its link with national history.[72]

Unlike social history, cultural history, economic history or even political history, colonial history is too often considered as limited either to a specific period or to a geographically defined space, such as Spanish history. Moving colonial history into mainstream national history will develop new perspectives both for colonial history and for national history. National history will be decentralised in some respects, while the exotic feeling and smell surrounding colonial history will be rooted out.

This is, from my point of view, the main outlook for the future of colonial history in France. Of course, historians from other countries, especially from the former colonies, may not share it, but they have already gone through their own post-colonial revolution. Political history has shown the way and the Algerian Mohamed Sahli has spoken of decolonising history.[73] France, on the other hand, has not really taken into account the fact that the empire is over. For some people, it seems as though the empire still exists, particularly because of the persistence of racial discrimination, while for others amnesia is so powerful that it seems that it never existed. I do not think that historians have to choose between these two positions, but that they should try to promote reflection on the role of empire in defining the national identity, whether from a cultural, social, political or economic point of view. Of course, this does not mean that colonial history is everywhere, and the empire in every part of French history. But we should no longer have to think of colonial history as parallel to national history, or that colonial history includes national history.

This reconsideration of colonial history should not only lead to linking the colonial era and a post-colonial era, questioning the never-ending issue of changes and continuities. It should also help us to understand the nature of Frenchness at the end of the colonial period. That is why colonial history is not over yet, and may never be.

Notes

1 Romain Bertrand, *Mémoires d'empire: la controverse autour du 'fait colonial'* (Paris, Editions du Croquant, 2006).

2 The full text of the law can be accessed on the website for Journal Officiel de la République Française at www.admi.net/jo/20050224/DEFX0300218L.html

3 The Algerian war lasted from 1954 to 1962. Fighting in Morocco and Tunisia began in 1952. Both achieved independence in 1956.

4 The petition, signed initially by Claude Liauzu, Gilbert Meynier, Gérard Noiriel, Frédéric Régent, Trinh Van Thao and Lucette Valensi, was put online at the website of the Toulon section of the League of the Rights of Man on 24 March 2005. By 4 May the number of supporters had reached 1001, at which point it was decided to close the petition to further signatures. The petition can be accessed at www.ldh-toulon.net. Claude Liauzu is the author of numerous articles, books and chapters on French colonialism. These include *Naissance du Salariat et du movement ouvrier en Tunisie* (Paris, CNRS, 1978), and *La société française face au racsime. De la Révolution à nos jours* (Brussels, Complexe, 1999). He died in May 2007.

5 The petition, entitled *Liberté pour l'histoire,* was published in the French daily *Libération* (13 December 2005), 35. The 23 February law was linked to other legislation outlawing the denial of crimes against humanity, recognising the Armenian genocide and condemning slavery as a crime against humanity, passed on 13 July 1990, 29 January 2001 and 21 May 2001 respectively.

6 The conference took place at Guelma in eastern Algeria on May 2005.

7 Bouteflika's speech can be found at www.Algeria-Watch.de. For Bouteflika, attacking the old colonial enemy was also a way of uniting Algerians behind him in the run-up to the referendum on his reconciliation policy on 29 September 2005. Through the proposed peace charter, Bouteflika hoped to bring an end to the huge violence that has dogged Algeria since 1992.

8 'Nous sommes les indigènes de la République', Appel pour les assises de l'anti-colonialisme post-colonial, published 19 January 2005. On this, see their website www.indigenes-republique.org/spip.php?article1

9 This link was underlined by the fact that the state of emergency law invoked by the government dated from the Algerian war.

10 President Chirac made these comments during a press conference for radio and television on 9 December 2005. For a resumé of the conference, go to the website of Radio France Internationale at www.rfi.fr/actufr/articles/072/article_40372

11 On this, see Martin Evans and John Phillips, *Algeria: Anger of the Dispossessed* (London, Yale University Press, 2007), 26–8.

12 Both have published prolifically on Algeria and colonialism. Key books by Gilbert Meynier include *L'Algérie révélée* (Geneva, Droz, 1981), *Histoire intérieure du FLN, 1954–1962* (Paris, Fayard, 2002) and *L'Algérie des origines* (Paris, La Découverte, 2007). Key books by Benjamin Stora include *Messali Hadj* (Paris, L'Harmattan, 1986), *La gangrène et l'oubli: la mémoire de la guerre d'Algérie* (Paris, La Découverte, 1992) and *Algeria 1830 to 2000* (Ithaca, Cornell University Press, 2001).

13 David Cannadine, *Ornamentalism: How the British Saw their Empire* (London, Allen Lane, 2001); Linda Colley, *Captives: Britain, Empire and the World 1600–1850* (London, Jonathan Cape, 2002); Niall Ferguson, *Empire: How Britain Made the Modern World* (London, Allen Lane, 2003); Catherine Hall, *Civilising Subjects: Metropole and Colony in the English Imagination* (University of Chicago Press, 2002); Stephen Howe, *Ireland and Empire: Colonial Legacies in Irish History and Culture* (Oxford University Press, 2000).

14 Edward Said, *Orientalism* (London, Routledge and Kegan Paul, 1978).

15 Homi Bhabha, *The Location of Culture* (London, Routledge, 1994); Gayatri Spivak, *In Other Worlds: Essays in Cultural Politics* (New York, Methuen, 1987); Robert Young, *Colonial Desire: Hybridity in Theory, Culture and Race* (London, Routledge, 1995). Born in Karachi in 1935, Rasheed Araeen is a London-based artist and cultural theorist. He is the author of *Making Myself Visible* (London, Kala Press, 1984) and the editor of the journal *Third Text*.

16 Ferguson, *Empire*, 381.

17 Stephen Howe, 'Tales of the imperial city', *The Independent, Arts & Books Review* (30 November 2007), 5.

18 Judith Herrin, *Byzantium: The Surprising Life of a Medieval Empire* (London, Allen Lane, 2007).

19 On the end of the British Empire, see Ronald Hyam's *Britain's Declining Empire* (Cambridge University Press, 2007) and Piers Brendon's *The Decline and Fall of the British Empire* (London, Cape, 2007). On Kenya, see David Anderson, *Histories of the Hanged: Britain's Dirty War in Kenya and the End of Empire* (London, Weidenfeld & Nicolson, 2005) and Caroline Elkins, *Britain's Gulag: The Brutal End of Empire in Kenya* (London, Cape, 2005).

20 Linda Colley, 'The difficulty of empire: present, past and future', *Historical Review* 79 (August 2006), 207.

21 In terms of global histories of empire, we can already look towards J. H. Elliot's monumental comparative study of Britain and Spain's empires, in the Americas, *Empires of the Atlantic World: Britain and Spain in America, 1492–1830* (London, Yale University Press, 2006) and John Darwin's *After Tamerlane: The Global History of Empire* (London, Allen Lane, 2007), which, in examining the six centuries since the 1405 death of Tamerlane, the semi-legendary Mongol conqueror, alters our focus of empire. By setting

Europe within the Eurasian landmass as a whole, he relates the Portuguese, Spanish, French, Dutch, Belgian, German and British empires to those of the Ottomans, the Safavids, the Mughals, the Manchus, the Russians and the Soviets and the Japanese. In doing so he shows how there is nothing peculiarly European, or western, about imperialism.

22 Linda Colley, 'The difficulty of empire: present, past and future'.

23 On this see Frederick Cooper, *Colonialism in Question: Theory, Knowledge, History* (Berkeley and Los Angeles, University of California Press, 2005).

24 The three conferences led to three books – François Bédarida and Etienne Fouilloux, eds., *La guerre d'Algérie et les chrétiens* (Paris, Les Cahiers de l'IHTP, 1988); Jean-Pierre Rioux and Jean-François Sirinelli, eds., *La guerre d'Algérie et les intellectuels français* (Paris, Les Cahiers de l'IHTP, 1988); and Jean-Pierre Rioux, ed., *La guerre d'Algérie et les Français* (Paris, Fayard, 1990).

25 These included Bertrand Tavernier's four-hour film portrait of French veterans from the Grenoble region, *La guerre sans nom*, and Richard Copan's television documentary, *Les frères des frères*, on the French resistance to the Algerian war. A major exhibition on the Algerian war was organised by Laurent Gervereau, Jean-Pierre Rioux and Benjamin Stora at the Bibliothèque de Documentation Internationale Contemporaine (BDIC) at Nanterre, and subsequently published as a book: Laurent Gervereau, Jean-Pierre Rioux and Benjamin Stora, eds., *La France en guerre d'Algérie* (Nanterre, BDIC, 1992). A major conference, *Mémoire et enseignement de la guerre d'Algérie*, was organised in Paris on 13 and 14 March 2002 by the Institut du monde arabe and La Ligue de l'enseignement. The conference proceedings were published by Gilles Manceron, ed., *Mémoire et enseignement de la guerre d'Algérie: actes du colloque* (2 vols., Paris, Institut du monde arabe, 1993).

26 For Benjamin Stora's own reflections on the reception of the series, see Benjamin Stora, 'Entre histoire, memoires et images: les années algériennes', *Vingtième siècle. Revue d'histoire* 35 (July–Sept 1992), 93–6.

27 On the relationship between colonialism and racism, see Max Silverman, *Deconstructing the Nation: Immigration, Racism and Citizenship in Modern France* (London, Routledge, 1992).

28 Nicolas Blancel, Pascal Blanchard and Sandrine Lemaire, *La fracture coloniale* (Paris, La Découverte, 2006) and Jean-Luc Einaudi, *La Bataille de Paris: 17 Octobre 1961* (Paris, Le Seuil, 1991).

29 Raphaëlle Branche, *La torture et l'armée pendant la guerre d'Algérie 1954–1962* (Paris, Gallimard, 2001) and Sylvie Thénault, *Une drôle de justice: les magistrats dans la guerre d'Algérie* (Paris, La Découverte, 2001).

30 The circular aimed to speed up responses to demands to consult restricted material, the so-called *dérogations*.

31 On this, see Raphaëlle Branche, *La guerre d'Algérie: une histoire apaisée* (Paris, Le Seuil, 2005), 172.

32 On this see Evans and Phillips, *Algeria: Anger of the Dispossessed*, 107.

33 John Parker and Richard Rathbone, *African History: A Very Short Introduction* (Oxford University Press, 2007).

34 Within the United Kingdom, Charles Forsdick and David Murphy, both working in languages departments, have been at the forefront of this intellectual trend. See Charles Forsdick, *Travel in Twentieth-century French and Francophone Cultures: The Persistence of Diversity* (Oxford University Press, 2005) and Charles Forsdick and David Murphy, eds., *Francophone Postcolonial Studies: A Critical Introduction* (London, Edward Arnold, 2003). See also Margaret Majumdar, ed., *Francophone Studies* (London, Edward Arnold, 2002).

35 Bernard Porter made these comments during a day conference entitled 'Comparative Empires' at the University of Sydney, 28 July 2006. The conference was organised by the Empire, Nation, Globe research cluster. On their work, go to www.arts.usyd.edu.au/research_projects/nationempireglobe. A key book by Bernard Porter is *The Absent-minded Imperialists: Empire, Society and Culture in Britain* (Oxford University Press, 2004).

36 John Mackenzie, *Orientalism: History, theory and the arts* (Manchester: Manchester University Press, 1995).

37 Frederick Cooper, *Colonialism in Question: Theory, Knowledge, History*, 14.

38 Edward Said, *Culture and Imperialism* (New York, Knopf, 1993).

39 Frederick Cooper, *Colonialism in Question: Theory, Knowledge, History*, 99.

40 Frederick Cooper, *Decolonization and African Society: The Labor Question in French and British Africa* (Cambridge University Press, 1996).

41 Key publications by Robert Aldrich include *France and the South Pacific since 1940* (Basingstoke, Macmillan, 1993); *Greater France: A History of French Overseas Expansion* (Basingstoke, Macmillan, 1996); *Colonialism and Homosexuality* (London, Routledge, 2002); *Vestiges of the Colonial Empire in France: Monuments, Museums and Colonial Memories* (Basingstoke, Macmillan, 2005).

42 See Tony Chafer, *The End of Empire in French West Africa* (Oxford, Berg, 2002); Nicola Cooper, *France in Indochina: Colonial Encounters* (Oxford, Berg, 2001); Martin O'Shaughnessy, 'Poor propaganda: French colonial films of the 1930s', in Martin Evans, ed., *Empire and Culture: The French Experience 1830–1940* (Basingstoke, Macmillan, 2004).

43 Rod Kedward, *La vie en bleu: France and the French since 1900* (London, Allen Lane, 2005).

44 The conference, organised by the École Normale Supérieure, took place on 20–22 June 2006 and was entitled *Pour une histoire critique et citoyenne: le cas de l'histoire franco-algérienne*. The conference proceedings can be accessed at http://ens-web3.ens-lsh.fr/colloque/france-algerie/

45 Claire Mauss-Copeaux, *Les appelés en Algérie: la parole confisquée* (Paris, Hachette, 1999); Natalya Vince, 'To be a moudjahida in independent Algeria: itineraries and memories of women combatants' (PhD thesis, University of London, 2008).

46 Ryme Seferdjeli, '"Fight with us, women, and we will emancipate you": France, the FLN and the struggle over women during the Algerian War of National Liberation' (PhD thesis, University of London, 2005).

47 The project can be accessed at www.ihtp.cnrs.fr/. The findings of the project will be published by Autrement.

48 Martin Thomas, *The French Empire Between the Wars: Imperialism, Politics and Society* (Manchester University Press, 2005).

49 Irwin M. Wall, *France, the United States and the Algerian War* (Berkeley and Los Angeles, University of California Press, 2001); Martin Shipway, *Decolonization and Its Impact: A Comparative Approach to the End of the Colonial Empires* (London, Blackwell, 2008).

50 In terms of those empires with which it shared time, the French Empire should be set alongside not only the Portuguese, Spanish, French, Dutch, Belgian, German and British empires, but also the Habsburg, the Russian and the Ottoman ones.

51 Arlette Heymann, *Les libertés publiques et la guerre d'Algérie* (Paris, Librairie générale de droit et de jurisprudence, 1972).

52 Sylvie Thénault, 'L'état d'urgence (1955–2005): de l'Algérie coloniale à la France contemporaine', *Le mouvement social* 218 (Jan–Mar 2007), 63–78.

53 'Nous sommes les indigènes de la République!…'. Appel pour les assises de l'anti-colonialisme post-colonial. Published 19 January 2005.

54 See, for example, Pascal Blanchard, Nicolas Bancel and Sandrine Lemaire, eds., *La fracture coloniale: la société française au prisme de l'héritage colonial* (Paris, La Découverte, 2005). Several journals have brought out special issues on the topic. For instance, *Politix. Revue des sciences et du politique*, 'La colonie rapatriée' 76/19 (2006); *ContreTemps*, 'Postcolonialisme et immigration', 16 (April 2006).

55 Raphaëlle Branche, *La guerre d'Algérie: une histoire apaisée?* (Paris, Le Seuil, L'histoire en débats series, 2005).

56 This article was later abolished. See Martin Evans' contribution above, pp. 145–7.

57 Sophie Dulucq and Colette Zytnicki, 'Penser le passé colonial français. Entre perspectives historiographiques et résurgence des mémoires', *Vingtième siècle. Revue d'histoire* (spring 2005), 59–69.

58 Sophie Dulucq and Colette Zytnicki, eds., *Décoloniser l'histoire?: de l'histoire coloniale aux histoires nationales en Amérique latine et en Afrique, XIXe–XX siècles* (Saint-Denis, Société française d'histoire d'outre-mer, 2003).

59 On a close topic, see Fanny Colonna, 'The nation's "unknowing other": three intellectuals and the culture(s) of being Algerian, or the impossibility of subaltern studies in Algeria', *Journal of Northern African Studies* 8/1 (Spring 2003), 155–70.

60 Djamila Amrane, *Les femmes algériennes dans la guerre* (Paris, Plon, 1991); Christelle Taraud , *La prostitution coloniale. Algérie, Tunisie, Maroc (1830–1962)* (Paris, Payot, 2003); Chérifa Bouatta, 'Feminine militancy: moudjahidates during and after the Algerian war', in Valentine Moghadam, ed., *Gender and National Identity – Women and Politics in Muslim Societies* (published for the United Nations University World Institute for Development Economics Research (UNU/WIDER) by Zed Books; Karachi, Oxford University Press, 1994), 18–39; Ryme Seferdjeli, 'French reforms and Muslim women's emancipation during the Algerian war', *The Journal of North African Studies* 9/4 (2004), 19–61.

61 Nicolas Bancel, Pascal Blanchard and Françoise Vergès, *La République coloniale: essai sur une utopie* (Paris, Albin Michel, 2003).

62 Pascal Blanchard, Nicolas Bancel and Sandrine Lemaire, eds., *La fracture coloniale. La société française au prisme de l'héritage colonial* (Paris, La Découverte, 2005).

63 Nicolas Bancel, Pascal Blanchard and Francis Delabarre, eds., *Images d'Empire: 1930–1960: trente ans de photographies officielles sur l'Afrique française* (Paris, La Martinière: la documentation française, 1997); Pascal Blanchard, Éric Deroo, Driss El Yazami et al. *Le Paris arabe: deux siècles de présence des Orientaux et des Maghrébins* (Paris, la Découverte: Génériques: ACHAC, 2003).

64 Homi Bhabha's *Location of Culture* (1994) was not translated into French until 2007.
65 André Nouschi, *Enquête sur le niveau de vie des populations rurales constantinoises, de la conquête jusqu'en 1919, essai d'histoire économique et sociale* (Paris, PUF, 1961).
66 Annie Rey-Goldzeiguer, *Le royaume arabe: la politique algérienne de Napoléon III, 1861–1870* (Algiers, Société nationale d'édition et de diffusion, 1977).
67 Charles-Robert Ageron, *Les Algériens musulmans et la France (1871–1919)* (2 vols., PUF, 1968).
68 Omar Carlier, Guy Pervillé, Benjamin Stora, Mohammed Harbi.
69 On the topic, see Benjamin Stora's first books: *Dictionnaire biographique des militants nationalistes algériens, 1926–1954* (Paris, L'Harmattan, 1985) and *Messali Hadj (1898–1974) pionnier du nationalisme algérien* (Paris, Sycomore, 1982).
70 For example, Laure Pitti's thesis, 'Ouvriers algériens à Renault-Billancourt de la guerre d'Algérie au grèves d'OS des années 1970. Contribution à l'histoire sociale et politique des ouvriers étrangers en France' (University of Paris VIII, 2002).
71 Linda Amiri, *La bataille de France: la guerre d'Algérie en métropole* (Paris, R. Laffont, 2004); Jim House and Neil MacMaster, *Paris 1961, Algerians, State Terror and Memory* (Oxford University Press, 2006).
72 Romain Bertrand, *Mémoires d'empire. La controverse autour du 'fait colonial'* (Broissieux, Editions du Croquant et Savoir/Agir, 2006).
73 Mohamed Chérif Sahli, *Décoloniser l'histoire* (Paris, F. Maspero, 1965).

8

Is there a 'tyranny of the present' in the writing of history today?

Alya Aglan and Robert Gildea

History has always been a dialogue between the present and the past. The questions historians ask of the past have traditionally been to undertand the present: how did this society, or nation, or religion get to where it is now? Today, however, there is arguably a 'tyranny of the present' in that the present dictates ways in which the past is understood: if people are suffering today, then the past needs to be rewritten as a story of oppression, and the oppressors or their heirs called upon to make amends in the present. The past is now rewritten not only by professional historians, but by groups who mobilise their group memory as a legitimate account of the past; the more they were oppressed, the more attention needs to be paid to their account. This mobilisation takes the form of commemoration, and the goal is achieved when the commemoration of a particular group is upheld as a commemoration by the society or nation as a whole. Historians are no longer required to write 'objective' accounts, but to endorse the account of one persecuted group or another. Alya Aglan examines the way in which French historians have been summoned by the French state to unearth the manner in which Jews were despoiled during the German occupation and yet have to find a way of reconciling group memories with a wider history of society. Robert Gildea explores the recourse to the past of nostalgics as well as victims and nations, and argues that one option for historians is to study precisely how societies come to terms with their painful pasts.

Alya Aglan

An excess of the present in the past

> Perhaps it would be proper to say that there are three times, the present of things past, the present of things present, and the present of things future. For these three are in the soul and I do not see them elsewhere: the present of things past is memory; the present of things present is immediate vision; the present of future things is expectation.
> (St Augustine)[1]

The present pervades history as it pervades historians. According to Marc Bloch, historians understand the past through the present, and the present through the past. 'In the last analysis, whether consciously or no, it is always by borrowing from our daily experiences and by shading them, if necessary, with new tints that we derive the elements which help us to restore the past. The very names we use to describe ancient ideas or vanquished forms of social organisation would be quite meaningless if we had not known living men.'[2] As R. G. Collingwood asserted, 'the past is not a dead past but lives on in the present, the historian's knowledge … is knowledge of the past in the present, the self-knowledge of the historian's own mind as the present revival and reliving of past experiences'.[3] Having considered such writers, Antoine Prost argues that 'this past time which is brought up to the present is explored by the historian in both directions, upstream from present to past and downstream from past to present', and he concludes that 'history is constructed by this continual movement between the present and the past and between different moments of the past'.[4]

Few historians would have any quarrel with this. The use of the present to ask questions of the past is perfectly legitimate, but the past is also increasingly called upon to provide answers for the present, which is much more controversial. Unfinished business in the present, such as the pain suffered by the victims of past persecution, has led to a mobilisation of the past in a particular way to highlight persecution and oppression, for which apology, compensation and justice are demanded in the present. The past becomes not an objective account of 'how things happened', but a moral drama in which champions of right and perpetrators of wrong are held to account for the benefit of a contemporary audience in search of redress. This is what is meant by a the 'tyranny of the present', in the sense of an excess of the present in the past, which imposes a 'duty' on the historian to rewrite history in light of present needs. It poses a challenge to the traditional role of the historian which will be examined.

The evolution of different ways in which society relates the past to the present has been explored by Reinhardt Koselleck.[5] For Koselleck, broadly, there are three distinct ways of viewing history. The first takes the perspective of the past. Each historical event is seen from the point of view of a changeless past which renews itself as tradition and gives a cyclical vision of the past, in constant repetition. It can be summarised as 'There is nothing new under the sun'. The past provides the framework for understanding events, as the myth of Atlantis gave Plato the framework for understanding the history of Athens. The second view, which coincides with the coming of the modern world, takes the perspective of the future. Each event is seen from the perspective of a final utopian state, as a stage leading to it. The history of humanity is that of progress in linear fashion. The third view, which developed from the nineteenth century, takes the perspective of the present. The present rather than the past is the lens through which the past is viewed. The past is in some way summoned by the present to serve as an analogy, an echo. History is sporadically replayed rather than allowed to unfold as a process. Koselleck argues that the present is conceived as the future of a past whose apirations – in terms of emancipation or identity – it can judge to see if they have been fulfilled or not. The present embraces those elements of the past with which it has an elective affinity and registers the success or failure of its hopes.

Seeking to explain the way in which revolutions seek legitimation in a past that seems to announce them, Walter Benjamin famously spoke of 'the tiger's leap into the past':

> History is the subject of a construction whose site is not homogeneous, empty time, but time filled by a now-time [*Jetztzeit*]. Thus, to Robespierre, ancient Rome was a past charged with now-time, a past which he blasted out of the continuum of history. The French Revolution viewed itself as Rome reincarnate. It cited ancient Rome exactly the way fashion cites a bygone mode of dress. Fashion has a nose for the topical, no matter where it stirs in the thickets of long ago. It is the tiger's leap into the past.[6]

The intensity of the present is explained by the selective way in which the past is plundered, and rescued from the monotonous succession of cause and effect. While Benjamin spoke of the messianic quality of certain events, the poet Baudelaire (explicitly quoted by Benjamin) spoke of the mystical concommitance in the present moment of the ephemeral and the eternal.[7] The tyranny of the present is this permeation of the present that can be found in the links made by contemporaries with history, a history that becomes the trace of aspirations that are never fulfilled.

History and memory

For a long time, this use of the past for the purposes of legitimation was undertaken above all by the victors in the historical process. During the French Third Republic (1870–1940), for example, the dominant school of French history, led by the historians Seignobos and Lavisse, placed an emphasis on 'great men', their decisions, the centres of power and important events. The past was to serve an edifying role, underpinning the Republic that had to be secured against political challenges, and rebuilding the nation's confidence in itself after the defeat of 1870.[8] 'The history of France in particular', said a decree of 1880, 'should highlight the development of institutions from which modern society has emerged. It should inspire respect for and loyalty to the principles on which these institutions have been founded'.[9] History is an 'instrument of political education',[10] wrote Seignobos, written 'not to tell a story or to prove but to answer questions about the past that are posed by contemporary society'.[11]

More recently, the use of the past for present purposes has been the work of social, religious or ethnic groups who feel that they have not been given justice by the outcome of history, and demand a replaying which recognises their identities and claims. Because they do not initially have access to 'official' history, these groups mobilise memory through the act of commemoration or remembering in common.

Since the end of the 1970s, 'memory' has taken over the social sciences. For Holocaust historian Enzo Traverso:

> Memory is often used as a synonym for history, and has a tendency to absorb it, becoming itself a metahistorical category. It trawls the past with a net whose mesh is coarser than that of the traditional discipline called history, and injects a much greater dose of subjectivity and experience. In a word, memory seems to be a less arid and more humane kind of history. Today it is invading public space in the western world. The past accompanies the present and occupies its collective imagination as a memory that is powerfully enlarged by the media, often controlled by the authorities ... The past becomes collective memory, selected and reinterpreted according to the cultural sensibilities, ethical questions and political conveniences of the present.[12]

With fascism and Nazism, the Holocaust and colonialism, there has been a mobilisation of memories, often in competition, and entirely solicited by a present, which is the future of this past. Memory becomes a sort of civil religion whose purpose is to recognise and apologise.

Tszvetan Todorov has described a 'commemorative mania' or a 'frenzy of historical liturgies' in France and elswehere. He points out that one museum a day is being opened in Europe. The 'militants of memory', he says, find in memory the most immediate way to obtain affirmation of their existence, to feel membership of a group.

> I am Catholic, or from Berry, or a peasant, or a communist; I am not nobody, so I won't be swallowed up by nothingness. Without being particularly observant, we can see that the contemporary world is tending to greater homogeneity and uniformity, and that this tendency threatens traditional identities and loyalties … The meeting of these two conditions – the need for collective identity and the destruction of traditional identities – explains in part the new cult of memory. It is by establishing a common past that groups can secure recognition.[13]

There is a danger that the identity of the historian is used to legitimate his or her academic interests, so that only Armenians are qualified to write about the Armenian massacres, African history can only be written by Africans, and Muslim history is monopolised by Muslims. In this way, history becomes purely empathetic rather than critical. The writing of history is not simply the defence of the memory of certain groups, nor does it require the identification of historians and their subject. As Eric Hobsbawm emphasises, 'History which is designed only for Jews (or African Americans, or Greeks, or women, or proletarians, or homosexuals) cannot be good history, though it may be comforting history to those who practise it'.[14] Nevertheless, a professional historian who, in the pursuit of a critical overview, goes against the common past asserted by a group risks provoking the anger of that group. Thus a West Indian group from Guiana recently sued the French historian Pétré-Grenouilleau for his book on the slave trade, provoking a number of historians to sign and publish a petition entitled 'Liberté pour l'histoire', 'Freedom for history'.[15]

The obsession with memory is less the fault of historians than of society and political power, but it has shaped historiographical movements such as the appearance of *Subaltern Studies* in India in the early 1980s, devoted to writing the history of 'peoples without history'.[16] In the West, historians are caught up in the contradictions of the present, required to respond to an increased and diversified social demand. They are called upon as expert witnesses in the trials of former collaborators, or as expert researchers to work in the archives of businesses suspected of collaboration with the Nazis, or they are summoned to advise the media in its hunger for commemoration.[17] This may jeopardise the academic freedom conventionally demanded by historians in order to pursue their research and writing. As experts they may be required to provide answers in the past to questions suggested by the present concerns of a particular aggrieved group or institution threatened with discredit, rather than to questions suggested by the evolving historiography of the discipline. They may also be required to provide answers under conditions and time constraints that are set by political rather than professional requirements. The summons to French historians to sort out the tangled past of occupied France serves as an eloquent example in this respect.

Vichy in the 1990s

After 1990 there was a painful return of unresolved questions about the Second World War in France. Issues raised by society exercised a huge pressure on professional historians. In order to understand the nature of these issues we have to go back to the context of those years.[18] Although the reunification of Germany on 3 October 1990, following the fall of the Berlin Wall in 1989, might have brought to an end the legacy of the Second World War, in France, paradoxically, debates around the memory of events relating to the German occupation became even more intense. In February 1990, judicial proceedings began into the case of the former militia leader Paul Touvier, who had been arrested and accused of crimes against humanity. On 27 April 1990, *L'express* led with an investigation into the French concentration camps of Pithiviers and Beaune-la-Rolande near Orléans, where Jews, including 3,500 Jewish children, were held after the round-up of 16–17 July 1942 and initial internment in the Vélodrome d'Hiver (Vel d'Hiv) in Paris. On 13 May 1990, there was a demonstration of Jewish associations in front of the house of René Bousquet, who had been Secretary-General of Police in the Vichy government in the period 1942–43. Judicial proceedings into his case began on 19 November 1990. On 14 May, there were massive demonstrations in Paris, protesting against the desecration of Jewish graves in a Carpentras cemetery. On 16 May, new accusations of crimes against humanity were brought against Maurice Papon, former secretary-general of the prefecture of Bordeaux under Vichy. On 13 November 1990, Serge Klarsfeld, president of the Association of the Sons and Daughters of Jewish Deportees from France, told *Le monde* that he had found, in the archives of the veterans' ministry, the census file listing Jews in the Paris area in 1940, which formed the basis of the round-ups of 1942. Finally, the question of confiscation of Jewish property arose when Klarsfeld revealed in *Libération* on 15 July 1995 that Jews interned at Drancy on the outskirts of Paris had not been compensated for property confiscated from them.

The French government responded to much of this pressure. A new penal code of 22 July 1991 brought in a distinction between crimes against humanity and genocide, lifting the time limit within which cases had to be brought to justice, and imposing a maximum life sentence. François Mitterrand came under pressure to admit the responsibility of the French state in the persecution of Jews in France during the war, with a petition submitted on 17 June 1992 by the Comité du Vel d'Hiv 42, and a bill tabled by Charles Lederman on its behalf by communist senators on the recognition of crimes against humanity committed by Vichy. A decree of 3 February 1993 inaugurated a national day of commemoration of racist and anti-Semitic persecution that would be held annually on 16 July, the anniversary of the Vel d'Hiv round-ups. On 16 July 1995, in a speech delivered in front of the monument to the victims of the Vel d'Hiv, President of the Republic Jacques Chirac accepted the responsibility of the French state and spoke of a 'collective wrong'. At the annual dinner of the Council of Jewish Organisations in France (the Conseil Représentatif des Institutions Juives de France, or CRIF) on 25 January 1997, its president asked the government to set up a commission of the great and the good to remove doubt and confusion about what happened to Jewish property confiscated during the war.

Immediately, on 5 February 1997, Prime Minister Alain Juppé invited Jean Mattéoli to chair a commission of enquiry, which would include historians, into the confiscation of Jewish property. Historians had recently had a great deal to do. The historians' commission chaired by René Rémond, which investigated the links between Paul Touvier and the Catholic Church, reported on 6 January 1992, and its findings were published by Fayard.[19] A commission of experts, again chaired by René Rémond, reported on 30 December 1992 on the census discovered by Serge Klarsfeld; it ruled that this was not the census of October 1940, which had been destroyed in 1948–49. In a new departure, historians were now summoned as witnesses at the Touvier trial at Versailles in 1994 and the Papon trial at Bordeaux in 1997.[20]

The example of the Deposit and Consignment Office

History caught up with the Deposit and Consignment Office (the Caisse des dépôts et consignations or CDC, which had been set up by the Vichy government in 1941 to hold confiscated Jewish property) in 1990. Two journalists began to investigate its role under the occupation, and one of them, Sabine Guez of the *Nouvel observateur*, met the Office's historical consultant. A report of 10 June 1990 to the Office's managing director, Robert Lion, stated that the interview had gone well in that the journalist had not been shown the documents she wished to see. These were no. 501, the accounts of judicial and administrative deposits, and no. 511, the accounts of the General Commission on Jewish Questions (the Commissariat général aux questions juives or CGQJ), which revealed the scale and nature of financial operations at the time. The Office's archivist replied that their archives could not be consulted before the elapse of 60 years, so that they would be opened gradually between 2001 and 2011, but because of the payment of deposits after 30 years and the shredding of accounts there was 'little hope of finding clear evidence'. The report ended by saying that research into the archives of the CDC had not begun, but 'while the few documents found – which have not been communicated or mentioned – make sorry reading, in some matters the Office conducted itself in a postive and honorable manner'. This report was annotated by managing director Robert Lion, 'Why not show the journalist the accounts 501 and 511 and talk about those? Thank you for acting in this way'.[21]

Once again, in October 1992, the Office was challenged by Serge Klarsfeld, who requested information about 'the possible rerouting of property of the French Jewish community to Germany'.[22] A limited search took place, but the archives reported that the documents had not been classified and were inaccessible. In December 1992, the Office received two letters, one from Serge Klarsfeld and the other from Jean Kahn, president of the Council of Jewish Organisations in France. These asserted that the Office still had assets originating from the confiscation of Jewish property under the Occupation. During the period 1992–93 the Office was afraid that it would be abolished, as announced by the new prime minister, Edouard Balladur, and did not wish to be incriminated. In self-defence, the office tried to bury the case. The Office's auditors and historical consultant (*conseiller*) undertook an investigation and declared in June 1993 that these were internal matters, the results of which would remain internal; citing the 1979 archive law, they announced that no documents would be made available for 60 years. The Office preserved a kind of faith in its own infallibility. 'On the question of whether the Office has ever retained funds entrusted to it and never reclaimed', read a note of the historical consultant in 1994, 'an examination of the rules and their execution shows that the Office made a full repayment either to individuals with claims or to the Treasury'.[23] Four years after the first scares, the office was still repeating the same story. The report of June 1993 was not sent to the Council of Jewish Organisations, the prime minister and the minister of finance until September 1995. In an article published in *Libération* on 17 July 1995, Serge Klarsfeld accused the Deposit and Consignment Office, the Bank of France, the National Estates office (the Administration des Domaines), the Paris Prefecture of Police and the Treasury of holding Jewish property in the form of money, jewellery and share titles which had been seized at the Drancy camp, after the Liberation.

In 1997, the Office discretely contacted the historians Jean-Pierre Azéma and René Rémond in order to show them the research they had undertaken. There was to be no publicity about either the work or the archives, which remained closed. In December 1996, at a conference, Michel Slitinsky, who escaped the Vel d'Hiv round-up at the age of 17 and joined the Resistance, challenged the Office's legal director, alleging that the Office's vaults contained a fortune derived from the confiscation of Jewish property. Another bombshell was the book of *Libération* journalist Brigitte Vital-Durand, entitled *Domaine privé*, which accused the City of Paris of holding in its private endowment part of the property seized from Jews under the Occupation.[24] The council for the City's private endowment, chaired by Noël Chahid-Nouraï, set up a commission, which reported. Most significant for the involvement of historians was the establishment in October 1997 of the Mattéoli Mission, set up by Prime Minister Alain Juppé and continued by his successor Lionel Jospin. Its brief was to advise the authorities and to 'evaluate the degree of confiscations', establish which kinds of person had benefitted, draw up a balance sheet, find out what had happened to the property, inventory the property that had not been reclaimed, and make recommendations about what should happen to properties that were currently in the hands of French institutions. The government was acting as a mediator between, on the one hand, pressure from society that was growing in the 1990s, and, on the other, the Office and other banks and insurance companies. It was a decisive intervention by the government which provided the researchers assigned to this enquiry with all the necessary means, in particular the freedom to consult all the documenation they required. Historians François Furet, Annette Wieviorka, Claire Andrieu and Antoine Prost, together with archivist Caroline Piketty, were allocated research assistants among those called up for military service to go through part of the AJ 38 section of the National Archives. The computerisation of individual files was begun. In response to social pressures, the Office accepted this enquiry, but with the presupposition that it had done nothing wrong, either then or now. In response to the government initiative, it launched its own research, modelled on the work of the Mattéoli Mission and employing 15 people on a full-time basis.

The Mattéoli Mission was required to establish an audit of confiscations, not a history of confiscations, which was left to historians. The pioneering work of Philippe Verheyde on the Aryanisation of large Jewish businesses,[25] and those of Jean Laloum on that of small businesses in the Paris region,[26] which appeared in 1997 and 1998, were followed by other studies.[27] The tasks were clearly divided up: historians were to establish the facts, to analyse and explain, while those appointed by the Mattéoli Mission, followed by the Office's own team, were to produce the accounts. Faced by the social pressure mediated by the government, the embarrassment of the Mattéoli Mission historians was evident. On several occasions they made clear their unease about the size of the task, the intensity of the social pressure and the constraints on their freedom of enquiry. In particular, they underlined the ambiguity of their position: the questions they were required to address were not their own, and yet to reply to social pressure they were obliged to answer them. This unease was underlined in the introduction to the final report submitted to the government early in 2000. 'The questions have not been framed by historians as they would prefer, in the freedom of their study, but by various national and international demands'.[28] In addition, the time allotted for research was voluntarily limited by respect for the victims and descendants of victims, who were awaiting their conclusions. The research was undertaken under close surveillance, interspersed by the periodic and virulent attacks of the World Jewish Congress on the working methods of the Mattéoli Mission. As every business that traded during the Second World War was challenged to publish its accounts, the pressure exerted on historians was intense. Some came from American law firms which took up cases and even encouraged litigation – although Robert Paxton, for one, refused – some from businesses accused of misdeeds which set up commissions of historians to trawl their archives. The German publisher Bertelsmann, for example, asked Saul Friedländer to form a team of researchers to investigate its activities during the Third Reich. An article in *Libération* on 11 March 1999, entitled, 'Historians, guarantors of businesses', listed a score of German firms which has already set up commissions of historians, alongside 18 commissions set up by the Austrian, Swiss, Argentinian, French and US governments. Pressure was even greater on the Deposit and Consignment Office. The World Jewish Congress initiated proceedings against certain French banks. Two collective actions were brought in December 1997 and December 1998 against the Société Générale, the Crédit Lyonnais, the Crédit Commercial de France, the Crédit Agricole, Indosuez, Natexis, and French branches of Chase Manhattan and J. P. Morgan. The Deposit and Consignment Office was cited as a witness and feared losing its precious AAA/AAA ranking, which was synonymous with financial solidity on the international markets. Any action brought by the World Jewish Congress might provoke a boycott in the American market, which would be disastrous for the Office's financial activities.

Since the Mattéoli Mission was of government origin, established to investigate the plundering of Jewish property under the Vichy regime, the questions historians had to address derived from the government itself, which in turn channelled and provoked questions raised in society. The historical commission of the Deposit and Consignment Office, set up at the same time, offers a powerful example of the gap between historical priorities and institutional imperatives. The conclusions of the historians employed on this enquiry were determined in advance, given that the Office in the 1940s was not seen differently from the Office of today. To reply to these different pressures, historians were obliged to navigate around the conclusions that were suggested to them, to return to their own questions and their own methodologies.[29]

Critical history

Following Maurice Halbwachs[30] and then Pierre Nora, French historians have increasingly distinguished between history and memory, stressing that history is not beholden to pressures outside itself and has no other object than knowledge. In his introduction to *Les lieux de mémoire,* Pierre Nora wrote:

> Memory and history, far from being synonymous are completely opposed. Memory is life, always cultivated by living groups and is thus in a state of permanent evolution, subject to the dialectic of remembering and forgetting, unaware of successive deformations, liable to be used and manipulated, sometimes lying quiet and then suddenly revived. History on the other hand is the difficult and incomplete reconstruction of that which is no more. Memory is always current, a living bond with the present; history is the representation of the past. Emotional and magical, memory only retains what comforts it. It is made up of vague, telescoping, general, floating, individual and symbolic memories, a prey to transference, censorship, screening-out and projection. History, which is an intellectual and rational practice, requires analysis and a critical approach ... memory is an absolute and history is relative. [31]

To be true to the discipline, Nora asserted, the historian must keep a critical distance from the subject in order to see all its facets, and not subject it to any moral standard or judgement.

In contemporary society, however, François Hartog has spoken of a 'presentism of the present', a refuge in the present when the future is seen to threaten, which results in the elision of the past and future in the present'.[32] This problem is central to the history of memory. There is a danger in the historiographical tendency which looks to the past to provide answers to questions relating to the present. 'For Halbwachs', says Enzo Traverso, 'history supposes an external perspective on events whereas memory implies an internal relationship with what is related. Memory fixes the past in the present, whereas history places it in a time that has passed, organised in a rational way which is the complete opposite of subjective experience'.[33] Historians of memory face the challenge of needing to remain outside the phenomena they are analysing but with which they are subjectively involved. The historian's craft, while being sensitive to what memory provides, must be able to hold it at a distance, in order to reconstruct as objectively as possible the relation between present and past.

One response to this delimma about the abuse of the past in the present has been suggested by Paul Ricoeur. He argued that memory could not be abolished, but that history could critique and contextualise individual and group memories because it has a responsibility to all the dead of the past. The historian has to acknowledge a deep dependency on memory, which is neither an archaic vestige nor a dangerous fiction, but a resource in which the critical work of the historian can take place.

> There is a privilege that cannot be refused to history; it consists not only of expanding collective memory beyond any actual memory but in correcting, criticising, even refuting the memory of a determined community, when it folds back upon itself and encloses itself within its own sufferings to the point of remaining blind and deaf to the suffering of other communities. It is along the path of critical history that memory encounters a sense of justice. [34]

To find the 'just memory' requires renouncing two forms of historical knowledge that are seen as absolute. In the first place, the historian can no longer assume the role of a judge, because history is constantly being rewritten. Second, the aim of history should not be complete objectivity, but rather a history which takes account of the subjective understandings of individuals and communities but subjects them to critical appraisal. Only in this way can a bridge be built between the discipline of the historian and society. Historians must relinquish their omnipotence and redefine history as 'a discipline which distances from lived experience', in order to give the present its rightful, self-conscious place.

Robert Gildea

There is a clear sense, at the beginning of the twenty-first century, of a unique obsession with the present. The past is driven away by pressing priorities of global competition, technological advances, market forces, mass media, consumerism, management and modernisation. Contemporary man needs to throw off the shackles of the past in order to survive. Economic man has become microchip man. And yet there is an opposite sense that the same globalising and modernising processes do not so much destroy the past as call it back to do work in the present, as groups at risk are challenged to defend their identities and interests by giving their own version of events. 'Since identity is shaped by memory', asserts Tzvetan Todorov, people today 'are obsessed by a new cult, that of memory.'[35] Similarly, François Hartog has asked, 'is memory not invoked all the more because it is disappearing?'[36]

This paper is divided into two parts. The first will examine the presence of the past in the contemporary world, under the three headings of commemoration, demands for recognition by the victims of history, and the obsession with national heritage and *patrimoine*. The second will explore the response of historians to the challenges by way of memory studies, which has become a branch of historiography in its own right over the last twenty or twenty-five years, and how historians can make the best use of memory.

Commemoration

Since the 1980s there has been a ceaseless round of commemoration. In 1991, the American historian William M. Johnston signalled 'the cult of anniversaries in Europe and the United States'.[37] The French have been at the forefront of this movement. The historian Pierre Nora described a 'commemorative bulimia' and 'commemorative obsession' in France, counting between 1985 and 1990 the 300th anniversary of the Revocation of the Edict of Nantes which began an era of persecution of Protestants, the 50th anniversary of the Popular Front, the 1000th anniversary of the Capetian monarchy, the 20th anniversary of May 1968, the Bicentenary of the French Revolution, and the centenary of the birth of General de Gaulle. This pattern has similarly been referred to by Jean-Claude Guillebaud as a 'commemorative mania', and by Henry Rousso as 'a frenzy of commemoration'.[38] The transfer of the remains of France's great men to the Panthéon in Paris, which fell into decay between 1964 and 1987, saw a renewal thereafter, under Mitterrand and Chirac, including the transfer of the remains of the first woman to the Panthéon, Marie Curie, in 1995.[39] Even in the UK, which worships at the altar of modernisation and affects an impatience with the past, due reverence is required on Remembrance Sunday following 11 November, and street parties and bunting mandatory to celebrate royal jubilees. Gordon Brown made a speech to the Fabian Society in January 2006 in which he argued that in the face of the challenges of globalisation and multiculturalism, there was even greater need for a British identity which must centre on the 'golden thread' of the 'ideal of liberty' which runs through British history from Magna Carta in 1215 to the 1689 Bill of Rights and the defeat of fascism in 1945.[40] A poll that followed on the best date for a national day for the BBC *History Magazine* put Magna Carta Day, 15 June, first, followed by VE Day and D-Day.

Great commemorations, when sponsored by the state, have the purpose of uniting the nation around the memory of a historic moment, defining its identity and legitimating its claim to combat on the side of right, to greatness, even to a divine mission. In his famous lecture of 1882, *What is a Nation?* Ernest Renan stated:

A nation is a soul, a spiritual principle. This is made up of two things which are really only one. One in the past, the other in the present. One is the collective ownership of a rich legacy of memories, the other is the present consent or desire to live together, the will to continue to develop the inheritance it has received intact … The nation, like the individual, is the culmination of a long past of striving, sacrifice and dedication. The cult of ancestors is of all cults the most legitimate; ancestors have made us who we are. A heroic past, great men, glory (I mean the real kind) are the social capital on which the national idea is based. To have common glories in the past and a common will in the present; to have done great things together and to wish to do more of them, that is the prerequisite of a people.[41]

The task of making great men and glory the common property of the nation has been the function of the state, which has claimed a monopoly of major acts of commemoration in order to dictate a single national story. Pierre Nora has demonstrated how the French Republic and Nation was dramatised by a panoply of symbols from 14 July to the Panthéon, from war memorials to colonial exhibitions. The commemoration of great moments and great men in a nation's history was designed to block out challenges to the legitimacy of the state and the unity of the nation.

In the construction of national identities, competing readings of the past by groups contesting state power or the nation as a single linguistic, cultural or historic entity have been occluded or repressed. After all, history is written by the victors. In the catechism of the French Revolution, the Vendée rebellion was a stab in the back, and no thesis on the Vendée was defended at the Sorbonne until 1985. Pieter Lagrou has shown how, after 1944 the experience of occupation, collaboration and latent civil war in France was overcome by the 'invented honour' of a national memory that glorified the Resistance and refused to acknowledge the specificity of the deportation of Jews over that of resisters.[42] The Algerian war of 1954–62 was defined as an internal disorder until 1999, because it was not a colony but constitutionally part of metropolitan France. The National Assembly's vote in 2002 of the date of the Evian agreement of 19 March 1962 to mark the end of the Algerian war was not endorsed by the government, on the grounds that Algerian independence triggered the expulsion of *pied noir* settlers and the massacre of *harkis* or Algerians who fought for France, and whose sensibilities as members of the French national community had to be taken into account.[43]

For the UK, David Cannadine has shown how the pageantry of the British monarchy, which was also a celebration of the British Empire, took off when Victoria became Empress of India in 1877, and was marked by her jubilees in 1887 and 1897, and promoted the monarchy as 'the embodiment of consensus, stability and continuity'.[44] In 2007, the UK celebrated the 300th anniversary of the Union with Scotland, and it has been reluctant to accommodate alternative readings of its noble imperial past of the integrity of the Union with Northern Ireland. Colonial atrocities such as the Amritsar massacre of 1919 in the Punjab, and the Bloody Sunday of 30 January 1972 in Londonderry, were the subject of perfunctory and politicised enquiries. The Bloody Sunday Justice Campaign was started on the twentieth anniversary of the massacre to overturn the unsatisfactory verdict of the Lord Chief Justice Widgery Tribunal of 1972. The Saville Inquiry was eventually set up by Tony Blair in 1998, in order to reinvestigate Bloody Sunday, and sat until 2005, but has yet to publish its verdict, perhaps because justice to the victims must at some level recognise the brutality of the British State and undermine the Union.[45]

Finally, in terms of national memories, the two German states were reluctant after 1945 to acknowledge the evils of the Third Reich and, in particular, the extermination of the European Jews. The Federal Republic designated 1945 as 'Year Zero', from which history would begin anew, while the Communist Democratic Republic legitimated itself by locating its birth in the struggle against fascism sponsored since 1941 by the Soviet Union, and continued to persecute Jewish communists as agents of Zionism or American imperialism.

Voices of the victims

In recent years, commemoration has no longer been the monopoly of governments, and their attempts to impose a single national story have been dramatically contested. Groups or peoples in civil society whose claims against the state or nation have been ignored have begun to fight back. 'Identity politics' has become the rage, and groups seeking to assert their identity and the legitimacy of their claims have had to construct their own memories and tell their own stories of repression and persecution, for there is no identity without memory.

Since history is written by the victors, the accounts of the repressed and persecuted have often not been written down, but have been transmitted orally. The testimony that they bring to the courtroom of history has claimed the right to be heard alongside the accounts of professional historians, and their ultimate goal is that their version of events becomes the new orthodoxy. Their discourse is always one of victimhood, of rights flouted, identities erased, lives lost. Their demands are for apology, compensation, and a justice now for what they were denied in the past. The greatest claim is that of genocide, the experience of an attempt to exterminate a people. Other groups have followed suit to obtain, in Todorov's words, 'not, as between countries, the most favoured nation clause, but that of the most oppressed group', the outcome being a 'hit-parade of suffering'. Jean-Claude Guillebaud has spoken of 'the rhetoric of victimhood' and Jean-Michel Chaumont of 'competition between victims'.[46]

The first and most powerful victim account is that of the Jewish people, above all the survivors of the Holocaust. For some time after the war they did not speak up, either because of the unspeakable nature of their suffering, or because of their desire to rebuild their lives and assimilate with the nations of which they were a part. Around the time of the Eichmann trial in 1961, it has been argued, Jewish survivors and the Jewish community began to speak out, demanding recognition of their suffering, the trial of individuals responsible for their suffering, and an admission of guilt by states involved in their persecution. Each 16–17 July, on the anniversary of the mass deportation of Jews from France in 1942, Jews have congregated on the site of the Vélodrome d'Hiver, where tens of thousands of them were held before being sent to Auschwitz. On the fortieth anniversary of the deportation, in July 1992, President François Mitterrand attended the cere-mony, but refused to acknowledge the responsibility of the French state, arguing that the deportation was the work of the Vichy regime, which no longer existed, not of the Republic. After Mitterrand's death, this casuistry was rejected by President Chirac, who acknowledged the responsibility of the French state, but in the same breath paid homage to the 'righteous among nations' – a title con-ferred by the Israeli Knesset after 1953 – who had saved three-quarters of Jews living in France during the war. In doing this, Chirac seized the opportunity to portray France not as an accomplice in the Holocaust, but as the country that had invented the rights of man and sponsored liberty and enlightenment in the world. This furthered the work of the Loi Gayssot of 13 July 1990, which outlawed racial and religious discrimination, and notably negation of the Holocaust. Commemoration of the Holocaust became global in nature with the establishment of Holocaust Memorial Day. The UK, whose hands were clean in the matter of the extermination of the Jews, although not in its reluctance to welcome persecuted Jews from the continent in the 1930s, has used Holocaust Memorial Day since 2001 as an opportunity for the prime minister to deliver a homily on the evils of racism and the tolerance of difference.

In the wake of the Jewish population, other ethnic minorities have been keen to be heard. Black communities, especially, argued that they were victims of a previous persecution, even genocide – the institution of slavery, sustained by the international slave trade in which all western maritime nations participated. In France, commemoration of the 150th anniversary of the revolution of 1848 in 1998 included homage paid by Prime Minister Jospin at the birthplace of Victor Schoelcher, who had sponsored the bill emancipating slaves in French colonies in 1848. This attempt to reinforce France's claim to be the country of the rights of man was contested by the black population of France, which organised a march in Paris in May 1998, and by the president of the regional council of France's overseas department of Martinique, who argued that the slaves had fought for their own liberty, and that France must recognise slavery and the slave trade as a crime against humanity. This was endorsed by the National Assembly, reclaiming

France's bid to pose as the country of the rights of man, in a law of 21 May 2001.[47] UNESCO's International Day for the Remembrance of the Slave Trade and its Abolition, on 23 August 2004, was marked by the launch of Rendezvous of Victory, which campaigned for a British apology for the slave trade and, through that, a revived black identity. In November 2006, Tony Blair called the slave trade a 'crime against humanity' and expressed his 'deep sorrow' for Britain's role, but stopped short of a formal apology to mark the 200th anniversary of the abolition of the slave trade in the British Empire.[48]

Heritage, *patrimoine* and living history

In parallel with the mania for commemoration since the 1980s has been an obsession with heritage or *patrimoine*. 'Instead of manufacturing goods, we are manufacturing *heritage*', wrote Robert Hewison in *The Heritage Industry* in 1987, 'a commodity which no-one seems able to define, but which everyone is eager to sell'. Appalled by the Wigan Pier Heritage Centre set up in 1984, which reconstituted an idealised working-class community of *c*.1900, he argued that the obsession with heritage was a response both to rapid modernisation and a sense of national decline. It was 'bogus history', he said, offering 'fantasies of a world that never was'.[49] Commenting on developments in the USA, Diana Barthel spoke of 'heritage machines', special interest groups marketing historical sites for profit. Deadwood, South Dakota, for instance, was rebuilt as a Wild West gold-rush town, which would permit gambling and increase local tax revenues, drawing on the media presence and commercial interest of Kevin Costner, who had celebrated Sioux culture in *Dances with Wolves*.[50] In France, the first *journée du patrimoine* was held in 1980, and *centres du patrimoine* have been spreading, celebrating the creative interaction of man and his environment from stately Loire châteaux to the maritime heritage of Brittany. One of the most successful is Le Puy-du-Fou, which opened in 1978, staging medieval jousting and falconry, but also celebrating the Vendean wars against the Revolution. In this way, it was both a commercial and a political phenomenon, which pulled in tourists and conveyed the political message of right-wing, Eurosceptic deputy Philippe de Villiers.[51]

A development of heritage and *patrimoine* has been 'living history', where the past is not just displayed in a museum or country house but re-enacted by enthusiasts in period costume. In Britain, enthusiasts can choose between dressing up and re-enacting battles involving Romans, Celts, Vikings, medieval knights, Civil War Roundheads and Cavaliers, Napoleonic or First World War soldiers. They can discover, according to the HISTORIC UK website, the 'romantic beauty of the legend of the Celts' and the 'golden age' of the Romans.[52] In France, the landing of Napoleon on his return from Elba at Golf-Juan is re-enacted each year on the first weekend in March, and the National Association of Mayors of the Napoleon Route organise re-enactments of his epic journey to Grenoble, Lyon and Paris, when old *grognards*, veterans of his campaigns who had been disbanded by the restored monarchy, flocked to his colours.[53]

It is easy to denounce the cult of heritage and living history as a combination of commercial rip-off and political manipulation. At best it is a romantic fantasy to bring back a mythical world of heroes rather than mere men, of poetry rather than prose, a purely escapist antidote to contemporary life that may be indulged in for a weekend. However, it is possible to argue that it is an anxious response to the threat of a loss of identity in the contemporary world, which has destroyed not only rural but industrial communities, tearing generations from their roots. It is significant that in France, eco-museums are nowhere more popular than in new towns like Villeneuve d'Asq outside Lille, or Saint-Quentin-en-Yvelines in the Paris region, where a new population has yet to lay down roots, build social networks and create a local identity. The emphasis is on recreating daily life with everyday domestic objects such as flat irons and coffee grinders, in an attempt to link up with the safe communities, familiar practices and shared norms of previous generations.[54] In her examination of the Rhondda Heritage Park, which opened in 1990, seven years after the Victorian colliery closed in 1983, Bella Dicks argues that this historic reconstruction of a 1950 'archetypal mining community' in South Wales is not just a tourist attraction, but models traditional notions of class and community solidarity, traditional gender division and a strong sense of place which pulls in the descendants of people who left the South Wales valleys and are keen to investigate their origins.[55]

Memory as a social construct

The first generation of historians of memory was keen to point out that memory was not individual and given, but a social construct. It shaped identity, which was a construct also. Their theoretical reference point was Maurice Halbwachs, a disciple of Durkheim who died in a German concentration camp in 1945. In his *Cadres sociales de la mémoire* of 1925, translated as *On Collective Memory* in 1992, he argued that whereas dreams are the random images of individual minds, what we remember is conditioned by those who surround us, whether a family, religious community or social class, and that these groups are themselves defined by their shared memories. Even more influential was his *La mémoire collective,* translated as *The Collective Memory* in 1980. This reiterated that we remember only in conjunction with others, more effectively in 'nearby milieus' like the family than distant ones like the nation. It also drew a distinction between memory, which is a living consciousness, and history, which divides up what has past into periods. Equally, said Halbwachs, memories are multiple and partial stories, whereas history is 'unitary', a 'single record', rising above the memories of groups.

The legacy of Halbwachs informed the great project of Pierre Nora, *Les lieux de mémoire,* which appeared in seven volumes between 1984 and 1992, divided into the Republic, the Nation, and *Les France.* Nora's was a nostalgic project, taking the view that traditional societies that perpetuated memory were dissolving as history accelerated, bringing with it 'globalisation, democratisation, massification, mediatisation', and that it was up to historians to pinpoint and explore and preserve the 'sites of memory' around which the identity of the Republic, nation and constituent facets of France were built. These included the festival of 14 July, Verdun, the Panthéon, Lavisse's *History of France,* the Gallic cockerel, and so on. British historians writing about memory at the same time, often together with anthropologists, preferred to use terms such as 'tradition' or 'myth'. *The Invention of Tradition,* edited by the historian Eric Hobsbawm and the anthropologist Terence Ranger in 1983, pointed out that traditions were not given and timeless, but socially constructed for a present purpose in order to inculcate beliefs, ensure group cohesion and legitimate institutions.[56] Highly influential too were the papers of the sixth International Oral History Conference, published in 1990 by Raphael Samuel and Paul Thompson as *The Myths We Live By,* using the term myth not in the sense of fiction, but of a story that society tells to itself, embodying notions of its founding, values and hopes.[57] Chris Wickham, in conjunction with anthropologist James Fentress, preferred the term 'social memory' in their 1992 book, in order not to 'render the individual a sort of automaton, passively obeying the interiorised collective will'.[58] The German version of *Les lieux de mémoire,* edited by Étienne François, a French historian working in Berlin, and Hagen Schulze, appeared in 2001 as *Deutsche Erinnerungsorte.* Although the editors had toyed with the idea of calling it 'German myths' or 'Historical signposts', they settled for the closest translation of Nora's term. The three volumes included 121 'sites of memory' to Nora's 130, ranging from Goethe to Marlene Dietrich, Grimm's *Fairy Tales* to 1968, Hitler's bunker to Willi Brandt's kneeling before the Warsaw Holocaust memorial.

The democratisation of history

A second generation of historians of memory became keenly aware that collective memory was less orchestrated by the state for the benefit of state and nation than heavily contested by competing communities seeking to legitimate their own claims to apology, compensation or justice by asserting their own memories, which (as we have seen) were generally of victimhood: oppression, persecution and massacre. It had to confront the claims of oral history, which tended to focus on the accounts of the 'disinherited' – ethnic minorities, working classes, women – whose stories tended to undermine 'official history' as white, middle-class and sexist. It also had to recognise that history was being told outside the academy, 'profession' or 'guild' of historians, and becoming ever more democratic.

In France, there has been a general opposition to oral history, to the claims of witnesses, and a powerful defence of academic history. As Alya Aglan has shown, the distinction made by Halbwachs between multiple, partisan memories and single, impartial history was taken up by Pierre Nora: 'there are as many memories as there are groups. Memory is by nature multiple and multiplied, collective, plural and individualised. History, on the contrary, belongs to everyone and to no-one, which gives it a calling to the universal'.[59] Jacques Le Goff argued in *History and Memory* that memory is not history, but both one of its objects and an elementary level of its development. He attacked Raphael Samuel's welcoming of the 'deprofessionalisation of history', holding that 'even if history only distantly approaches scientific status, it is a science that depends on knowledge that is professionally acquired'.[60] For a younger generation, Henry Rousso, director of the Institut d'Histoire du Temps Présent (IHTP), distinguished between memory as 'the presence or the present of the past … a phenomenon that operates in the present tense', and history, 'a scholarly reconstruction of the past [which] focuses on individuals and social facts which perhaps have completely disappeared from collective memory'. The IHTP, he argued, has avoided 'oral history' and refused 'to grant testimony a sacred character simply because the words are those of the victims or those forgotten by history'.[61]

The rearguard defence by historians came to a climax over the 'lois mémorielles' or 'lois de mémoire', such as the Loi Gayssot on negationism, and the law declaring slavery and the slave trade a crime against humanity. History and memory clashed once, when legal proceedings were brought by a lobby against a historian who had published a book about the slave trade, arguing that it was not just rape by the West but profit for African and Arab kings and traders. They clashed again over the law of 23 February 2005, which recognised the claims of *pieds noirs* and *harkis*, and then famously required school syllabuses to teach the 'positive role of the French presence overseas and notably in North Africa'. This provoked the formation of a Liberté pour l'histoire group, set up in France in 2005 under the presidency of René Rémond and including Pierre Nora, to fight for the repeal of all the 'lois de mémoire'. Its manifesto declared that 'history is not memory … The historian collects people's memories, compares them, sets them against documents, objects and traces, and establishes the facts. History takes account of memory, but is not reduced to it'. It denied that history was only for historians, but it said that it was even less for politicians.[62]

British and Anglo-Saxon historians, by contrast, have had a generally positive view of oral history. Recovering the voices of forgotten or marginal groups silenced or ignored by official or dominant historical accounts was the original purpose of the oral history movement in the 1960s and 1970s, and they have not been denounced as being at the service of political claims for recognition or compensation. Alistair's Thomson's *Anzac Memories* (1994) demonstrated how the Anzac legend, the founding myth of Australia, was subverted by the stories of 'diggers' or veterans' interviews in the working-class suburbs of Melbourne in the early 1980s, who remembered not glory but the pain of leaving home, suffering and fear.[63] Alongside oral history, meanwhile, grew up 'public history', which started with the family histories of the students themselves, as representative of the broader social and cultural history of 'ordinary people', and studied everyday life through family albums, libraries, domestic objects, and a powerful sense of place.[64]

This gives rise to the question whether there is now such a thing as a single, universal, objective history, which listens to but is not a tool of conflicting memories, or do we now have to speak of a democratisation of history, under which all sorts of groups write their own histories in a search for their identity, and one narrative is just as valid as another? The advent of postmodernism has given a new legitimacy to these alternative readings of history. Elizabeth Deeds Ermath, for example, has attacked the notion of history as a 'single public medium, to which private histories are tributaries or "in" which they operate'. 'Multilevel thinking', she continues, 'holds out the possibility of re-imagining "the past", not only by pluralizing it but by releasing it from the dialectical and linear relationships to which it is constrained by historical narrative'.[65]

Memory as working through

There is another theoretical model for memory studies, perhaps not so much used, which is that of Freud. This concentrates on the notion of traumatic memory, the memory of a bodily or more often psychological wound, which is buried in the unconscious. This memory is deep and fragmented and not accessible to normal thinking processes, but also threatens to overwhelm the subject, to erupt into the present again, since it has not been processed and 'filed' as a past event. In his 1914 essay, 'Remembering, repeating and working through', Freud argued that the traumatised patient was condemned to react in one of two ways, either by what he called the 'compulsion to repeat', an obsessive repetition of the same gesture, inhibition or attitude without thinking, or by retreat into silence or amnesia, shutting off from the real world. The only way round this is the working-through of memory, coming back to the blockage but metabolising it, so that the patient can be 'reconciled with the repressed material', overcome it, master it, move on and shelve it as a past event.[66]

Whereas the risk in the democratisation of history is to drive a wedge between professional historians and wider communities, working through a difficult past offers a challenge for historians and communities to work together. This is particularly the case when a society is confronted by historical burdens such as the Holocaust, the slave trade or colonial oppression. In recent years, historians have tapped a rich vein of enquiry into how societies have come to terms with a difficult and painful past and produced a dynamic account of the work and reconstruction of memory.

Work on the German past has led the way. In *Divided Memories* (1997), Jeffrey Herf explored the silence of Adenauer's Germany, which wanted to forget the Nazi era in favour of the new war against communism, and to amnesty war criminals, while the communist DDR regarded Nazism as not its problem, since it was founded by the anti-fascist struggle led by the Soviet Union. In *War Stories* (2003), Robert G. Moeller argued that Germans in the Federal Republic took refuge not only in silence but in the portrayal of themselves as victims, of Allied bombing, but above all of the collapse of Reich in the East at hands of the USSR, foregrounding ethnic Germans expelled from countries liberated from German rule by the Soviets and POWs kept in Soviet camps until 1955. In this sense, the underlying trauma was the defeat, occupation and partition of 1945, not the evils of the Third Reich. In the significantly titled *The Work of Memory* (2002), Alon Confino and Peter Fritzsche investigated the way in which the Germans have finally come to terms with their Nazi past, not in the sense of 'reconciliation with Nazi crimes', but a mastery of the past, the 'process in which Germans internalise this past as an integral part of their national identity', and stop resisting it.[67] It is in this light that the François-Schulze *Deutsche Erinnerungsorte* was constructed. It was conceived in 1996, six years after the reunification of Germany, arguing that for the first time the question of Ernst Moritz Arndt, 'what is the German nation?', could be answered. It was also a response to two other challenges; the need to come to terms with the 'national catastrophe' of Auschwitz, and the European and global challenge to German national identity. Rather than hagiographical, unitary and hexagonal, like Nora's, the François-Schulze version is 'an open, pluralistic and European history'. It has sections on revolution and freedom, law and discipline, but also on guilt, which includes Auschwitz and the Berlin Holocaust memorial.

Coming to terms with the French past has been a considerable challenge to French historians. Alya Aglan argues that French historians are unhappy about the ways they have been mobilised by the government and society to investigate the contribution of the state, banks and insurance companies to the persecution and plundering of the Jews. But investigate they have, and government authorisation has opened up official and business archives to teams of researchers in ways that would have been inconceivable without government backing. In a similar way, Martin Evans and Raphaëlle Branche have explored how the French, and indeed the Algerians, have begun to come to terms with their colonial past, moving beyond 'amnesia and hagiography', as part of a 'therapeutic process'.[68]

Rather than bask in guilt, however, the French have made new use of an old narrative for themselves, that of a country committed since 1789 to upholding the rights of man. Although President Chirac recognised the responsibility of the French state in deporting Jews during the German occupation, much was made of the fact that two-thirds of Jews in France were not deported and survived the war. How the French rebranding as hosts to the 'just among nations' who saved Jews from destruction has replaced that of the French as resisters, has been explored by a number of young historians, both French and non-French.[69]

'The trouble with the Engenglish', says Bombay film producer Mr 'Whiskey' Sisodia in Salman Rushdie's *Satanic Verses*, 'is that their hiss hiss history happened overseas, so they dodo not know what it means'.[70] The British do not have to flagellate themselves for responsibility for the Holocaust, and some historians have explored how they elevated their resistance to German invasion in 1940 to a myth of embattled isolation, symbolised by the *Daily Mail* photograph of St Paul's towering above the smoking inferno of the Blitz.[71] The British historical burden has rather been one of colonial exploitation and oppression. The 'subaltern studies' group of historians from the subcontinent were keen to demonstrate that the pressure for national independence in India came as much from popular movements as from political elites, although more recently mainstream historians have tended to rewrite the colonial experience as one of cultural encounter and exchange rather than oppression.[72] One area where exceptionally the 'working-through' of Britain's colonial past has been studied is the story of Northern Ireland. In *Making Peace with the Past?* (2007), Graham Dawson has investigated how the divided communities of Northern Ireland have overcome the fear of recurrent violence which has driven them apart, through a process of remembering together at local level and securing recognition from the other community of its own pain. He cites the journalist Virginia Ironside: 'You have no power over the death, but you do have power over the story'.[73]

The role of historians in regard to memory has thus changed. In the nineteenth century, they elaborated a national narrative of liberation and greatness, and in the twentieth, chronicled the ways in which states and nations represented the past for present unity and legitimacy. In recent years, they have been called upon to act on behalf of victimised communities, to discover the 'truth' about their victimisation, and to provide evidence for compensation and apology. Here they feel they have been 'instrumentalised', although during this process they have been able to rewrite history from multiple perspectives, not only from that of the state. Today they have a new role, investigating how societies have come or are coming to terms with their painful pasts, listening to the testimony of witnesses, exploring bridges between different communities, and finally laying the past to rest.

Notes

1   St Augustine, *Confessions* (New York, Fathers of the Church, 1953), Book 11, Chapter 20, 350.
2   Marc Bloch, *The Historian's Craft* (Manchester University Press, 1954), 44–5.
3   R. G. Collingwood, *The Idea of History* (Oxford, Clarendon Press, 1946), 175.
4   Antoine Prost, *Douze leçons sur l'histoire* (Paris, Le Seuil, 1996), 180–1.
5   Reinhart Koselleck, *L'expérience de l'histoire* (Paris, Gallimard, Le Seuil, 1997).
6   Walter Benjamin, 'On the concept of history' [1940], in Benjamin, *Selected writings 4. 1938–1940* (Cambridge, Mass. and London, Belknap Press of Harvard University Press, 2003), 395.
7   Reinhart Koselleck, *Le futur passé. Contribution à la sémantique des temps historiques* (Paris, EHESS, 2000); Jürgen Habermas, *Le discours philosophique de la modernité* (Paris, Gallimard, 1988).
8   Jean Bodin, *La méthode de l'histoire*, trans. P. Mesnard (Paris, Belles Lettres, 1941); Jules Michelet, *Histoire de France*, preface of 1869.
9   Paul Gerbod, 'La place de l'histoire dans l'enseignement secondaire de 1802 à 1880', *L'information historique* 130 (1965), quoted by Antoine Prost, *Douze leçons*, 23.
10 Charles Seignobos, 'L'enseignement de l'histoire comme instrument d'éducation politique', in *Conférences du Musée pédagogique* (Paris, Imprimerie nationale, 1907), 1–24, quoted by Charles Seignobos, *Études de politique et d'histoire* (Paris, PUF, 1934), 109–32, quoted by Antoine Prost, *Douze leçons*, 295–7.
11 Cf. Charles Seignobos, 'L'enseignement de l'histoire dans les facultés. III. Méthodes d'exposition', *Revue internationale de l'enseignement* (15 July 1884), 35–60, 60, quoted by Antoine Prost, *Douze leçons*, 26.
12 Enzo Traverso, *Le passé, modes d'emploi. Histoire, mémoire, politique* (Paris, La Fabrique éditions, 2005), 10–11.
13 Tzvetan Todorov, *Les abus de la mémoire* (Paris, Arléa, 1995), 51–4.
14 Eric J. Hobsbawm, 'Identity history is not enough', *On History* (London, Weidenfeld & Nicolson, 1997), 277.
15 Olivier Pétré-Grenouilleau, *Les traites négrières. Essai d'histoire globale* (Paris, Gallimard, 2004).
16 Ranajit Guha, 'The small voice of history', *Subaltern Studies* 9 (Delhi, Oxford University Press, 1996), 1–12.
17 Olivier Dumoulin, *Le rôle social de l'historien. De la chaire au prétoire* (Paris, Albin Michel, 2003.)
18 Eric Conan and Henry Rousso, *Vichy, An Ever-present Past* (Hanover, University Press of New England, 1998).
19 René Rémond, *Touvier et l'Église: rapport de la Commission historique instituée par le cardinal Ducourtray* (Paris, Fayard, 1992).
20 Jean-Noël Jeanneney, *Le passé dans le prétoire: l'historien, le juge et le journaliste* (Paris, Le Seuil, 1998), analyses in detail the new relationship of the historian and the justice system. See also Annette Wieviorka, *The Era of the Witness* (Ithaca and London, Cornell University Press, 2006), 145–9.
21 Archives of the Caisse des dépôts et consignations (CDC).
22 Archives of the CDC, J. M. Thiveaud, extract from a 'mémorandum sur la question des consignations des biens israélites', 17 Feb. 1993.
23 Archives of the CDC, extract from summary by J. M. Thiveaud to director-general Philippe Lagayette, 20 July 1994.
24 Published by First Editions, 1996.
25 Philippe Verheyde, *Les mauvais comptes de Vichy: l'aryanisation des entreprises juives* (Paris, Perrin, 1999).
26 Jean Laloum, *Les juifs dans la banlieue parisienne des années vingt aux années cinquante. Montreuil, Bagnolet et Vincennes à l'heure de la Solution finale* (Paris, CNRS éditions, 1998).
27 See among other works Jean-Marc Dreyfus, *Pillages sur ordonnances: aryanisation et restitution des banques en France 1940–1953* (Paris, Fayard, 2003).
28 Antoine Prost, ed., *Aryanisation économique et restitutions, mission d'étude sur la spoliation des juifs de France* (Paris, La Documentation française, 2000); Annette Wieviorka, ed., *Les biens des internés des camps de Drancy, Pithiviers et Beaune-la-Rolande, mission d'étude sur la spoliation des juifs de France* (Paris, La Documentation française, 2000); Claire Andrieu, ed., *La persécution des juifs de France 1940–1944 et le rétablissement de la légalité républicaine, recueil des textes officiels 1940–1999*, mission d'étude sur la spoliation des juifs de France (Paris, La Documentation française, 2000); Claire Andrieu, ed., *La spoliation financière, mission d'étude sur la spoliation des juifs de France* (Paris, La Documentation française, 2000); Caroline Piketty, ed., *Guide des recherches dans les archives des spoliations et des restitutions, mission d'étude sur la spoliation des juifs de France* (Paris, La

Documentation française, 2000).

29 Cf. Alya Aglan, Michel Margairaz and Philippe Verheyde, eds., *La Caisse des dépôts, la Seconde Guerre mondiale et le XXe siècle. Actes du colloque international des 28, 29 et 30 novembre 2001* (Paris, Albin Michel, 2003).

30 Maurice Halbwachs, *La mémoire collective* (Paris, Albin Michel, 1997) and *Les cadres sociaux de la mémoire* (Paris, Albin Michel, 1994 [1925]), translated as *Collective Memory* (1980) and *On Collective Memory* (1992).

31 Pierre Nora, 'Entre histoire et mémoire. La problématique des lieux', *Les lieux de mémoire,* I (Paris, Gallimard, 1984), XIX–XX. See also Henry Rousso, 'La mémoire n'est plus ce qu'elle était', in François Bédarida, ed., *Écrire l'histoire du temps présent* (Paris, CNRS éditions, 1993).

32 François Hartog, *Régimes d'historicité: présentisme et expériences du temps* (Paris, Le Seuil, 2003).

33 Enzo Traverso, *Le passé, modes d'emploi*, 26.

34 Paul Ricœur, *Memory, History, Forgetting* (Chicago and London, University of Chicago Press, 2004), 500. See also Olivier Abel, Enrico Castelli-Gattinara, Sabina Loriga and Isabelle Ullern-Weité, eds., *La juste mémoire. Lectures autour de Paul Ricœur* (Geneva, Labor et Fides, 2006).

35 Tzvetan Todorov, *Les abus de la mémoire* (Paris, Arléa, 1995), 51.

36 François Hartog, *Régimes d'historicité. Présentisme et expériences du temps* (Paris, Le Seuil, 2003), 126.

37 William M. Johnston, *Celebrations. The Cult of Anniversaries in Europe and the United States Today* (New Brunswick and London, Transaction Publishers, 1991).

38 Pierre Nora, *Les lieux de mémoire,* III.1 (Paris, Gallimard, 1992), 977–8; Jean-Claude Guillebaud, *La trahison des lumières. Enquête sur le désarroi contemporain* (Paris, Le Seuil, 1995), 21; Henry Rousso, *The Haunting Past. History, Memory and Justice in Contemporary France* (Philadelphia, University of Pennsylvania Press, 2002), 3, 10.

39 Patrick Garcia, 'Les panthéonisations sous la Ve République: redécouverte et metamorphoses d'un rituel', in Jean-Luc Bonniol and Maryline Crivello, *Façonnons les passé. Repésentations et cultures de l'histoire XV1e–XX1e siècle* (Aix, 2004), 88–91.

40 www.fabian-society.org.uk/press_office/display.asp?id=520&type=news&cat=43

41 Ernest Renan, 'Qu'est-ce qu'une nation?' Sorbonne lecture, 11 March 1882, in *Oeuvre Complètes* I (Paris, Calmann-Lévy, 1882), 12–28.

42 Pieter Lagrou, *Mémoires patriotiques et occupation nazie* (Brussels, Editions Complexe, 2003), 11–23, 240–4, 281–3.

43 Claire Andrieu, 'La commémoration des dernières guerres françaises: l'élaboration de politiques symboliques, 1945–2003', in Claire Andrieu, Marie-Claire Lavabre and Danielle Tartakowsky, eds., *Politiques du passé. Usages politiques du passé dans la France contemporaine* (Aix, Publications de l'Université de Provence, 2006), 43.

44 David Cannadine, 'The context, performance and meaning of ritual: the British monarchy and the invention of tradition', in Eric Hobsbawn and Terence Ranger, eds., *The Invention of Tradition* (Cambridge University Press, 1983), 140.

45 *The Amritsar Massacre, 1919. General Dyer in the Punjab, 1919* (London, The Stationery Office, 2000); Patrick Hayes and Jim Campbell, *Bloody Sunday. Trauma, Pain and Politics* (London, Dublin and Ann Arbor, Pluto Press, 2005); www.bloody-sunday-inquiry.org

46 Todorov, *Les abus*, 57; Guillebaud, *La trahison*, 84; Jean-Michel Chaumont, *La concurrence des victimes: genocide, identité, reconnaissance* (Paris, La Découverte, 1997, 2002).

47 Jean-Luc Bonniol, 'Échos politiques de l'esclavage colonial des départements d'outr-mer au coeur de l'État', in Andrieu et al., *Politiques du passé*, 59–69.

48 *The Observer*, 26 Nov. 2006.

49 Robert Hewison, *The Heritage Industry* (London, Methuen, 1987), 10.

50 Diane Barthel, *Historic Preservation: Collective Memory and Historical Identity* (New Brunswick, NJ, Rutgers University Press, 1996), 117–23.

51 See, for example, Sarah Blowen, Marion Demoissier and Jeannine Picard, eds., *Recollections of France. Memories, Identities and Heritage in Contemporary France* (Oxford and New York, Berghahn Books, 2000).

52 www.historic-uk.com

53 Maryline Crivello, 'Les braconniers de l'histoire. Les reconstitutions historiques, nouveaux lieux de politique', in Maryline Crivello, Patrick Garcia and Nicolas Offenstadt, *Concurrences des passées. Usages politiques du passé dans la France contemporaine* (Aix, Publications de l'Université de Provence, 2006), 53–7.

54 Hervé Glevarec, 'Le nouveau regime d'historicité porté par les Associations du patrimoine', in Crivello et al., *Concurrences des passes*, 23–36.

55 Bella Dicks, *Heritage, Place and Community* (Cardiff, University of Wales Press, 2000), 109–18, 209–16.

56 Hobsbawn and Ranger, eds., *The Invention of Tradition*.

57 Raphael Samuel and Paul Thompson, *The Myths We Live By* (London and New York, Routledge, 1990).

58 Chris Wickham and James Fentress, *Social Memory* (Oxford, Blackwell, 1992), ix.

59 Pierre Nora, *Les lieux de mémoire I. La République* (Paris, Gallimard, 1984), xix.

60 Jacques Le Goff, *History and Memory* (New York, Columbia University Press, 1920), 129.

61 Rousso, *Haunting Past*, 7, 36.

62 www.ldh-toulon.net/article.php3?id_article=1086 and see above, pp. 144, 157.

63 Alistair Thomson, *Anzac Memories. Living with the Legend* (Melbourne, Oxford University Press, 1994).

64 Hilda Kean, *London Stories. Personal Lives, Public Histories* (London, Rivers Oram Press, 2004).

65 Elizabeth Deeds Ermath, *Sequel to History. Postmodernism and the Crisis of Representational Time* (Princeton University Press, 1992), 87–8, 213.

66 Freud, 'Remembering, repeating and working-through' [1914], in *The Complete Psychological Works* XIII (London, Hogarth Press, 1964), 145–56.

67 Jeffrey Herf, *Divided Memory. The Nazi Past in the Two Germanies* (Harvard University Press, 1997); Alon Confino and Peter Fritsche, *The Work of Memory. New Directions in the Study of German Society and Culture* (Urbana and Chicago, University of Illinois Press, 2002); Robert G. Moeller, *The Search for a Usable Past in the Federal Republic of Germany* (Berkeley, University of California Press, 2003).

68 See above, pp. 149-50, 153-4, 159-61.

69 S. Gensburger, 'Usages politiques de la figure du juste: entre mémoire historique et mémoires individuelles', in Andrieu et al., *Politiques du passé*; S. Gensburger, 'Les figures du juste et du résistant et l'évolution de la mémoire historique française de l'Occupation', *Revue française de science politique* 52/2–3 (April–June 2002).

70 Salman Rushdie, *The Satanic Verses* (New York, Viking, 1989), 343, cited by Homi K. Bhaba, *The Location of Culture* (London and New York, Routledge, 1994), 6, 167.

71 Malcolm Smith, *Britain and 1940. History, Myth and Popular Memory* (London and New York, Routledge, 2000), 81–2.

72 Maria Misra, *Vishnu's Crowded Temple. India since the Great Rebellion* (London, Allen Lane, 2007), 186, argues that no popular movements in India 'succeeded in breaking the bounds of locality or province to create nationwide networks or leadership to compete with Congress'.

73 Graham Dawson, *Making Peace with the Past? Memory, Trauma and the Irish Troubles* (Manchester University Press, 2007). Quotation from Virginia Ironside, *You'll Never Get Over It! The Rage of Bereavement* (London, Hamilton, 1996), is on p. 31.

Conclusion: Does history have a French accent?[1]

Anne Simonin

In 1966, the *Times Literary Supplement* asked 'some of the younger and middle generation of [British] historians', together with historians from Europe and the so-called 'underdeveloped countries', about 'New Ways in History'. Three issues and thirty articles allow today's readers to make up their own mind on what was going on with the frontiers, topics and methods of history.[2] The views expressed by academics from those of antiquity to the very contemporary demonstrated a wide discrepancy between French and British approaches to history. In Britain, argued Keith Thomas, 'history [used to be] a training for politicians and administrators, and the constitution was England's greatest contribution to the world ... Politics and the constitution therefore remained the central concern of academic historians ... In doing so [British historians] are decades behind their colleagues in [other] countries. In France, the *Annales* school founded by Marc Bloch and Lucien Febvre has long urged the historical study of *la psychologie collective*. Britain has no medievalist to compare with Bloch, no monument of demographic study to rival Goubert's great work on Beauvais ... There is no English counterpart to the French historical school of religious sociology with its regional studies and its *Archives des sociologies des religions*'.[3]

An explanation of this fundamental gap between the two countries was suggested by Antoine Prost: history had been so creative in France because history was something more than an academic field. It had a responsibility for building national identity and was given resources and attention unknown to the other disciplines by the higher authorities of the state.[4] Chapter 8 of this volume, by Alya Aglan and Robert Gildea, explores the link between national identity and history which has seen a revival in recent years in France with the importance given to 'memory' and the spread of commemoration practices. The gap between the French and British views of history may also have another and maybe less ideological explanation: history has been written in France by individuals who belonged to the same corporation of 'specialists' who have been trained in the same schools, the *grandes écoles*, and taken the same degree, the *agrégation*, created in 1830.[5] A reviewer of *Vingt-cinq ans de recherche historique en France (1940–1965)* wrote,

> To the professional study and writing of history modern French scholars bring a coherence of method that is peculiarly their own. If French historical learning since the war has enjoyed something of a renaissance, it is mainly because of this coherence and self-consciousness. Not for French men the easy-going individuality of English historians, each following his personal method in amiable anarchy. The French tradition is that professional academics heavily predominate, that they form schools, and that they have a prevalent theory about how and why history should be written.[6]

If the *agrégation* is still in force today, it has nevertheless lost its monopoly of the training of historians, and no new school of thought can claim to exert a unifying influence over French historians similar to that of the *Annales* or even of Marxism from the 1930s to the 1960s.[7] This loss of singularity has probably contributed to bring French and British historians closer, as the papers gathered in this volume suggest. But if, forty years after the *TLS* inquiry, differences between the two communities of historians have diminished, they nevertheless remain. French historians are still more under the influence of theory or in search of a 'conceptual history' (*histoire conceptualisante*) than their English counterparts, as suggested by the contribution in this volume from Sophie Wahnich and by the methodological postulates of 'socio-history' outlined by Gérard Noiriel.[8] As Michael Kelly has pointed out: 'National identities [still] play the primary role in differentiating scholars' gaze. At the very least, it is visible that perspectives focused on gender, class or other social differences are more widely recognized in British academic discourse than in the French scholarly community, where the aspiration to universal academic values remains strong'.[9]

The lasting influence of theory

The return of the event heralded by Pierre Nora in 1974 may be considered a major shift in the *Annales* tradition.[10] The ambition of 'total history', to display the whole scope of historical studies, both in time and space, was vanishing: was not the present, until then drowned in the *longue durée*, worthy of being studied for its own sake in its political and cultural dimension? Jacques Le Goff nevertheless clarified that the rediscovery of political history was not a return to the traditional approach, focussed on the biography of 'great men' or military 'heros', following a linear narration and considering politics as a major cause of historical development. The *Annales* called for a 'new political history' in an anthropological perspective focussed on the notion of power: 'The models of the new general history must accord the dimension of politics the same place as is occupied in society by the phenomenon of power ... To pass from the age of anatomy to that of the atom, political history is no longer the backbone of history, but its nucleus'.[11] That is probably why François Dosse, in his attack on the *Annales* in 1987, could write, 'Rejecting political analysis caused the *Annales* to miss the major historical phenomena of its day...'.[12]

The response was quick to come. In an editorial published in the 1988 issue of *Annales, économies, sociétés, civilisations*, the editors criticised the distorted vision of the *Annales* school attacked by François Dosse the year before, and called for a new critical direction (*un tournant critique*) structured around two main questions: 'the level of analysis' and 'the writing of history'.[13] The *Annales* was conscious of the fading of a model which had shaped the making of French history for half a century. It was also aware of the criticism voiced at international level against the 'social-scientifically oriented historians, of whom the members of the French *Annales* group may be considered exemplary. This group (Braudel, Furet, Le Goff, Le Roy Ladurie, and so on) regarded narrative historiography as a non-scientific, even ideological representational strategy, the extirpation of which was necessary for the transformation of historical studies into a genuine science'.[14] The *Annales* were moving on. In 1988, the 'primacy of the quantitative and the series' was over for them: 'It was [now] necessary to take seriously forms of the historical writing'.[15]

To measure the shift in the *Annales* tradition induced by this return of the 'event' and to a narrative tradition, one has to bear in mind Fernand Braudel's well-known essay, 'The situation of history in 1950', in which the head of the *Annales* had been very critical of narrative history for its archaic views of social realities, dismissing the 'meagre images that chronicles, traditional history, the narrative history so dear to the heart of Ranke offer us of the past and of the sweat of men. A gleam but no illumination; facts but no humanity'.[16] For years to come, 'The *Annales* school loathed the trio formed by political history, narrative history or episodic (*événementielle*) history. All this for them was mere pseudo-history, history on the cheap, a superficial affair which preferred the shadow to the substance'.[17]

Paradoxically, however, it is in that quest for new narrative forms respectful of the logic of the proof at work in history that the contemporary *Annales* has been most successful since the eighties. Their call for the establishment of 'new alliances' with art history or the history of science has not succeeded in decompartmentalising (*décloisonner*) those disciplines in France, unlike in Britain, where Michael Kelly's contribution to this volume shows the close links forged by cultural history with the history of art and music.[18] Neither has their ambition to federate a 'collective enterprise' given them back the academic authority they used to exercise.[19] However, their new attention to historical writing and their repeated commitment to interdisciplinarity, as exemplified by Dominique Kalifa's demonstration in this volume of the reappropriation of judicial practice by the cultural historian, has kept the contemporary *Annales* still at the core of the major research questions asked by French historians.

British historians were not always at ease with the challenge of the *Annales* school. As Eric Hobsbawm pointed out, 'What has been influential in England ... is not so much *Annales* specifically as what might be called the French *nouvelle vague* in history'. The *Annales* stood for the place where 'this concentration of French historical (if you prefer, intellectual) energies, this historical phase, found its most significant and concentrated expression'.[20] In other words, no one could take as representative the devastating review of François Furet and Denis Richet's book, *La Révolution française*,[21] published anonymously according to the then custom in the *TLS* of 1966 by the Oxford historian Richard Cobb. A specialist of the 'history from below' of the French Revolution, Richard Cobb was probably the most French of British historians, or the least British among French ones. Louis Chevalier, who considered Cobb 'an *habitué*' of the past as well as of the present of Paris history and contemporary debates, called him 'As familiar with the Paris crowd as might be a Parisian historian, a *piéton de Paris*; having discovered the one appropriate method of approach and having instinctively adopted the right tone and vocabulary, he is just as naturally at home in the Paris of the Revolution as in the Paris of today'.[22] Published a year after Alfred Cobban's *The Social Interpretation of the French Revolution* (1964), Furet and Richet's *La Révolution française* embodied what has been called 'the revisionist crisis of the historiography of the French revolution', as David Andress has explained in this volume. It promoted a dual vision of the Revolution: the 'good' Revolution, the legacy of the Enlightenment, illustrated by the year of 1789, and the 'bad' one starting with the end of the constitutional monarchy on 10 August 1792, the eruption of popular forces onto the political stage, and the bloodshed of the Terror of 1793–1794. This *TLS* review offered Cobb less the opportunity to argue in favour of a different conception of the Revolution than the opportunity to disgorge what he thought about the *Annales* school:

> It is hardly suprising that, after nearly forty years of existence – the
> review was founded in the 1920s – and after twenty years of imperial
> power, by virtue of the famous Sixième Section of the École Pratique des
> Hautes Études, the *Annales* school ('Nous des Annales', the opening
> words of so many articles) should have acquired not only the mentality

of a dedicated and close fraternity, but also a language of its own which is almost immediately recognizable ... The *Annales*, after conquering the Mediterranean and colonizing the Baltic, have now moved into the French Revolution ... The school does not hold any monopoly of new subjects [but] *Annales* must be the first in every new field. Novelty can often result in vulgarity and pretentiousness. M. Furet and M. Richet are two very representative members of the school. The most obvious characteristic is the style, very much *style Annales*. This might be described, at its worst, as the faculty to restate obscurely and in a French almost Sartrean in its muddiness, what previous, non-juror historians have stated clearly and simply.[23]

If, to my knowledge, no other British historian was so harsh about the *Annales,* the school has always raised reservations among non-orthodox Marxists, the New Left historians like E. P. Thompson who were committed to a much more empirical tradition. In his famous and controversial attack on the Althusserian school in *The Poverty of Theory or an Orrery of Errors* (1978),[24] Thompson attacked the *Annales* in a footnote by establishing the direct line between them and the most visible representative of the most radical quantitative history: Robert William Fogel, the American historian, author of *Railroads and American Economic Growth. Essays in Econometric History* (1964) and of the very debatable *Time on the Cross. The Economics of American Negro Slavery* (1974), whose work has been discussed in this volume by Michel Margairaz and Robert Gildea. Thompson took Fogel as the symbol of the excesses of quantitative history and its inability to explore certain topics which were most important for history, regretting that 'the French historical profession (to judge by the *Annales E.S.C.* in recent years) has not always offered the same principled defence against the universalist claims of the computer'.[25] Confronted by this assault of quantitative history from France and the United States, Thompson urged British historians to keep their faith in empiricism. In a sophisticated empiricism, however, since 'Any serious historians know that facts are liars',[26] the model for which could be found in the chapter on 'Exploitation' in his classic *The Making of the English Working Class* (1963):

There is, first, the very real difficulty of constructing wage-series, price-series, and statistical indices from the abundant but patchy evidence ... But at this point a further series of difficulties begin, since the term 'standard' leads us from data amenable to statistical measurement (wages or articles of consumption) to those satisfactions which are sometimes described by statisticians as 'imponderables' ... The first is a measurement of quantities: the second a description (and sometimes an evaluation) of qualities. Where statistical evidence is appropriate to the first, we must rely largely upon 'literary evidence' as to the second ... It is at times as if statisticians have been arguing: 'the indices reveal an increased *per capita* consumption of tea, sugar, meat and soap, *therefore* the working class was happier', while social historians have replied, 'literary sources show that people were unhappy, *therefore* their standard-of-living must have deteriorated'.

   This is to simplify. But simple points must be made. It is quite possible for statistical averages and human experiences to run in opposite directions. A *per capita* increase in quantitative factors may take place at the same time as a great qualitative disturbance in people's way of life, traditional relationships, and sanctions ... Thus it is perfectly possible to maintain two propositions which, on a casual view, appear to be contradictory. [27]

Promoting 'literary sources' as of equal weight to the statistics then so prominent, this sophisticated empiricism, theorised in the 1960s by one of the leading figures among British social historians, unknowingly paved the way to the reception of the 'linguistic turn' in the 1980s.[28] It is, then, in no way surprising that interest in the 'linguistic turn' and the shift to a cultural history inspired by it, as Chris Waters argues in Chapter 1, began among the British social historians inspired by Marxism and, as Dominique Kalifa has shown, spread through them to other historical disciplines which were open to 'interdisciplinarity'.[29]

   At the beginning of the 1980s, French and British historians, through different paths, and under the influence of different, if not opposite, intellectual traditions, would probably both have subscribed to the view of Croce that 'Where there is no narrative, there is no history'.[30] Probably because of the largely accepted history of *mentalités,* which has allowed easier exchanges between social and cultural history, this conclusion was reached with less rhetorical violence in France than in Britain.[31]

The pervasive influence of the literary

Among French and British historians, the 1980s were, as Lawrence Stone announced, those of 'the revival of narrative', that is 'the organization of material in a chronologically sequential order and the focusing of the content into a single coherent story, albeit with sub-plots', more focussed on man than on circumstances. After years of scientific certainty based on statistics, 'the revival of narrative', under the influence of anthropology and Freudian ideas as the most influential of the social sciences, aimed to reconcile historians to 'the principle of indeterminacy'.[32] Destined for great success, this formula was nevertheless misleading, according to Carlo Ginzburg, because it blurred the frontiers between fiction and history instead of helping to define new relationships between them:

> A century needed to pass before historians began to take up the challenge issued by the great novelists of the nineteenth century – from Balzac to Manzoni, from Stendhal to Tolstoy – confronting a previously disregarded field of research, with the aid of more subtle and complex explanatory models than the traditional ones. Historians' increasing predilection for the themes and, in part, for the expository forms once reserved for novelists, a phenomenon inappropriately defined as the 'rebirth of narrative history' is nothing but a new chapter of a lengthy conflict on the terrain of the knowledge of reality.[33]

Ginzburg has blamed 'the revival of narrative' for having been unable to capture 'the discernible cognitive nucleus in fictional narratives', and having limited its scope to the analysis of the traces of the scientific or historical pretensions of the novels. Neither the 'rhythms of historical narrative', nor the 'cognitive of various types of narration' have been interrogated by historians who use literature as a source or to establish comparison between literary text and other types of documentation:

> Today the insistence on the narrative dimension of any historiographic work, however much it may differ from another, accompanies... relativistic postures which tend to annul, *de facto*, every distinction between fiction and history. In opposition to these tendencies it must be stressed that an increased awareness of a narrative dimension does not imply an attenuation of the cognitive possibilities of historiography but, on the contrary, their intensification. Indeed, it is exactly from this point that a radical critique of historiographic language... will have to commence.[34]

As Jean-Frédéric Schaub points out in Chapter 5, in his analysis of a seventeenth century novel, *Oroonoko*, writing must be understood in both its 'textual' and 'contextual' dimension to highlight the contribution of the literary to the total history of a period, in this case English society in the early modern period.

The most 'narrative-minded' historians may not, in fact, be those who have chosen literary forms to express historical views – like the adaptation for the theatre of Simon Schama's book, *Rough Crossings*, in 2007, or *La Nuit blanche*, a play written by Arlette Farge in 2002 which tells the story of a young man of eighteen who was executed in Cambrai in 1770 because he had spread bad rumours about the town worthies and had blasphemed against the king[35] – but economic historians like Robert William Fogel who have encapsulated a literary vision of their subject.[36] Paradoxically, there could be no more literary historical work than Fogel's *Railroads and American Economic Growth. Essays in Econometric History* (1964). For if this book epitomised the peak of quantitative history, it also opened the way to a new form of narrative. Echoing the words of Morris Raphael Cohen, 'To say that the thing happened the way it did, is not at all illuminating. We can understand the significance of what did happen only if we contrast it with what might have happened', Robert William Fogel was 'opening up a new branch of literature', as one reviewer observed, more than he was returning to Manzoni's thought about the extension of the realm of narrative history.[37]

In a text of 1842, 'On the historical novel, and in general on works where history and fiction are intertwined', the Italian writer Alessandro Manzoni pointed out an original solution to enforce the way of thinking of literature in historical writing :

> It might be not out of place to mention that history sometimes also uses
> the verisimilar, and can do so harmlessly if it uses it properly and
> presents it as such, thereby distinguishing it from the real ... In fact, all
> that is needed to clarify the relationship between the factual and the
> verisimilar is that the two appear distinct. History acts almost like
> someone who, when drawing a city map, renders in a distinctive colour
> the streets, plazas and buildings planned for the future and who, while
> distinguishing the potential form from the actual, lets us see the logic of
> the whole. History, at such moments, I would say, abandons narrative,
> but only in order to produce a better narrative. History aims to present
> reality, as much in conjecturing as in narrating; therein lies its unity.[38]

What Manzoni was asking for and called 'verisimilar' or 'conjecturing' history is surprisingly close to the counter-factual history experimented with by Fogel in *Railroads in American Economic Growth*. Discussing 'the possibility of technological adaptation to a non-rail situation' in America in the nineteenth century, Fogel explored two ways to prove that the 'axiom of indispensability' of the railroad was a fallacy. One way was 'the improvement of the country road', the other one 'the extension of internal navigation'. To illustrate the last solution, Fogel drew, without knowing it, Manzoni's map, distinguishing what he called 'the proposed canals' – ones that might have been constructed in the absence of the railroads – from the 'connecting rivers' and the 'connecting canals' already there.[39] Manzoni's call did not remain unanswered. It has found an unexpected posterity in the work of one of the harder 'cliometricians', who is a long way from fictitious history expressed through literary forms in the theatre.

The blind eye of history to 'middle-brow' literature

Using literature, historians very often do not seem to be aware that 'a stylistic canon selects certain aspects of reality and not others, highlights certain connections and not others, establishes certain hierarchies and not others'.[40] The literary authors they refer to are generally classical authors with an international reputation, or even more fundamentally authors who figure in school textbooks or who have been the subject of academic research. The popular literature and bestsellers studied by cultural history seem to be of little use for 'intellectual' history.

Let us turn first to the British context, and to a very famous subset of popular literature: the Victorian novel. To quote but a few names among the famous Victorian novelists, Dickens was a solicitor's clerk, Robert Louis Stevenson studied law at Edinburgh, and Charles Reade and Wilkie Collins were called to the Bar, but never practised. If John Sutherland has noticed the obvious link existing between this so-called 'middle-brow' literature and law, he has not – according to him – really caught the 'convincing explanation of the wide bridge connecting Victorian law and Victorian fiction':

> Some reasons for the law–fiction link may be guessed at... the study and practice of law is punctuated by absurdly long vacations... the young barrister emerged from his training without any clear next step. He waited, hopefully, for briefs. Often they were slow in coming. Typically, in this awkward interval, the lawyer would marry, incurring new debts. And typically, in this interval, the drift to writing would occur. Finally, although it is a hard link to discern, there is probably an affinity between the mentalities of jurisprudence and Victorian fiction, shaped as both were by the study of individual cases and the canons of (poetic) justice.[41]

In his illuminating book, *Fiction and the Law. Legal Discourse in Victorian and Modernist Literature* (1999), Kieran Dolin offers a different interpretation. He starts with the 'common mentality' of Victorian fiction and jurisprudence, showing clearly their common matrix, that is Bentham's utilitarian thought and what had been known as 'the reform movement'. This convergence gave law a new function in the nineteenth century, an instrumental one. It was because law appeared both to the judges and Victorian novelists as 'a means of consciously achieving particular social goals', and was regarded as 'an instrument of social improvement' and not simply the abstract regulation of social life, that Victorian fictions were so effective. 'Victorian novelists used the form to bring social abuses to light and convince readers of the need for reform… adding an affective dimension to the intellectual and religious mainsprings of social improvement. Many fictional representations of the law in this age… were actuated by reformist sentiment.'[42]

Dolin's analysis confirmed the intuition of an American lawyer, the dean of Northwestern University, John Henry Wigmore, who paid a great deal of attention to Victorian fiction and in the early twentieth century invented a new literary genre, Legal Novels:

> Was jail-reform more aided by Bentham's essay or by Charles Reade's *Never Too Late To Mend*? How soon would the right to imprison sane people in the private lunatic asylums have been abolished if *Hard Cash* had not been written?[43]

What is shown by the link between Victorian fiction and the reform in law is not only that this kind of fiction is worthy of attention from intellectual historians, but, on a more general scale, that middle-brow literature 'constitutes a bridge between several discourses' and is at the core of an 'interdiscourse' which produces 'collective symbolism', in this case, a widespread agreement about the necessity of the reform of the Common Law in Victorian England.[44]

In a similar way, popular literature is of little interest to French 'intellectual' history. I will take but one example.

On 20 September 1940, Louis Rougier, a French academic, met Marshal Pétain at the Pavillon Sévigné in Vichy, and was given a letter of introduction to Winston Churchill, whom he met on 24 October 1940 in London. That 'secret mission' might have succeeded in concluding a 'gentleman's agreement', summed up by Jeffrey Mehlman:

> The French would cede neither their (undefeated) fleet nor their colonial bases to the Germans. In exchange, the British would relax the blockade on foodstuffs from the French empire, put an end to *ad hominem* attacks on Pétain over the BBC... and allow de Gaulle to take military actions against as many Germans and Italians as he might like, but... not against Frenchmen.[45]

This so-called 'protocol', published by Rougier in 1945, made a huge splash, and was used by Pétain's lawyers during his trial as a decisive proof of the defendant's *double jeu*, negotiating with Britain and Germany at the same time for the sake of France. According to careful research in the British National Archives by the historian Robert Frank, this 'protocol' never existed.[46] The British government nevertheless lied when, in 1945, it denied on several occasions that secret negotiations had taken place between the British Prime Minister, Winston Churchill, and the Vichy Government, first in London, then in Madrid in 1940 and 1941. In 1957, the 'protocol' was examined by military experts to establish it as a hoax. But the task was singularly complicated by the intrusion of an uninvited guest in the shape of the fictitious *Clotilde*, invented by a writer who went under the pseudonym of Cecil Saint Laurent.

Cecil Saint Laurent was, in reality, Jacques Laurent, who had served under Vichy as a civil servant, and at the end of the Second World War was one of the most talented young writers from the political right. He told the story of a pretty teenage girl who, thanks to the exodus of French people fleeing ahead of the German invasion in 1940, which she experiences not as a trauma, but as a complete liberation of the stifling world of provincial respectability, discovers life. *Clotilde* does not fit in any frame. It does not belong to the kind of literary testimony used by Hanna Diamond in her recent *Fleeing Hitler. France 1940*. In particular, it differs from *Jeux interdits*, a novel published in 1947 and made into a famous film by René Clément in 1952, which showed 'the horrors of war through the eyes of children who become caught up in an obsession with death. The opening scenes of the film show queues of terrified refugees under attack from the air by machine-gunners, and these images have become the key iconic representation of the exodus in French collective memory'.[47] The experience of the exodus of Clotilde and her brother was not so tragic. For them, according to Richard Cobb, '*l'Exode* took the form of a voyage of discovery *à l'intérieur* ... For children, especially, the hazards of living for months out of suitcases contained elements of a game of adventure to be recalled nostalgically years after. So there is a Literature of *l'Exode* which has something of the spice and excitement of an eighteenth-century picaresque novel'.[48] Without doubt, Cecil Saint Laurent's work belongs to that tradition:

> To their left, amid the cornfields, the long train stood motionless ... There were more soldiers lying in the grass beside the road, smoking their pipes and drinking wine from their water-bottles. They were unshaven... They laughed as they watched the civilians' cars go by. Knife in hand, they were sharing out a whole Gruyère cheese.
>
> A bee was buzzing inside the car. Clotilde, squashed between the door and her brother, who was eating chocolate, was fighting down her nausea. Her eyes were glued to the dusty trail of the truck in front. It sported a huge advertisement for a brand of biscuit which a bear was eagerly devouring. 'Do as the bear does, ask for Nours, the biscuit for connoisseurs.' But a hastily improvised placard, hand-written in ink, bore the words: 'Priority. Evacuation of pregnant women'. [49]

We may ask whether these two conflicting views of the same event through the same medium, popular literature, have not done more to erase the exodus as 'a pivotal moment for the people of France' in the collective memory than the lack of interest of historians in this event.[50] As Hanna Diamond has pointed out, for the exodus, 'The very nature of the event… meant that the archives upon which professional historians normally depend, such as prefect's reports, are either not available or incomplete. So the historian is largely dependant on journals, memories, oral accounts and novels to piece together the collective experience of this event'.[51]

The power of the literary gaze for defining attitudes to the Second World War brings us back to the Rougier Mission. Clotilde, in Cecil Saint Laurent's 1957 novel, is what would later be called 'liberated'. She is in close contact not only with Vichy, but also with the Resistance, in occupied France and overseas, joining the Free French in London. She discovers the existence of Rougier's 'protocol', also known as the 'gentlemen's agreement', while hiding in a corridor listening to her lover, Guy de Vise, talking with a woman, Mme d'Alvala, who turns out to be a Gaullist agent:

> There was a rustle of paper.
> – What is it ?
> – It is a copy of the Pétain–Churchill Agreement. It was stolen in
> Madrid from the British Ambassador … But read the secret agreement!
> she exclaimed.

So Guy de Vise does, and Cecil Saint Laurent gives a lengthy and precise account of the text.

> – Did Churchill write that himself ?
> – Yes. Don't you recognize the violence of his style? It is probable that
> Rougier had several conversations not only with the Minister for Foreign
> Affairs, Halifax, but also with Churchill, that he then drew up a draft
> and that Churchill wished to amend certain points of the draft as it was
> presented to him.
> – It's fascinating…[52]

And so convincing, that although Churchill never annotated this 'scrappy document' (*torchon de papier raturé*),[53] the English publisher had to insert a 'publisher's note' to make things clear: 'It is now a matter of common knowledge that no such "agreement" was ever drawn up … Of course, since there was never a "Rougier Agreement", the statement that a copy of this document was stolen from the safe of the British Ambassador is quite untrue'.[54] If, in 1958, things for a British audience were of 'common knowledge', why was it necessary to re-assert this, if not because Cecil Saint Laurent had masterfully succeeded in instilling doubts again and reaffirming the existence of what has been called by Jeffrey Mehlman 'principled Petainism',[55] a Petainism based upon the certainty that

Pétain was collaborating with the Germans, but at the same time planning the resistance of the Empire with the British? This turned out to be completely false, but was nevertheless believed in some sectors of French public opinion. Literature in a 'literary' nation like France[56] has always been more than literature: here it is the site of the production of a counter-history by writers from the right who, in the 1950s, developed that counter-history very effectively for political ends, to weaken, not to say shatter, the glorious Gaullist narrative of the occupation years.[57]

Colonial and 'gendered history'

In two fields there is evidence of enduring discrepancy between French and English historians: in colonial and gender studies. A French reader of the *TLS* enquiry of 1966 could not but be struck by the importance given to the outside world, not limited to the former Empire, in British history.[58] Much earlier than the French, British historians problematised a colonial history which could be defined as 'an account of the activities of Europeans in various parts of the world which they controlled, written for their own point of view'.[59] Two things seemed to have played a key influence. First there was 'the stimulus of anthropology' in the form of a book like Evans-Pritchard's *Witchcraft, Oracles and Magic among the Azande* (1937), which, according to Keith Thomas, 'disposed [British historians] to see analogies between their history and that of "underdeveloped" African countries in a way that Victorians could never have done. That gain in under-standing and comparative sense is incalculable'.[60] The other main factor of this openness of British history to the notion of 'the other' may have been the influence of the *Annales* school. As Jack P. Greene has pointed out:

> Inspired by the demands for an *histoire totale* articulated by Marc Bloch and Lucien Febvre and other members of the *Annales* school in France as early as the 1920s, as well as by post-World War II social and political changes, historians of British America have been on the forefront of the effort, emerging in the 1960s and still going strong, to recover the histories of those people – Amerindians, Africans and people of mixed races – whose stories had largely been neglected in the construction of grand narratives of the development of colonial British America and the emergence of the American nation.[61]

The *Annales* school did not obviously have a similar influence in France. If one looks at the bibliography gathered by the Centre National de Recherche Scientifique (CNRS) in 1965 to showcase *Vingt cinq ans de recherche historique en France*, colonial history was reduced to a set of 'lives of great men', the so-called colonial heros such as Lyautey and Bugeaud. The overseas world was of interest because the empire exemplified France's economic strength and symbolic grandeur. While British historians, influenced by Indian scholars, started to 'colonise British history' by imposing the colonised view in national histori-ography, French historians were still writing an epic history summed up in 144 books as diverse as Auguste Pavie, *À la conquête des coeurs* (1947), Jean Frédet, *Quand la Chine s'ouvrait: Charles de Montigny, consul de France (1848–1859)* (1953) and Albert Lougnon, *Sous le signe de la tortue: voyages anciens à l'île de Bourbon* (1958).[62] A sub-category of the history of international relationships, colonial history was clearly of minor importance for historians. In their defence, it has to be said that colonisation was explored by other scientific fields such as historical geography and economic history.[63] As the Marxist historian Pierre Vilar, author of the classic *La Catalogne dans l'Espagne moderne* (1962), put it: 'The main questions which we were confusedly thinking might be dominant in our century – colonisation, the crisis within the British world – were asked of us through the teaching of our influential geographers'.[64]

In 1964, Charles-Robert Ageron published a slim *Histoire de l'Algérie contem-poraine* which went through eleven editions in thirty years.[65] As the preface to the English edition proclaimed:

> His *Histoire de l'Algérie contemporaine*, published for a wide audience in the PUF *Que sais-je?* series, was not only a balanced and scholarly account for its subject, but a firm contribution to the controversy inseparable from the subject-matter. In measured terms, and measured tones, it put the blame for the Algerian war firmly on the European population of the country. Such a view was inevitably attacked by those who held that France itself was the culprit, who blamed the Muslim enemy, or conversely regarded the war of liberation as the necessary triumph of the Muslim people ... The judgement, however, still stands, buttressed over the years by the author's immense scholarly output. Supported in this way, the *Histoire* of 1964 has become a classic statement of its case, and a classic in its own right.[66]

Ageron's posterity was long to come, but nevertheless took off in the last ten years or so, when a new generation of historians was permitted access to the archives of the Algerian war and went further, starting to 'nationalise colonial history' by including the Algerian conflict in the shaping of the modern state of the Vth Republic, especially from the cultural and the legal point of view.[67] The chapter by Martin Evans and Raphaëlle Branche demonstrates the dramatic advances made in historiography in this period. If, as Bertrand Taithe put it in 2006, 'the Algerian war was a conflict that dared not speak its name and, for an entire generation... was not a subject for measured discussion in either France or Algeria,' it is now far too severe to conclude that, 'Despite a multitude of books and narratives, the Algerian War remained a complex unspoken page of French history'.[68]

The chapter by Ruth Harris and Laura Lee Downs suggests that if 'gender' lies in the past of British and American cultural history understood in its broader sense, it is still the future of the French one. For in what other country would it have been possible to write the history of the history of the last fifty years 'without gender'? The French academic's oversight of gender has but one significance, as Laura Lee Downs says – it reveals 'gender's potential as a critical tool' and allows 'French historians to re-think their tools of analysis' in key areas of research.

The issue of women and collaboration was, until the end of the 1990s, a non-issue for historians, except one: Richard Cobb. In his *French and Germans. Germans and French. A Personal Interpretation of France under Two Occupations 1914–1918/1940–1944* (1983), a maverick book in the period chosen, and in his tone, a mix of personal views and historical analysis, Richard Cobb raised a new question: 'What was a *collaboratrice*?' He sketched her in this way:

> Collaborationism of [the] extreme kind, as well as previous enrolment in the uniformed ranks of the PPF, the RNP, the Milice and the Francistes, was confined to males, these various bodies not possessing women's sections. So it is difficult to quantify feminine collaborationism and to assess the impact of feminine participation in collaborationist activities. Let us exclude, once and for all, the prostitutes ... Let us also exclude the nonprofessional *horizontales*, who lay down for a variety of motives, few of them ideological. Let us exclude the 80,000 mothers who claimed German nationality for their offspring ... Numerically, the most important element in feminine collaboration would be supplied by the secretarial personnel employed by the various German organizations in Paris. Secretaries were extremely well-paid – double the wages offered in the civilian sectors ... They might also have ready access to the favours of good-looking or high-ranking German officers ... Michel points out that one-fifth of those... brought to trial in the Département de la Seine after the Liberation were women, no doubt most of them secretaries, typists and interpreters in German organizations.
>
> But, undoubtedly, much the greatest service rendered by women to the German and French repressive authorities was in the ancient form of delation... the work of the dark battalions of yellow-faced *dénonciatrices*, the bile and slime of times of disaster; the work too, however, of women of substance, wreaking vengeance on some neighbour who had gossiped

about them, had hinted that they had been showing undue favours to members of the German forces, or who had insulted them in food queues.[69]

If Cobb repeatedly put the sexual factor aside, by doing so he unwittingly underlined it, mentioning the seduction exerted upon the French secretaries by their German employers, and writing that in 1943 the eighty thousand French women who 'had claimed children's benefits from the German military authorities and had requested German nationality for their offspring' in the Occupied zone had taken 'the first step towards collaborationism, whether at a personal or at a public level, being a desire to opt out of one's own nationality and to cross the frontiers of an alien and adopted one'.[70] Since then, until the release of Hanna Diamond's *Women and the Second World War in France 1939–1948* (1999), which devoted a chapter to the study of French women's *political* collaboration,[71] the sexual dimension or *collaboration horizontale* has been the most explored as far as women's behaviour under the Occupation is concerned.[72] In fact, women were politically committed, and, contrary to what Cobb argued, and as Laura Lee Downs shows, joined feminine associations created by the pro-collaborationist movements, in the direct line of the Catholic conservative political movement of the thirties.[73] A quantitative analysis of the data of the Civic Chambers of the Département de la Seine, the exceptional jurisdictions which were set up to sentence a new crime, national unworthiness, and only empowered to deprive defendants of civic and civil rights (national degradation), shows that women accounted for 25 per cent of defendants and that the accusations faced could be divided between: 'membership of an anti-national movement', 56 per cent; 'lack of national dignity' (including sexual intercourse with Germans), 26 per cent; 'denunciation or delation', 3 per cent. 'Denunciation or delation' was therefore not the main feature of women's collaboration.[74] As Julie Chassin has pointed out in a local study of the Cour de Justice of the Calvados, if women formed a slight majority (52 per cent) of denouncers there, it was for a practical reason. Prisoners in Germany, requisitioned by the Service du Travail Obligatoire, voluntary workers for the Germans, men were largely absent during the war. The over-representation of women among the denouncers reflected the specific constraints of the historical situation, and was by no means evidence that denounciation or delation were a 'woman's business'.[75]

The Civic Chambers of the Seine acquitted 48 per cent of women, as against 42 per cent of men. The indulgence of the courts, based both on a statistical approach and on a qualitative investigation of the personal files of defendants, shows that the judges – all men – did not take women's political commitment seriously. The 'social citizenship' (Magali della Sudda) women demonstrated by their actions within pro-collaborationist movements was again dismissed, since only a political citizenship which had triumphed in the French Revolution was taken into account. The Civic Chamber could acquit, sanction with national degradation, but also *relever*, which means sanction with a punishment with no effect. This *relèvement* was a kind of judicial forgiveness which involved 4 per cent of the women, but 10 per cent of men. This discrepancy is very telling: it shows that women were questioned far more than men about their moral behaviour under the Occupation, and condemned more for 'lack of dignity', a judicial crime created by the jurisprudence of the courts, than for the political crime of 'national indignity' conceived by the jurists of the Resistance.

At the end of this survey orientated by the questions asked to the historians, I am forced to conclude that history has more than a French accent: it has a sex and a colour. Will they vanish with the opening to the main trends of Anglo-Saxon approaches? As Keith Thomas observed in 2006, 'Above all, it has become mandatory for all historians to consider the gender aspect of their topic, whatever it may be, with the strong implication that not to do so is as much a moral failure as an intellectual one'.[76]

Since the 1960s, French history has become marginalised among British historians, who are more interested in issues and approaches developed by American historians, such as gender and post-colonial studies. American historians' 'enduring fascination' with France does not seem to have any equivalent among contemporary British historians.[77] In two long studies, Perry Anderson, the iconic thinker of the British New Left, has explored the '*dégringolade*' of the 'Great nation', a nation which in the 1960s and the 1970s embodied 'the world of ideas'. While 'two unstoppable forces: the worldwide advance of neo-liberalism and the rise of English as universal language' have been at work, French culture has been fixated by its own peculiarities which, according to him, rely on 'the formative role of the rhetoric in the upper levels of the French system':

> The potential cost of a literary conception of intellectual disciplines is obvious enough: arguments freed from logic, propositions from evidence. Historians were least prone to such an import substitution of literature, but even Braudel was not immune to the loosening of controls in a too flamboyant eloquence. It is this trait of the French culture of the time that has so often polarised foreign reactions to it, in a seesaw between adulation and suspicion.[78]

Merciless as he was, and up to date with the most recent developments of French culture, Anderson has nevertheless remarked on 'the continuing native vitality of French history'.[79] Insisting upon the central importance of the contemporary in the shaping of new historical subjects, for example, French historians have undertaken path-breaking work in memory studies, as Alya Aglan and Robert Gildea show in Chapter 8, which has opened up a rich new seam of research in Britain and the United States. Instead of re-nationalising historical questions, French historians have sought to de-territorialise them, to put an end to the French genre of 'auto-descriptive'. Why not study something other than France?

The 1966 *TLS* investigation of 'New Ways in History' has unfortunately not been collected and published separately. Our enterprise has been more limited in scope, but has had two ambitions: to get rid of national stereotypes or *clichés*, but to take account of the real discrepancies at work in historical research, shaped consciously or otherwise by national traditions. Instead of signing some new manifesto, contemporary historians on each side of the Channel and the Atlantic have agreed, in a field 'characterized by an astonishing diversity of approach', as Keith Thomas puts it, to keep an eye open on what their colleagues are thinking.

Notes

1 Editor's Introduction, 'History with a French accent', *Journal of Modern History* 44/4, December 1972, special issue on Fernand Braudel, 447.
2 *Times Literary Supplement (TLS)*, 7 April 1966, 28 July 1966 and 8 September 1966.
3 Keith Thomas, 'The tools and the job', *TLS*, 7 April 1966.
4 Antoine Prost, *Douze leçons sur l'histoire* (Paris, Le Seuil, coll. 'Points-Histoire', 1996), 16–17.
5 Prost, *Douze leçons*, 19.
6 'The French way of research', *TLS*, 8 September 1966.
7 Guy Bourdé and Hervé Martin, 'L'école des Annales', in *Les Écoles historiques* (Paris, Le Seuil, coll. 'Points-Histoire', 1997), 215–43.
8 Paul Veyne, 'L'histoire conceptualisante', in Jacques Le Goff and Pierre Nora, eds., *Faire de l'histoire* (Paris, Gallimard, 1974), I, 66–72.
9 Michael Kelly, 'Comparing French and British intellectuals: towards a cross-Channel perspective', *French Cultural Studies* vol. 14, part 3, number 42 (October 2003), 340.
10 Pierre Nora, 'Le retour de l'événement', in Jacques Le Goff and Pierre Nora, eds., *Faire de l'histoire* I, 210–27.
11 Jacques Le Goff, 'Is politics still the backbone of history?', in Felix Gilbert and Stephen R. Graubard, eds., *Historical Studies Today* (New York, Norton and Company, 1972), 349.
12 François Dosse, *New History in France. The Triumph of the Annales* (Chicago, University of Illinois Press, 1994), 196. This is a translation of *L'Histoire en miettes: des Annales à la Nouvelle Histoire* (Paris, La Découverte, 1987), 195.
13 'Histoire et sciences sociales: un tournant critique?', *Annales. Économies, Sociétés, Civilisations* 2 (March–April 1988), 292.
14 Hayden White, 'The question of narrative in contemporary historical theory', in *The Content of the Form. Narrative, Discourse and Historical Representation* (Baltimore, Johns Hopkins University Press, 1987), 31.
15 'Histoire et sciences sociales: un tournant critique?', 293.
16 Fernand Braudel, 'The situation of history in 1950', in *On History* (London, Weidenfeld and Nicolson, 1980), 11. Translation of *Écrits sur l'histoire* (Paris, Flammarion, 1969).
17 Jacques Le Goff, 'Is politics still the backbone of history?', 340.
18 See the special issue for the sixtieth birthday of the review 'Histoire et sciences sociales: un tournant critique', *Annales, Économies, Sociétés, Civilisations* 6, (November–December 1989), which exemplified the 'new critical direction'.
19 Gérard Noiriel, *Sur la 'crise' de l'histoire* (Paris, Belin, 1996), 150–4.
20 Eric Hobsbawm, 'British history and the *Annales*: a note', in *On History* (London, Weidenfeld and Nicolson, 1997), 178, 181.

21 François Furet and Denis Richet, *La Révolution française* (Paris, Hachette, coll. 'Réalités', 1965), vol. 1, *Des états-généraux au 9 thermidor*. Translated in an abridged version as *The French Revolution* (London, Weidenfeld and Nicolson, 1970).

22 Louis Chevalier, 'A reactionary view of urban history', *TLS*, 8 September 1966.

23 [Richard Cobb], 'Annalists' Revolution', *TLS*, 8 September 1966. This has recently been translated by Julien Louvrier, 'Nous des Annales: un compte rendu de Richard Cobb dans le Times Literary Supplement en 1966', http://rcvolution-française.net/2006

24 In E. P. Thompson, *The Poverty of Theory and Other Essays* (London, Merlin Press, 1978). Susan Magarey, 'That hoary old chestnut, free will and determinism: culture vs. structure, or history vs. theory in Britain. A review article', *Comparative Studies in Society and History*, 29/3 (July 1987), 627–39, gives an account of the controversial reception of Thompson's book and of his attack on the new 'New Left' through the reprinted essay 'The peculiarities of the English', 1965, where Thompson had pastiched Dickens to mock 'Messrs. Anderson and Nairn' (op. cit., 36–7).

25 E. P. Thompson, *The Poverty of Theory and Other Essays*, op. cit., 386, footnote 28.

26 Ibid., 220.

27 E. P. Thompson, *The Making of the English Working Class* (London, Victor Gollancz, 1963, Penguin, 1968), 230–1.

28 The 'linguistic turn' was popularized by a conference on European intellectual history held at Cornell University, chaired by Dominick LaCapra and Steven Kaplan, in 1980, and published in 1982 as *Modern European Intellectual History. Reappraisals and New Perspectives* (Ithaca and London, Cornell University Press). According to Gérard Noiriel, this expression has never been properly defined, but its vagueness was part of its success among the Anglo-Saxon historical community. The 'linguistic turn' may be identified with 'historical works which pay attention to the question of language'. See Gérard Noiriel, 'Le linguistic turn', *Sur la crise de l'histoire*, 126. More radically, the 'linguistic turn' suggests that if reality is mediated by language and by texts, then historical research is nothing but a reflection upon discourse, and a 'dialogical relationship' (Dominick LaCapra) must take over from the documentary approach used by historians (Noiriel, 137).

29 Geoff Eley, 'De l'histoire sociale au "tournant linguistique" dans l'historiographie anglo-américaine des années 1980', *Genèses. Histoire et sciences sociales* 7 (1982), 179, considers that the pre-Marxian Raymond Williams' *Culture and Society 1780–1950* (London, Columbia University Press, 1958) and *The Long Revolution* (London, Columbia University Press, 1961) played a key part in the development of cultural history as a history of 'a whole way of life'. But, as Susan Magarey has pointed out ('That hoary old chestnut', 627), 'Thompson's essays in *The Poverty of Theory* represent everything that had become known as culturalism by 1979 in Britain'.

30 Quoted in Hayden White, 'The value of narrativity in the representation of reality', in *The Content of the Form*, 5.

31 Jacques Le Goff, 'Mentalities: a history of ambiguities', in Jacques Le Goff and Pierre Nora, eds., *Constructing the Past* (Cambridge University Press/Paris, Maison des Sciences de l'Homme, 1985), 167. 'The notion of "mentality"… refers to a kind of historical beyond. Its function, as a concept, is to satisfy the historian's desire to "go further" and it leads to a point of contact with the other human sciences.' See the conclusion of Laura Lee Downs' paper in this volume.

32 Lawrence Stone, 'The revival of narrative: reflections on a new old history', *Past and Present* 85 (November 1979), 3, 13. French translation: 'Retour au récit ou réflexions sur une Nouvelle Vieille Histoire', *Le Débat* 4 (September 1980), 116–42. See also E. J. Hobsbawm, 'The revival of narrative: Some comments', *Past and Present* 86 (February 1980), 3–9, reprinted in *On History*, 186-91, and Robert Gildea's Introduction to this volume.

33 Carlo Ginzburg, 'Proofs and possibilities: in the margins of Nathalie Zemon Davis' *The Return of Martin Guerre*', *Yearbook of Comparative and General Literature* 37 (1988), 121.

34 Ginzburg, 'Proofs and possibilities', 118–22.

35 Arlette Farge, *La Nuit blanche* (Paris, Le Seuil, coll. 'Librairie du XXe et du XXIe siècle', 2002)

36 See Robert Gildea's paper on literature in this volume.

37 Charlotte Erikson, review of '*Railroads and American Economic Growth* by Robert William Fogel', *Economica* 33/129 (February 1966), 107. See Robert Gildea's paper in this volume.

38 Quoted in Carlo Ginzburg, 'Proofs and possibilities', 123.

39 Robert William Fogel, 'Proposed canals', in *Railroads and American Economic Growth*, 93.

40 Carlo Ginzburg, 'Proofs and possibilities', 119.

41 John Sutherland, *Victorian Fiction. Writers, Publishers, Readers* (New York, Palgrave MacMillan, 1985, 2006), 171.

42 Kieran Dolin, *Fiction in the Law. Legal Discourse in Victorian and Modernist Literature* (Cambridge

University Press, 1999), 31.

43 John H. Wigmore, 'A list of one hundred legal novels', *Illinois Law Review*, 17/1 (May 1922), 29.

44 The concept of 'interdiscourse' is borrowed from the German scholar Jürgen Link. See Peter Schötler, 'Historians and discourse analysis', *History Workshop Journal* 27 (Spring 1989), 53 and 64, footnote 111.

45 Jeffrey Mehlman, 'Louis Rougier and the "Pétain-Churchill Agreement"', in *Émigré New York. French Intellectuals in Wartime Manhattan, 1940–1944* (Baltimore, Johns Hopkins University Press, 2000), 125–6. Translated as *Émigrés à New York: les intellectuels français à Manhattan 1940–1944* (Paris, Albin Michel, 2005).

46 Robert Frank, 'Vichy et les Britanniques 1940–1941: double jeu ou double langage?', in Jean-Pierre Azéma and François Bédarida, eds., *Le Régime de Vichy et les Français,* (Paris, Fayard, 1992), 146–50.

47 Hanna Diamond, *Fleeing Hitler. France 1940* (Oxford University Press, 2007), 213.

48 Richard Cobb, '*L'Exode* and after', in *Promenades. A Historian's Appreciation of Modern French Literature* (Oxford University Press, 1980), 53.

49 Cecil Saint Laurent, *Clotilde* (London, Weidenfeld and Nicolson, 1958), 29.

50 Hanna Diamond, *Fleeing Hitler*, 12.

51 Ibid, 217.

52 Cecil Saint Laurent, *Clotilde*, op. cit., 150–1.

53 Robert Frank, 'Vichy et les Britanniques 1940–1941', 149. The writings are from Strang and Halifax.

54 'Publisher's note', in *Clotilde*, V–VI.

55 Jeffrey Mehlman, 'Louis Rougier and the "Pétain-Churchill Agreement"', 132.

56 Priscilla Parkhurst Ferguson, *Literary France: the Making of a Culture* (Berkeley, University of California Press, 1987).

57 Henry Rousso, *Le Syndrome de Vichy* (Paris, Le Seuil, 1987), 83–7. Translated as *The Vichy Syndrome: History and Memory in France since 1944* (Cambridge, Harvard University Press, 1991); Nicholas Hewitt, *Literature and the Right in Postwar France: The Story of the Hussards* (Oxford, Berg, 1996) and Anne Simonin, 'The right to innocence : literary discourse and the postwar purges', *Yale French Studies* 98, March 2000, special issue on 'The French Fifties', 5–29.

58 Raymond Carr, 'New openings. Latin America', *TLS*, 7 April 1966. See in the same edition Rachel F. Wall, 'New openings. Asia', and Thomas Hodgkin, 'New openings. Africa'.

59 Elsa V. Goveia and F. R. Augier, 'Colonialism from within', *TLS*, 28 July 1966. See in the same edition E. U. Essien-Udom, 'The coming of colour', Irfan Habib, 'India looks at herself' and Joseph Levanson, 'Ideas of China'.

60 Keith Thomas, 'The tools and the job', *TLS*, 7 April 1966.

61 Jack P. Greene, 'Colonial history and national history: reflections on a continuing problem', *The William and Mary Quarterly*, 3rd series, 64/2 (April 2007), 239. I am indebted for this development to Jean-Frédéric Schaub, who has been kind enough to let me read an article in progress to be published in the *Annales, Histoire, Sciences Sociales*, under the title 'La catégorie "études coloniales" est-elle indispensable?'

62 *Vingt-cinq ans de recherche historique en France* (Paris, CNRS, 1965), II, 449–54.

63 Pierre Chaunu, 'Economic history: past achievements and future prospects', in Jacques Le Goff and Pierre Nora, eds., *Constructing the Past*, 28–47.

64 Quoted in Jean Glénisson, 'L'historiographie française contemporaine: tendances et réalisations', in *Vingt-cinq ans de recherche historique en France* I, XV.

65 Charles-Robert Ageron, *Histoire de l'Algérie contemporaine* (Paris, PUF, coll. 'Que sais-je', 1964), translated as *Modern Algeria: A History from 1830 to the Present* (London, Hurst, 1991).

66 Michael Brett, 'Preface to the English edition', *Modern Algeria*, VI–VII.

67 See as examples Raphaëlle Branche, *La Torture et l'armée pendant la guerre d'Algérie* (Paris, Gallimard, 1991); Laure Blévis, 'La citoyenneté française au miroir de la colonisation: étude des demandes de naturalisation des "sujets français" en Algérie coloniale', *Genèses* 53 (December 2003), 25–47; and Sylvie Thénault, 'L'état d'urgence (1955–2005): de l'Algérie coloniale à la France contemporaine: destin d'une loi', *Le Mouvement social* 218 (January–March 2007), 63–78.

68 Bertrand Taithe, 'Introduction: an Algerian history of France?', *French History* 20/3 (September 2006), 236.

69 Richard Cobb, *French and Germans, Germans and French. A Personal Interpretation of France under Two Occupations 1914–1918/1940–1944* (London, University Press of New England, 1983), 104–5, translated as *Vivre avec l'ennemi: la France sous deux occupations 1914–1918 et 1940–1944* (Paris, Éditions du Sorbier, 1985). See the fall-out from Cobb's analysis in Philippe Burrin, 'The French and the Germans', in *Living with Defeat: France under the German Occupation 1940–1944* (London, Arnold, 1996), 204–9, translated from *La France à l'heure allemande 1940–1944* (Paris, Seuil, 1992).

70 Cobb, *French and Germans,* 66–7.
71 Hanna Diamond's *Women and the Second World War in France 1939–1948: Choices and Constraints* (Harlow, Longman, 1999), 71–98. See also Françoise Leclerc and Michèle Wendling, 'Des femmes devant les cours de justice', in Liliane Kandel, ed., *Féminisme et nazisme* (Paris, Publications de l'Université Paris VII-Denis Diderot, 1997), 77, and Cheryl Koos and Daniella Sarnoff, 'France', in Kevin Passmore, ed., *Women, Gender and Fascism in Europe 1919–1945* (Manchester University Press, 2003), 168–88.
72 Alain Brossat, *Les Tondues: un carnaval moche* (Levallois-Perret, Manya, 1993) and Fabrice Virgili, *La France virile: des femmes tondues à la Libération* (Paris, Payot, 2000), translated as *Shorn Women: Gender and Punishment in Liberation France* (Oxford, Berg, 2002).
73 See Laura Lee Downs' paper in this volume.
74 Anne Simonin, *L'Honneur dans la République. Une histoire de l'indignité (1789–1958)* (Paris, Grasset, forthcoming, 2008).
75 Julie Chassin, 'La délation sous l'Occupation dans le Calvados', *Annales de Normandie* 54/1 (January 2004), 82–3.
76 Keith Thomas, 'New ways revisited. How history's borders have expanded in the past forty years', *TLS*, 13 October 2006.
77 Laura Lee Downs and Stephane Gerson, eds., *Why France? American Historians Reflect on an Enduring Fascination* (Ithaca, Cornell University Press, 2007).
78 Perry Anderson, 'Dégringolade', *London Review of Books*, 2 September 2004, translated in *La Pensée tiède. Un regard critique sur la culture française* (Paris, Le Seuil, 2005).
79 Perry Anderson, 'Union sucrée', *London Review of Books*, 23 September 2004.

Bibliography

Abel, Olivier, Castelli-Gattinara, Enrico, Loriga, Sabina and Ullern Weité, Isabelle (eds.), *La juste mémoire. Lectures autour de Paul Ricœur* (Geneva, Labor et Fides, 2006).

Abélès, Marc, *L'Échec en politique* (Belval, Circé, 2005).

Abraham, David, *The Collapse of the Weimar Republic* (Princeton University Press, 1981).

Acton, Lord (ed.), *The Cambridge Modern History, I: The Renaissance* (Cambridge University Press, 1904), vii.

— *Lectures in Modern History* (London, Macmillan, 1906).

— *Lectures on the French Revolution* (London, Macmillan, 1910).

Agamben, Giorgio, *Homo sacer. Le pouvoir souverain et la vie nue* (Paris, Le Seuil, 1997).

Ageron, Charles-Robert, *Histoire de l'Algérie contemporaine* (Paris, PUF, 1964).

— *Les Algériens musulmans et la France (1871–1919)* (2 vols., Paris, PUF, 1968).

Aglan, Alya, Margairaz, Michel and Verheyde, Philippe (eds.), *La Caisse des dépôts, la Seconde Guerre mondiale et le XXe siècle. Actes du colloque international des 28, 29 et 30 novembre 2001* (Paris, Albin Michel, 2003).

Agulhon, Maurice, *Marianne into Battle: Republican Imagery and Symbolism in France, 1789–1880*, trans. J. Lloyd (Cambridge University Press, 1981).

Aldrich, Robert, *France and the South Pacific since 1940* (Basingstoke, Macmillan, 1993).

— *Greater France: A History of French Overseas Expansion* (Basingstoke, Macmillan, 1996).

— *Colonialism and Homosexuality* (London, Routledge, 2002).

— *Vestiges of the Colonial Empire in France: Monuments, Museums and Colonial Memories* (Basingstoke, Macmillan, 2005).

Allen, Nathan, *The Opium Trade* (Lowell, MA, Harvard, 1853).

Amiri, Linda, *La bataille de France. La guerre d'Algérie en métropole* (Paris, R. Laffont, 2004).

Amrane, Djamila, *Les femmes algériennes dans la guerre* (Paris, Plon, 1991).

Anderson, Benedict, *Imagined Communities: Reflections on the Origin and Spread of Nationalism*, 2nd revised ed. (London, Verso, 1991).

Anderson, David, *Histories of the Hanged: Britain's Dirty War in Kenya and the End of Empire* (London, Weidenfeld & Nicolson, 2005).

Andreano, Ralph A., *La Nouvelle Histoire économique. Exposé de méthodologie* (Paris, Gallimard, 1974).

Andress, David, *Massacre at the Champ de Mars: Popular Dissent and Political Culture in the French Revolution* (London, Royal Historical Society, 2000).

Andrieu, Claire (ed.), *La persécution des Juifs de France 1940–1944 et le rétablissement de la légalité républicaine. Recueil des textes officiels 1940–1999* (Paris, La Documentation française, 2000).

— *La spoliation financière. Mission d'étude sur la spoliation des Juifs de France* (Paris, La Documentation française, 2000).

— 'La commémoration des dernières guerres françaises: l'élaboration de politiques symboliques, 1945–2003', in Andrieu, Lavabre and Tartakowsky (eds.), *Politiques du Passé*.

—, Lavabre, Marie-Claire and Tartakowsky, Danielle (eds.), *Politiques du Passé. Usages politiques du passé dans la France contemporaine* (Aix-en-Provence, Publications de l'Université de Provence, 2006).

Ankersmit, F. R., *Narrative Logic: A Semiotic Analysis of the Historian's Language* (The Hague, M. Nijhoff, 1983).

— 'Historiography and postmodernism', *History and Theory*, 28 (1989), 137–53.

Appiah, Kwame, *Cosmopolitanism: Ethics in a World of Strangers* (New York, W. W. Norton, 2006).

Appleby, Joyce, 'One good turn deserves another: moving beyond the linguistic; a response to David Harlan', *American Historical Review*, 94 (1989), 1326–32.

—, Hunt, Lynn and Jacob, Margaret, *Telling the Truth about History* (London, W. W. Norton, 1995).

Arnold, Dana (ed.), *The Metropolis and Its Image: Constructing Identities for London 1750–1950* (Oxford, Blackwell, 1999).

— *Cultural Identities and the Aesthetics of Britishness 1750–1950* (Manchester University Press, 2004).

Arnold, Odile, *Le corps et l'âme: la vie des religieuses au XIXe siècle* (Paris, Le Seuil, 1984).

Artières, Philippe and Kalifa, Dominique, *Vidal le tueur de femmes. Une biographie sociale* (Paris, Le Perrin, 2001).

Asthana, Anushka, 'What links the British Empire, witch-hunts and the Wild West?', *The Observer*, 21 October 2007.

Atack, Margaret, *Literature and the French Resistance: Cultural Politics and Narrative Forms 1940–1950* (Manchester University Press, 1989).

— *May 68 in French Fiction and Film* (Oxford University Press, 1999).

Atkinson, Antony B. and Stiglitz, Joseph E., *Lectures on Public Economics* (New York, Mcgraw Hill, 1980).

Augustine, St, *Confessions* (New York, Fathers of the Church, 1953).

Aumann, Robert J., 'Game theory', in *The New Palgrave: A Dictionary of Economics* (London, Palgrave Macmillan, 1987), vol.2, 460–82.

Baker, Keith M., *Inventing the French Revolution: Essays on French Political Culture in the Eighteenth Century* (Cambridge University Press, 1990).

—, Lucas, Colin and Furet, François, *The French Revolution and the Creation of Modern Political Culture* (4 vols, Oxford, Pergamon, 1987–94).

Bancel, Nicolas, Blanchard, Pascal and Delabarre, Francis (eds.), *Images d'Empire, 1930–1960. Trente ans de photographies officielles sur l'Afrique française* (Paris, La Martinière, 1997).

—, Blanchard, Pascal and Vergès, Françoise, *La République coloniale. Essai sur une utopie* (Paris, Albin Michel, 2003).

Barciela, Carlos, Chastagnaret, Gérard and Escudero, Antonio (eds.), *La Historia economica en Espana y Francia (siglos XIX y XX)* (Alicante University, 2006).

Barthel, Diane, *Historic Preservation: Collective Memory and Historical Identity* (New Brunswick, NJ, Rutgers University Press, 1996).

Barthes, Roland, *Michelet* (Paris, Le Seuil, 1954).

— *S/Z, Tel Quel* (Paris, Le Seuil, 1970).

— *The Rustle of Language*, trans. R. Howard (Oxford, Blackwell, 1989).

Bayly, C. A., 'The Orient: British historical writing since 1890', in Peter Burke (ed.), *History and Historians in the Twentieth Century* (Oxford University Press, 2002), 88–119.

Bédarida, François (ed.), *L'histoire et le métier de l'historien en France 1945–1995* (Paris, Maison des sciences de l'homme, 1995).

— and Fouilloux, Etienne (eds.), *La guerre d'Algérie et les chrétiens* (Paris, Les Cahiers de l'IHTP, 1988).

Bender, Thomas (ed.), *Rethinking American History in a Global Age* (Berkeley, University of California Press, 2002).

Bénichou, Paul, *Le temps des prophètes. Doctrines de l'âge romantique* (Paris, Gallimard, 1977).

— *Les mages romantiques* (Paris, Gallimard, 1988).

— *L'école du désenchantement. Sainte-Beuve, Nodier, Musset, Nerval, Gautier* (Paris, Gallimard, 1992).

— *Le sacre de l'écrivain, 1750–1830. Essai sur l'avènement d'un pouvoir spirituel laïque dans la France moderne* (Paris, Gallimard, 1996 [1973]).

Benjamin, Walter, *Charles Baudelaire: A Lyric Poet in the Era of High Capitalism*, trans. H. Zohn (London, New Left Books, 1973).

— 'The work of art in the age of mechanical reproduction', in *Illuminations*, trans. H. Zohn (London, Fontana, 1992), 211–44.

— 'On the concept of history' [1940], in *Selected Writings, IV: 1938–1940*, trans. E. Jephcott *et al.*, (Cambridge, MA, Belknap Press of Harvard University Press, 2003).

Bennett, Judith, 'Feminism and history', *Gender and History*, 1 (1989), 251–72.

— *History Matters: Patriarchy and the Challenges of Feminism* (Philadelphia, University of Pennsylvania Press, 2006).

Berg, Maxine, *A Woman In History: Eileen Power, 1889–1940* (Cambridge University Press, 1996).

Bergfelder, Tim, Carter, Erica and Göktürk, Deniz (eds.), *The German Cinema Book* (London, BFI Publishing, 2002).

Berkhofer, Robert, 'A point of view on viewpoints in historical practice', in F. R. Ankersmit (ed.), *The New Philosophy of History* (London, Reaktion Books, 1995), 174–91.

Berr, Henri, 'Avant propos', in Georges Weill, *Le Journal. Origines, évolution et rôle de la presse périodique* (Paris, La Renaissance du livre, 1934), XVII.

Berstein, Serge, 'La France allergique au fascisme', *Vingtième siècle: revue d'histoire*, 2 (April 1984), 84–94.

Bertrand, Romain, *Mémoires d'empire. La controverse autour du 'fait colonial'* (Paris, Editions du Croquant et Savoir/Agir, 2006).

Besley, Timothy, 'The New Political Economy', Keynes Lecture, British Academy, 13 October 2004.

— and Ghatak, Maitreesh, 'Competition and incentives with motivated agents', *Centre for Economic Policy Research Discussion Paper*, 4641 (September 2004).

Bhabha, Homi, *The Location of Culture* (London, Routledge, 1994).

Bidelman, P. K., *Pariahs Stand Up! The Founding of the Liberal Feminist Movement in France 1858–1889* (Westport, CT, Greenwood Press, 1982).

Blanchard, Pascal, Bancel, Nicolas and Lemaire, Sandrine (eds.), *La fracture coloniale. La société française au prisme de l'héritage colonial* (Paris, La Découverte, 2005).

—, Deroo, Éric, El Yazami, Driss, *et al.*, *Le Paris arabe: deux siècles de présence des Orientaux et des Maghrébins* (Paris, La Découverte, 2003).

Blassingame, John, *The Slave Community. Plantation Life in the Antebellum South* (New York and Oxford, Oxford University Press, 1972).

Blaufarb, Rafe, *The French Army, 1750–1820: Careers, Talent, Merit* (Manchester University Press, 2002).

Blévis, Laure, 'La citoyenneté française au miroir de la colonisation. Etude des demandes de naturalisation des "sujets français" en Algérie coloniale', *Genèses*, 53 (December 2003), 25–47.

Bloch, Ernst, *Le principe espérance*, (3 vols, Paris, Gallimard, 1976–1991).

Bloch, Marc, *La Société féodale* (2 vols, Paris, Albin Michel, 1939–40).

— *The Historian's Craft*, trans. P. Putnam (Manchester University Press, 1954).

Blowen, Sarah, Demoissier, Marion and Picard, Jeannine (eds.), *Recollections of France: Memories, Identities and Heritage in Contemporary France* (Oxford and New York, Berghahn Books, 2000).

Bodin, Jean, *La méthode de l'histoire*, transl. P. Mesnard (Paris, Belles Lettres, 1941).

Bonnell, Victoria and Hunt, Lynn (eds.), *Beyond the Cultural Turn: New Directions in the Study of Society and Culture* (Berkeley and London, University of California Press, 1999).

Bonniol, Jean-Luc, 'Échos politiques de l'esclavage colonial des départements d'outre-mer au cœur de l'État', in Andrieu, Lavabre and Tartarowsky (eds.), *Politiques du Passé*, 59–69.

Bony, Anne, *Les Années 40. Collection Couleur du XXe Siècle* (Paris, Editions du regard, 1985).

Bossenga, Gail, *The Politics of Privilege: Old Regime and Revolution in Lille* (Cambridge University Press, 1991).

Bouatta, Chérifa, 'Feminine militancy: moudjahidates during and after the Algerian War', in Valentine Moghadam (ed.), *Gender and National Identity: Women and Politics in Muslim Societies* (Zed Books for UNU/WIDER; Karachi, Oxford University Press, 1994), 18–39.

Bourdé, Guy and Martin, Hervé, *Les Écoles historiques* (Paris, Le Seuil, 1997).

Bourdieu, Pierre, 'L'illusion biographique', *Actes de la Recherche en Sciences sociales*, 62–63 (1986), 69–72.

— *Homo Academicus*, trans. P. Collier (Cambridge, Polity, 1988).

— *The Logic of Practice*, trans. R. Nice (Cambridge, Polity Press, 1990).

Boureau, Alain, 'La compétence inductive. Un modèle d'analyse des représentations rares', in Bernard Lepetit (ed.), *Les formes de l'expérience. Une autre histoire sociale* (Paris, Albin Michel, 1995), 23–38.

Bourguignon, André, *Essais de psychanalyse* (Paris, 1981).

Bourguignon, François and Lévy-Leboyer, Maurice, *L'économie française au XIXe siècle. Analyse macro-économique* (Paris, Économica, 1985).

Bouza, Fernando, *Corre manuscrito. Una historia cultural del Siglo de Oro* (Madrid, Marcial Pons, 2001).

Branche, Raphaëlle, *La Torture et l'Armée pendant la Guerre d'Algérie 1954–1962* (Paris, Gallimard, 2001).

— *La guerre d'Algérie: une histoire apaisée?* (Paris, Le Seuil, 2005).

Braudel, Fernand and Labrousse Ernest (eds.), *Histoire économique et sociale de la France* (8 vols, Paris, PUF, 1970–82).

— *The Mediterranean and the Mediterranean World in the Age of Philip II*, trans. S. Reynolds (New York, Harper & Row, 1972).

— *On History*, trans. S. Matthews (London, Weidenfeld & Nicolson, 1980).

Brendon, Piers, *The Decline and Fall of the British Empire* (London, Cape, 2007).

Bridenthal, Renate and Koonz, Claudia, *Becoming Visible: Women in European History* (Boston, MA, Houghton Mifflin, 1977).

Brossat, Alain, *Les Tondues. Un carnaval moche* (Levallois-Perret, Manya, 1993).

Brown, Howard G., 'Echoes of the Terror', *Historical Reflections/Réflexions historiques*, 29 (2003), 529–58.

— *Ending the French Revolution: Violence, Justice and Repression from the Terror to Napoleon* (Charlottesville, University of Virginia Press, 2006).

Browning, Christopher, *Ordinary Men: Reserve Police Battalion 101 and the Final Solution in Poland* (New York, HarperCollins, 1992).

Burke, Peter, *Varieties of Cultural History* (Cambridge, Polity Press, 1997).

— *What is Cultural History?* (Cambridge, Polity Press, 2004).

Burnett, John, *Plenty and Want: A Social History of Diet in England from 1815 to the Present Day* (London, Nelson, 1966).

Burrin, Philippe, *Living with Defeat: France under the German Occupation 1940–1944*, trans. J. Lloyd (London, Arnold, 1996).

Burstin, Haim, 'Pour une phénoménologie de la violence révolutionnaire. Réflexions autour du cas parisien', *Historical Reflections/Réflexions historiques*, 29 (2003), 389–407.

Burton, Antoinette, 'Thinking beyond the boundaries: empire, feminism and the domains of history', *Social History*, 26 (2001), 60–71.

Burton, Richard D. E., *Holy Tears, Holy Blood: Women, Catholicism and the Culture of Suffering in France, 1840–1909* (New York, Cornell University Press, 2004).

Campbell, Peter R., Kaiser, Thomas E. and Linton, Marisa (eds.), *Conspiracy in the French Revolution* (Manchester University Press, 2007).

Cannadine, David, 'The context, performance and meaning of ritual: the British monarchy and the invention of tradition', in Hobsbawm and Ranger (eds.), *The Invention of Tradition*, 101–164.

— *Ornamentalism: How the British Saw their Empire* (London, Allen Lane, 2001).

Caplan, Jane, 'Contemporary history: reflections from Britain and Germany', *History Workshop Journal*, 63 (Spring 2007), 230–8.

Carbonell, Charles-Olivier and Livet, Georges, *Au Berceau des Annales. Le Milieu strasbourgeois, l'histoire en France au début du XXe siècle* (Toulouse, Presses de l'Institut d'Études Politiques de Toulouse, 1983).

Carlyle, Thomas, *The French Revolution* (Oxford University Press, 1989 [1837]).

Carpenter, Kirsty and Philip Mansel (eds.), *The French Emigrés in Europe and the Struggle Against Revolution, 1789–1814* (Basingstoke, Macmillan, 1999).

Carr, Raymond, 'New openings: Latin America', *TLS*, 7 April 1966.

Carré, Jean-Jacques, Dubois, Paul and Malinvaud, Edmond, *La croissance française. Un essai d'analyse économique causale de l'après-guerre* (Paris, Le Seuil, 1972).

Carroll, Stuart, *Blood and Violence in Early Modern France* (Oxford, Clarendon Press, 2006).

— (ed.), *Cultures of Violence: Interpersonal Violence in Historical Perspective* (Basingstoke, Palgrave Macmillan, 2007).

Cartledge, Paul, 'What is social history now?', in David Cannadine (ed.), *What is History Now?* (Basingstoke, Palgrave Macmillan, 2002).

Chafer, Tony, *The End of Empire in French West Africa* (Oxford, Berg, 2002).

Chakrabarty, Dipesh, *Provincializing Europe: Postcolonial Thought and Historical Difference* (Princeton University Press, 2000).

Chandler (Jr.), Alfred D., *The Visible Hand: The Managerial Revolution in American Business* (Cambridge, MA, and London, Belknap Press of Harvard University Press, 1977).

Chang, Gordon H., 'History and postmodernism', *Amerasia Journal*, 21 (1995).

Chapman, James, *Licence to Thrill: A Cultural History of the James Bond Films* (New York, Columbia University Press, 2000).

— *Past and Present: National Identity and the British Historical Film* (London, I. B. Tauris, 2005).

Charle, Christophe (ed.), *Histoire sociale, histoire globale?* (Paris, Maison des sciences de l'homme, 1993).

Chartier, Roger, 'Le monde comme représentation', *Annales E.S.C*, 44 (1989), 1505–20.

— *L'Ordre des livres. Lecteurs, auteurs et bibliothèques en Europe entre XIVe et XVIIe siècles* (Aix-en-Provence, Alinéa, 1992).

— *Au bord de la falaise. L'histoire entre certitudes et inquiétudes* (Paris, Albin Michel, 1998).

— *Inscrire et effacer. Culture écrite et littérature (XIe-XVIIIe siècle)* (Paris, Gallimard-Seuil, 2005).

Chassin, Julie, 'La délation sous l'Occupation dans le Calvados', *Annales de Normandie*, 54/1 (January 2004).

Chaumont, Jean-Michel, *La Concurrence des victimes: genocide, identité, reconnaissance* (Paris, La Découverte, 1997).

Chaunu, Pierre, 'L'économie. Dépassement et prospective', in Le Goff and Nora (eds.), *Faire de l'histoire*, vol. 2, 51–73.

Chérif Sahli, Mohamed, *Décoloniser l'histoire* (Paris, F. Maspero, 1965).

Chevalier, Jean-Claude, 'La langue', in Le Goff and Nora (eds.), *Faire de l'histoire*, vol. 3, 95–114.

Chevalier, Louis, 'A reactionary view of urban history', *TLS*, 8 September 1966.

Clark, Elizabeth A., *History, Theory, Text: Historians and the Linguistic Turn* (Cambridge, MA, Harvard University Press, 2004)

Clark, T.J., *Farewell to an Idea: Episodes from a History of Modernism* (New Haven, CT, Yale University Press, 2001).

Clavero, Bartolomé, *Razón de Estado, Razón de Individuo, Razón de Historia* (Madrid, Centro de Estudios Políticos y Constitucionales, 1991).

— *La Grâce Du Don. Anthropologie catholique de l'économie moderne* (Paris, Albin Michel, 1996).

Clavin, Patricia, 'Defining transnationalism', *Contemporary History*, 14/4 (2005), 421–39.

— and Wessels, Jens-Wilhelm, 'Transnationalism and the League of Nations: understanding the work of its economic and financial organisation', *Contemporary European History*, 14/4 (2005), 465–92.

Clifford, Rebecca, 'Creating official Holocaust commemorations in France and Italy, 1990–2005', PhD thesis (University of Oxford, 2008).

CNRS, *Vingt-cinq ans de recherche historique en France* (2 vols, Paris, 1965).

Coates, Jim, *The Amritsar Massacre, 1919: General Dyer in the Punjab* (London, Stationery Office, 2000).

Cobb, Richard, *Terreur et subsistances, 1793–1795* (Paris, Clavreuil, 1965).

— 'Annalists' Revolution', *TLS*, 8 September 1966.

— *A Second Identity: Essays on France and French History* (Oxford University Press, 1969).

— *The Police and the People: French Popular Protest, 1789–1820* (Oxford, Clarendon Press, 1970).

— *Reactions to the French Revolution* (Oxford University Press, 1972).

— *Promenades: A Historian's Appreciation of Modern French Literature* (Oxford University Press, 1980).

— *French and Germans, Germans and French: A Personal Interpretation of France under Two Occupations, 1914–1918/1940–1944* (London, University Press of New England, 1983).

— *The People's Armies: The Armées Révolutionnaires, Instrument of the Terror in the Departments, April 1793 to Floral Year II*, trans. M. Elliott (New Haven, CT, Yale University Press, 1987).

Cobban, Alfred, *The Social Interpretation of the French Revolution* (Cambridge University Press, 1964).

Cole, G. D. H., *An Intelligent Man's Guide Through World Chaos* (London, Victor Gollancz, 1932).

— *The Common People, 1746–1938* (London, Methuen, 1938).

— and Cole, M. I., *The Condition of Britain* (London, Victor Gollancz, 1937).

Colley, Linda, *Captives: Britain, Empire and the World 1600–1850* (London, Jonathan Cape, 2002)

— 'The difficulty of empire: present, past and future', *Historical Review*, 79/207 (August 2006).

Collingwood, R. G., *The Idea of History* (Oxford, Clarendon Press, 1946).

Collini, Stefan, *Absent Minds: Intellectuals in Britain* (Oxford University Press, 2006).

Collins, Jane, *Threads: Gender, Labor and Power in the Global Apparel Industry* (Chicago University Press, 2003).

Colonna, Fanny, 'The Nation's unknowing Other: three intellectuals and the culture(s) of being Algerian, or the impossibility of subaltern studies in Algeria', *Journal of Northern African Studies*, 8/1 (Spring 2003), 155–70.

Comninel, George C., *Rethinking the French Revolution: Marxism and the Revisionist Challenge* (London, Verso, 1987).

Conan, Eric and Rousso, Henry, *Vichy, an Ever-Present Past*, trans. N. Bracher (Hanover, University Press of New England, 1998).

Confino, Alon and Fritsche, Peter, *The Work of Memory: New Directions in the Study of German Society and Culture* (Urbana and Chicago, University of Illinois Press, 2002).

Cook, Pam (ed.), *Cinema Book* (London, BFI Publishing, 1985).

— *Screening the Past: Memory and Nostalgia in Cinema* (London and New York, Routledge, 2005).

Cooper, Frederick, *Decolonization and African Society: The Labor Question in French and British Africa* (Cambridge University Press, 1996).

— *Colonialism in Question: Theory, Knowledge, History* (Berkeley and Los Angeles, University of California Press, 2005).

Cooper, Nicola, *France in Indochina: Colonial Encounters* (Oxford, Berg, 2001).

Coward, Barry and Swann, Julian (eds.), *Conspiracies and Conspiracy Theory in Early Modern Europe: From the Waldensians to the French Revolution* (London, Ashgate, 2004).

Coward, David, *A History of French Literature from Chanson De Geste to Cinema* (Oxford, Blackwell, 2004).

Crafts, Nicholas F. R., *British Economic Growth during the Industrial Revolution* (Oxford, Clarendon Press, 1985).

— and Mills, Terence C., 'Was nineteenth-century British growth steam-powered? The climacteric revisited', *Explorations in Economic History*, 41 (2004), 156–71.

Crivello, Maryline, 'Les braconniers de l'histoire. Les reconstitutions historiques, nouveaux lieux de politique', in Crivello, Garcia and Offenstadt (eds.), *Concurrences des passés*, 49–58.

—, Garcia, Patrick and Offenstadt, Nicolas (eds.), *Concurrences des passés. Usages politiques du passé dans la France contemporaine* (Aix-en-Provence, Publiciations de l'Université de Provence, 2006)

Crouzet, Denis, *Les guerriers de Dieu. La violence au temps des troubles de religion (vers 1525–vers 1610)* (Seyssel, Champ Vallon, 2005).

Crow, Thomas E., *Modern Art in the Common Culture* (New Haven, CT, and London, Yale University Press, 1996).

— *The Rise of the Sixties: American and European Art in the Era of Dissent, Perspectives* (London, Weidenfeld & Nicolson, 1996).

Cumming, Mark, *A Disimprisoned Epic: Form and Vision in Carlyle's French Revolution* (Philadelphia, University of Pennsylvania Press, 1988).

Darnton, Robert, *The Great Cat Massacre and Other Episodes in French Cultural History* (London, Penguin, 1985).

Darwin, John, *After Tamerlane: The Global History of Empire* (London, Allen Lane, 2007).

Dasguptha, Partha, *An Inquiry into Well-being and Destitution* (Oxford, Clarendon Press, 1993).

Dauphin, Cécile *et al.*, 'Culture et pouvoir des femmes. Essai d'historiographie', *Annales E.S.C.*, 41 (1986), 271–93.

Davies, Andrew, *Leisure, Gender and Poverty: Working-class Culture in Salford and Manchester, 1900–1939* (Milton Keynes, Open University Press, 1992).

— 'The Scottish Chicago? From "hooligans" to "gangsters" in inter-war Glasgow', *Cultural and Social History*, 4 (2007), 511–27.

Dawson, Graham, *Making Peace with the Past? Memory, Trauma and the Irish Troubles* (Manchester University Press, 2007).

de Barros, Françoise and Charbit, Tom (eds.), 'La colonie rapatriée', *Politix. Revue des sciences et de la politique*, 76/19 (2006).

de Benedictis, Angela, *Politica, governo e istituzioni nell'Europa moderna* (Bologna, Il Mulino, 2001).

de Certeau, Michel, *L'écriture de l'histoire* (Paris, Gallimard, 1975).

— *The Practice of Everyday Life* (Berkeley and Los Angeles, University of California Press, 1984).

de Grazia, Victoria, *Irresistible Empire: America's Advance through Twentieth-century Europe* (Cambridge, MA, Belknap Press of Harvard University Press, 2005).

Deeds Ermath, Elizabeth, *Sequel to History: Postmodernism and the Crisis of Representational Time* (Princeton University Press, 1992).

della Sudda, Magali, *Une activité politique féminine conservatrice avant le droit de suffrage en France et en Italie. Socio-histoire de la politisation des femmes catholiques au sein de la Ligue Patriotique des Françaises (1902–1933) et de l'Unione tra le donne cattoliche d'Italia (1909–1919)* (doctoral thesis, EHESS, 2007).

Deloye, Yves and Voutat, Bernard (eds.), *Faire de la science politique. Pour une socio-histoire du politique* (Paris, Belin, 2002).

Demartini, Anne-Emmanuelle and Kalifa, Dominique (eds.), *Imaginaire et sensibilités au XIXe siècle* (Paris, Créaphis, 2005).

Derrida, Jacques, *Of Grammatology*, trans. G. C. Spivak (Baltimore, MD, Johns Hopkins University Press, 1997).

Desan, Suzanne, *The Family on Trial in Revolutionary France* (Berkeley, University of California Press, 2006).

Descimon, Robert and Guéry, Alain, 'Un État des Temps modernes?', in André Burguière and Jacques Revel (series eds.) and Jacques Le Goff (vol. ed.), *Histoire de la France. La longue durée de l'État* (Paris, Le Seuil, 2000), 209–534.

Desrosières, Alain and Thévenot, Laurent, *Les catégories socioprofessionnelles* (Paris, La Découverte, 1988).

Diamond, Hanna, *Women and the Second World War in France 1939–1948: Choices and Constraints* (Harlow, Longman, 1999).

— *Fleeing Hitler: France 1940* (Oxford University Press, 2007).

Dickens, Charles, *A Tale of Two Cities* (London, Penguin, 1985 [1859]).

Dicks, Bella, *Heritage, Place and Community* (Cardiff, University of Wales Press, 2000).

Dine, Philip, *Images of the Algerian War: French Fiction and Film 1954–1992* (Oxford, 1994).

Dobry, Michael, *Le mythe de l'allergie française au fascisme* (Paris, Albin Michel, 2003).

Dolin, Kieran, *Fiction in the Law: Legal Discourse in Victorian and Modernist Literature* (Cambridge University Press, 1999).

Dosse, François, *New History in France: The Triumph of the Annales*, trans. P. Conroy (Jr.) (Chicago, University of Illinois Press, 1994).

Downs, Laura Lee, 'Reply to Joan Scott', *Comparative Studies in Society and History* (April 1993), 444–58.

— *Childhood in the Promised Land: Working-class Movements and the Colonies de Vacances in France, 1880–1960* (Durham, NC, Duke University Press, 2002).

— *Writing Gender History* (London, Hodder Arnold, 2004).

— (forthcoming), 'To re-unite the national family in the folds of the tricolour: gender and the social politics of working-class childhood on the extreme right, 1930–39', *Journal of Modern History*, special issue on European childhood.

Doyle, William, *Origins of the French Revolution* (Oxford University Press, 1980).

Dreyfus, Jean-Marc, *Pillages sur ordonnances. Aryanisation et restitution des banques en France 1940–1953* (Paris, Fayard, 2003).

Duby, Georges, *The Legend of Bouvines: War, Religion and Culture in the Middle Ages*, trans. C. Tihanyi (Cambridge, Polity Press, 1990).

— and Perrot, Michelle (eds.), *A History of Women in the West* (5 vols, Cambridge, MA, Belknap Press of Harvard University Press, 1992–4).

Duchen, Claire, *Women's Rights and Women's Lives in France 1944–1968* (London, Routledge, 1994).

Dulucq, Sophie and Zytnicki, Colette (eds.), *Décoloniser l'histoire? De l'histoire coloniale aux histoires nationales en Amérique latine et en Afrique, XIXe-XXe siècles* (Saint-Denis, Société française d'histoire d'outre-mer, 2003).

— 'Penser le passé colonial français. Entre perspectives historiographiques et résurgence des mémoires', *Vingtième Siècle. Revue d'histoire*, 86 (Spring 2005), 59–69.

Dumoulin, Olivier, *Le rôle social de l'historien. De la chaire au prétoire* (Paris, Albin Michel, 2003).

Duroselle, Jean-Baptiste, *La Grande Guerre des Français. L'incompréhensible* (Paris, Le Perrin, 1995).

Editorial, 'History with a French accent', *Journal of Modern History*, 44/4 (December 1972), 447–538.

Editorial, 'Histoire et sciences sociales. Un tournant critique?', *Annales E.S.C.*, 2 (March–April 1988), 291–3.

Editorial, *Cultural and Social History*, 1 (2004), 1–5.

Editorial, *History Workshop Journal*, 1 (1976).

Einaudi, Jean-Luc, *La Bataille de Paris. 17 octobre 1961* (Paris, Le Seuil, 1991).

Eley, Geoff, 'De l'histoire sociale au "tournant linguistique" dans l'historiographie anglo-américaine des années 1980', trans. M. Charlot, *Genèses. Histoire et sciences sociales*, 7 (1982), 163–93.

— *The Crooked Line: From Cultural History to the History of Society* (Ann Arbor, University of Michigan Press, 2005).

Elias, Norbert, *Engagement et distanciation* (Paris, Fayard, 1983).

Elkins, Caroline, *Britain's Gulag: The Brutal End of Empire in Kenya* (London, Cape, 2005).

Elliot, J. H., *Empires of the Atlantic World: Britain and Spain in America, 1492–1830* (London, Yale University Press, 2006).

Englund, Steven, 'The ghost of nation past', *Journal of Modern History*, 44 (1992), 299–320.

— *Napoleon, a Political Life* (Cambridge, MA, Harvard University Press, 2004).

Epstein, James, 'Understanding the cap of Liberty: symbolic practice and social conflict in early nineteenth-century England', *Past & Present*, 122 (1989), 75–118.

Erikson, Charlotte, review of Fogel, *Railroads*, *Economica*, 33 (1966), 106–9.

Evangelisti, Silvia, 'Rooms to share: convent cells and social relations in early-modern Italy', in *The Art of Survival: Gender and History in Europe, 1450–2000*, *Past & Present* Supplement 1 (Oxford, 2005), 55–71.

Evans, Martin (ed.), *Empire and Culture: The French Experience, 1830–1940* (Basingstoke, Macmillan, 2004).

— and Phillips, John, *Algeria: Anger of the Dispossessed* (London, Yale University Press, 2007).

Evans, Richard, *In Defence of History* (London, Granta, 1997).

Evans-Pritchard, E. E., *Anthropology and History* (Manchester University Press, 1961).

Farcy, Jean-Claude, Kalifa, Dominique and Luc, Jean-Noël (eds.), *L'Enquête judiciaire en Europe au XIXe siècle. Acteurs, imaginaire, pratiques* (Paris, Créaphis, 2007).

Farge, Arlette, *Le goût de l'archive* (Paris, Le Seuil, 1989).

— *La nuit blanche* (Paris, Le Seuil, 2002).

— and Revel, Jacques, *Logiques de la foule. L'affaire des enlèvements d'enfants, Paris 1750* (Paris, Hachette, 1988).

Fass, Paula S., 'Cultural history/social history: some reflections on a continuing dialogue', *Journal of Social History*, 37 (2003), 39–46.

Febvre, Lucien, *Combats pour l'histoire* (Paris, A. Colin, 1953).

Feiertag, Olivier and Margairaz, Michel (eds.), *Politiques et pratiques des banques d'émission en Europe (XVIIe–XXe siècles). Le bicentenaire de la Banque de France dans la perspective de l'identité monétaire européenne* (Paris, Albin Michel, 2003).

Ferguson, Niall, *Empire: How Britain Made the Modern World* (London, Allen Lane, 2003).

Fernández Sebastián, Javier, *Diccionario politico y social del siglo XIX español* (Madrid, Alianza, 2003).

Fitzsimmons, Michael P., *The Remaking of France: The National Assembly and the Constitution of 1791* (Cambridge University Press, 1994).

— *The Night the Old Regime Ended: August 4, 1789, and the French Revolution* (University Park, Penn State University Press, 2003).

Fogel, Michèle, *Les cérémonies de l'information dans la France du XVIe siècle au XVIIIe siècle* (Paris, Fayard, 1989).

Fogel, Robert W., *Railroads and American Economic Growth: Essays in Econometric History* (Baltimore, MD, Johns Hopkins University Press, 1964).

— and Engerman, Stanley L., *The Reinterpretation of American Economic History* (2 vols, Boston, Little, Brown, 1971–4).

— and Engerman, Stanley L., *Time on the Cross: the Economics of American Negro Slavery* (Boston-Toronto, Little, Brown, 1974).

Forrest, Alan, *Society and Politics in Revolutionary Bordeaux* (Oxford University Press, 1975).

— *The French Revolution and the Poor* (Oxford, Blackwell, 1981).

Forsdick, Charles, *Travel in Twentieth-century French and Francophone Cultures: The Persistence of Diversity* (Oxford University Press, 2005).

— and Murphy, David (eds.), *Francophone Postcolonial Studies: A Critical Introduction* (London, Edward Arnold, 2003).

Foucault, Michel, *Madness and Civilisation: A History of Insanity in the Age of Reason*, trans. R. Howard (London, Tavistock, and New York, Mentor, 1965).

— *Discipline and Punish: The Birth of the Prison*, trans. A. Sheridan (New York, Pantheon, 1977).

— (ed.) *Herculine Barbin: Being the Recently Discovered Memoirs of a Nineteenth-century Hermaphrodite*, trans. Richard McDougall (Brighton, Harvester Press, 1980).

— 'Polémique, politique et problématisation' [1984], in *Dits et écrits* (Paris, Gallimard, 1994).

— *Naissance de la Bio-politique* (Paris, Le Seuil-Gallimard, 2004).

Frank, Robert, 'Vichy et les Britanniques, 1940–1941. Double jeu ou double langage?', in Jean-Pierre Azéma and François Bédarida (eds.), *Le Régime de Vichy et les Français* (Paris, Fayard, 1992), 146–50.

Freud, Sigmund, 'Remembering, repeating and working-through' [1914], in *The Complete Psychological Works, XIII* (London, Hogarth Press, 1964), 145–56.

Fridenson, Patrick, 'Les organisations. Un nouvel objet', *Annales E.S.C.*, 6 (November–December 1989), 1461–77.

Friedman, Lester D., *British Cinema and Thatcherism: Fires Were Started* (London, UCL Press, 1993).

— *American Cinema of the 1970s: Themes and Variations*, Screen Decades (New Brunswick, NJ, Rutgers University Press, 2007).

Frye, Northrop, *Anatomy of Criticism: Four Essays* (Princeton University Press, 1957).

Fukuyama, Francis, *The End of History and the Last Man* (Harmondsworth, Penguin, 1992).

Furet, François, 'Le Catéchisme révolutionnaire', *Annales E.S.C.,* 26/2 (March–April 1971), 255–89.

— *Interpreting the French Revolution*, trans. E. Forster (Cambridge University Press, 1981).

— and Ozouf, Mona (eds.), *A Critical Dictionary of the French Revolution*, trans. A. Goldhammer, (Cambridge, MA, Belknap Press of Harvard University Press, 1989).

— and Richet, Denis, *La Révolution* (2 vols, Paris, Hachette, 1965–6).

Garcia, Patrick, 'Les Panthéonisations sous la Ve République: redécouverte et metamorphoses d'un rituel', in Jean-Luc Bonniol and Maryline Crivello, *Façonner le Passé. Représentations et cultures de l'histoire, XVIe–XXIe siècle* (Aix-en-Provence, Publications de l'Université de Provence, 2004).

Gaspard, Françoise and Khosrokhavar, Farhad, *Le foulard et la République* (Paris, Le Découverte, 1995).

Gay, Peter, *The Enlightenment: An Interpretation* (2 vols, New York, W. W. Norton, 1966).

Geertz, Clifford, *The Interpretation of Cultures* (New York, Basic Books, 1973).

Genette, Gérard, *Palimpsests: Literature in the Second Degree* (Lincoln, University of Nebraska Press, 1997)

Gensburger, Sarah, 'Les figures du Juste et du résistant et l'évolution de la mémoire historique française de l'Occupation', *Revue française de science politique*, 52/2–3 (April–June 2002), 291–322.

— 'Usages politiques de la figure du Juste: entre mémoire historique et mémoires individuelles', in Andrieu, Lavabre and Tartarowsky (eds.), *Politiques du passé*.

Gerbod, Paul, 'La place de l'histoire dans l'enseignement secondaire de 1802 à 1880', *L'Information historique*, 3 (1965).

Gervereau, Laurent, Rioux, Jean-Pierre and Stora, Benjamin (eds.), *La France en guerre d'Algérie* (Nanterre, BDIC, 1992).

Gilbert, Felix, *History: Politics or Culture? Reflections on Ranke and Burckhardt* (Princeton University Press, 1990).

Ginzburg, Carlo, 'Proofs and possibilities: in the margins of Natalie Zemon Davis' *The Return of Martin Guerre*', *Yearbook of Comparative and General Literature*, 37, (1988), 114–27.

— *Myths, Emblems, Clues*, trans. J. and A. Tedeschi (London, Hutchinson, 1990).

Glevarec, Hervé, 'Le nouveau régime d'historicité porté par les Associations du patrimoine', in Crivello, Garcia and Offenstadt, *Concurrences des passés*, 23–36.

Godechot, Jacques, *France and the Atlantic Revolution of the Eighteenth Century, 1770–1799*, trans. H. H. Brown (New York, Free Press, 1965).

Goodman, Dena (ed.), *Marie Antoinette: Writings on the Body of a Queen* (London, Routledge, 2003).

Gossman, Lionel, *Between History and Literature* (Cambridge, MA, and London, Harvard University Press, 1990.

Goveia, Elsa V. and Augier, F. R., 'Colonialism from within', *TLS*, 28 July 1966.

Grafton, Anthony, *The Footnote: A Curious History* (London, Faber and Faber, 2003).

Greenblatt, Stephen, *Marvelous Possessions: The Wonder of the New World* (University of Chicago Press, 1991).

Greene, Jack P., 'Colonial history and national history: reflections on a continuing problem', *The William and Mary Quarterly*, 3rd series, 64/2 (April 2007), 235–50.

Gross, Jan, *Neighbors: the Destruction of the Jewish Community in Jedwabne, Poland* (Princeton University Press, 2001).

Grossi, Paolo, *L'Ordine giuridico medievale* (Rome, Laterza, 2001).

Gueniffey, Patrice, *La Politique de la Terreur. Essai sur la violence révolutionnaire, 1789–1794* (Paris, Fayard, 2000).

— 'La Terreur: circonstances exceptionnelles, idéologie et dynamique révolutionnaire', *Historical Reflections/Réflexions historiques*, 29 (2003), 433–50.

Guerreau, Alain, *L'avenir d'un passé incertain. Quelle histoire du Moyen Âge au XXIe siècle?* (Paris, Le Seuil, 2001).

Guha, Ranajit, 'The small voice of history', *Subaltern Studies*, 9 (Delhi, 1996), 1–12.

— and Spivak, Gayatri Chakravorty (eds.), *Selected Subaltern Studies* (New York and Oxford, Oxford University Press, 1988).

Guillebaud, Jean-Claude, *La trahison des Lumières. Enquête sur le désarroi contemporain* (Paris, Le Seuil, 1995).

Habermas, Jürgen, *Le discours philosophique de la modernité* (Paris, Gallimard, 1988).

Halbwachs, Maurice, *On Collective Memory*, trans. L. Coser (University of Chicago Press, 1997).

Hall, Catherine, 'Politics, post-structuralism and feminist history', *Gender and History*, 3 (1991), 204–10.

— *Civilising Subjects: Metropole and Colony in the English Imagination* (University of Chicago Press, 2002).

— and Davidoff, Leonore, *Family Fortunes: Men and Women of the English Middle Class, 1780–1850* (London, Routledge, 1987).

Hardman, John, *French Politics 1774–1789: From the Accession of Louis XVI to the Fall of the Bastille* (London, Longman, 1995).

Harlan, David, 'Intellectual history and the return of literature', *American Historical Review*, 94 (1989), 581–609.

Harley, C. Knick, 'British industrialisation before 1841: evidence of slower growth during the Industrial Revolution', *Journal of Economic History*, 42 (1982), 267–89.

Harris, Ruth, *Murders and Madness: Medicine, Law and Society in the Fin de Siècle* (Oxford, Clarendon Press, 1989).

— *Lourdes: Body and Spirit in the Secular Age* (Harmondsworth, Allen Lane, 1999).

Hartog, François, *Régimes d'historicité. Présentisme et expériences du temps* (Paris, Le Seuil, 2003).

— and Revel, Jacques (eds.), *Les usages politiques du passé* (Paris, Editions de l'EHESS, 2001).

Harvey, David, *The Condition of Postmodernity: an Enquiry into the Origins of Cultural Change* (Oxford, Blackwell, 1989).

Hause, Steven C. and Kenny, Anne R., 'The development of the Catholic women's suffrage movement in France 1896–1922', *Catholic Historical Review*, 68 (1981), 11–30.

— *Women's Suffrage and Social Politics in the French Third Republic* (Princeton University Press, 1984).

Hayes, Patrick and Campbell, Jim, *Bloody Sunday: Trauma, Pain and Politics* (London, Dublin and Ann Arbor, MI, Pluto Press, 2005).

Hayward, Susan, *French National Cinema* (London, Routledge, 1993).

Heller, Henry, *The Bourgeois Revolution in France, 1789–1815* (New York, Berghahn Books, 2006).

Herf, Jeffrey, *Divided Memory: The Nazi Past in the Two Germanies* (Cambridge, MA, Harvard University Press, 1997).

Herrin, Judith, *Byzantium: The Surprising Life of a Medieval Empire* (London, Allen Lane, 2007).

Herzog, Dagmar, *Sexuality and German Fascism* (Oxford and New York, Berghahn Books, 2004).

Hespanha, António Manuel, *La gracia del derecho. Economía de la cultura en la Edad Moderna* (Madrid, Centro de Estudios Políticos y Constitucionales, 1993).

Hesse, Carla, 'Revolutionary historiography after the Cold War: Arno Mayer's "Furies" in the French context', *Journal of Modern History*, 73 (2001), 897–907.

Hewison, Robert, *The Heritage Industry* (London, Methuen, 1987).

Hewitt, Nicholas, *Literature and the Right in Postwar France: The Story of the Hussards* (Oxford, Berg, 1996).

Hexter, J. H., *Doing History* (London, Allen & Unwin, 1971).

Heymann, Arlette, *Les libertés publiques et la guerre d'Algérie* (Paris, Librairie générale de droit et de jurisprudence, 1972).

Higonnet, Patrice, *Goodness Beyond Virtue: Jacobins during the French Revolution* (Cambridge, MA, Harvard University Press, 1998).

Hobsbawm, Eric, 'The revival of narrative: some comments', *Past and Present*, 86 (February 1980), 3–9.

— *Worlds of Labour: Further Studies in the History of Labour* (London, Weidenfeld & Nicolson, 1984).

— *On History* (London, Weidenfeld & Nicolson, 1997).

— and Ranger, Terence (eds.), *The Invention of Tradition* (Cambridge University Press, 1983).

Hodgkin, Thomas, 'New openings: Africa', *TLS*, 7 April 1966.

Hogan, Michael, *The Marshall Plan: America, Britain and the Reconstruction of Western Europe, 1947–1952* (Cambridge University Press, 1989).

Hollier, Denis and Bloch, R. Howard (eds.), *A New History of French Literature* (Cambridge, MA, Harvard University Press, 1989).

Horn, Jeff, *The Path Not Taken: French Industrialization in the Age of Revolution, 1750-1830* (Cambridge, MA, MIT Press, 2006).

House, Jim and MacMaster, Neil, *Paris 1961: Algerians, State Terror and Memory* (Oxford University Press, 2006).

Howe, Stephen, *Ireland and Empire: Colonial Legacies in Irish History and Culture* (Oxford University Press, 2000).

— 'Tales of the imperial city', *Arts & Books Review: The Independent*, 30 November 2007, 5.

Hudson, Pat (ed.), *Living Economic and Social History* (Glasgow, Economic History Society, 2001).

Hufton, Olwen H., *The Poor of Eighteenth-century France, 1750–1789* (Oxford, Clarendon Press, 1974).

— *Women and the Limits of Citizenship in the French Revolution* (University of Toronto Press, 1992).

— 'Femmes/hommes: une question subversive', in Jean Boutier and Dominique Julia (eds.), *Passés recomposés: champs et chantiers de l'histoire* (Paris, Autrement, 1995), 235–42.

— *The Prospect before Her: A History of Women in Western Europe, 1500–1800* (London, HarperCollins, 1995).

Hulten, Pontus (ed.), *Paris–Paris 1937–1957* (Paris, Centre Georges Pompidou, 1981).

Hunt, Lynn, *Politics, Culture and Class in the French Revolution* (Berkeley and London, University of California Press, 1984).

— (ed.) *The New Cultural History* (Berkeley, University of California Press, 1989).

— *The Family Romance of the French Revolution* (London, Routledge, 1992).

— *The French Revolution and Human Rights: A Brief Documentary History* (New York, Bedford/St Martin's Press, 1996).

— 'Where have all the theories gone?', *Perspectives*, 40 (2002), 5–7.

Hyam, Ronald, *Britain's Declining Empire* (Cambridge University Press, 2007).

Iggers, Georg G., *The German Conception of History* (Middletown, CT, Wesleyan University Press, 1968).

Ignatieff, Michael, *A Just Measure of Pain: The Penitentiary in the Industrial Revolution, 1750–1850* (London, Macmillan, 1978).

INSEE, *Pour une histoire de la statistique* (2 vols, Paris, INSEE, 1977).

Ireland, Craig, 'The appeal to experience and its consequences: variations on a persistent Thompsonian theme', *Cultural Critique*, 52 (2002), 87–107.

Ironside, Virginia, *You'll Never Get Over It! The Rage of Bereavement* (London, Hamilton, 1996).

Jameson, Frederic, *The Political Unconscious: Narrative as a Socially Symbolic Act* (New York, Routledge, 1981).

— *The Cultural Turn: Selected Writings on the Postmodern, 1983–1998* (London and New York, Verso, 1988).

— *Postmodernism: Or, the Cultural Logic of Late Capitalism* (London, Verso, 1991).

Jeanneney, Jean-Noël, *Le passé dans le prétoire. L'historien, le juge et le journaliste* (Paris, Le Seuil, 1998).

Jefferson, Anne and Robey, David, *Modern Literary Theory*, 2nd ed. (Batsford, 1988).

Jenkins, Brian (ed.), *France in the Era of Fascism: Essays on the French Authoritarian Right* (New York, Berghahn Books, 2005).

Johnson, Douglas W. J. and Johnson, Madeleine, *The Age of Illusion: Art and Politics in France, 1918–1940* (London, Thames & Hudson, 1987).

Johnston, William M., *Celebrations: The Cult of Anniversaries in Europe and the United States Today* (New Brunswick and London, Transaction Publishers, 1991).

Jones, Colin, *Paris: Biography of a City* (London, Allen Lane, 2004).

Jouhaud, Christian, *Les pouvoirs de la littérature. Histoire d'un paradoxe* (Paris, Gallimard, 2000).

Joyce, Patrick, *Visions of the People: Industrial England and the Question of Class, 1840–1914* (Cambridge University Press, 1991).

— 'The imaginary discontents of social history: a note of response', *Social History*, 18 (1993), 81–6.

— *Democratic Subjects: The Self and the Social in Nineteenth-century England* (Cambridge University Press, 1994).

— 'The end of social history', *Social History*, 20 (January 1995), 73–91.

— 'The return of history: postmodernism and the politics of academic history in Britain', *Past & Present*, 158 (1998), 207–35.

Julliard, Jacques, 'La Politique', in Le Goff and Nora (eds.), *Faire de l'histoire*, vol. 1, 210–28.

Kalifa, Dominique, 'L'expérience, le désir et l'histoire. Alain Corbin, ou le "tournant culturel" silencieux', *French Politics, Culture & Society*, 22/2 (2004), 14–25.

— 'Criminal investigators at the fin de siècle', *Yale French Studies*, 108 (2005), 36–47.

— 'L'histoire culturelle contre l'histoire sociale?', in Martin and Venayre (eds.), *L'Histoire culturelle du contemporain*.

— and Vaillant, Alain, 'Pour une histoire culturelle et littéraire de la presse française au XIXe siècle', *Le Temps des médias. Revue d'histoire*, 2 (2004), 197–214.

Kaplan, Steven, *The Famine Plot Persuasion in Eighteenth-century France* (Philadelphia, PA, American Philosophical Society, 1982).

Kean, Hilda, *London Stories: Personal Lives, Public Histories* (London, Rivers Oram Press, 2004).

Keane, John, *Reflections on Violence* (London, Verso, 1996).

— *Violence and Democracy* (Cambridge University Press, 2004).

Kedward, Rod, *La vie en bleu: France and the French since 1900* (London, Allen Lane, 2005).

— and Wood, Nancy (eds.), *The Liberation of France: Image and Event* (Oxford, Berg, 1995).

Kelly, Michael, 'Comparing French and British intellectuals: towards a cross-channel perspective', *French Cultural Studies*, 14/3 (October 2003), 336–48.

— *The Cultural and Intellectual Rebuilding of France after the Second World War* (London, Palgrave Macmillan, 2004).

Klegman, L. and Rochefort, F., *L'egalité en marche* (Paris, Editions des Femmes, 1989).

Klein, Melanie, *Love, Guilt and Reparation and Other Works, 1921–45* (London, Virago, 1991).

Koos, Cheryl, and Sarnoff, Daniella, 'France', in Kevin Passmore (ed.), *Women, Gender and Fascism in Europe 1919–1945* (Manchester University Press, 2003), 168–88.

Koselleck, Reinhart, 'Begriffsgechichtliche Anmerkungen zur "Zeitgeschichte"', in V. Conzemius, M. Greschat and H. Kocher (eds.), *Die Zeit nach 1945 als Thema kirchlicher Zeitgeschichte* (Göttingen, PUB, 1988), 17–31.

— *Le Futur-passé. Pour une sémantique des temps historiques*, trans. J. and M.-C. Hoock (Paris, Editions EHESS, 1990).

— *L'expérience de l'histoire*, trans. A. Escudier (Paris, Gallimard, Le Seuil, 1997).

Kuisel, Richard F., *Capitalism and the State in Modern France: Renovation and Economic Management in the Twentieth Century* (Cambridge, MA, and London, Cambridge University Press, 1981).

Kwass, Michael, *Privilege and the Politics of Taxation in Eighteenth-century France: Liberté, Egalité, Fiscalité* (Cambridge University Press, 2000).

Labrousse, Ernest, *Esquisse du mouvement des prix et des revenus en France au XVIIIe siècle* (2 vols, Paris, Dalloz, 1933).

— *La crise de l'économie française à la fin de l'Ancien Régime et au début de la Révolution* (Paris, PUF, 1944).

— '1848–1830–1789. Comment naissent les révolutions', in *Congrès historique du centenaire de la révolution de 1848* (Paris, PUF, 1948), 1–20.

LaCapra, Dominick, *Rethinking Intellectual History: Texts, Contexts, Language* (Ithaca, NY, Cornell University Press, 1983).

— and Kaplan, Steven (eds.), *Modern European Intellectual History: Reappraisals and New Perspectives* (Ithaca, NY, and London, Cornell University Press, 1982).

Laferté, Gilles, *La Bourgogne et ses vins. Image d'origine contrôlée* (Paris, Belin, 2006).

Laffargue, Bernard and Robert, Phillippe, *L'image de la justice criminelle dans la société. Le système pénal vu par ses clients* (Paris, SEPC, 1977).

Lagrou, Pieter, *Mémoires patriotiques et occupation nazie* (Brussels, Editions Complexe, 2003).

Lahire, Bernard, 'Remarques sociologiques sur le *linguistic turn*', *Politix*, 27 (1994), 189–92.

Lake, Marilyn and Reynolds, Henry, *Drawing the Global Colour Line: White Men's Countries and the International Challenge of Racial Equality* (Cambridge University Press, 2008).

Laloum, Jean, *Les Juifs dans la banlieue parisienne des années vingt aux années cinquante. Montreuil, Bagnolet et Vincennes à l'heure de la Solution finale* (Paris, CNRS, 1998).

Lancaster, Roger N., *Life is Hard: Machismo, Danger and the Intimacy of Power in Nicaragua* (Berkeley, University of California Press, 1992).

Landes, David, *The Unbound Prometheus: Technological Change and Industrial Development in Western Europe from 1750 to the Present* (London, Cambridge University Press, 1969).

Landes, Joan, *Women and the Public Sphere in the Age of the French Revolution* (Ithaca, NY, Cornell University Press, 1988).

Langlois, Charles-Victor and Seignobos, Charles, *Introduction to the Study of History* (London, Duckworth, 1898).

Langlois, Claude, *Le Catholicisme au féminine: Les congregations françaises à supérieure générale au XIXe siècle* (Paris, Le Cerf, 1984).

Latham, A. J. H., 'An Interview with Douglas Farnie', *The Newsletter of the Cliometric Society*, 21/2 (Autumn 2006), 4–12.

Le Goff, Jacques, 'Is politics still the backbone of history?', in Felix Gilbert and Stephen R. Graubard (eds.), *Historical Studies Today* (New York, Norton and Company, 1972), 337–55.

— 'Mentalités. Une histoire ambiguë', in Le Goff and Nora (eds.), *Faire de l'histoire*, vol. 3, 76–98.

— *History and Memory*, trans. S. Rendall and E. Claman (New York, Columbia University Press, 1992).

—, Chartier, Roger and Revel, Jacques (eds.), *La Nouvelle Histoire* (Paris, CEPL, 1978).

— and Nora, Pierre (eds.), *Faire de l'histoire* (3 vols, Paris, Gallimard, 1974).

Le Roy Ladurie, Emmanuel, 'L'historien et l'ordinateur', *Le Nouvel Observateur*, 8 May 1968.

— *Montaillou: Cathars and Catholics in a French Village*, trans. B. Bray (London, Scolar Press, 1981).

— *The Mind and Method of the Historian*, trans. S. and B. Reynolds (Brighton, Harvester Press, 1981).

Leclerc, Françoise and Wendling, Michèle, 'Des femmes devant les cours de justice', in Liliane Kandel (ed.), *Féminisme et nazisme* (Paris, Publications de l'Université Paris VII-Denis Diderot, 1997).

Lee, Ching Kwan, *Gender and the South China Miracle: Two Worlds of Factory Women* (Berkeley, University of California Press, 1998).

Leech-Wilkinson, Daniel, *The Modern Invention of Medieval Music* (Cambridge University Press, 2002).

Lefebvre, Georges, 'Le Mouvement des prix et la Révolution Française', *Annales d'histoire économique et sociale*, 44 (1937), 139–70.

— *Quatre-vingt-neuf* (Paris, Maison du livre français, 1939).

— *The Great Fear of 1789: Rural Panic in Revolutionary France*, trans. J. White (New York, Pantheon Books, 1973).

Léonard, Jacques, 'Femmes, religion et médicine: Les religieuses qui soignent en France au XIXe siècle', *Annales, ESC*, 32 (1977), 887–907.

Lepetit, Bernard, *Les formes de l'expérience* (Paris, Albin Michel, 1995).

Levasseur, Émile, *Histoire des classes ouvrières en France depuis 1789 jusqu'à nos jours* (2 vols, Paris, Hachette, 1867).

Lévi-Strauss, Claude, *La pensée sauvage* (Paris, Plon, 1962).

Lévy, Bernard-Henri, *Les aventures de la liberté* (Paris, Grasset, 1991).

Lewis, Gwynne, *The Advent of Modern Capitalism in France, 1770–1840: The Contribution of Pierre-François Tubeuf* (Oxford, Clarendon Press, 1993).

Liauzu, Claude, *Naissance du salariat et du mouvement ouvrier en Tunisie* (Paris, CNRS, 1978).

— *La Société française face au racisme. De la Révolution à nos jours* (Brussels, Complexe, 1999).

'Liberté pour l'histoire', *Libération*, 13 December 2005, 35.

Lilti, Antoine, *Le monde des salons. Sociabilité et mondanité à Paris au XVIIIe siècle* (Paris, Fayard, 2005).

Locher, Fabien, *Le Nombre et le temps. La météorologie en France (1830–1880)*, PhD thesis (EHESS Paris, 2004).

Loraux, Nicole, 'Eloge de l'anachronisme en histoire', *Le Genre Humain*, 27 (1993), 23–39.

Loriga, Sabina, 'La biographie comme problème', in Jacques Revel (ed.), *Jeux d'échelles. La micro-analyse à l'expérience* (Paris, Seuil-Gallimard, 1996).

— 'Tolstoï dans le scepticisme de l'histoire', *Esprit*, June 2005, 6–25.

Lovejoy, Arthur O., *The Great Chain of Being: A Study of the History of an Idea: The William James Lectures Delivered at Harvard University, 1933* (Cambridge, MA, Harvard University Press, 1998).

Lucas, Colin, 'Nobles, bourgeois and the origins of the French Revolution', *Past and Present*, 60 (1973).

— *The Structure of the Terror: The Example of Javogues and the Loire* (Oxford University Press, 1973).

MacKenzie, D. F., *Bibliography and the Sociology of Texts* (London, British Library, 1986).

Mackenzie, John, *Orientalism: History, Theory and the Arts* (Manchester University Press, 1995).

Magarey, Susan, 'That hoary old chestnut, free will and determinism: culture vs. structure, or history vs. theory in Britain. A review article', *Comparative Studies in Society and History,* 29:3 (July 1987), 627–39.

Maier, Charles, *In Search of Stability: Explorations in Historical Political Economy* (Cambridge University Press, 1987).

Majumdar, Margaret (ed.), *Francophone Studies* (London, Edward Arnold, 2002).

Manceron, Gilles (ed.), *Mémoire et enseignement de la guerre d'Algérie: actes du colloque* (2 vols, Paris, Institut du monde arabe, 1993).

Mani, Lata, *The Debate on Sati in Colonial India* (Berkeley, University of California Press, 1998).

Margadant, Ted W., 'Summary justice and the crisis of the Old Regime in 1789', *Historical Reflections/Réflexions historiques,* 29 (2003), 495–528.

Margairaz, Michel and Olivier Dard (eds.), 'Le service public, l'économie, la République (1780–1960)', *Revue d'Histoire moderne et contemporaine,* 52/3 (July–September 2005).

Mariot, Nicolas, *Bains de foule. Les voyages présidentiels en province, 1880–2002* (Paris, Belin, 2006).

Marrison, Andrew, *British Business and Protection, 1903–1932* (Oxford, Clarendon Press, 1996).

Martin, Laurent and Venayre, Sylvain (eds.), *L'Histoire culturelle du contemporain* (Paris, Nouveau Monde, 2005).

Mathiez, Albert, *Les grandes journées de la Constituante* (Paris, Hachette, 1913).

Mauss-Copeaux, Claire, *Les Appelés en Algérie. La parole confisquée* (Paris, Hachette, 1999)

Mayer, Arno J., *The Furies: Violence and Terror in the French and Russian Revolutions* (Princeton University Press, 2000).

Mayfield, David and Thorne, Susan, 'Social history and its discontents: Gareth Stedman Jones and the politics of language', *Social History,* 17 (1992), 165–88.

McMahon, Darrin M., *Enemies of the Enlightenment: The French Counter-Enlightenment and the Making of Modernity,* (Oxford University Press, 2001).

McMillan, James, 'Religion and gender in modern France: some reflections', in Frank Tallett and Nicholas Atkin, *Religion, Society and Politics in France since 1789* (London, Hambledon Continuum, 1991).

Mehlman, Jeffrey, *Émigré New York: French Intellectuals in Wartime Manhattan, 1940–1944* (Baltimore, MD, Johns Hopkins University Press, 2000).

Meinecke, Friedrich, *Historicism* (London, Routledge and Kegan Paul, 1972).

Merlin-Kajman, Hélène, *Public et littérature en France au XVIIe siècle* (Paris, Les Belles Lettres, 1994).

— *L'excentricité académique. Littérature, histoire, société* (Paris, Les Belles Lettres, 2001) .

Meynier, Gilbert, *L'Algérie révélée* (Geneva, Droz, 1981).

— *Histoire intérieure du FLN, 1954–1962* (Paris, Fayard, 2002).

— *L'Algérie des origines* (Paris, La Découverte, 2007).

Michel, Hélène, *La cause des propriétaires. Etat et propriété en France, fin XIXe–XXe siècle* (Paris, Belin, 2006).

Michelet, Jules, *Histoire de la Révolution Française* (Paris, Robert Laffont, 1979 [1847]).

— *Correspondance Générale, V (1846–48)* (Paris, Honoré Champion, 1996).

Misra, Maria, *Vishnu's Crowded Temple: India since the Great Rebellion* (London, Allen Lane, 2007).

Moeller, Robert G., *The Search for a Usable Past in the Federal Republic of Germany* (Berkeley, University of California Press, 2003).

Morgan, Robert P. (ed.), *Modern Times: From World War I to the Present (Music and Society)* (Englewood Cliffs, NJ, Prentice Hall, 1994).

Morris, Frances (ed.), *Paris Post War: Art and Existentialism 1945–55* (London, Tate Gallery, 1993).

Mouton, Michelle and Pohlandt-McCormick, Helena, 'Boundary crossings: oral history of Nazi Germany and apartheid South Africa', *History Workshop Journal*, 48 (1999), 41–63.

Munslow, Alun, 'The postmodern in history: a response to Professor O'Brien', in Institute of Historical Research, *Reviews in History* (London, 1999).

Murphy, Robert (ed.), *The British Cinema Book*, 2nd ed. (London, BFI Publishing, 2001)

Negus, Keith, *Music Genres and Corporate Cultures* (London and New York, Routledge, 1999).

Noiriel, Gérard, *Sur la 'crise' de l'histoire* (Paris, Belin, 1996).

— *Introduction à la socio-histoire* (Paris, La Découverte, 2006).

— *Immigration, antisémitisme et racisme en France (XIXe–XXe siècle). Discours publics, humiliations privées* (Paris, Fayard, 2007).

— (ed.) *L'identification. Genèse d'un travail d'Etat* (Paris, Belin, 2007).

Nora, Pierre, 'Le retour de l'événement', in Le Goff and Nora (eds.), *Faire de l'histoire*, vol. 2, 229–50.

— 'Entre histoire et mémoire. La problématique des lieux', in Nora (ed.), *Les lieux de mémoire,* vol. 1 (Paris, Gallimard, 1984), xix–xx.

— (ed.), *Les lieux de mémoire* (3 vols, Paris, Gallimard, 1984–92).

Nouschi, André, *Enquête sur le niveau de vie des populations rurales constantinoises, de la conquête jusqu'en 1919. Essai d'histoire économique et sociale* (Paris, PUF, 1961).

Novick, Peter, *That Noble Dream: The 'Objectivity Question' and the American Historical Profession* (Cambridge University Press, 1988).

Nye, Robert, *Masculinity and Male Codes of Honor in Modern France* (Oxford University Press, 1993)

— 'Western masculinities in war and peace', *American Historical Review*, 112 (2007), 417–38.

O'Shaughnessy, Martin, 'Poor propaganda: French colonial films of the 1930s', in Evans (ed.), *Empire and Culture*.

Offen, Karen, 'Depopulation, nationalism and feminism in the *fin de siècle*', *American Historical Review*, 89 (1984), 648–76.

Offerlé, Michel (ed.), *La profession politique* (Paris, Belin, 1999).

Orléan, André, *Analyse économique des conventions* (Paris, PUF, 1994).

Ory, Pascal, 'Pour une histoire culturelle de la France contemporaine', *Bulletin du centre d'histoire de la France contemporaine*, 2, (1981), 5–32,

— 'L'Histoire culturelle de la France contemporaine. Questions et questionnement', *Vingtième siècle. Revue d'histoire* (1987), 67–82.

— *L'Histoire culturelle* (Paris, PUF, 2004).

Otter, Chris, 'Making liberalism durable: vision and civility in the late Victorian city', *Social History*, 27 (2002), 1–15.

Overy, Richard, *Why the Allies Won* (London, Pimlico Press, 1996).

Ozouf, Mona, *Festivals and the French Revolution*, trans. A. Sheridan (Cambridge, MA, Harvard University Press, 1988).

Palmer, Bryan D., *Descent into Discourse: The Reification of Language and the Writing of Social History* (Philadelphia, PA, Temple University Press, 1990).

Palmer, Robert R., *The Age of the Democratic Revolution: A Political History of Europe and America, 1760–1800* (2 vols, Princeton University Press, 1959–64).

Parker, John and Rathbone, Richard, *African History: A Very Short Introduction* (Oxford University Press, 2007).

Parkhurst Ferguson, Priscilla, *Literary France: The Making of a Culture* (Berkeley, University of California Press, 1987).

Passeron, Jean-Claude, *Le raisonnement sociologique* (Paris, Nathan, 1991).

Passmore, Kevin, 'Planting the tricolor in the citadels of communism. Women's social action in the Croix de Feu and Parti social français', *Journal of Modern History*, 71 (December 1999), 814–51.

— (ed.), *Women, Gender and Fascism in Europe 1919–1945* (Manchester University Press, 2003).

— (forthcoming), 'The gendered genealogy of political religions theory', *Gender & History*, special 20th anniversary issue.

Pérez Garzón, Juan Sisinio, *La gestión de la memoria. La historia de España al servicio del poder* (Barcelona, Crítica, 2000).

Perkin, Harold, *The Making of a Social Historian* (London, Athena Press, 2002).

Perrot, Michelle, *Les femmes ou les silences de l'histoire* (Paris, Flammarion, 1998).

Perrot, Jean-Claude, 'Rapports sociaux et villes au XVIIIe siècle', *Annales E.S.C.*, 23/2 (March–April 1968), 241–67.

Petit, Carlos, *Pasiones del jurista. Amor, memoria, malancolía, imaginación* (Madrid, Centro de Estudios Políticos y Constitucionales, 1997).

Pétré-Grenouilleau, Olivier, *Les traites négrières. Essai d'histoire globale* (Paris, Gallimard, 2004).

Pick, Daniel, *Faces of Degeneration: A European Disorder, c. 1948– c.1914* (Cambridge University Press, 1989).

Piketty, Caroline, Dubois, Christophe and Launay, Fabrice (eds.), *Guide des recherches dans les archives des spoliations et des restitutions. Mission d'étude sur la spoliation des Juifs de France* (Paris, La Documentation française, 2000).

Pitti, Laure, 'Ouvriers algériens à Renault-Billancourt de la guerre d'Algérie au grèves d'OS des années 1970. Contribution à l'histoire sociale et politique des ouvriers étrangers en France', PhD thesis (Université de Paris-VIII, 2002).

Poirrier, Philippe, *Les enjeux de l'histoire culturelle* (Paris, Le Seuil, 2004).

Pollock, S., Bhabha, H., Breckenridge, C. and Chakrabarty, D., 'Cosmopolitanisms', *Public Culture*, 12/3 (2000), 577–89.

Popkin, Jeremy D., *Press, Revolution and Social Identity in France, 1830–1835* (University Park, Penn State University Press, 2002).

Porter, Bernard, *The Absent-Minded Imperialists: Empire, Society and Culture in Britain* (Oxford University Press, 2004).

'Postcolonialisme et immigration', *ContreTemps Special Issue*, 16 (April 2006).

Powrie, Phil, *French Cinema in the 1980s: Nostalgia and the Crisis of Masculinity* (Oxford, Clarendon Press, 1997).

Price, Munro, *The Fall of the French Monarchy: Louis XVI, Marie Antoinette and the Baron De Breteuil* (Basingstoke, Macmillan, 2002).

Prochasson, Christophe, 'La guerre en ses cultures', in Jean-Jacques Becker (ed.), *Histoire culturelle de la Grande Guerre* (Paris, A. Colin, 2005), 255–71.

Prost, Antoine, *Douze leçons sur l'histoire* (Paris, Le Seuil, 1996).

— (ed.), *Aryanisation économique et restitutions. Mission d'étude sur la spoliation des Juifs de France* (Paris, La Documentation française, 2000).

— and Winter, Jay, *Penser la Grande Guerre. Un essai d'historiographie* (Paris, Le Seuil, 2004).

Quint, David, *Epic and Empire: Politics and Generic Form from Virgil to Milton* (Princeton University Press, 1993).

Rancière, Jacques, *Les mots de l'histoire* (Paris, Le Seuil, 1992).

Reed-Danahay, Deborah, *Education and Identity in Rural France: The Politics of Schooling* (Cambridge University Press, 1996).

Rémond, René, *Touvier et l'Église: rapport de la Commission historique instituée par le cardinal Ducourtray* (Paris, Fayard, 1992).

Renan, Ernest, 'Qu'est-ce qu'une nation?' [1882], in *Oeuvres Complètes I* (Paris, Calmann-Lévy, 1947), 887–907.

Retort, *Afflicted Powers: Capital and Spectacle in a New Age of War* (London, Verso, 2005).

Revel, Jacques (ed.), *Jeux d'échelles. La micro-analyse à l'expérience* (Paris, Le Seuil, 1996).

Rey-Goldzeiguer, Annie, *Le Royaume arabe. La politique algérienne de Napoléon III, 1861–1870* (Algiers, Société nationale d'édition et de diffusion, 1977).

Reynolds, David, 'International history, the cultural turn and the diplomatic twitch', *Cultural and Social History*, 3 (2006), 75–91

Reynolds, Siân, *France between the Wars: Gender and Politics* (London, Taylor and Francis, 1996).

— review of Downs, *Writing Gender History*, *Clio HSF*, 23 (2006).

Ricœur, Paul, *Temps et récit* (3 vols, Paris, Le Seuil, 1983–5).

— *Memory, History, Forgetting*, trans. K. Blamey and D. Pellauer (Chicago and London, University of Chicago Press, 2004).

Riley, Denise, '*Am I that Name?' Feminism and the Category of 'Women' in History* (London, Palgrave Macmillan, 1981).

Rioux, Jean-Pierre (ed.), *La Guerre d'Algérie et les Français* (Paris, Fayard, 1990).

— and Sirinelli, Jean-François (eds.), *La Guerre d'Algérie et les intellectuels français* (Paris, Les Cahiers de l'IHTP, 1988).

Rochefort, Florence, 'Foulard, genre et laïcité en 1989', *Vingtième siècle. Revue d'histoire*, 75 (July-September 2000), 145–56.

Roper, Lyndal, *Oedipus and the Devil: Witchcraft, Religion and Sexuality in Early Modern Europe* (New York, Routledge, 1994).

— *Witch Craze: Terror and Fantasy in Baroque Germany* (New Haven, CT, and London, Yale University Press, 2004).

Rorty, Richard, *Consequences of Pragmatism* (Minneapolis, University of Minnesota Press, 1982).

— (ed.) *The Linguistic Turn: Recent Essays in Philosophical Method* (University of Chicago Press, 1992).

—, Skinner, Quentin and Schneewind, J. B., *Philosophy in History: Essays on the Historiography of Philosophy* (Cambridge University Press, 1984).

Rosenberg, Emily S., *Financial Missionaries to the World: The Politics and Culture of Dollar Diplomacy, 1900–1930* (Cambridge, MA, Harvard University Press, 1999).

Roudinesco, Elisabeth, *Jacques Lacan & Co : A History of Psychoanalysis in France, 1925–1985*, trans. Jeffrey Mehlman (London, Free Association Books, 1990).

Rousso, Henry (ed.), *De Monnet à Massé. Enjeux politiques et objectifs économiques dans le cadre des quatre premiers plans (1946–1965)* (Paris, Éditions du CNRS, 1986).

— *Le syndrome de Vichy* (Paris, Le Seuil, 1987).

— 'La mémoire n'est plus ce qu'elle était' in François Bédarida (ed.), *Ecrire l'histoire du temps présent* (Paris, CNRS, 1993).

— *The Haunting Past: History, Memory and Justice in Contemporary France*, trans. R. Schoolcraft (Philadelphia, University of Pennsylvania Press, 2002).

Rushdie, Salman, *The Satanic Verses* (New York, Viking, 1989).

Russell, Bertrand, *A History of Western Philosophy and its Connection with Political and Social Circumstances from the Earliest Times to the Present Day* (London, George Allen and Unwin, 1946).

Sabatier, Gérard, *Versailles ou la figure du roi* (Paris, Albin Michel, 1999).

Sahlins, Marshall, *Islands of History* (University of Chicago Press, 1985).

Said, Edward, *Orientalism* (London, Routledge and Kegan Paul, 1978).

— *Culture and Imperialism* (New York, Knopf, 1993).

Saint Laurent, Cecil, *Clotilde*, trans. H. Hare (London, Weidenfeld & Nicolson, 1958).

Salais, Robert, Baverez, Nicolas and Reynaud, Bénédicte, *L'invention du chômage. Histoire et transformation d'une catégorie en France des années 1890 aux années 1980* (Paris, PUF, 1986).

— and Storper, Michael, *Les mondes de production. Enquête sur l'identité économique de la France* (Paris, EHESS, 1993).

Saldaña-Portillo, María Josefina, 'The authorized subjects of revolution: Ernesto "Che" Guevara and Mario Payeras', in Saldaña-Portillo, *The Revolutionary Imagination in the Americas* (Durham, NC, Duke University Press, 2003), 63–108, 299–303.

Samuel, Raphael and Thompson, Paul, *The Myths We Live By* (London and New York, Routledge, 1990).

Schaeffer, Jean-Marie, *Pourquoi la fiction?* (Paris, Le Seuil, 1999).

Schama, Simon, *Dead Certainties (Unwarranted Speculations)* (London, Granta Books, 1991).

— *Rough Crossings: Britain, the Slaves and the American Revolution* (London, BBC Books, 2003).

— *Citizens: A Chronicle of the French Revolution* (London, Folio Society, 2004 [1989]).

Schaub, Jean-Frédéric, 'Le temps et l'Etat. Vers un nouveau régime historiographique de l'Ancien Régime français', *Quaderni Fiorentini per la Storia del Pensiero Giuridico Moderno*, 25 (1996).

— *Oroonoko, prince et esclave. Roman de l'incertitude coloniale* (Paris, Le Seuil, 2008).

— (forthcoming), 'La catégorie "études coloniales" est-elle indispensable?', *Annales Histoire, Sciences Sociales* (2008).

Schöttler, Peter, 'Historians and discourse analysis', *History Workshop Journal*, 27 (Spring 1989), 37–65.

Scott, James C., *Weapons of the Weak: Everyday Forms of Peasant Resistance* (New Haven, CT, and London, Yale University Press, 1985).

Scott, Joan W., '"Gender": a useful category of historical analysis', *American Historical Review*, 91 (1986), 1053–75.

— 'The evidence of experience', *Critical Inquiry*, 17 (1991), 773–97.

— 'If "Woman" is just an empty category, then why am I afraid to walk alone at night? Identity politics meets the postmodern subject', *Comparative Studies in Society and History* (April 1993), 414–37.

— *Gender and the Politics of History* (New York, Columbia University Press, 1999 [1st ed. 1988]).

— 'Millenial fantasies: the future of "gender" in the 21st Century', in Claudia Honegger and Caroline Arni (eds.), *Gender-die Tüken einer Kategorie* (Zurich, Chronos Verlag, 2001), 19–37.

— 'Feminism's history', *Journal of Women's History*, 16/2 (2004), 22.

Scurr, Ruth, *Fatal Purity: Robespierre and the French Revolution* (London, Metropolitan Books, 2006).

Seferdjeli, Ryme, 'French reforms and Muslim women's emancipation during the Algerian War', *The Journal of North African Studies*, 9/4 (2004), 19–61.

— '"Fight with us, women, and we will emancipate you": France, the FLN and the struggle over women during the Algerian War of National Liberation', PhD thesis (University of London, 2005).

Seignobos, Charles, 'L'enseignement de l'histoire dans les facultés. III. Méthodes d'exposition', *Revue internationale de l'enseignement*, 15 juillet 1884.

— *Histoire politique de l'Europe contemporaine. Evolution des parties et des formes politiques* (Paris, A. Colin, 1897).

— 'L'enseignement de l'histoire comme instrument d'éducation politique', in *Conférences du Musée pédagogique* (Paris, Imprimerie nationale, 1907), 1–24.

— *Etudes de politique et d'histoire* (Paris, PUF, 1934).

Sen, Amartya, *Poverty and Famine: An Essay on Entitlement and Deprivation* (Oxford, Clarendon Press, 1981).

Sewell, William H., *Work and Revolution in France: The Language of Labour from the Old Regime to 1848* (Cambridge University Press, 1980).

— *A Rhetoric of Bourgeois Revolution. The Abbé Sieyès and 'What is the Third Estate?'* (Durham and London, Duke University Press, 1994).

Shipway, Martin, *Decolonization and its Impact: A Comparative Approach to the End of the Colonial Empires* (London, Blackwell, 2008).

Silverman, Maxim, *Deconstructing the Nation: Immigration, Racism and Citizenship in Modern France* (London, Routledge, 1992).

Siminand, François, *Les fluctuations économiques à longue durée et la crise mondiale* (Paris, Alcan, 1932).

'Simon Schama: history in the flesh', *The Daily Telegraph*, 12 September 2007.

Simonin, Anne, 'The right to innocence: literary discourse and the postwar purges', *Yale French Studies*, 98 (March 2000), 5–29.

— *L'Honneur dans la République. Une histoire de l'indignité (1789–1958)* (Paris, Grasset, 2008).

Skidelsky, Robert, *John Maynard Keynes: III, Fighting for Britain, 1937–1946* (London, Macmillan, 2000).

Smith, Bonnie G., *Ladies of the Leisure Class. The Bourgeoises of Northern France in the Nineteenth Century* (Princeton University Press, 1981).

Smith, Jay M., *The Culture of Merit: Nobility, Royal Service, and the Making of Absolute Monarchy in France, 1600–1789* (Ann Arbor, University of Michigan Press, 1996).

— *Nobility Reimagined: The Patriotic Nation in Eighteenth-century France* (Ithaca, NY, Cornell University Press, 2005).

Smith, Malcolm, *Britain and 1940. History, Myth and Popular Memory* (London and New York, Routledge, 2000).

Soucy, Robert, *French Fascism: The Second Wave* (New Haven, CT, Yale University Press, 1995).

Sowerwine, Charles, *Sisters or Citizens? Women and Socialism in France since 1876* (Cambridge University Press, 1984).

Sparrow, Elizabeth, *Secret Service: British Agents in France, 1792–1815* (Woodbridge, Boydell Press, 1999).

Spiegel, Gabrielle M., *The Past as Text: The Theory and Practice of Medieval Historiography* (Baltimore, MD, Johns Hopkins University Press, 1997).

— *Practicing History. New Directions in Historical Writing after the Linguistic Turn* (New York and London, Routledge, 2005).

Spivak, Gayatri Chakravorty, *In Other Worlds: Essays in Cultural Politics* (New York, Methuen, 1987).

— *The Post-Colonial Critic: Interviews, Strategies, Dialogues* (New York and London, Routledge, 1990).

Starobinski, Jean, 'Le mot civilisation', in *Le remède dans le mal. Critique et légitimation de l'artifice à l'âge des Lumières* (Paris, Gallimard, 1989), 11–59.

Stearns, Peter, 'Social history present and future', *Journal of Social History*, 37 (2003), 9–19.

Stedman Jones, Gareth, *Outcast London. A Study of the Relationship between Classes in Victorian London* (Oxford, Clarendon Press, 1971).

— *The Languages of Class: Studies in English Working-slass History, 1832–1982* (Cambridge University Press, 1983).

Steedman, Carolyn, *Landscape for a Good Woman: A Story of Two Lives* (London, Virago, 1986).

Stone, Lawrence 'The revival of narrative: reflections on a new old history', *Past & Present*, 85 (1979), 3–24.

— 'History and postmodernism', *Past & Present,* 131 (1991), 217–18.

Stora, Benjamin, *Dictionnaire biographique des militants nationalistes algériens, 1926–1954* (Paris, L'Harmattan, 1985).

— *Messali Hadj* (Paris, Sycomore, 1982).

— 'Entre histoire, mémoires et images. Les années algériennes', *Vingtième Siècle. Revue d'histoire,* 35 (July–September 1992), 93–6.

— *La Gangrène et l'oubli. La mémoire de la guerre d'Algérie* (Paris, La Découverte, 1992).

— *Algeria 1830 to 2000,* trans. J. M. Todd (Ithaca, NY, Cornell University Press, 2001).

Strange, Susan, 'Transnational Relations', *International Affairs,* 52/3 (July 1976), 333.

Summerfield, Penny, 'Culture and composure: creating narratives of the gendered self in oral history interviews', *Cultural and Social History,* 1 (2004), 65–93.

Summers, Lawrence H., 'Development lessons from the 1990s', in Tim Besley and Roberto Zagha (eds.), *Development Challenges in the 1990s: Leading Policy Makers Speak from Experience* (Washington, DC, The World Bank, 2004).

Sutherland, John, *Victorian Fiction: Writers, Publishers, Readers* (New York, Palgrave Macmillan, 1995).

Tackett, Timothy, *Priest and Parish in Eighteenth-century France: A Social and Political Study of the* Curés *in a Diocese of Dauphiné, 1750–1791* (Princeton University Press, 1977).

— *Religion, Revolution and Regional Culture in Eighteenth-century France: The Ecclesiastical Oath of 1791* (Princeton University Press, 1986).

— *Becoming a Revolutionary: The Deputies of the French National Assembly and the Emergence of a Revolutionary Culture (1789–1790)* (Princeton University Press, 1996).

— 'The flight to Varennes and the coming of the Terror', *Historical Reflections/Réflexions historiques,* 29 (2003), 469–93.

— *When the King Took Flight* (Cambridge, MA, Harvard University Press, 2003).

Taithe, Bertrand, 'Introduction: an Algerian history of France?', *French History,* 20/3 (September 2006), 235–9.

Taraud, Christelle, *La prostitution coloniale. Algérie, Tunisie, Maroc (1830–1962)* (Paris, Payot, 2003).

Taylor, Miles, 'The beginnings of modern British social history', *History Workshop Journal,* 43 (1997), 155–76.

Temple, Michael and Witt, Michael (eds.), *The French Cinema Book* (London, BFI Publishing, 2004).

Thébaud, François, *Écrire l'histoire des femmes et du genre* (Saint-Cloud, ENS Editions, 2007).

— 'Writing women's and gender history in France: a national narrative?', *Journal of Women's History,* 19/1 (spring 2007), 167–72.

Thénault, Sylvie, *Une drôle de justice. Les magistrats dans la Guerre d'Algérie* (Paris, La Découverte, 2001).

— 'L'état d'urgence (1955–2005). De l'Algérie coloniale à la France contemporaine: destin d'une loi', *Le Mouvement social,* 218 (January–March 2007), 63–78.

Thérenty, Marie-Ève and Vaillant, Alain, *1836. L'an I de l'ère médiatique* (Paris, Nouveau Monde, 2001).

— *Presse et plume. Journalisme et littérature au XIXe siècle* (Paris, Nouveau Monde, 2004).

Thomas, Keith, 'History and anthropology', *Past & Present,* 24 (1963), 3–24.

— 'The tools and the job', *TLS,* 7 April 1966.

— *Religion and the Decline of Magic: Studies in Popular Belief in Sixteenth- and Seventeeth-century England* (London, Weidenfeld & Nicolson, 1971).

— *Man and the Natural World: Changing Attitudes in England, 1500–1800* (London, Allen Lane, 1983).

— 'New ways revisited: how history's borders have expanded in the past forty years', *TLS,* 13 October 2006.

Thomas, Lynn M., 'Imperial concerns and "women's affairs": state efforts to regulate clitoridecto-my and eradicate abortion in Meru, Kenya, *c.* 1910–1950', *Journal of African History*, 39 (1998), 121–45.

— *Politics of the Womb: Women, Reproduction, and the State in Kenya* (Berkeley, University of California Press, 2003).

Thomas, Martin, *The French Empire Between the Wars: Imperialism, Politics and Society* (Manchester University Press, 2005).

Thompson, E. P., *The Making of the English Working Class* (London, Victor Gollancz, 1963).

— *The Poverty of Theory and Other Essays* (London, Merlin Press, 1978).

Thomson, Alistair, *Anzac Memories. Living with the Legend* (Melbourne and Oxford, Oxford University Press, 1994).

Todd, Selina (forthcoming), 'Domestic servants and social relations in England, 1900–1950', *Past & Present*.

Todorov, Tzvetan, *Les abus de la mémoire* (Paris, Arléa, 1995).

Tooze, Adam, *The Wages of Destruction: The Making and Breaking of the Nazi Economy* (London, Allen Lane, 2006).

Topalov, Christian, *'Naissance' du chômeur, 1880–1910* (Paris, Albin Michel, 1994).

Traverso, Enzo, *Le passé, modes d'emploi. Histoire, mémoire, politique* (Paris, La Fabrique éditions, 2005).

Turin, Yvonne, *Femmes et religieuses: Le féminisme 'en religion'* (Paris, Nouvelle Cité, 1989).

van der Linden, Marcel, 'Gaining ground', *Journal of Social History*, 37 (2003), 69–75.

Van der Pol, Lotte, with Rudolf Dekker, *Vrouwen in mannenkleren. De geschiedenis van een tegen-draadse traditie* (Amsterdam, Wereldbibliotheek, 1989).

Verdier, Raymond, *La vengeance. Etudes d'ethnologie, d'histoire et de philosophie* (Paris, Editions Cujas, 1980).

Verga, Marcello, *Storie di Europa. Secoli XVIII–XXI* (Rome, Carocci, 2004).

Verheyde, Philippe, *Les mauvais comptes de Vichy. L'aryanisation des entreprises juives* (Paris, Perrin, 1999).

Vernon, James, 'Who's afraid of the "linguistic turn"? The politics of social history and its discon-tents', *Social History*, 19 (1994), 81–97.

— *Hunger: A Modern History* (Cambridge, MA, Harvard University Press, 2007).

Veyne, Paul, 'L'histoire conceptualisante', in Le Goff and Nora (eds.), *Faire de l'histoire*, vol. 1, 66–72.

— *Comment on écrit l'histoire* (Paris, Le Seuil, 1971).

Vince, Natalya, 'To be a moudjahida in independent Algeria: itineraries and memories of women combatants', PhD thesis (University of London, 2008).

Virgili Fabrice, *La France virile. Des femmes tondues à la Libération* (Paris, Payot, 2000).

von Ranke, Leopold, *Zur Kritik neuerer Geschichtschreiber* (Leipzig and Berlin, G. Reimer, 1824).

— *The History of the Popes, their Church and State in the Sixteenth and Seventeenth Centuries*, trans. W. K. Kelly (London, 1843).

— *Memoirs of the House of Brandenburg and History of Prussia during the Seventeenth and Eighteenth Centuries*, trans. Sir A. and Lady D. Gordon (3 vols, London, J. Murray, 1849).

— 'The Great Powers' [1833], in Theodore von Laue, *Leopold von Ranke: the Formative Years* (Princeton University Press, 1950), 181–218.

— *The Secret of World History: Selected Writings on the Art and Science of History*, trans. R. Wines (New York, Fordham University Press, 1981).

Wachtel, Nathan, *Vision of the Vanquished. The Spanish Conquest of Peru seen through Indian Eyes, 1530–1570* (Hassocks, Harvester Press, 1977).

Waelti-Walters, J. and Hause, Steven C., *Feminisms of the Belle Epoque: A Historical and Literary Anthology* (Lincoln, University of Nebraska Press, 1994).

Wahnich, Sophie, 'De l'économie émotive de la Terreur', *Annales Histoire sciences sociales* (2002), 889–913.

— *La Longue patience du peuple. 1792, naissance de la première République* (Paris, Payot, 2008).

Walker Bynum, Caroline, *Holy Feast and Holy Fast: Religious Significance of Food to Mediaeval Women* (Berkeley, University of California Press, 1987).

— *Fragmentation and Redemption: Essays on Gender and the Human Body in Mediaeval Religion* (New York, Zone Books, 1991).

Wall, Irwin M., *France, the United States and the Algerian War* (Berkeley and Los Angeles, University of California Press, 2001).

Wall, Rachel F., 'New openings: Asia', *TLS*, 7 April 1966.

Waters, Chris, 'Autobiography, nostalgia, and the practices of working-class selfhood', in George K. Behlmer and Fred M. Leventhal (eds.), *Singular Continuities: Tradition, Nostalgia, and Identity in Modern Britain* (Stanford University Press, 2000), 178–95.

Werner, Michael and Zimmermann, Bénédicte, 'Penser l'histoire croisée. Entre empirie et réflexivité', *Annales, Histoires Sciences Sociales*, 1 (2003), 7–36.

Wesseling, Henk, 'Overseas history', in Peter Burke (ed.), *New Perspectives on Historical Writing* (Cambridge, Polity Press, 1991), 67–92.

White, Hayden, *Metahistory: The Historical Imagination in Nineteenth-century Europe* (Baltimore, MD, and London, Johns Hopkins University Press, 1973).

— *The Content of Form: Narrative Discourse and Historical Representation* (Baltimore, MD, and London, Johns Hopkins University Press, 1987).

Wickham, Chris and Fentress, James, *Social Memory* (Oxford, Blackwell, 1992).

Wieviorka, Annette (ed.), *Les biens des internés des camps de Drancy, Pithiviers et Beaune-la-Rolande. Mission d'étude sur la spoliation des Juifs de France* (Paris, La Documentation française, 2000).

— *The Era of the Witness* (Ithaca, NY, and London, Cornell University Press, 2006).

Wigmore, John H., 'A list of one hundred legal novels', *Illinois Law Review*, 17/1 (May 1922), 26.

Williams, Raymond, *Culture and Society: Coleridge to Orwell* (London, Chatto and Windus, 1958).

— *The Long Revolution* (London, Chatto and Windus, 1961).

Winch, Donald, 'The disputatious pair: economic history and the history of economics', paper presented to the Centre for Economics and History at the University of Cambridge, November 2001.

Windschuttle, Keith, *The Killing of History: How Literary Critics and Social Theorists are Murdering our Past* (New York, Free Press, 1997).

YMCA National Thrift Committee, *Tenth Anniversary Report on the National Thrift Movement* (New York, 1927).

Young, Robert, *Colonial Desire: Hybridity in Theory, Culture and Race* (London, Routledge, 1995).

Zagorin, Perez, 'Historiography and postmodernism: reconsiderations', *History and Theory*, 29 (1990), 263–74.

Zemon Davis, Natalie, *The Return of Martin Guerre* (Cambridge, MA, and London, Harvard University Press, 1983).

— *Fiction in the Archives: Pardon Tales and their Tellers in Sixteenth-century France* (Cambridge, Polity Press, 1987).

— *Women at the Margins: Three Seventeenth-century Lives* (Cambridge, MA, and London, Harvard University Press, 1995).

Zunz, Olivier, *Reliving the Past: The Worlds of Social History* (Chapel Hill, University of North Carolina Press, 1985).

Index